ECSTASY IN THE CLASSROOM

FORDHAM SERIES IN MEDIEVAL STUDIES
Mary C. Erler and Franklin T. Harkins, series editors

ECSTASY IN THE CLASSROOM

Trance, Self, and the Academic Profession in Medieval Paris

AYELET EVEN-EZRA

FORDHAM UNIVERSITY PRESS

New York   2019

Copyright © 2019 Fordham University Press

All rights reserved. No part of this publication may be reproduced, stored in a retrieval system, or transmitted in any form or by any means—electronic, mechanical, photocopy, recording, or any other—except for brief quotations in printed reviews, without the prior permission of the publisher.

Fordham University Press has no responsibility for the persistence or accuracy of URLs for external or third-party Internet websites referred to in this publication and does not guarantee that any content on such websites is, or will remain, accurate or appropriate.

Fordham University Press also publishes its books in a variety of electronic formats. Some content that appears in print may not be available in electronic books.

Visit us online at www.fordhampress.com.

Library of Congress Cataloging-in-Publication Data

Names: Even-Ezra, Ayelet, author.
Title: Ecstasy in the classroom : trance, self, and the academic profession in medieval Paris / Ayelet Even-Ezra.
Description: First edition. | New York, NY : Fordham University Press, 2019. | Series: Fordham series in medieval studies | Includes bibliographical references and index.
Identifiers: LCCN 2018024882| ISBN 9780823281923 (cloth : alk. paper) | ISBN 9780823281916 (pbk. : alk. paper)
Subjects: LCSH: Ecstasy—History of doctrines—Middle Ages, 600–1500. | Paul, the Apostle, Saint. | Visions in the Bible. | Altered states of consciousness—Religious aspects. | Experience (Religion)
Classification: LCC BV5091.E3 E94 2019 | DDC 248.2—dc23
LC record available at https://lccn.loc.gov/2018024882

Printed in the United States of America

21 20 19   5 4 3 2 1

First edition

CONTENTS

*As its title suggests, this book does three things:
(1) It describes the discourse about Paul's trance and other modes of cognizing God through key questions raised by early thirteenth-century theologians; (2) It discusses the perceptions of the self implied by this discourse; (3) It suggests these questions resonate concerns of theologians regarding the nature of their academic profession. Each chapter, therefore, has accordingly three titles.*

Introduction / 1

1 Why was Paul ignorant of his own state, and how do various modes of cognizing God differ? / 23
  The experiencing self and the observing self
  Theology among other modes of cognizing God

2 How could Paul remember his rapture? / 59
  Memory and the continuity of the self
  Theology between experience and words

3 Can a soul see God or itself without intermediaries? / 81
  The self as distinct from its habits and actions
  Theology between experience and observation

4 Does true faith rely on anything external? / 111
  The self as an ultimate source of authority
  Theology between internal and external authority

5 What happens to old modes of cognition when new ones are introduced during trance and other transitions? / 135
  The self and its ability to manipulate parts of it during transitions
  Theology between reasoned knowledge and simple faith

6 Can knowledge qua knowledge be a virtue? / 158
The self in society
Theology between theory and practice

Summary and Epilogue / 189
Appendix / 199
Acknowledgments / 205
Notes / 207
Bibliography / 265
Index / 291

Introduction

Not long after her falling down the rabbit hole, Lewis Carroll's Alice attempts to adjust to this wonderful altered state of consciousness. In order to understand who she is and whether she had become one of her friends, she tries to see what she knows, rather poorly, as it turns out:

> I wonder if I've been changed in the night? Let me think: was I the same when I got up this morning? . . . But if I'm not the same, the next question is, Who in the world am I? Ah, THAT's the great puzzle! . . . I'm sure I can't be Mabel, for I know all sorts of things, and she, oh! she knows such a very little! Besides, SHE's she, and I'm I, and—oh dear, how puzzling it all is! I'll try if I know all the things I used to know. Let me see: four times five is twelve . . . oh dear! . . . let's try Geography. London is the capital of Paris . . . no, THAT's all wrong, I'm certain! I must have been changed for Mabel![1]

What and how we know becomes part of us and defines, to a certain degree, who we are. Not only does knowledge make part of our individual identity, certain forms of knowledge have socially recognized agents whose public identity and social role center around this specific form of knowledge. Those experiencing ecstatic knowledge of the other world may become shamans or religious authorities; those mastering knowledge of a particular discipline may assume the role of university professors or scientific authorities.

While shamans and ecstatic forms of trance experiences have been in existence in almost every human culture for thousands of years, professors and study experiences in university classrooms are a comparatively recent phenomenon. This strange, peculiarly European institution took shape in the Western Europe of the twelfth and thirteenth centuries.[2] For hundreds of years beforehand, learning in all forms and sources in Christian Europe had been intertwined with the religious life of the community. Monastic environments allowed for free slippage between critical study, observation, contemplation, and ecstasy. But the twelfth century saw dramatic changes of two particular types of knowledge of the divine: the ecstatic and the scholastic.

Together with proliferating interest in prophecies like those attributed to the legendary figure of Merlin, flesh-and-blood prophets began to appear on the stage of Western Europe.[3] They were distinguishable both from the traditional shamans who still operated in parts of Europe and from earlier monks and nuns who experienced altered modes of consciousness.[4] Individuals such as Hildegard of Bingen and Joachim of Fiore had repeated, powerful experiences that they put in writing with new force and expression, both verbal and visual, weaving them into their exegetical works in creative ways that far exceeded the established *topos* of soliciting Christ or the Holy Spirit for assistance in writing. Society, including fellow monks and abbots, churchmen, nobles, and kings regarded them as sources of knowledge and counsel. In the urban centers of the same period, masters and students in the increasingly popular schools of Paris, Bologna, and Oxford, which were to develop into the institutional form of the university, established themselves as another new type of agent of knowledge.

At the beginning of the thirteenth century, both tendencies proliferated energetically: visionaries of a new kind flourished, forming what is now called "the new mysticism";[5] the schools turned into universities all over Europe. With the institutionalization of the second type of knowledge agency and its semi-independence from the church and the monastery, the gap between the two deepened. True, religious practice and experience wrapped the schools. There was significant variation with regard to the extent to which societies comprising masters and students were independent from religious institutions, authorities, and atmosphere.[6] The medieval faculty of theology in Paris enjoyed the least degree of autonomy. Bishops and chancellors had usually been regent masters themselves, and the majority of other faculty members held ecclesiastical positions. The papacy endeavored to exercise both direct and indirect influence and control over the faculty and all university affairs. Apart from classes, both students and masters participated in joint religious ceremonies. They preached and listened to sermons as a central part of their studies, and undoubtedly experienced the divine through these practices. Selling teaching licenses for money was considered by many simony, just as with any other ecclesiastical office. Teaching theology was "a spiritual matter" (*res spiritualis*).[7]

At the same time, however, even theology masters were subject to the general corporation of masters and its decisions. A layman could, at least theoretically, teach theology.[8] During the first decades of the thirteenth century, progress of study became ever more structured, monitored, regulated, and ritualized by internal government. Written and unwritten customs and the establishment of ceremonies and degrees created an institutional sphere unto itself. Most of all, teaching was done with increasingly sophisticated instruments and methods of human ingenuity, structured around texts, dialectic, divisions, and definitions. Live prophecy or ecstatic experience had no place there.

The history of the dynamic relationship between rationalist and ecstatic approaches to the divine and between their human representatives in medieval society is a complex, intriguing one. This book tells one of its most fascinating chapters. But first, the following three short cases, in which masters and students engaged with others having altered states of consciousness or experienced such themselves, will give a taste of this borderline zone.

SCHOLARS AND ECSTATIC VISIONS IN THE REAL WORLD: THREE NON-EXEMPLARY CASES

Master Odo and the Sybille of the Rhine

Among Hildegard of Bingen's correspondents was one, Odo of Soissons, a Parisian master.[9] In a letter whose date is difficult to determine precisely,[10] Odo addressed her with a theological question as a bride of Christ, one who has attained perception of heavenly things. In his letter, Odo prefaced his question with a long paragraph urging secrecy. Hildegard knew the secrets of the virginal bridal chamber, and Odo reminded her that the prophetic soul says, "My secret to myself, my secret to myself."[11] There is a danger in revealing secrets, he continues, alluding to the way "King Hezekiah grievously offended God by opening up the storerooms of spices and the treasuries of the Temple to the Babylonian messengers." A few lines further down, he remarks that "certain things which might distress the apostolic and ecclesiastical institution are kept under seal and not made known." Not very encouraging, considering Hezekiah's fate.

Only in the final sentences does Odo present his petition, asking her "to resolve a certain problem for us: Many contend that God is not both paternity and divinity." Would she explain in a letter what she has perceived in the heavens about this matter? This is not an innocent question, and warning was indeed necessary. The problem posed by the Parisian master stood at the center of a dispute involving complex structures of knowledge, authority, and power that focused on Gilbert of Poitiers (d. 1154). Gilbert, a renowned Parisian master, argued that an abstraction like "'Fatherhood' was distinct from 'that which the father was.'" Scholarly controversy turned serious as, according to Otto of Freising and John of Salisbury, local archdeacons in Poitiers, who were presumably masters themselves, resented their new bishop. Apparently, this conflict spiraled into a public dispute regarding this opinion in Paris in the 1140s and later in 1148, with Bernard of Clairvaux taking their side at a trial at the Council of Reims.[12] The unknown date of the letter makes it hard to assess its relation to these events. Constant Mews estimates that in 1147 Odo was already opposing Gilbert. He probably learned about Hildegard in 1148, just after her claim of prophecy was approved in Trier with the endorsement of the same Bernard. Odo was therefore interested in her refuting Gilbert's claims. Stover, on the other hand, argues that the letter, which does not refer to Gilbert, could have been written either before or after the trial, but not after the 1150s when Odo took the monastic habit. The warning tone, however, seems to me to support Mews's position.

Odo carefully establishes their respective positions: Hildegard is a virgin, he is a sinner. Accordingly, she possesses heavenly knowledge even though she has not studied, while he is a learned master who professes no visionary claims. In her reply to Odo, Hildegard establishes this contrast with equal care. She describes herself as an ignorant little woman, who is "not endowed with great powers or human education," like a feather that flies only as the air bears it along. In the same breath, she depicts herself on the top of the lofty mountain where the sun sends down its rays. She addresses Odo as a respected concomitant, who enables access to scripture and provides instruction. She writes that another very learned man consulted her, the little one, about the same issue, and she looked carefully at the light of truth in order to find the answer. "In the true light, certainly not from [her] own cogitation," she saw the orthodox truth—that is, that divinity and paternity are both God. As one who has just petitioned Bernard of Clairvaux and Eugenius III for legitimization, and perhaps reading Odo's warning between the lines, she said precisely what the authorities wished her to. Intriguingly, she did so partly with the very terms, phrasing, and examples of learned discourse with which she was clearly familiar.[13] Nevertheless, although she and Odo had more in common than it seems at first glance, both make exceptional efforts to delineate their respective social positions as agents of different sources of knowledge, participants in a fascinating moment in the dance of knowledge, authority, and politics in the West.

This seems to be a unique, perhaps circumscribed affair. It is the only known such letter from a theology master. Hildegard's position, as much as can be assessed, did not exert any decisive influence upon the Parisian scene. As Stover has demonstrated, this controversy extended at least until after 1185.[14] Moreover, a few decades later, probably in the 1220s, it was the intellectual descendants of Odo and Gilbert who were to examine Hildegard's visions. The monastery of Rupertsberg petitioned for the canonization of their abbess, and an inquiry was set on 1228. Bruno, a priest and guard of the church of St. Peter, told the inquirers that some years before, intending to go to Tours, he decided to stop at Paris with the intention of submitting Hildegard's writing to an examination so as to be sure he could securely read them (that is, to remove any doubt concerning their orthodoxy). Bruno had copied therefore the *Scivias*, the *Liber vitae Meritorum*, and the *liber divinorum Operum*, and with that precious volume traveled to Paris. There he persuaded the bishop to assemble all the masters of theology and submitted to each of them a copy in three quires for review. After the copies were examined and returned to the bishop, he gave them to Master William of Auxerre, one of the protagonists of this book, who announced that the opinion of the masters was that these words were purely divine. Now, it was for them to discern and legitimize.[15] Years passed and someone, perhaps in the fourteenth-century monastery of St. Victor, chose to bind Hildegard's writings together in the same codex with an early collection of theological *quaestiones*, some of which were excerpted from William of Auxerre, alongside excerpts from Aristotle's writings and a variety of prophecies by Joachim of Fiore, Merlin, and others.[16]

Amalricians

A different encounter between scholarly learning and ecstatic experience occurred a few decades later, just when the university was granted its first privileges. Amaury of Bena was a master of arts and then theology in Paris around 1200.[17] He was undoubtedly exceptional. The chronicler of Lyon remarks that he was close to the royal family, and, although very subtle, he lacked reason (*vir subtilissimus set ingenio pessimus*). He relates that the opinions he taught in both the faculty of arts and the faculty of theology were contrary to those of others. Seeing that controversies and disputes were the bread and butter of the schools, this observation emphasizes his true outsider position.[18] Guillaume of Breton also notes that Amaury differed from the other masters in both method and doctrine: he had "a mode of himself for teaching and studying" and "a private opinion." Amaury, Guillaume relates, asserted that each Christian must believe he is a member of Christ in order to be saved. Unlike any other scholarly opinion, he endeavored to make this an article of faith. The pope, however, accepted the opposing opinion of his fellow colleagues and decided against him. He was forced to confess what was contrary to his judgment before the university in an act that was the first of its kind for this community and died soon after of sorrow.[19]

This, however, was only the first act in a drama, the final scene of which would see the flames burn several heretics in a field near Paris. Amaury's students developed his ideas much further and formed a sect. The core group came undoubtedly from the university's ranks, although later they seem to have spread their doctrine to the unlearned as well. According to all sources, it consisted mainly of theology students.[20] According to Caesar of Heisterbach, even their prophet, William the Goldsmith, was such a student. Their meetings, however, were far from casual gatherings of classmates, as the term "prophet" might have already hinted. Master Ralph, who was sent to spy on the group, maintained that these meetings included ecstatic elements, and, in order to convince them of his pure intentions, he himself had pretended that his soul was rapt to heaven in order to be able to relate afterward what he had supposedly seen there.[21] An excluded scholarly opinion had become a prophetic, obliging truth.

This practice was closely tied to their doctrines. One of their fundamental heretical opinions was that all three persons of the Trinity had been incarnated throughout history. The third incarnation, that of the Holy Spirit, had occurred in none other than the members of their own group. Another opinion they held was that he who had God's knowledge in him had heaven in himself. Yet it is difficult to assess the respective roles they established for theological studies and tools in their meetings on the way to attaining this liberating truth.[22] According to one source, they believed that the Holy Spirit was incarnated in them, had revealed everything to them, and the resurrection of the dead was to be understood as that revelation.[23] Their condemnation by church authorities was explicitly linked to that of Aristotle's and his commentators' natural philosophy, but the surviving evidence does not allow us to determine the precise place of

Aristotelian, Eriugenian, or Joachimite ideas in the formation of their doctrine.[24] One way or another, dialectical methods and philosophical ideas were intertwined with ecstatic raptures and prophecies such as those of William the Goldsmith to both create and legitimize their doctrine. Although the persons involved were members of the university and their activities originated in classroom practices, their group ceased to be part of the masters' community. This separation occurred as they formed themselves as a distinct sect holding private meetings. It was surely accomplished by 1210, when their opinions were publicly condemned and they were severely punished. Even if this were a case of ecstasy in school *par excellence*, it was unique in the eyes of all around them, and it ended terribly.

An enraptured master: Thomas Aquinas's hagiographical portrait

The last case I would like to examine in this partial list occurred in a later period than the one studied in this book. It involves tales about Thomas Aquinas, the most famous of scholastic theologians, related by witnesses and hagiographers a few decades after his death.[25] Although Thomas himself reports no visionary or exceptionally inspirational experiences in his writings, his hagiographers, according to the genre, made considerable efforts to embellish his life with anecdotes suggesting divinely inspired knowledge. The principal testimony to this comes from Reginald of Piperno, Thomas's close friend and secretary. Right after Thomas's passing, Reginald ascended to the cathedra in school and told everybody that the master's knowledge was not due to natural ingenuity alone, but to the inspiration of the Holy Spirit. He used to intersperse his writing with exemplary religious practices, including prayer, fasts, and revelations. According to Reginald, Thomas never approached writing without first praying beforehand. Whenever he encountered difficulties and doubts, he would fast, pray, and shed tears and would return from prayer with miraculous clarity.[26]

According to Thomas's hagiographers, a few texts in particular emerged from this admixture of reason and inspiration, especially his *Summa against the Gentiles* and *Commentary on Isaia*. Both Calo and Tocco relate that the *Summa* was written partly from Thomas's proper reason and partly from his heavenly rapture (*quid ex proprio ingenio habuit, et quid ex raptu mentis in deum*).[27] As Thomas composed, he seemed frequently at a remove from his senses and entirely concerned with divine matters. What made Thomas's hagiographers attribute this to the *summa* in particular? The text itself betrays no mystical nature, but this might well be the very reason. They might have felt a need to justify its explicitly philosophical and rational character. Support for this hypothesis is found in a lengthy remark of Bernard Gui. It is not absurd, he argues, that Thomas used secular and philosophical knowledge to buttress his arguments, for "the subjects of all sciences proceed from the same divine intellect from which the truths of divine wisdom."[28] A similar apologetic sense arises from Calo's remark regarding another text that Thomas allegedly wrote while filled with the Holy Spirit and that was composed so quickly that it seemed to be the result of divine inspiration rather than human ingenuity. This second text is none other than Thomas's treatise refuting William of St. Amour (*Contra impugnantes*), which was written during the controversies between seculars and mendicants.[29]

Thomas's exposition of Isaia was the subject of another legendary embellishment. Reginald relates that while composing it Thomas faced a difficulty and immersed himself in prayer. One night, Reginald heard a strange conversation taking place in Thomas's cell. Just a few minutes later, he was summoned to fulfill his office as Thomas's amanuensis. After imploring Thomas several times to explain the strange conversation he overheard, Thomas confided that it had taken place with Peter and Paul, who clarified the textual difficulty.[30] Bernard Gui, again, takes the opportunity to glorify Thomas's revelatory knowledge, which exceeded the limited human intellect, citing his ability to speak with heavenly citizens while still here on earth, indeed depicting him as a sort of shamanic master.[31]

According to these sources, Thomas experienced several ecstasies and raptures that supported his intellectual profession. All hagiographers are careful to describe the phenomenon of mental abstraction (*abstractio mentis*) that would occur when Thomas was too focused on his thoughts to notice his surroundings. In the midst of a royal dinner with King Louis IX, he was so entirely taken by the *imaginatio* of writing, he struck the table with satisfaction when the perfect argument against the Manicheans occurred to him.[32] On another occasion, ignoring the presence of a distinguished cardinal, he smiled to himself as he found the solution to another problem. In each case, he required someone to pull on his cape physically to bring him back to reality. These anecdotes reveal how easily eager hagiographers could depict ordinary scholarly daydreaming as a "wonderful and unheard of mental abstraction" (*miranda et inaudita abstractio mentis*), to use the words of Tocco on the royal dinner.

There are also descriptions of more powerful raptures, which rather than inform Thomas's theological activity were opposed to it. Some appeared too powerful to be processed further as scholastic theology. During one Mass, for instance, Thomas reportedly experienced a long rapture and floated up into the air. When he returned to his senses, the knights around him implored him to divulge what he had seen. With a clear allusion to Paul, who heard "things that cannot be told to human beings," Thomas refused.

In two separate legends Thomas discusses theological conjunctures with the crucified Christ. In one, he was frustrated by scholarly disputations among the masters of theology regarding the Eucharist. With his notebook in hand, he approached the altar. Christ revealed himself and praised his work, remarking that his opinion was the correct one, as far as one can ascertain in this life. Thomas presented the solution in front of the university, and Tocco added that clearly Christ had illuminated his doctor with truth.[33] Gui concludes the same anecdote by saying that Thomas lectured in front of the university as one taught by Truth himself.[34]

The most famous legend, featuring the endorsement "you have written well," combines harmony and opposition.[35] There are different versions, but the general lines are similar in all hagiographies. They relate how Thomas once mystically conversed with the crucified Christ, who praised his writing as he was composing the third part of the *summa* dealing with incarnation and offered recompense for his efforts. The only thing Thomas asked for was "you." Theological writing won Thomas high spiritual reward, but this very reward was its cessation. The most certain indication of the fulfillment of Thomas's wish was, according to all hagiographers, him ceasing to write the *summa*: "He wrote little because of the wonderful things shown to him by God," they all concluded. Nothing was the same from then on. Thomas became subject to frequent raptures. In response to Reginald's inquiries as to why he left off composing such a great work, he replied that he simply could not continue. All the things he had written before seemed like a straw. While visiting his sister's castle, he experienced another extended rapture that worried his sister terribly. Reginald persisted in asking him about his cessation from writing, and Thomas explained further that what he was writing paled in comparison to what he had been shown. Earthly knowledge and earthly life were now mixed with heavenly counterparts, and Thomas disclosed his hope that with the end of his teaching his life would soon end as well.[36] Like Moses and Paul, Calo reflected, Thomas had enjoyed exceedingly rare understanding, and like them he died a short time thereafter.[37]

Readers of any version of this story are given the impression, therefore, that from a certain point the gap between theological cognition of God and a higher divine inspiration became so extreme that it was no longer bridgeable. At the same time, these hagiographic narratives create explicit continuity between these cognitions. Mental abstraction nourishes writing, and good writing is rewarded with an exceptional experience of rapture that discloses a beatific vision of life in heaven after death.

Both the gap and the bridge are fully expressed in a dream that Paul of Aquilla had at the time of Thomas's death. In his dream, Thomas is teaching a multitude of students when suddenly Paul the Apostle and his entourage enter the classroom. The doctor hurries down from his cathedra to greet his quite unexpected honored guests, but Paul nods to him to continue lecturing. Nevertheless, no professor of literature who has his author present in his class would miss such an opportunity, and in this dream, Thomas is no exception. He asks the apostle to confirm that he has understood his epistles well. Paul replies, "You've understood [them] very well, as much as a man living in the body can know. But I want you to come with me, and I will lead you to a place where you would have a clearer understanding of all things." Paul then takes Thomas by the cape, leading him outside the school. At this point, the dreamer woke up crying.[38]

Hagiographers took care to weave Thomas's scholastic teaching and writing together with threads of knowledge achieved and confirmed through revelations and raptures so that school, rapture, and heaven form one continuous path to understanding. As echoes of the harsh controversies over Thomas's opinions still hung in the air, this admixture served the Dominicans—Bernard Gui in particular—in their efforts to establish Thomistic doctrine, truthfulness, and authority on a higher level, one far above earthly magisterial disputes. Nevertheless, this amalgam of ecstasy and reasoning seems the exception that proves the rule. They are stories told precisely because of their unusual and wondrous nature, part of a considerable effort to present a dry, analytical academic as a colorful saint. Rather than demonstrate a common, institutionalized association between different states of consciousness, they betray this amalgam's exceptional character. It is a remarkable wonder, a secret revealed only to intimate friends such as Reginald and disclosed publicly only after the master's death. Normally, determinations in theological disputations on the Eucharist were not performed in front of altars.

These three cases represent exceptional moments in which scholarly masters were reported to have engaged with live prophesy and ecstasy. During the controversies about the orthodoxy of Gilbert of Poitiers, about that of Thomas Aquinas, or regarding the deviant students of Amaury, the common mechanisms of disputation and argumentation were depicted as being exceeded in order to lend additional authority to certain opinions and strengthen positions in conflicts over the politics of truth. The entire affair of Peter John Olivi's doctrine and his heretical followers could easily fit this list as well. A former master (d. 1298), he, too, it was believed, disclosed a few hours before his death that all his knowledge was divinely infused during a sudden illumination in the Paris cathedral. According to Bernard Gui (now under the hat of the inquisitor), his writings were held as authoritative prophecies by certain deviant Franciscans.[39] And yet, although exceptional, they attest that masters of scholastic theology, the only authorized group of professionals who were formally, specifically, and institutionally trained to apprehend the divine, had a complex relationship with other forms of apprehension.

TRANCE, SELF, AND THE ACADEMIC PROFESSION

While the classrooms of masters may not have witnessed any actual ecstasies, at least not institutionally intended, ecstasy was certainly present in them as an object of learning. As the book's subtitle suggests, it seeks to do three things. The first is to map and analyze the scholastic discourse about rapture and other modes of cognition in the first half of the thirteenth century. The second is to explicate the perception of the self they imply. The third is to read these discussions as a window on the predicaments of a newborn community of medieval professionals and thereby elucidate foundational tensions in the emergent academic culture and its social and cultural context. With this triple aim, it joins the latest attempts in the historiography of medieval universities, seeking to answer the recent call, which has been loudly heard, for a unified approach to intellectual creation, the conditions of its production, and its key instruments.[40]

Paul the Apostle was the archetype of an ecstatic throughout the Middle Ages, and his account of his rapture to heaven, a key text describing Altered States of Consciousness in Christian tradition, is the center of this inquiry. Together with a cluster of related modes of cognitions like prophecy and faith, it was subject to meticulous scholastic debates held with the standard professional tools of definitions, divisions, arguments, and up-to-date theories of the nature of the soul and of the body. This thick body of scholastic debates constitute the core body of primary sources: *quaestiones* about rapture, prophecy, faith, wisdom, and beatific vision that were written by regent masters of theology at the university of Paris, in the years 1215–45. Parts of this corpus were studied by historians of historical theology and philosophy who followed changing views concerning prophecy alone, or of beatific vision as well, and by scholars who explored one or two theologians in detail, but never together and as a product of a defined community of practice and in light of its social and cultural context.[41]

In the first place, this is a study of a community of professionals. Perhaps the term most appropriate for clarifying my purpose is "community of practice." This term, coined by Lave and Wenger while inquiring into the nature of situated learning, indicates a group of people who interact with each other both in texts and in life, who share a common "domain," who develop a collective repertoire of resources—metaphors, examples, tools, ways of handling typical problems—and who constantly negotiate meanings and professional identities.[42] John Baldwin's classic work on Peter the Chanter and his circle in the late twelfth century represents an exemplary study of such a group in the field of medieval studies.[43] Working on a community of practice rather than focusing on one figure or one school/circle enables one to map the most comprehensive picture possible of a discourse in a specific period and thus to recognize and locate various monologues as parts of a multi-participant interplay. It enables understanding, not only of what one says about something, but that about which one chooses to remain silent. Furthermore, the community's repertoires of questions, answers, loci of references, their various modes of actualization, and the changes within them become objects of inquiry themselves.

The theologians who were regent masters in the Parisian faculty of theology in the thirteenth century undoubtedly constitute such a community.

Although diverse in geographical and social background, by the 1220s the identity of the community of masters and students, in both legal and intellectual respects, was already in advanced stages of crystallization.[44] Already their predecessors, as Baldwin demonstrated, "exhibit self awareness as a professional group." They sought to evaluate their proper functions, to distinguish their activities from those of other groups, and to legitimate their contributions to society.[45] This generation lately received renewed scholarly attention in studies by Gorochov and Young, who presented a social and historical portrait of the group.[46] These studies, especially Gorochov's, include the most comprehensive and up-to-date bibliographic and biographical information on each of the figures populating these pages. Repetition would be superfluous here. I avoided therefore as much as possible throughout the book long chains of footnote references on each master and his work.

Studying a discourse of a community of professionals cannot be satisfied with examining one practitioner's thought or even that of one group with a particular agenda. Ideally, therefore, relevant texts would have been gathered from all active regent masters to form the corpus. Yet, due to the state of the sources, reconstruction of a complete, balanced picture is impossible. Many masters are known to us only by name, while others left almost nothing, or at least no materials related to rapture, prophecy, or faith. Thus, out of more than forty masters who are known to scholarship as active regent masters in the period from 1215 to 1245, only twelve left relevant materials: Godfrey of Poitiers, William of Auxerre, Philip the Chancellor, Alexander of Hales (OFM from 1236), William of Auvergne, William of Durham, Guiard of Laon, Roland of Cremona (OP), Guerric of St. Quentin (OP), Hugh of St. Cher (OP), John of La Rochelle (OFM), and Odo Rigaldi (OFM).[47]

This number becomes even smaller when we take into account that not all of them left *quaestiones* about each of the relvant issues. William of Durham and Guiard of Laon are the most underrepresented, while others, whose *summae* or commentaries survived in their entirety, are well represented in all spheres of the discourse, and their place in this picture is much clearer. This imbalance is not accidental: the mendicant orders did a better job of transmitting their masters' texts over the years, and thus their share is disproportionately large compared with their respective place in the faculty. Several anonymous tractates were included in the corpus as well, most of them from codices Douai 434 I and II.[48] These two highly valuable volumes, which were copied in the late 1230s, contain a treasury of contemporary *quaestiones* from the 1220s and the early 1230s on the issues at stake here, and they enrich our understanding of the discourse to a large degree.

The reader should therefore keep in mind that the full spectrum of opinions and practices and the estimation of their respective weight are necessarily partial and biased. I analyzed more than twelve *quaestiones "de fide"* (on faith) for this study, faith being consistently compared with rapture. All but William of Auvergne's tractate display a large number of common elements: issues, authorities, metaphors, arguments, and types of solutions. And yet each new *quaestio* I examined contains one or more elements that were not found in any of the others, whether a new little problem, a slightly different order of questions, or a new argument. It is possible, therefore, that Nicolas de Flavigny or Simon d'Authie, of whom no theological tractate has been identified so far, presented an entirely different set of problems and solutions in their discussions of faith. Yet it is also very likely that echoes of their positions left impressions in the discourse as counterarguments or as options excluded. The fact that the work of such eminent theologians as William of Auxerre and Philip the Chancellor survived allows us to assume that even though many pieces of the puzzle are missing, the already rich discussions treated here more than hint at the nature of the entire picture, or at least substantial and influential parts of it.

The 1240s constitute a different phase, marked by the rise of a new generation of theologians such as Albert the Great, Bonaventure, and Thomas Aquinas. While many historical theologians tend to end their investigations with these figures (Thomas Aquinas in particular), I believe this generation deserves a separate study. The *Summa Halensis (SH)*, compiled by John of La Rochelle and the anonymous *Considerans* and based on texts of Alexander of Hales, is still the product of the generation under investigation. It was accordingly included in the corpus. The attribution of the commentary on the *Sentences* in MS Vat. Lat. 691 has long been contested, but it is certain that it came from the circles of John of La Rochelle or Guerric of St. Quentin.[49] Although I tend to agree with the earlier attribution to Guerric, the author will be referred to just as "the author of Vat. Lat. 691."

The discussion of Paul's rapture is the point of departure of all the chapters of the book. But as I soon found out, it cannot and should not be separated from a larger array of issues concerning other human *cognitiones dei*, including prophecy, faith, the gifts of understanding and wisdom, and the beatific vision. When one enters into the forest of these *quaestiones*, reading each of the mini questions that comprise them, several common hidden themes and predicaments appear, crossing through the entire discourse and inviting a closer look at related problems in different places of the corpus and beyond it. I chose, therefore, to present this discourse neither arranged according to scholars (one chapter on William of Auxerre, another on Alexander of Hales) nor according to the grand types of cognitions of God analyzed here (one chapter about rapture, another chapter about prophecy). Rather, these small-scale problems or questions form the guiding principle of the chapters. The first title of each chapter is the question that guides it.

The two other parts of the subtitle hint at two further lines running through the book. Altered states of consciousness like those experienced through rapture or prophetic visions, once one is back to one's senses, challenge perceptions of the continuity, identity, and unity of the self. A community's approach to such experiences may therefore reveal much about the perceptions of the self that dominate it. Finally, these predicaments about knowledge and the self are set in the specific historical setting of Parisian university and elite culture and read as reflecting its inner conflicts. Some words about contextual awareness are in order, as I suspect this would be the more controversial part of my argument. The fact that a certain idea or question in any field of knowledge appears or changes its shape at a certain moment or that agents make markedly intensive use of a certain distinction is a historical fact calling for explanation. Furthermore, it is a cultural fact that can provide a glimpse into the values and concerns of the culture in which this development occurred. Historians of thought tend to explain such events in two manners that complete one another. The first of these has both its legs in the field of ideas. It explains changes either as a result of internal development of scholarly discussion, assertions, refutations, and reconciliations that generate new problems and the like or as a result of acquaintance with old or new ideas. There are excellent studies focusing on questions of epistemology from the point of view of historians of medieval philosophy, such as Robert Pasnau's *Theories of Cognition in the Later Middle Ages* and Steven Marrone's study of the cognition of God in the thirteenth century.[50] Works such as Decker's and Schlosser's on theories of prophecy or Bieniak on the Soul-Body problem employ this approach to a large degree as well.[51] In our specific case, a classic such explanation would focus on the debt owed to patristic thought and specific twelfth-century schools of thought and put emphasis on the growing acquaintance with, and use of, the Aristotelian corpus, the natural works, and the *Ethics* in particular, as well as of Avicenna and some others. This sort of analysis, but to a limited degree, shall be found in the first part of each of the book chapters. But as it continues, the second one comes to the fore. This complementary approach attempts to link ideas and books to their users and producers. Its basic assumption is that books are read actively and selectively by people who belong to a specific culture and who respond to political, social, and spiritual changes around them. In both old and new texts, they seek and highlight certain elements over others, and these focuses echo their own contemporary concerns, needs, fears, and hopes. The first kind of explanation is therefore never fully satisfying without the second, nor is the second without the first.

Theoretical discussions about marriage, money, or government lend themselves more easily to contextualization. Such topics have indeed been the subject of beautiful studies of medieval intellectual history.[52] Explicit remarks about theologians are readily accessible for those interested in studying the self-presentation of theologians as well.[53] The subject of ecstasy and of other modes of cognition, I suggest, may benefit from a contextual awareness as well. Certainly, not every idea about knowledge and cognition is the reflection of the position of its human agent or creator in the social field of knowledge production. Yet it is rewarding and thought-provoking to follow such a hypothesis when there are promising signs that it may be and see where this investigation leads us.[54]

The schoolmen were members of a nascent, emergent guild of knowledge transmitters. To use the term coined by Gieryn in the sociology of science, they had to carve out a niche and perform a "boundary-work" to demarcate their peculiar position in the broader field of knowledge production and authority. In the case of academic theology, this boundary-work was done while having in mind visionaries, believers, and philosophers.[55] It is reflected, I argue, in their discussions of these modes of apprehension. Furthermore, despite the incredibly powerful homogenizing force of scholastic training—one cannot tell an English nobleman from the son of an Italian merchant based on their literary products—the schoolmen did not live in a void. They heard jongleurs singing about love adventures, and their teaching trinkled outside the classroom in various ways; they preached and traveled, molding and being molded by different value systems. Awareness to this context is worth serious consideration.

The quest for a broader, richer context of ideas began with explicit references to theology and theologians in the first body of primary sources, as well as questions about theology's nature. The increasing number and length of questions on cognition of God and the appearance of systematic questions about the science of theology occurred simultaneously, and that is anything but mere coincidence.[56] Furthermore, I searched for the themes and concerns revealed by the first inquiry in documents including chronicles, hagiography, and romance literature. Central to this investigation were documents illuminating the culture, values, and concerns of the direct producers—that is, the masters who constituted the faculty of theology as such, such as university documents, exempla on academic life, and students' guides. When appropriate and relevant, early thirteenth-century texts from the world outside the university proper, such as hagiography and courtly romance, were called in as well.

A typical structure of each chapter therefore starts by identifying a question that troubles the members of the community regarding Paul's rapture or related experiences and elaborates on the different forms, treatment, and solutions each author of the community provided. It then reconstructs the perception of the self embedded in these treatises or another strong theme revealed in the more descriptive part and follows its relations to the self-fashioning of the community of theologians and beyond the classroom's windows.

CHAPTER OUTLINES

The problem that intrigued medieval masters the most concerning Paul's rapture was how to define his mode of cognition during rapture, while he himself confessed not to have known whether his soul was in or out of his body. Chapter 1 examines the attempts of our group of theologians to classify this ecstatic mode of vision while being aware of the tension between the rational theologian-observer and the experiencing subject. Augustine took Paul's self-ignorance regarding his body-soul relation as a point of departure for a threefold categorization of visions into corporeal, imaginative, and intellectual types. Augustine's classification was modified and developed further in the twelfth century, in which Paul's mode of vision was framed between the earthly vision of believers and the heavenly vision of the blessed souls. In the early thirteenth century, more and more cognitions joined the taxonomic parade: the visions of prophets, contemplators, Christ, Moses, scriptural exegetes, angels, and even God's knowledge of himself. This intense preoccupation with the taxonomy of agents of knowledge around them, and with the self as both experiencing and observing, I argue, served this community of theologians to map the field in which they operate and to explain to themselves and to others their place in it and their own mode of cognizing the divine.

Chapter 2 addresses a problem that was first introduced in the 1220s: the recollection of trance experience when the enraptured person returns to his/her senses. Traditionally, Paul was thought to have seen God in an immediate manner—that is, without any images mediating the seen object. Yet, if no images had been involved, no images could have remained following his rapture, and therefore, there would have been no imprint in his mind by which he could have recalled and shared with the audience what he had seen. Various explanations were suggested for the possible residues that enabled memory and further mediation to others. For example, it was claimed that all Paul had when he returned from ecstasy were mere words and definitions; or, in opposition, that he possessed real residues of the light in which he had been illuminated.

The chapter places the previous discussions in the context of the university faculty. As scholastic culture centered on words and texts as both tools and media for further transmission, it considers the relative places and the roles, within the faculty, of experience and experiment on the one hand and words on the other. That encompasses not only the genuinely limited place of learning through experience in university life (as depicted in anecdotes and statutes) but also the desire, within academic theology, for an equivalent to the direct, lived experience of objects, as enjoyed by natural philosophers and mystics.

Are our habits and knowledge an inseparable part of "us"? Or is there a certain primal self, concealed beneath, that remains constant, while habits may be lost or changed? Do habits like knowledge stand between the knowing subject and its object? Paul's ecstatic mode of consciousness was said to resemble the heavenly vision of blessed souls. In discussions of both issues, the problem of whether direct cognition of an essence was possible— that is, stripped of any intermediary images or any other means—was hotly discussed. In 1241, the opinion that no one can see God's essence directly headed the list of condemned opinions. In Chapter 3 I approach this controversy from a new perspective, arguing that what was at stake was the perception of what should be considered the self. According to some, the seeing subject did constitute one unified unit, but was composed of two layers—namely, a naked potency to know, which was regarded as the new "self," and a *habitus*, which stood between it and its object. Doubts over whether something's essence can be known through its image were raised not only with regard to the knowledge of God, but also with regard to man's ability or inability to know his own soul. This controversy is read against two cultural contexts: academic experience and courtly codes of behavior. First, I propose, a flood of philosophical and medical texts on the soul created estrangement and uneasiness among the learned regarding one's ability to know one's own soul *without* the mediation of this professional discourse. Away from the university, the idea that the fundamental self cannot be apprehended through its behavior finds surprising parallels in contemporary French romances that depict perfect disguises of gender, as well as in the courtly ideal of falling in love with nothing but an image.

The next two chapters continue to delve into the topics of transformation and identity by exploring different models of the relationship between inspiration and formally acquired learning. Departing from discussions of Paul's definition of faith, Chapter 4 examines the ways in which several masters recast the certitude of faith as a private intellectual illumination similar to that of the first principles assumed by Aristotle. They strongly contrasted this to the weak faith that relies on authorities and that is rooted in the ecclesiastical power structure while simultaneously aiming to strengthen the scientific image of theology and its distinction from simple belief. This discussion is then read against historical changes in the history of education and religion. First, it is related to a change in the balance between the roles of authority and of love, on the one hand, and between individual and natural judgment, on the other, as charismatic school culture transformed into the institution of the university. Subsequently, the chapter follows the complex problem of relying on oneself or on one's prelate in the context of the war on heresy.

Chapter 5 examines the intense queries of the masters about whether previous modes of cognition remain when a new one is introduced, such as during the dramatic transition of entering trance, or during less dramatic transitions, such as learning a proof for what was formerly only believed. Different masters suggested varying solutions to this problem while employing sophisticated notions taken from Aristotle's model of scientific knowledge and dependent sciences. Their discussions of a person's ability to hold to two different, contradicting, *habitus* (pl.) is then interpreted against two challenges university theologians faced. One was the masters' need to distinguish themselves from simple believers, and the other was the need to hold to the ideal of simplicity in the face of sophistication—that is, to be simultaneously simple and learned. This difficult reconciliation and its implications for the perception of a man's social performance were highly relevant to university masters of all orders. The chapter demonstrates these issues to have been particularly relevant to the conflicts over learning and simplicity among the Franciscans of the first and second generations (1218–50).

Some theologians defined Paul's cognition during his trance as purely intellectual and unmatched by the same degree of love, contrasting it to another form of cognition, which engages the affective part of the soul. Chapter 6 examines this dichotomy, thereby examining the moral aspects of knowledge in scholastic society and thought. A comparative investigation of questions concerning the meritorious value of prophecy and other modes of knowledge reveals the formulation of a new concept of grace: grace of a type that does *not* make one worthy for salvation and that may well reside in a sinner. The prominent examples of such grace were the pure intellectual talent of pagans or sinners and the charisma of gifted preachers. A dominant metaphor for sterile knowledge was of "remaining standing in the truth, without moving further to the good deed" (which is like knowing you must go the gym—but remaining on the sofa). These and related theoretical discussions lead to a discussion of charisma, ethic in the academic sphere, and the value of personal example in teaching within the newly formed institution; to reflections about the internal search for truth on the one hand, and external pressure on university members to supply for the needs of society—tensions that have been accompanying the academy ever since.

A SHORT NOTE ON *HABITUS*

Theology students of the early thirteenth century were well versed in Aristotle's *Categories*, *Topics*, and the first books of the *Ethics*. They were therefore fully acquainted with a highly significant term that will frequent the following pages: *habitus* (Greek: *hexis*. Note that, unfortunately, *habitus* belongs to the group of Latin nouns whose plural looks exactly like the singular.) Modern readers, however, are less familiar with it, though have probably encountered the English *habit* and *habitus* as a concept employed by sociologist Pierre Bordieu. Both bear family resemblance to their classical-medieval ancestors, and the latter's modern birth even relates directly to scholastics.[57] This is not the proper place to review scholarly literature on this concept or its meaning and use by Aristotle or by medieval thinkers.[58] For our purposes, it will suffice to define it briefly and point out its principal aspects that are particularly relevant for this book.

According to Aristotle and medieval theories, *habitus*, like emotions and potencies, lie in the soul. They divide into two species: knowledge and virtue. Like many other concepts, in order to understand what *habitus* is, it helps to note the concepts to which it is opposed. There are two such principal oppositions: an undeveloped, potential ability and a sporadic, individual action. Let us take Aristotle's example of the *habitus* of playing a cithara. To say "John can play" connotes two different things. There is the natural potential ability that exists in almost each person—even those who never saw a cithara—to learn how to play. Stones do not have such potential, while John does. The *habitus*, however, is the already acquired ability, that which is possessed by the one who has already studied and practiced playing.

This skill is also distinguished from the specific action of playing cithara at a certain time. Long after the sounds fade, the ability is still there. It exists in the minds of cithara players even when they sleep. In ethics, this distinction makes the difference between a sporadic, even coincidental good deed and the abiding good character of the generally good man. "Morally significant actions are rooted in more permanent principles or traits that regulate the behavior of the agent."[59] In the field of learning, *habitus* is neither one's potential ability to learn French one day nor the actual speaking of one sentence or another at this or another moment. Rather, it is one's complete, internalized skill at speaking French.

Habitus (pl.), therefore, occupy the gray zone between the substantial and the mere accidental. On the one hand, they are qualities that are so deeply rooted that they become second nature, "something permanent and not easily subject to change."[60] They become part of one's continuous character and identity. On the other hand, they are distinguished from innate, natural abilities. A second nature indeed, the *habitus* is not a product of nature, for it is acquired through significant effort, through long hours of practicing playing scales and doing good deeds.

This second educational aspect makes the *habitus* not only an interior "thing" in the soul, but a secret agent of external environment and society within the soul. Something of this externality resides in the twelfth-century idea of grace-given *habitus*. The meritorious virtues granted by divine grace are prior to the actions they produce (no need to practice cithara) and by that may be seen as contradicting a substantial feature of the *habitus*. Nevertheless, the interior and permanent features remain to a large degree: *habitus* is a matter of lasting character, fixed in the believers' soul; it is distinguished from their natural, innate abilities on the one hand and from their sporadic, virtuous actions on the other. And last but not least, its source is somewhat external.

Intriguingly, we can interpret the history of visionary activity in the twelfth century as the emergence of a "vision" *habitus*. Peter Dinzelbacher has argued convincingly that a significant shift has occurred in this period. One of the changes was that while visions reported in the early Middle Ages emphasized the uniqueness of the unexpected transportation to heaven or to hell, the type that became predominant since the twelfth century tended to be a repeatable experience.[61] As other scholars have noted, Theodor, the hagiographer of Hildegard, used the single word *visio* to connote not only what she had seen or the particular instances of her visions, but also to refer to her permanent visionary gift.[62] In the discourse investigated here, Hugh of St. Cher is the only one of the masters to suggest that prophecy is neither knowledge nor virtue. It is not a *habitus* at all, but rather a complex of mental acts and impressions.[63] Much like our modern habits, the permanent nature of *habitus* poses obvious difficulties to dramatic changes and transformations, all the more so due to the extreme, abrupt transformative experience of rapture. This fundamental complex of identity, self, and transformation flows underneath the next chapters, whether through the question of Paul's memory or his ability to hold to both faith and knowledge during rapture.

As noted earlier, *visio* denotes *what* one sees—that is, cognizes—but frequently it refers to *the mode in which* one sees. A *quaestio* denotes a common genre of scholastic writing that includes arguments to both sides, solution, etc. Whenever "question" is not italicized, it has the broader, normal, sense.

CHAPTER ONE
Why was Paul ignorant of his own state, and how do various modes of cognizing God differ?
The experiencing self and the observing self
Theology among other modes of cognizing God

There is always a stake in where things are placed: tell me how you classify and I'll tell you who you are. (Roland Barthes on the importance anthropologists assign to taxonomies, *The Semiotic Challenge*, 47)

In the second Epistle to the Corinthians, Paul writes:

It is doubtless not profitable for me to boast. I will come to visions and revelations of the Lord: I know a man in Christ who fourteen years ago—whether in the body I do not know, or whether out of the body I do not know, God knows—such a one was caught up to the third heaven. And I know such a man—whether in the body or out of the body I do not know, God knows—how he was caught up into Paradise and heard inexpressible words, which it is not lawful for a man to utter. Of such a one I will boast; yet of myself I will not boast, except in my infirmities. (II Cor. 12:1–5)

Paul's brief and enigmatic account of his rapture is caught between multiple binaries: power and infirmity, pride and humility, unveiling and secrecy.[1] At this point in his letter, Paul is turning to a new source of power in order to establish his authority among the "genuine" apostles and against the crowd of boasting false apostles he addresses in the preceding paragraphs. He wishes to divulge his intimate, occult knowledge of God, but at the same time to keep the position of anti-hero, which is prevalent throughout the entire epistle. This dialectical play between these binaries is enhanced by a sophisticated alternation between first and third person that organizes the temporal structure of the discussion. Use of the third person denotes the subject who experienced rapture fourteen years ago, whereas the first person denotes the narrator in the present.[2] Alienating his past self allows Paul to engage in an intricate game of boasting, for "of such a one I will boast, yet of myself I will not boast." Only after several verses does the reader realize that these two stand for the same person: "And lest *I* should be exalted above measure by the abundance of the revelations, a thorn in the flesh was given to me." This alienation increases as Paul the observer twice asserts his ignorance as to whether he was taken "in the body or out of the body." His lack of self-awareness during this experience stands in sharp contrast to the superior knowledge he has gained in heaven, hearing words that remain inexpressible to human ears.

The thing that interested medieval masters of theology the most about Paul's trance experience was how to classify it among other states of consciousness. None omitted this from his discussion. This chapter traces their engagement with this difficult task, a task that remains challenging for modern research of trance and ecstatic experience until today.[3] Three deeply entangled questions organized this task: how could Paul not know his own state?; is heavenly vision possible in this physical body?; and how does this form of cognition compare to other modes of cognizing the divine?

Then as now, categorizing mental phenomena was complicated by the strained relationship between the observer who classifies and defines and the passive subjectivity, or frequently the refusal of passivity by the experiencing subject(s). Writing and analysis assume activity on the part of the writer and passivity on that of its subject, the word "subject" itself suggesting the power relationship between the two. This is an obvious thing for those who construct taxonomies of minerals. Observers of mental phenomena, however, which are essentially inaccessible to an outsider beyond their physical indicators such as Rapid Eye Movement, must listen to what their subjects relate regarding their private experience and adjust their own descriptions accordingly. Most modern anthropologists and even psychiatrists, even those who do not wish to accept native, emic, categories such as "possession" or "heavenly journey," would still depend on the shaman's descriptions to record his heavenly journey.[4] The question of Paul's doubt or ignorance highlighted this tension, reflecting it in both of his two personae, as well as in the manner in which it confused the theologians who tried to understand Paul's state without pretending to know better than him. This doubt constitutes one center of the present chapter.

The question of Paul's state of consciousness relates strongly to the question of the possibility of experiencing a heavenly cognition in this life, in this body. Trance, in every culture, is conceived as a dramatic movement between worlds or roles. Mary Douglas hypothesizes a correlation between attitudes toward dissociative phenomena and social control. Dissociation, she has suggested, is viewed positively in societies with weakly defined social roles and boundaries.[5] Yet other studies have found statistical correlation between the level of stratification and complexity of a society and the occurrence of possession trances, whether viewed negatively or positively. These results were sometimes explained by claims that in a rigid social structure such journeys or possessions allow access to the freedom that is limited in "normal" states. Medieval theologians' attitudes to Paul's rapture were necessarily positive. But tensions arose regarding the relative freedom by which one might entirely slide from one role to the other, and these tensions stand at the center of their efforts to classify such experiences. Douglas's insights, as well as Carolyn Walker Bynum's arguments, about perceptions of changing social roles and of hybrids in late twelfth- and early thirteenth-century religious thought, will enable us to reflect upon these debates in the context of an age in which roles and institutions were consolidating. Finally, it must be remembered that the first half of the thirteenth century saw the culmination of a wave of religious attempts to realize spiritual perfection *within* the world, to live the apostolic ideal. This explicitly contrasted with the traditional ideal of perfection, which required withdrawal from the world. The possibility of total abstraction from sensory experience—that is, of detachment while living on earth—is reflected in this mirror as well.

Augustine, who was troubled and intrigued by these tensions, laid the foundations for a taxonomy with an influential tripartite classification of corporeal, spiritual, and intellectual visions. Twelfth-century theologians developed this framework further. Yet in the first half of the thirteenth century its discussion rose to a peak, culminating in a rich proliferating discourse in which theology masters compared a variety of modes of cognition to one another, employing various criteria in order to differentiate them. These comparisons form the subject of the last part of this chapter.

Augustine's categories enabled the medieval erudite to explain to themselves various visionary phenomena around them. But they did more than that. In twelfth-century Western Europe, not only were there different ways to apprehend Christ, God, and the divine realm, but experts emerged who mastered one of these ways in particular. While ordinary believers apprehended divine issues in one way, visionaries like Hildegard of Bingen, Elisabeth of Schönau, Francis of Assisi, and Marie d'Oignies experienced long ecstasies on a regular basis, thereby cognizing God differently from both ordinary believers and theologians. The special knowledge obtained by visionaries enhanced their influence and legitimacy for inspiring and counseling their surrounding community. At the same time, experts of another rational mode flourished: the masters of the sacred page who possessed esoteric knowledge about God, the angels, and Christ. During the late twelfth century and the first decades of the thirteenth, they too grew in power and influence. There was a need to impose order on this variety of roles.

The work of definition and classification (sociologists of knowledge would refer to this as "boundary-work"), which forms the subject of this chapter, I suggest, informed this entire field in which knowledge of the divine was sought by diverse kinds of seekers. It thereby provided a site for theologians and their students to negotiate their peculiar position among visionaries, philosophers, prophets, and simple believers. This becomes even clearer when we take into account the affinity of this discourse with the same figures' systematic reflection on theology as a discipline. First, these discourses flourished simultaneously. In the same years that questions regarding "differences" between modes of visionary cognition began to accumulate, so did the first distinct questions about theology, its aim, and its scientific nature. The first known drafts of *quaestiones* that deal with the nature of theology in a scholastic manner are from the Douai 434 collection (1220s–30s), and the practice of systematically addressing these issues at the beginning of the course on Peter Lombard's *Sentences* became common, though perhaps not yet fully established, in the 1240s.[6] Second, a question regarding the genus of all these diverse modes of cognition was chosen to open the most ambitious *summa* of the time together with a *quaestio* on theology. The author-compilers of the *Summa Halensis* composed its introductory treatise from a *quaestio* on theology (Q. I: *De doctrina theologiae*), which was immediately followed by a *quaestio* on the cognition of God in this life (Q. II: *De cognitione dei in via*). The latter enumerated such earthly cognitions as faith and the gifts of understanding and wisdom, as well as those of prophecy and rapture—precisely the cluster of issues presented earlier.⁷ Both sets of issues were thought of as the proper introductory material for all following theological work.

AUGUSTINE: PAUL'S DOUBT AND THE FIRST TRIPLE CLASSIFICATION OF VISIONS

Augustine chose Paul's short, loaded account of his rapture as his point of departure for a careful analysis and classification of visions, found in the twelfth book of his *De genesi ad litteram*. Doubt and certitude play central roles in this text, first with regard to Augustine himself, then with regard to Paul. Reflecting on the previous eleven books, Augustine assures the reader that he distinguishes there clearly between what he is sure about and what he doubts.⁸ From there, he moves immediately to discuss Paul's own uncertainties and distinctions.⁹ Throughout the first chapters, Augustine rephrases time and again three problematic relations of knowledge.

1. What is the relation between his own knowledge as the interpreter and Paul's as the visionary? Who would dare to say he knows something the apostle himself said he had not known?
2. What is the relation between Paul's knowledge as an outside observer and his knowledge as the experiencing subject? Why did he not deduce his own state through the things that he had seen? How could he be sure about the heaven he saw but unsure about the mode in which he saw it?, Augustine asks in frustration.¹⁰
3. What is the relation between Paul's firm certitude that what he experienced was in fact the third heaven and his uncertainty regarding his own body and soul? That third would also be the key to the solution.

The first problem is clear: Paul is not only the experiencing subject, he is also *the* apostle. Unlike the ignorant young boys and women whose visionary experiences Augustine relates and analyzes later, Paul is a superior authority; one should not presume to know better. Augustine's second problem may be termed "correlation awareness." It supposes correlation between the perceived object and the perceiving faculty. Scents are perceived by the faculty of smell, and thus when we perceive the smell of a rose, we simultaneously know that it was through the sense of smell that we perceived it. But when we perceive the solution for an abstract mathematical problem, we know that it was not with the sense of smell that we perceive it. Furthermore, when we see, we are also aware of the *way* we see. If one is used to wearing glasses, one knows perfectly well when one has them on and when not, based on the quality of one's vision. Similarly, if Paul saw bodies, it was with his bodily eyes, and therefore he must have concluded that rapture occurred "in the body." If these were hidden intelligibles—that is, abstract objects of understanding—it was through his intellect that he grasped them. Augustine devotes some passages to demonstrating how one may mistakenly fail to distinguish between mental images of bodies and real bodies, as happens in dreams or other states when persons cannot clearly say whether what they saw was an illusion or not. But he eschews this distinction until his final answer.

In his role as the interpreter, Augustine returns to a close reading of II Corinthians and distinguishes between what Paul claims to know and to not know. Paul *knows* it was a third heaven for certain; he *does not know* whether his soul was in the body. That means that these two facts do not share the same status, for "if both appeared as images, they were known or unknown in the same way." The third heaven, therefore, could not be an image of a corporeal heaven, a kind of a dream in which one climbs from one heaven to another. Indeed, the third heaven cannot be an object at all. It denotes the third kind of vision among three, which Augustine enumerates later. It is an intellectual vision through which one perceives abstract, intelligible objects, such as love or hope, rather than bodies like trees and houses or their mental images.

In the fifth chapter, Augustine solves all three problems. Paul saw intellectually, and he knew this extremely well. What he was not sure about was whether his soul left behind a dead body or dwelt there in a way that vivified it while it was caught up in the third heaven, in the same manner it does during sleep or ecstasy.[11] Paul could not have deduced his body-soul state from his vision, since this vision is equal in both states. From this point, Augustine is free to develop his arguments regarding Paul's vision without presuming to know more than Paul himself.

Indeed, Augustine dedicates the remainder of his twelfth book to a thorough discussion of visions. The tripartite division of the heavens implied by Paul's mention of a third heaven represents three distinct kinds of vision. They are distinguished based on the type of perceived objects in a manner similar to the way the senses are distinguished by their objects

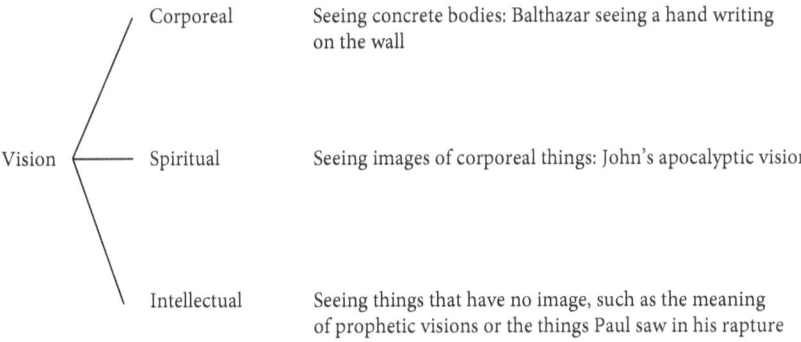

Figure 1-1

(color/shape, sound, etc.). These are: (1) a corporeal vision in which one sees actual, concrete bodies; (2) a spiritual-imaginary vision in which one sees corporeal images in one's mind, although the actual object is absent, and (3) an intellectual vision in which one sees the meaning of the aforementioned images or ponders abstract things that "have no image" at all, like love, the virtues, or the soul itself.[12] The most evident characteristic of the third heaven—namely, the intellectual vision—is its lack of signs, likenesses, or images of any kind. There the brightness of the Lord is seen, neither through a signifying vision or corporeal one, as it was seen in Mount Sinai, nor through a spiritual vision, as Isaiah had seen, or Johannes in the Apocalypse, but through a species, not through riddles.[13]

This is the clearest vision possible, without any obscuring riddles or metaphors. The prototype for such direct perception in Augustine's eyes is the manner in which we see our own thoughts and feelings—that is, when the intellect apprehends itself.[14]

MEDIEVAL CLASSIFICATIONS AND DOUBTS

Augustine's scheme was repeatedly referred to in almost every commentary on II Corinthians throughout the early Middle Ages. Yet the systematic theology of the late twelfth and early thirteenth centuries located Paul's vision in another setting as well. The two coordinates of this new frame were earth and heaven, which corresponded to different modes of knowing God: the faith of the believers or the wayfarers (*viatores*), on the one hand, and the firm knowledge of the blessed souls dwelling in paradise, their homeland

TABLE 1-1

Place	Earth, way (*via*)	Paradise, homeland (*patria*)
Status	wayfarer (*viator*)	Comprehensor
Body-soul relation	soul in body	soul separated from body
Habitus *of knowing God*	faith (*fides*)	knowledge (*scientia*)
Mode *of cognition*	enigmatic, through mirror	face to face, seeing through species

(*patria*), on the other. These binaries can be summarized as shown in Table 1-1.

The two extremes represent normal states of being. But Paul's ascension to paradise in the middle of his life and his ignorance concerning the state of his soul during that rapture threw this system into disorder. What is the *status* of a wayfarer who visits his homeland for a short period and then returns? What is his mode of seeing? Here, there, or somewhere in between? And is there an intermediary for each of these categories?

It had not disturbed earlier twelfth-century theologians to attribute to Paul the clear face-to-face vision of a *comprehensor* or an angel, regardless of his being a wayfarer and of his status as a body-soul. But in the second half of the century and toward 1200, an uneasiness emerged. Several theologians could not accept that the wayfarer's soul could stay in the body without this obscuring his heavenly vision. If Paul's soul was in his body, his vision must have been obscured. They still confessed to not knowing where his soul was, like Paul himself. But the least they could do was to assign each possible body-soul state a matching mode of vision. Thus, Master Martin, Stephen Langton, and others argued that if the soul was out of the body, it possessed the angelic vision of one who comprehends: a *visio comprehensoris*. If, however, it was in the body during rapture, it was an intermediary vision, *visio mediastina*.

This innovative "intermediary vision" stood midway between the vision of wayfarers and that of blessed souls.[15] Yet they clarified nothing but its position. While Augustine's first division relies on the objects and the semiotic principle of thing/image/imagelessness, this new classification of levels of clarity centers on the state of the cognizing person and the degree of separation of soul from body. Visions were characterized by their

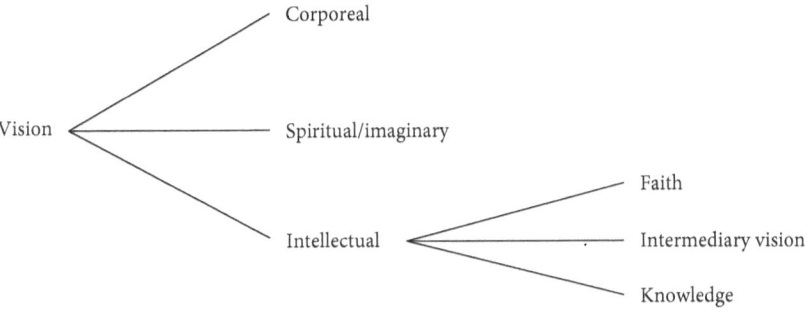

Figure 1-2

beholders: the wayfarer's vision, the *comprehensor*'s vision, Paul's vision, Adam's vision, etc.

The idea of the intermediary vision fits well with lively twelfth-century interest in sharp dichotomies and in the expanses between their extremes, as expounded in recent scholarship.[16] The wonder of union between body and soul was the prototype for such conjunctions. Thus, Alcher of Clairvaux's *De spiritu et anima*—a frequently quoted text in early thirteenth-century treatises on the soul that was thought to be Augustine's—expresses a deep sense of wonder. Alcher moves constantly between opposing principles—interior and exterior, spirit and flesh, soul and God—expressing the wondrous nature of each of these conjunctions.[17] *De unione corporis et spiritus*, attributed to Hugh of St. Victor, revolves as well around the Augustinian gulfs between interior and exterior and between signifier and signified and at the same time aims to bridge them by the rhythm of the words and metaphors of ascent and descent and by looking for a "medium" to explain the miracle of conjunction.[18] As James Bono has shown,[19] Hugh does not construct a separate ontological medium between these oppositions. Rather, an interior division in each enables connection: the inferior part of the spirit, *sensualitas*, and the most spiritual part of the body, the sense, draw near each other: "There is something by which the body ascends in order to approach the spirit, and accordingly something by which the spirit descends in order to approach the body."[20] Hugh uses the scene of Mount Sinai, in which God descends and Moses ascends, to demonstrate this type of connection. They "meet" in the middle, without requiring a third intermediary

However, the option of a third, independent intermediary, based on a hybrid model, was suggested as well. In the realm of body and soul, it was constructed around the term *spiritus*, close to the Galenic meaning of the word, which had recently been introduced to the West and was later employed, as we shall see, by the Dominican masters. Authors in the twelfth century modified the Galenic notion of *spiritus* as "subtle matter" into "an intrinsically essential substance in itself,"[21] a mediator effecting a "gentle shading from matter to spirit," uniting body and soul.[22] The treatise *De discretione animae, spiritus et mentis* by Gilbert of Poitiers presented such a triad of *mens* at one end, *anima* at the other, and *spiritus* between the two.[23]

Such ontologically independent intermediaries were proposed not only between body and soul but for other binaries. One well-known example is purgatory, which, according to Le Goff's thesis, was born in the late twelfth century as a separate place midway between hell and paradise and between this world and the next.[24] In her meticulous investigation of concepts of change that circulated around 1200, Bynum highlights the late twelfth-century fascination not only with binaries, but with the dynamic aspect of these gulfs—that is, with radical movements from one component of the binary to the other. Her earlier work on resurrection had also noticed preoccupation with the unity of body and soul and refusal to argue for complete loss of identity.[25] The discourse of trance and the "intermediary vision" fits extremely well into these two observations.

BETWEEN HEAVEN AND EARTH

New solutions always bring new problems. They may also raise older ones anew. What is this "middleness" or obscurity? Is it right in the middle or closer to one of the ends? Is there also a matching middle *status*, a middle between image and species, a middle cognitive certitude between faith and knowledge? Then, if the body-soul state is associated with clarity, it leads back to the "correlation awareness" problem of Paul's doubt: couldn't he deduce from the way in which he saw—obscurely or clearly—whether his soul was in the body or not?

An anonymous writer of a *quaestio* on Paul's rapture found in a collection from the 1220s and 1230s, which was possibly compiled by the same writer, spelled out this very problem, stating that "a separated soul knows itself to be separated." Paul, he determined, knew that his soul was separated according to its potency rather than its essence. However, his knowledge was not a result of information achieved by the senses, but by divine revelation, and that is why he said he does not *know*.[26] *Scientia* is taken, it seems, in its most strictly Aristotelian definition: rational knowledge obtained through the senses. Nevertheless, the main problem remained unanswered. If indeed a separated soul knows that it is separated, why should it need divine revelation?

This anonymous *quaestio* was part of an intense early thirteenth-century discourse focused on Paul's rapture found in commentaries on the Epistles, as well as in distinct *quaestiones de raptu*, whose volumes kept growing. Let us turn now in more detail to the generation of masters that stands at the center of this book, with an eye to both the problem of classifying Paul's vision and of his ignorance, which was inevitably, implicitly or explicitly, compared with the knowledge of his interpreters. Godfrey of Poitiers studied theology at the beginning of the thirteenth century, probably under Stephen Langton, Praepositinus of Cremona, and Robert de Courçon.[27] As the older generation of masters left Paris and the younger took the lead, he was one of the few who bridged the two. He seems to have completed his *summa* before 1215 but remained active in university affairs until at least 1231.[28] In his *quaestio* on rapture, like some of his predecessors but unlike Augustine, Godfrey strives to preserve the correspondence between the body-soul state and the clarity of vision. He therefore employs the intermediary vision solution. Were Paul "in the body," he would have seen with a mode of vision that was between that of the wayfarer and that of the blessed souls. Godfrey expresses, however, several doubts about this solution. First, he notes, the glosses provided an additional interpretation to Paul's "third heaven"—that is, "a vision similar to that of angels of the third hierarchy."[29] Such angels, however, could not be said to have an intermediary vision. He solves this difficulty by claiming that the similarity between Paul and the angels did not lie in clarity, but in immediacy. In neither case does a creature mediate the vision of God.

Unlike previous supporters of the intermediary view, Godfrey tackles the problem of Paul's ignorance, although somewhat surprisingly, he only turns to the correlation awareness problem later. His more urgent concern is to determine how one who enjoyed such great knowledge of God did not have what seems to be an inferior form of knowledge: that of himself. Knowledge, this argument implicitly assumes, is gathered in an orderly fashion, from bottom up. In order to resolve this rather new difficulty and show that a high form of knowledge does not necessarily presuppose a lower one, Godfrey chooses a most intriguing example: one can excel at preaching theology without knowing the alphabet.[30] This is "most intriguing," because it was far from a consensus. In fact, Waldensians were being persecuted in these years as heretics for their ardent desire (and supposed presumption) to do just that. A few decades earlier, Walter Map scorned their "ignorance" and illiteracy, judging them unfit thereby to preach and deliver the Word of God, which they could not even properly receive.[31] As heresy spread, charismatic preachers without proper education were becoming unwelcome. Even the Friars Minor, whose numbers grew during Godfrey's life from a small group into an international movement, were not authorized to preach doctrine until rather late, several decades into the order's formative period.[32] No doubt, this example directed the students' attention toward the tense relationship between formal training and inspiration that informed their theological studies. This tension and its relation to changes in perspectives on preaching, simplicity, and erudition will be dealt with at length in the coming chapters.

Godfrey spells out the correlation awareness problem explicitly at a later point with a remark on the problematic position of the theologian-observer in relation to that of Paul, the experiencing subject. Paul is assumed to know the psychotheological principle as much as his analyzers did: "We know that if he saw with an intermediary vision his soul was in the body, and if with a comprehensive vision, it was out of the body; *we* know that, and so did *he*." In order to solve this quandary, Godfrey separates Paul's cognition during ecstasy from his knowledge afterward.[33] In addition, he applies a distinction between knowledge in act and knowledge *in habitu*, the latter being the knowledge that lies in the back of the mind but is not activated at the moment, like your knowledge of geometry while reading Harry Potter. Paul, he proclaims, undoubtedly knew his state, but only in a latent, inactivated manner. He was too focused on divine secrets to consider such matters. As he came back to his senses, this knowledge had disappeared, and thus he was entirely honest when saying that he did not know how his soul was taken to that third heaven. His attention made him unaware of himself. Imagine that you see a film so remarkable that you do not even notice whether you saw it through green glasses or red ones. Somewhere, your brain did catch these colors, but the conscious part of it was too focused to process this information. When the film was over, it was lost. That latent awareness puts the returned Paul and the theologian on the same ground: neither had access to that knowledge.

William of Auxerre (d. 1231) was the best-known and most influential master of the 1220s.[34] Memories of his rare talent in theological disputation remained years after his death, and his high position was well recognized by Parisian bishops, the papacy, and the French crown alike.[35] His *Golden Summa* (*Summa aurea*, or *Summa magistri Guillelmi*, as it was called by his contemporaries), was written in the early 1220s and had an enormous influence in the ensuing decades.[36] More than 130 manuscripts survive, attesting to its wide distribution, along with the multiple references and quotations in his contemporaries' works and various abridgments prepared in the following decades by Ardengus (ca. 1227–29), Herbert of Auxerre (d. 1259), William of Montaigu (d. 1246), and perhaps several anonymous scholars.[37]

William opens his question of whether Paul had the vision of a *comprehensor* or of a wayfarer with the intermediary opinion.[38] His first argument against this, supporting an absolute *comprehensor*'s vision, rests on the difficulty to define this middle "clarity" and find an intermediary between the "through mirror" and "face-to-face" modes of apprehension. Since Paul did not see through a mirror, he must have seen face-to-face—that is, as a *comprehensor*. The second argument recalls Augustine's classical description of intellectual vision, claiming that it is not different from that of the *comprehensor*.

Three counterarguments are now brought forth. The first views Paul's experience in a traditional manner, shared by almost all commentators, in the context of Exodus 33:20, where God tells Moses that "no one may see me and live." If the apostle were alive during his rapture, the argument goes, he could not see God as a *comprehensor* would. The second argument puts a new twist on this same argument by combining it with Paul's own doubt. If Paul had seen God, he must have known it. Since he knew this biblical passage, he should have inferred that he was not alive and therefore would have known that his soul was "outside the body." The last argument addresses Paul's ignorance with a slight variation. While Godfrey compared Paul's ignorance of his soul with his high-quality vision, William claims that a face-to-face vision is equivalent to "reading things in the mirror of eternity" (*legere res in speculo eternitatis*). The "mirror of eternity" was a relatively new term for the divine Word or for the exemplar of all things, sometimes called the "book of life" (*liber vitae*) as well. This is the reason one is said not only to "see" in it but also to "read."[39] This is not only a high form of knowledge, but one that evidently and more precisely encompasses, or is supposed to encompass, everything. If Paul had this kind of vision and was capable of seeing the exemplar of all things, William asks, couldn't he have seen the condition of his own soul as well?

There are subtle differences between the problems that concerned Augustine, Godfrey, and William. For Godfrey and William, Paul was supposed to be aware of his body-soul state, just in part due to his mere experience of seeing ("I see obscurely, therefore my soul is in the body"). His self-knowledge was expected to be included in the highest, all-embracing knowledge he acquired. Furthermore, they imagined him combining the knowledge he had as an experiencing subject with other external, literary sources of information, such as the scriptures (Ex. 33:20) or the mirror of eternity, somewhat as they did, when attempting to reconcile his account with relevant verses.

Doubts aside, William agrees that flesh must impede clarity. Consequently, Paul could not have seen as clearly as if his soul were completely separated from his body. He is not willing, however, to label this "an intermediary vision." Paul saw face-to-face like a *comprehensor*, he contends, just less clearly (*non ita limpide*), for there are different levels of clarity in that category. Now if "comprehensive yet a little obscure" is what the masters intend by "intermediary vision," so be it, but William is not content with this term. On the spectrum, Paul seems to him much closer to the heavenly end than to the earthly one.[40] As to Paul's ignorance, William explains that the exterior sources of information did not help Paul. Exodus 33:20 has been interpreted by theologians for centuries as relating only to "using sense and imagination," which Paul did not do, whether in the body or out of it. Paul, like William, knew that. The mirror of eternity, on the other hand, shows only what it wants to show. It could hide from Paul his soul's state. Feeling perhaps that this reply is unsatisfactory, William suggests another solution, similar to that of Godfrey. Paul did indeed see his soul's state in the mirror during his rapture. He simply forgot it on his return.[41]

Unlike William, Alexander of Hales (d. 1245), an influential English-born master, had no problem ascribing Paul an "intermediary vision" in his *quaestio de raptu*, written before he became a Franciscan friar and the founding father of Franciscan thought.[42] Like Godfrey, therefore, he had to encounter the interpretation of the third heaven as a vision equal to that of third-hierarchy angels. Were Paul's vision identical to that of the third hierarchy's angels, which possess comprehensive, clear vision, Paul should have seen in the same manner. On the other hand, he still holds the *status* of wayfarer. Hence the *habitus* of faith, which is an obscure vision, remained in his soul. But should one truly have to choose between the two? Can there perhaps be two *habitus* simultaneously in the same soul, one blurred and the other clear? Yes, replies Alexander, as long as only one of them is active. Chapter 5 will expand on this idea and its implications. For now, the important thing is that as the *habitus* of faith is inhibited and full, clarity remains still impeded. The potency of seeing is not entirely purified, Alexander claims, so as to enable seeing in an entirely "comprehensive" way.[43] Paul, therefore, had an intermediary vision, between that of the wayfarer and that of the *comprehensor*. Like William, Alexander solves the comparison to third-hierarchy angels by arguing that the feature Paul shared with them was not clarity but immediacy.

When Alexander faces the predicament of comparing Paul's knowledge to that of theologians such as himself, he too replies that during rapture Paul's power of *intelligentia* was directed solely to God. He knew that the sensible parts of his soul were not in use for this purpose, but he couldn't know whether they were using phantasms for other purposes. Afterward, however, he *did* know.[44] Alexander does not comment on how Paul knew, but it is likely that he assumed that Paul followed the same line of thought he did. If Paul had not died, then he was a wayfarer still and remained so throughout this experience. Therefore, Alexander deduced, he still had faith. Alexander does not bother to explain the scriptural fact that Paul, the narrator, is the one who repeats in present tense, "I do not know." Nor does the problem of awareness of correlation arise in its simple formulation: "I saw God obscurely therefore my soul was in my body."

Alexander joined the Friars Minor in 1236 as, not long after their foundation, the orders of the Preachers and the Friars Minor arrived in Paris and at its university. This was far from a typical move for those aspiring to a pure life. In 1201, four masters of theology still felt obliged to leave Paris and retire to an isolated place to fulfill their religious ideals in a context of peace and solitude. Along with thirty-seven of their students, they established the Order of the Valley of Disciples (*Val Scolarium*). But the followers of Dominic and Francis moved in the other direction: into the cities and into the world while remaining committed, according to their new formulation of spiritual perfection.

When I tell my students about traditional Eastern or Benedictine monks turning their backs to the world of earthly, temporal temptations, I occasionally remind them that when one wishes to engage in a strict diet, living above a bakery shop might not be the best idea. The new friars, however, eager to follow the apostolic life as they interpreted it, did exactly that. Despite attracting obvious suspicions, they insisted on being able to keep to their purity of life while saving the souls of others. Their involvement with the university was an integral part of the life they sought. The Dominican agenda of preaching the gospel and fighting heresy did not lead them to monastic schoolmasters, but to the urban schools of Paris and Bologna to be properly trained for these tasks. When the monks of the Valley of Disciples returned to Paris in 1234, Dominican and Franciscan houses were already well established, and they were gaining further influence in the scholarly life of the faculty of theology.

Roland of Cremona was the first of the Dominican order to incept as master in theology in Paris. He entered the order earlier in Bologna, where he lectured on philosophy and perhaps medicine as well.[45] His tenure in Paris around 1230 was rather short, as he soon left for Toulouse. Internal evidence seems to indicate that his *summa* or "*liber quaestionum*" was perhaps not completed until 1244, rather than during his regency in Paris. It is nevertheless a typical product of his studies there, being a constant dialogue with William of Auxerre's *Summa Aurea*.

Roland is the first among the known masters of this generation to question the assumption that flesh necessarily impedes intellectual clarity. The degree of abstraction that the soul can reach while still in the body, he contends, equals that which it achieves in a state of absolute separation. This complete abstraction of the soul is possible due to an inner separation of the faculties that enliven the body and enable understanding. "In this vision the soul is taken up so that it is not impeded by any means by the flesh. The body can *be enlivened* so that by no means the soul will be intent to the body from the aspect in which it understands."[46] Since an absolutely clear face-to-face vision of God is therefore possible in this life and in this body, Paul had the same comprehensive vision in both cases. Accordingly, his doubt posed no problem. The concept of "intermediary vision" or the degrees of clarity suggested by William thus prove unnecessary, though Roland accepts such a middle state as possible and conceives angels in their first *status* as perhaps somewhere between the wayfarer and the *comprehensor*.[47]

Nevertheless, toward the end of the *quaestio* Roland provides a different angle, which presents an intriguing dialogue between Paul's knowledge and Roland's. Rephrasing the question as "whether Paul was alive or dead" during rapture, and drawing on contemporary medical knowledge, Roland points out that in this world men may suffocate and die from extreme joy. Both according to Galen and holy scripture, intensity of joy may cause the vital spirit to evaporate entirely from the heart. The superlative joy experienced by Paul in his vision must therefore have caused a natural death.[48] Where William implicitly juxtaposes Paul's subjective and formal information, Roland makes this juxtaposition explicit. Paul knew that he died, he argues here, "*both through experience and through knowledge*" ("et per experientiam, et per scientiam"). This extra knowledge was neither of biblical verses nor due to the exemplary mirror but was medical. Paul must have known the aforementioned medical fact by *scientia*, for "Paul was very skilled in the art of medicine and in the natural art as well."[49] Experiencing this overabundance of joy, Paul must have died and must have known it.

Yet Paul twice proclaims his ignorance, and if the common theologian is not to be presumptuous, he must not pretend to know better. At the end of a long series of arguments involving other scientific authorities, Roland comes up with two possible solutions:

1. Paul died and knew it. What he didn't know was *how* his soul left his body, with pain or without it, since like a soldier in battle his soul was not attending to his body, and therefore he did not feel any pain.
2. Paul was kept alive during rapture through a miracle, in an unnatural manner, as God kept his vital spirit in his heart despite his joy. Knowing that such a miraculous option is possible, Paul withheld judgment.[50]

Although different from each other, both solutions rehabilitate the correspondence between Paul's knowledge and that of Roland. Both know their medicine, both know miracles can happen, and both choose to profess doubt.

In the midst of a dramatic university sermon in 1231, Master John of St. Gilles took the Dominican habit as well, thus giving the Dominicans their second chair of theology. When he left Paris to succeed Roland in Toulouse, Guerric of St. Quentin took his place. Guerric, a former master of arts in the University of Paris and perhaps a doctor of medicine as well, entered the order in 1225.[51] He was sent to lecture in Bologna, but from 1232–33 until his death in 1242 was a regent master in Paris.[52] His views on rapture can be found in his commentary to II Corinthians,[53] as well as in a *quaestio* found in MS Prague IV D 13.[54] Although the author is not designated by the copyist of the latter, the fact that many other *quaestiones* in the manuscript are attributed to him and the judgments, vocabulary, and views in this *quaestio* there correspond neatly to the commentary makes the attribution highly plausible.

Like Roland, he employs contemporary philosophical-medical knowledge to support full clarity during Paul's rapture even if the soul was in the body. Guerric focuses on the understanding of the third heaven as a "vision equal to that of the third-order angels." This is his principal, persistent opposition to the intermediary vision, together with a general refusal to accept intermediaries on other levels, such as "middle status" or a middle sort of cognition.[55] He knew well the attempts of Godfrey, William, and others to attribute to Paul a vision that is angelic in respects aside from clarity or limpidity but is not satisfied with them. The third heaven means nothing but "clarity equal to that of Seraphim," he insists. How is that clarity possible in the body? Guerric dismisses this central difficulty with a light hand: "No problem" (*non est questio*). The soul is both the form of the body and its mover. During rapture it could have remained in the body as a form, but not as a mover. This state can be considered life, thanks to the Galenian vital spirit already invoked by Roland.

While rejecting intermediary visions and *status*, Guerric willingly admits a medium in the body-soul level, and the vital spirit is characterized as a medium *par excellence*.[56] While the soul is from God and the body is from an inferior nature, the vital spirit is a medium that holds the one within the other. It must therefore relate to a supercelestial body that lies between the two ends.[57] Being perpetually moved by this heavenly body, it infuses heat into the human body. During rapture, this natural heat stops, but the perpetual motion originating in the celestial body persists. The body is thus kept alive while the soul is free to see as clearly as if it were totally separated from it. In the *quaestio*, Guerric addresses Alexander's arguments in more detail.[58] The *habitus* of faith and the corruption of the natural body do not *in themselves* hinder full clarity, as Guerric maintains there, but only when they are active (*in actu*).[59] In addition, he opposes the assertion that only Seraphim receive unmediated illuminations. In the commentary he does not say why, but in the *quaestio* he explains that superior angels do not deliver every kind of illumination to their inferiors. The Trinity, for instance, is not delivered in this way, but is apprehended equally and immediately by all angels. Immediacy, therefore, cannot be the special feature that Paul's vision shared with the Seraphim. As a last resort, the respondent of the question turns to a new line of defense: Paul is compared to angels from the third hierarchy regarding their *ardor* and love (*caritas, dilectio*), not regarding their vision. This argument, however, is cut short by Guerric, who contends that matters of love (*ea quae caritatis sunt*) are irrelevant when differentiating modes of cognition, thus:

> In this place, the comparison was not regarding the immediacy of the vision, because this is common to all angels, but regarding its clarity. In the same manner, it was not a comparison regarding ardor, because it is not accepted as the difference in the category of vision.[60]

In Chapter 6, I will return to this statement in more detail.

Guerric does not mention the medical effects of extreme joy suggested by Roland, and thus Paul and the angels see with exactly the same clarity "whether in the body whether out of the body." Paul's self-ignorance is not a problem, for he could not deduce his situation. Other sources of information that could pose a problem regarding this ignorance, such as those addressed by Godfrey and William, are not mentioned.

Hugh of St. Cher, Guerric's fellow Dominican whose *quaestio de raptu* is found in Douai 434 as well, embraced the basic mechanism suggested by his two fellow Dominicans.[61] Paul did not experience a total, substantial separation of soul from body. Yet a soul can remain in the body as a form but not as a mover, and in this state the body has no effect on the lucidity of the vision.[62] John of La Rochelle, a Franciscan master who was very close to Guerric and cooperated with Alexander of Hales in the friars' Parisian *studium*, adhered to the same opinion. Although he did not elaborate the mechanism, he too argued in his commentary against the old opinion of his master—that is, that Paul had a *comprehensor* vision.[63]

Thus, the general picture that emerges is that many of the theologians of the first half of the thirteenth century—Godfrey of Poitiers, William of Auxerre, Alexander of Hales, and the authors of q. 230, 338, 454 in Douai 434—could not accept the possibility of heavenly vision in the body and on earth. Like their immediate predecessors, they assumed that if one's soul were in the body, one's cognition must be obscured to a certain degree.[64] Emphasizing the static concepts of *status* and *habitus*, they refused to accept transit: a wayfarer who visits his homeland remains identical to himself. Like Bynum's not-really-metamorphoses, his cognition was not transformed into an angelic one. Dominican masters, however, along with the Franciscan John of La Rochelle, were willing to accept absolute abstraction of the intellect while in the body and therefore to ascribe an entirely clear and heavenly cognition to the enraptured subject. Subtle differentiations within the soul, which were explicitly borrowed from medical and natural sources, supported this view. William of Auvergne, bishop from 1228 and a prolific, influential theological author, did not write a *de raptu*, but discusses Paul's rapture briefly in his *De anima*. In there, he remarks that Paul could easily know that if it mattered—he just did not judge this information necessary for either magnifying the creator or edifying the church.[65]

I would like to propose a hypothetical contextualization for this mendicant belief in the possibility of full transition, one that is consistent with their turn to an apostolic ideal in the early thirteenth century. A common medieval analogy likened the solitary monastery to heaven, imagining it to be the secluded place of angelic human beings, and contrasted it with the earthly secular mode of being. Since the best manner to present analogies, as medieval scholars themselves recognized, is visual, let us draw a simple table (see Table 1-2).

Following the Gregorian reform, the gap between secular life and the ideal of monastic perfection deepened. Hermits, traditional Benedictines, and innovative Cistercians all believed that pure life upon earth could be led only when sequestered from the earthly mode of existence in a forest or in a highly secluded monastery. At the gate, one must leave this world behind in a metaphorical death. But the twelfth century was a golden age, not only for extreme expressions of *contemptus mundi*, but also for the cultivation of various other experimental forms of religious life, both within monastic orders and outside their ranks. It witnessed a proliferation of

TABLE 1-2

Earth	Secular, earthly life
Heaven	Monastery
Death	Permanent entry into the monastery, leaving everything behind in pursuit of angelic life
An angelic vision is/is not possible on earth	Living a pure perfect life in the secular world is/is not possible

options for combining elements of the secular clergy's vocation with spiritual perfection, whether in the form of itinerant preachers, of groups of regular canons, or the order of the Praemonstratensians. Toward the end of the twelfth century, apostolic winds swept up lay persons such as Peter Waldo and Francis of Assisi. In the first decades of the thirteenth century, the mendicant friars developed and institutionalized the full model of the friar/monk-in-the-world in all its radical force, to the continuous distaste of both traditional monks and secular clergy. Undefined, informal groups of lay men and women living holy lives in the heart of the cities without taking any monastic vows flourished. Although occasionally despised and suspected, the mendicants, as well as Mary of Oignies and her like, promoted and modeled the idea that a life of perfection could be practiced *in* the secular world. Jacques de Vitry accurately described them "leading a celibate—indeed, an angelic—life, they were so much more worthy of the crown *since they did not burn when put in the fire*" (my italics).[66]

This tension mirrored in the sphere of educational ideals as well. In the first decade of the twelfth century, as well as the first decade of the thirteenth, groups of scholars wished for isolated contemplative life, away from the pleasures of Paris: the followers of William of Champeaux and the people of the Valley of Students represent this sentiment. But eventually, neither community could escape Paris's influence. The Victorines lived very near the city gates and played an eminent role in the intellectual sphere of the period, and in 1237 asked for a university teacher; the group of the Valley of Students returned to Paris in 1234. The mendicant "houses" were already established there as the mendicant ideal tacitly assumed that detachability is possible while engaging in the world.[67] This accords very well with the Dominican masters' opinion regarding man's ability to achieve momentary angelic nature and to see like a heavenly *comprehensor* while his body and his older mental *habitus* remained.

INTERPRETERS, BELIEVERS, PROPHETS, ADAM: FURTHER KNOWERS AND DISTINCTIONS

The central question of the discourse considering Paul's mode of vision compared it with the vision of heavenly inhabitants such as blessed souls and angels. With the establishment of the idea of intermediary vision, the earthly intellectual vision of believers was explicitly positioned as the opposite coordinate. Around 1220, however, theologians began using questions regarding rapture and other altered states of consciousness to expound subtle differences among even more kinds of cognition.

William of Auvergne compared the mental state of rapture with powerful astonishment and even drunkenness. It was distinguished from them by the addition of new illumination to abstraction of the senses. Another state he thought similar was that of being in love: a man falling in love is so enraptured that he finds it difficult to think of anything but the woman he loves. Unlike love, however, which alienates the mind, rapture directs and illuminates it.[68] Godfrey of Poitiers devoted a large part of his question on prophecy to the distinction between different kinds of divine inspiration, which could be defined as prophecy as well. Belief and understanding may, he objects, be considered prophecy, as they are also divinely inspired. Strangely, the only difference he suggests in this case is that prophecy entails publicizing the received message to others, whereas belief does not. The cognitive mode plays no role. However, a majority of the discussion is dedicated to the question of whether interpreters of scriptures—to which Godfrey himself belongs as a master who lectures on the Bible—can be called "prophets." Exegetes, a range of authoritative arguments suggests, merit designation as prophets, receiving divine inspiration of immutable truth even regarding future events such the coming of the Antichrist. This latter position was shown to be far from merely theoretical. Less than thirty years after Godfrey, the controversial views of Joachim of Fiore, an exegete and a prophet, were to ignite some Franciscan minds. More than fifty years after Godfrey's *summa*, Master Peter John Olivi's commentary on the Apocalypse was regarded by the radical party of the spiritual Franciscans as an authentic, scriptural prophecy.[69]

Godfrey addressed this objection at length. Human beings were capable of seeing the truth naturally, but sin and earthly habitation veiled their mental eyes, impeding correct comprehension of scripture. This veil was partially removed from the apostles' eyes by Christ. Even today it is what prevents "us"—Godfrey explicitly employs the first-person plural—from understanding scripture in full. It can partially be removed in this life by either teaching (*beneficio doctrine*) or grace (*beneficio gratie*), both operations of divine revelation. Interpreters experience such a removal when they comprehend correctly, a phenomenon that is familiar to us all when we suddenly understand something as if a veil has been removed. Yet this gift can be regarded only as prophecy in the very broad application of the term. In order to differentiate this from prophecy precisely, Godfrey distinguishes the prophet from the interpreter-theologian according to the existence or absence of an inner voice. Invoking etymology, he explains inspiration as an intimate, inner speaking, through which one spirit mysteriously expresses a message to another in a manner unknown to us. An account such as Zachariah's "Now the angel who talked with me came back" (4:1) exemplifies the personal aspect of this experience. Mere interpreters receive no such voice. Intriguingly, and in contrast with all other masters, Godfrey reduces the visual aspect of prophecy to a minimum. Immediately after this, when he compares angelic knowledge with prophetic inspiration, he distinguishes them on this very ground: angels look into the mirror of eternity or read the book of life directly, while the prophet receives a message transmitting what is written there but does not see it himself.

Alexander of Hales took a different path, employing every opportunity to elaborate comparisons. At the end of his *quaestio* on rapture, he raises a series of short questions regarding "difference." Here he explores the differences between the vision of the enraptured and the vision of contemplatives, prophets, angels, glorified souls, Moses, Adam, and John of Patmos. In "on the difference of rapture from the vision of angels and glorified souls," he maintains that glorified souls and angels see glory inside themselves in act. This *habitus* of glory is different from Paul's, since it has the power to remove the *habitus* of faith altogether and thus to elucidate the psychological potency of the intellect entirely.[70] Different cognitions, therefore, have different abilities for removing others (Chapter 5 will discuss these "removals" in detail). Compared with both prophetic vision and contemplation, the three are differentiated according to the degree in which the intellect is separated from phantasms and imagination. Prophetic vision includes corporeal images for the benefit of the prophet's audience and therefore involves imagination, while the contemplator's mind still requires phantasms, unlike rapture, which is entirely devoid of them. Moses' vision was not completely abstract either.

When Alexander treats Adam's cognition in his *Sentences*' commentary, he referred to both abstraction and content. The *Ordinary Gloss* on Adam's sleep (Gen. 2) directs the mind of its readers to perceive it as an altered state of consciousness, similar to ecstasy or rapture.[71] Alexander's category of intermediary vision, therefore, includes not only Paul's rapture but also that of prophets and of Adam during his sleep. These three are distinguished by both the object of their vision and the degree of separation of the soul from the body. Adam saw the initial state of the church, Paul saw its progress, and John—separated here from other prophets—saw its consummation. As to their body-soul state, Paul's vision is the most noble and abstract, while the prophets' intellect remains connected to their imagination. Alexander breaks the dyad "through mirror and enigma" into two in order to create a middle mode of vision: Adam saw through the mirror, but not in an enigmatic manner.[72] The resulting scale of cognitions is something like that shown in Figure 1-3.

Abstraction plays a major role in this discussion, yet when Alexander compares Paul's vision to the clear cognition enjoyed by the blessed souls in heaven, he introduces a new element: a distinction between pure intellectual cognition and cognition accompanied by action. The vision of the enraptured belongs, he maintains, to the cognitive faculty alone. It is mere

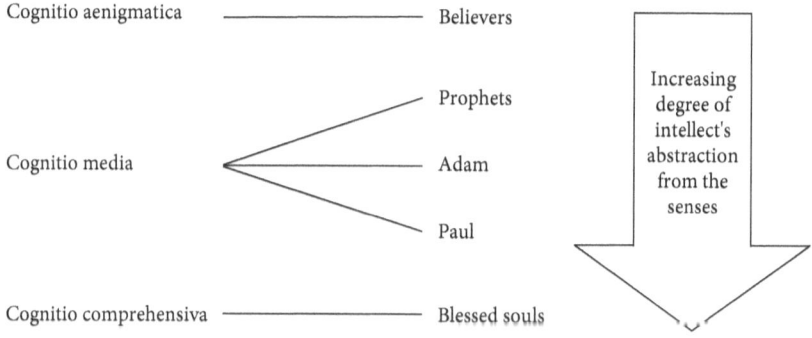

Figure 1-3

"seeing," while that of glorified souls belongs to both the cognitive and operative faculties and is designated as "seeing and having" (*videre et habere*). This new parameter is associated with abstraction. Since love (*caritas*) controls the measure of abstraction, the greater it is, the better it unites the intellect with God and abstracts it from phantasms.[73] These are precisely the "love affairs" (*ea quae caritatis sunt*) that Guerric did not find suitable for his discussion.

The desire to classify and differentiate modes of cognition is evident in Alexander's *De prophetia* as well, where other visionaries and seers join the parade.[74] There are several earthly modes of looking in the mirror: that of believers, that of interpreters of scriptures, that of the enraptured, and those of Moses and prophets.[75] Assuming that all five wayfarers look into the same mirror and the mirror presents itself equally to all, Alexander concludes that the difference must be sought in the receiving mind. Unfortunately for him, the psychological potency seems to be the same as well: the intellect: "If those visions were in diverse potencies of the soul, then it would have been easy to assign their difference!"[76] Alexander turns therefore to "reception mode" (*modus recipiendi*) as his difference maker. Abstraction still plays a major role, yet with a subtler distinction between abstraction according to essence, *habitus*, and act, rather than mere degrees of connection to the imagination. At the same time, other faculties of the soul enter the game through the concept of cooperation: whether they operate together with cognition or not, as can be seen in Figure 1-4.

Thus, when the *affectus* is operating together with the intellect, the cognitive *habitus* we are speaking of is the virtue of faith, or the Holy Spirit's gifts of understanding and wisdom. When interpreters of scripture "see" God through correct understanding of the text, it is with the cooperation of thinking alone.[77] The intellect that "looks" into the mirror can therefore be separated in different manners from the body, as well as cooperate or not with the affective, cogitative, or interpretive powers.

Alexander's comparative approach was embraced by additional theologians who argued for an intermediary vision. *Quaestio* 230 in Douai 434 is a short question *de raptu Pauli*, attributed to G, who is assumed to be the principal compiler of the codex.[78] G begins by asking if Adam was enraptured by sleep and proceeds to articulate a classical tripartite division. Christ and the glorified souls enjoy a manifest vision (*visio aperta*); prophets and contemplators see through an enigmatic vision (*visio enigmatica*); while

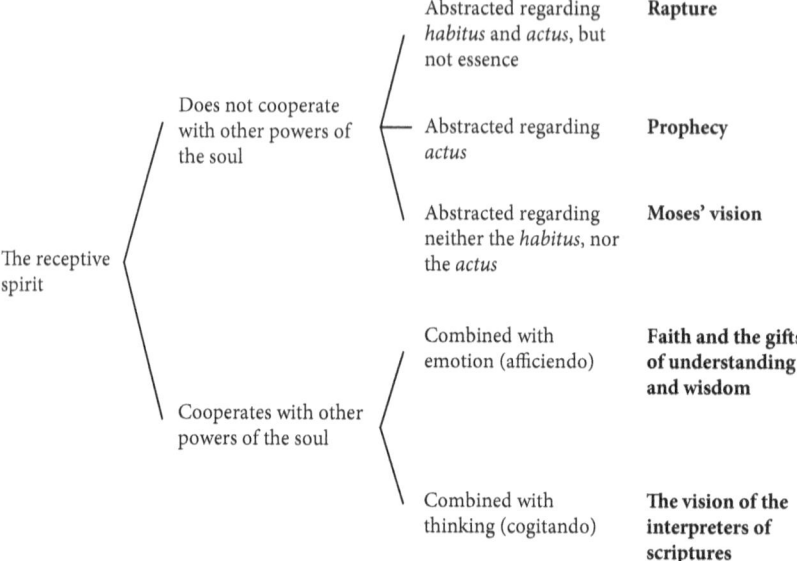

Figure 1-4

Paul and Adam experienced an intermediary vision.[79] His classification is guided not only by abstraction, but by the experience's relation to one's nature. The first two groups, G observes, are not called "enraptured," because their vision accords with their nature, whereas Adam and Paul were violently taken "against their nature," or "above their nature."[80] Since the *status* of the latter two was not changed during the experience, the correspondence between their *status* and mode of vision was damaged. This parameter of nature also served Guerric of St. Quentin when he compared Paul's vision to faith. Both faith and rapture are, according to him, elevations "beyond nature." Yet the object of this attribute is different: while the believer is elevated in order to see an *object* that is "beyond nature" (the Trinity, for instance), rapture is an elevation beyond the earthly nature of the *subject*, the human nature.[81]

Whether one is beyond or against nature is not the only difference between occasional visitors and natives of the homeland. G suggests further clarifications, similar to those found in Alexander's writings. The glorified souls, he determines, use both their cognitive and operative intellects, while the enraptured use the cognitive intellect alone. In addition, Adam saw "what he had," but not "that he had it," nor "through what he had."[82] The enraptured see God face-to-face, but without actual spiritual contact, again unlike the blessed souls, who enjoy unmediated contact.[83] A separate passage differentiates the visions of Paul, Adam, and John according to their content, in the same way as does Alexander.

The anonymous *quaestio* 454 in codex Douai 434 develops the difference-discourse even further. It opens with a question regarding intellectual vision and rapture in general, then turns to an accelerating series of *differentia* questions:

> What is the difference between the cognition of the glorified soul and of he who was enraptured? *Item*, what is the difference between the cognition of the angels and Paul's rapture? *Item*, what is the difference between the cognition of Christ's soul that knew everything and rapture or cognition during rapture? *Item*, what was the difference between prophets' vision and rapture? *Item*, what was [the difference] between the vision in Adam's ecstasy and rapture? *Item*, what was the difference between Moses' vision and that of Jacob, who saw God face-to-face, and rapture? *Item*, what is the difference between the vision treated in the Gloss on II Cor. 12 towards the end, where it is said "this is the third heaven, that is, the vision in which God is seen face-to-face and paradise of paradises," and the vision of which it is said in I Cor 12 "Now we see through species but then face to face"?[84]

The author begins by distinguishing the concepts of intellectual vision, contemplation in the strict sense, and rapture. Intellectual vision is considered as a most general concept, defined as abstraction of the mind from the senses. It comprises three types, however, that are differentiated both by the way one reaches one's conclusion and by its particular fallibility. Thus, one can know something through its accident (*per comprehensionem accidentis*), a conclusion that can be false; through a sign (*per aprehentionem signi*), a conclusion that is sometimes fallible and sometimes not; or by knowing its cause, a type of knowledge that is infallible.[85] All these fit within the intellectual activity of ordinary persons.

Rapture is, however, quite different. It involves an entire change of one's *status*. The abstraction from the senses is so vehement that not only does one not care for sensible things, but all vital operations are suspended except one's heartbeat. As in Douai 230, rapture is distinguished from angelic vision and all other wayfarers' visions primarily by this violent, unnatural change of *status*.[86] Prophets and believers require divine grace for their illuminations as well, but this grace is not given to them contrary to their nature. Nor does it change their *status*. Their visions are therefore only "beyond nature" (*preter naturam*), but not, as Paul's, in contradiction to it. Nevertheless, the enraptured use the dominant natural power in humans: the intellect. Like Alexander, the author finds the old Augustinian categories of imaginary and intellectual vision satisfactory regarding rapture and prophecy. The enraptured have only intellectual vision, while prophets see corporeal images, which are given them so that they can transmit the message to their audience.

The next question introduces Christ's vision into the comparison. This is an unusual move, for when Christ's cognition is mentioned in this context it is usually put in the same category with that of angels. In order to make this comparison, the author refers to the distinction between knowing something by its genus or its universal (*in proprio genere*) and knowing it through looking at its exemplar (*cognitio in verbo*), the mirror of eternity. Paul could not have seen in both manners; Christ's soul could.[87]

At this point, the author turns to distinguishing between face-to-face visions, employing parameters similar to those of Alexander and Douai 230. Paul and Moses experienced rectification of the speculative intellect alone, but not of the practical intellect, as happens to a glorified soul. This, the author concludes, led to an unequal degree of love and knowledge in Paul, while glorified souls enjoy equal "quantities," according to the principle "the more I love the more I see" (*quo magis amo tamto plus inspicio*).[88] Paul's vision, however, was a pure intellectual cognition unmatched by the respective amount of love. His inconsistent *status*, between "way" (earthly existence) and "homeland" (heaven), is traced as the cause of this imbalance.[89] The author of Douai 454 employs, therefore, several criteria and differences among visions, summarized as follows:

> *Contemplators and believers* see through signs and created mirror—*Enraptured* do not.
> *Prophets* usually see through images—*Enraptured* always without images.

Contemplators, believers, and angels see beyond their nature—
Enraptured see against their nature.
Enraptured see in the mirror of eternity—*Christ* sees both in the mirror of eternity and in the proper genus.

Enraptured see when their speculative intellect is rectified—*blessed souls* see when both the speculative and the active intellects are rectified.

Quaestio 338 in this same codex similarly unfolds the theme of rapture into a rich discussion of differences,[90] stating at the beginning of its solution that, although one usually distinguishes three grades of intellectual visions, there are actually seven.[91] Like the authors of questions 230 and 454, he emphasizes the unnatural character of rapture (*contra naturam*) as opposed to visions "beyond nature" (*praeter naturam*). At first, he seems to attribute to Paul a momentary comprehensive vision, in spite of his wayfarer's nature, with the interesting argument that the fact that one is comprehending at one moment does not make one a *comprehensor*, just as the fact that one sings does not make one a professional singer.

Can an occasional action be independent from a fixed *status*? The author is not clear on this point, but later he provides another reason that Paul's vision was different from that of proper citizens of heaven. The glorified soul, he determines, sees God in itself and knows that it is God, while the enraptured sees God and has him in himself without knowing that this is the case.[92] This point echoes Alexander and Douai 230. It is brought up again later in the description of the contemplator, who has God in himself but neither sees him nor sees that God is really *in* there.[93]

Comparing rapture with prophecy, three principal points of dissimilarity are enumerated. One is the direction of the inspiration (downward or upward), a distinction that is central to modern classification systems between heavenly journey and possession trance but is intriguingly marginal in this discourse. The aim of this inspiration, whether to deliver the information further or not, is another factor, as is the manner in which the things seen were seen, as future beings or as beings folded "in their cause." Last but not least, the reader meets an unexpected member in a group of visionaries: the "active" visionary. "Note that he sees through deeds," the author adds, offering no further explanation for this somewhat unclear coupling of *theoria* and *praxis*.[94]

Despite the different parameters used in each distinction, the anonymous author of Douai 338 concludes with an attempt to order all these cognitions by degree of divine presence. As I can watch the light when it is in the sun and when it is present in a color, a mirror, or a candle, so can I see God in different objects in which he is present to a greater or lesser degree. The contemplative sees in a more present manner, the prophet more, and Christ even more.[95]

For Hugh of St. Cher, it was the philosophers who urged him and his students to enter the "find the difference" game with full force. Augustine's triple visions, they noticed, were mentioned also in the Ordinary Gloss on Romans 1:20, where the vision of those who see the invisible through visible creation is interpreted as an intellectual one. Since philosophers see God in an intellectual vision, Hugh or one of his students inferred, they were rapt to the third heaven like Paul. Philosophers and the enraptured were never until this point so closely equated. From here, Hugh turns immediately to the question of different classes of vision: "Angels see God, Paul saw God, philosophers saw God through creatures, saints see God through contemplation; indeed all believers see God through faith; the prophets saw God. What is the difference between all these?"[96]

Hugh solves the question about philosophers and any who see their own soul by making several distinctions. First, between secret knowledge and common knowledge; second, between knowing through image, through species, or through the presence of the seen object itself; and finally, between labored reasoning and quiet intuition, for reasoning entails labor while heaven is quiet. He defines rapture as seeing both one's mind and God solely through intuition and without any ratiocination. Seeing through presence and not through image or species is not enough for an intellectual vision to be considered a third heaven. It also must be something hidden from others. Philosophers, therefore, see differently from the enraptured for two reasons: they do not see through presence, but through the image of creation, and they work hard to get to this knowledge by ratiocination, rather than by intuition.[97] One could further develop this point, though Hugh does not spell it out, to position theologians who employ ratiocination in a similar manner as differentiated on this ground as well. The enraptured, however, like angels, see through presence and quiet intuition. Hugh's final scheme of cognitions includes therefore two parameters in each category (see Table 1-3).

TABLE 1-3

Angels and Paul	see through	species	and	Intuition
Philosophers	see through	creation	and	reasoning
Prophets	see through	imagination	and	revelation
Contemplators	see through	pre-tasting	and	imagination
Believers	see through	Mirror	and	enigma[a]

[a] Hugh of St. Victor, Faes de Mottoni, "Il ms. Douai Bibliothéque Municipale 434/II e la questio N. 480 *De raptu*," 199–200.

TAXONOMY AND IDENTITY

Interest in classifications can issue from different social and historical motives. Anthropologists have invested effort in decoding classification systems and searching for their deeper meaning. Roland Barthes's quotation in the epigraph for this chapter, "Tell me how you classify and I'll tell you who you are," summarizes the common view of anthropologists in his eyes. Bourgignon suggested that the new intensity of scholarly interest in altered states of consciousness in the 1960s and 1970s was motivated in part by the American drug culture of these years.[98]

Paul's ecstasy raised plenty of questions in the theology classroom. For a few moments, the firm borders between heaven and earth, body and soul, and faith and knowledge were transgressed. The account itself indicated a break between experience and later report, between sublime knowledge and ignorance, and theologians since Augustine have found in it a place to treat distinctions among different cognitive states in an increasingly complex manner. Paul's vision was not only compared to that of the heavenly citizens and believers, but to others as well. This comparative approach was not developed by all authors to the same extent. For instance, William of Auvergne did not follow this line of inquiry at all.[99] Although he discusses rapture in his *De anima*, he neither asks nor answers the majority of the typical questions from the repertoire on rapture. Nor does he use its common vocabulary or compare rapture with any other kind of vision.[100] He prefers to compare it with intoxication, with a strong astonishment that leads to abstraction from the senses and with ecstatic love. William of Auxerre, Roland, and Guerric compare Paul to angels and believers alone. Godfrey compares prophets to exegetes and believers. Philip the Chancellor compares prophecy and faith. But theologians such as Alexander, G., the anonymous authors of *quaestiones* 454, 338, and Hugh use the *quaestio de raptu* as a locus through which the variety of *cognitiones dei* could be fully shown, including those of Christ, the prophets, Adam, Moses, and John. Some introduce peculiar figures like Hugh's philosophers or even the "actives" of Douai 338. Alexander's interest in this is particularly prominent and is evident not only in questions on prophecy, rapture, and in his gloss, but also in an entire later *quaestio* regarding the differences among different cognizers of God in heaven, including God himself, the angels, the blessed souls, and Christ.[101]

I propose that in the very different historical circumstances of the early thirteenth century, the context was that of the formation of academic theologians as a distinct group of agents of knowledge who, with the rise of the university, sought to legitimize their claim to influence and justify its practice. The world they saw around them proposed forms of divine apprehension that were different from theirs. As they dealt with rapture, they gathered these diverse players under one roof, the common genus of cognition of God, of which all those seemingly different and previously scattered phenomena were now conceived as species. They ordered this field and drew coordinates in which they could set their own position.[102]

Indeed, academic discussions of Paul's ecstasy included more and more knowers of God. Yet one such knower seems to be missing from this group photo: the theologian who held the camera. His object was the same as that of all of the aforementioned, but his mode of vision seemed to differ. Roland of Cremona made this quite clear when he expounded on the arcane nature of what Paul saw during his heavenly journey. These are not things that cannot be talked about, he proclaims, for *we* are talking about God, the Trinity, and the angels all day (*de talibus tota die loquimur*).[103] The only unspeakable aspect, he concludes, is the mode of seeing, not the objects. But *exactly how* do university theologians who speak all day about God see him, as philosophers, as believers, as contemplators, or through the gift of wisdom?

The label closest to theirs is that of "interpreters of scriptures." Divinely inspired writing had been a *topos* since the days of the church fathers. In the twelfth century, visionaries like Hildegard of Bingen asserted that their visions were in fact exegetical. They opened their eyes to the true meaning of the holy scriptures. Rupert of Deutz even claimed that exegesis *is* seeing God face-to-face.[104] Among the masters seen here, Godfrey provided several fine arguments to argue that interpreters should be considered prophets. Later, he distinguished their divine inspiration from pure prophecy, but in the same breath demonstrated their proximity. Similarly, Alexander included them among those who look into the mirror of eternity with their intellect and distinguished them from prophets or believers by application of thinking or interpretive faculties. Hugh of St. Cher did not address theology, but his distinction between quiet intuition and ratiocination points to a similar direction.

Contemplators constitute a proximate niche to academic theology, yet one that cannot simply be identified with it. Contemplation is underrepresented in these discussions, and this lacuna joins two intriguing facts. The first is that in contrast to the relatively large number of questions regarding rapture, prophecy, and faith, I found no questions on contemplation. The second is the almost total absence of the twelfth-century writer Richard of St. Victor's rich insights on visions, contemplation, ecstasy, and related material in this discourse. Is it the association of contemplation with the monastic, as opposed to magisterial contact with the divine? The best monastic treatment of visions from this period strengthens this impression. Caesar of Heisterbach devoted a long chapter to visions in his *Dialogus Miraculorum*, a collection of exempla. He begins with Augustine's distinction of corporeal, spiritual, and intellectual visions and even recalls, albeit extremely briefly, the triple division of intellectual visions, which includes intermediary vision.[105] Nevertheless, he shifts focus to corporeal and spiritual visions alone and orders these according to their subject matter. Mostly it is monks who experienced visions in ecstasy, which was often associated with contemplation. In his explanation of spiritual vision during ecstasy, Caesar clearly alludes to Richard's *Benjamin Minor*.[106]

Similarly, theologians share features with believers and philosophers but are not to be entirely identified with either of them. Nevertheless, being behind the camera is a position of power in its own right, and thus, while the theologian is not fully present in this discourse, his shadow is. This elusive position behind and in front of the analytical eye of the camera is mirrored in the manner in which his person emerged through Paul's doubt. Paul's account amplifies the ambiguity of one who simultaneously occupies the position of the experiencing subject and that of the observer. Since

Augustine, Paul's ignorance invited the theologian-observer to refer to, and be painfully aware of, his own position as he presumes to understand what his subject could not. Almost all theologians who address his doubt were well aware of this problematic situation. Most of them, however, refused to accept ignorance and ascribed to him the knowledge of an observant subject, even if that knowledge was hidden and inactive.

As demonstrated earlier, simple awareness of the type that claims "I see obscurely, therefore my soul is not separate," was not the only thing that concerned them. They presented different possibilities for man to know and not know his self, both body and soul, options that intensified the duality within Paul and contributed to conception of his persona as an academic observer who relies not only on his experience, but also on formal knowledge. Godfrey wondered how to reconcile Paul's ignorance with the higher knowledge he received and, by his example, set his disciples to position learned theology against the talent of preaching. William of Auxerre took into account not only the possibility that Paul knew that inhabiting the body affects intellectual clarity, but that Paul knew other literary sources, such as the scriptures, as well as the all-comprehensive mirror of eternity. Both reconciled these new doubts and finally suggested that Paul *did know*, but as a later observer he forgot. Roland of Cremona equated his knowledge with that of Paul, attributing to both familiarity with natural philosophy and medicine. Taking into account the supernatural, he therefore preferred to profess doubt. The author of *quaestio* Douai 230 was certain that Paul's soul was separated from his body only according to potency and that Paul knew this as well as he did, although their sources may differ.

The diverse dividing lines and coordinates drawn by these theologians created a single grid. This grid, woven out of considerations of Paul's rapture, is the very heart of this book. Its unity confirms that Paul's ecstasy and the array of issues it raised may serve both as a key to and as the center of a much broader discourse on knowledge and cognition. The Pauline distinction between seeing "through a mirror enigmatically" and "face-to-face" or the Augustinian division into seeing "through image" and "through species" remained current but was no longer sufficient for our theologians. Presence had become a much more subtle and complicated issue, as is best seen in *quaestio* 338 of the Douai codex. In addition, while the degree of abstraction from the body remained an important metric, many other distinctions were suggested, such as exemplary cognition vs. universal cognition, labored reasoning vs. quiet intuition, knowledge of cause vs. knowledge through sign or through accident, cognition based on exterior, or revelatory knowledge vs. that based on sense experience.

Two of these distinctions are of particular centrality and prominence: against vs. beyond nature and purely speculative vs. affective knowledge. The first reveals how much the subject of rapture involves problems of change, transition, and identity. Paul's vision is described as contradicting nature, while the illuminations of contemplators, prophets, blessed souls, and angels are compatible with their natural positions and happen just "beyond" their nature. Intriguingly, the discussions lack explicit or implicit dealing with the idea of natural prophecy and natural disposition for prophecy expressed in the Arabic peripatetic tradition, the dilemma that preoccupied the next generation of scholars.[107] Nature here is human nature in large, without those whose capacities are extremely well attuned to receiving the light or seeing. All revolves around the question of whether one exceeds one's nature but still within this nature's limits or, like Paul, totally trangresses it and sees against nature. The element of violence and involuntary rise by an external force is eminent in the definitions of rapture, even if one assumes Paul prepared himself for the lift.

For Alexander, Paul's fixed status as wayfarer shades the clarity of his vision even when temporarily inactive, but issues of *habitus* or *status* are almost left out of the discussion entirely by these authors and by William of Auxerre. While reflecting concerns (and motivations) about the ability to conduct pure, angelic life on earth, as noted earlier, these matters of identity will be elaborated in the next chapters to present a fuller account of perceptions on identity at this period.

The second distinction introduces noncognitive elements such as love and affectivity. The vision of the enraptured was distinguished as purely cognitive or speculative. It does not involve the practical or the operative intellect, and the affective parts of the soul do not cooperate with the intellect as they do in faith or in the gifts of understanding and wisdom. This distinction has a deep ground in the tensions regarding the social and moral expectations of agents of knowledge in the early thirteenth century, and it will guide the last chapter of this book.

The compressed Pauline account became a focal point for developing and refining ideas about knowledge and cognition. It is time, therefore, to enter through this gate, to examine in detail these issues as they emerge from the respective *quaestiones* about rapture, but also those about faith, prophecy, and beatific vision. The following chapters trace different threads highlighted here and develop issues raised only briefly, such as different degrees of presence, the possibility of having two cognitive *habitus* at the same time, and the relation of cognition to love or care for society, searching within this interlacing for the shadow of its creators.

CHAPTER TWO
How could Paul remember his rapture?
Memory and the continuity of the self
Theology between experience and words

The question of "through what" we know or "see" something was fundamental to the scholastic discourse of knowledge. Traditionally, the most powerful difference between earthly and heavenly cognition, such as the one enjoyed by Paul in II Corinthians, was that of either knowing "through image" or "enigmatically through a mirror" on one hand versus direct, face-to-face knowing on the other. Paul's intellectual vision was characterized by Augustine, first and foremost, as one devoid of the mediation of images, for he saw "things as they are."

The knowledge we have after a face-to-face meeting with someone supersedes what we previously knew about him based only on seeing his picture. The picture or the image is a substitute, a useful aid, but it cannot equal reality. We use it in the absence of the actual thing. Absence compels us to rely on something other than the absent thing and other than ourselves. Belief is therefore the archetype of this mediated, uncertain knowledge. We believe ancient chronicles provide us with knowledge of times in which we have not lived; we believe visual depictions and stories about places we have never visited; we trust the gestures and words of a friend to communicate her inner thoughts and feelings, an interior realm we will never access.

Who or what "other" can function as a reliable transmitter of information about someone who is not present or proximate to us? It could be someone else, such as a common friend or a messenger who just saw her. It could be something else, such as a letter she had written, a portrait of hers, or something that she made. One category may be termed, therefore, "mediating creatures," or, in Alexander of Hales's terms, a medium belonging to the hierarchy of creatures in the universe ("*in ordine universi*"; "*in ordine creaturarum*"). The classic example of such mediators is angels that convey illuminating messages to inferior angels and also to humans. Thus, one of the interpretations for "the third heaven" that Paul visited in II Corinthians contends that his vision shared the immediacy of vision proper to third-hierarchy angels, for he similarly did not receive his knowledge about God from someone else, such as another angel. A different mediator, who is not a creature but certainly a "who" rather than a "what," was the primary Christian mediator, Christ himself. Human messengers, such as prophets, prelates, preachers, and teachers mediate information as well: Chapter 4 will discuss mediation by those who inform us "through hearing."

The other category of media was that of intermediate propositions or objects of knowledge that support or lead to another object of knowledge. Sometimes, we reach conclusions only through intermediate propositions and thus, according to Aristotle, the only immediate knowledge is that of the first principles. This category may host other media, such as pictures, images, or vestiges by which we learn of an absent thing. When we see a picture of a lion, we know what it looks like even if we have never met one face-to-face. Absence is not always absolute but can connote contiguity across distance. Furthermore, even when we see an object that is present before our eyes, images are already involved in our perception and cognition. Its *species* or image is imprinted on the eye and is thus transmitted to the perceiving subject, to the imagination or the memory, so that it can be accessed when the actual thing is no longer present. Is this considered an "other" as well? An image of a corporeal object in our memory differs substantially and ontologically from the corporeal thing itself. One may conclude, therefore, as Augustine did, that genuine direct access can only be achieved where no distance obtains at all. The soul gazing inside its own interior realm was considered such a case. Introspection was Augustine's typical example of intellectual vision, since the soul was thought to be present to itself without any barriers. Its contents, such as joy, sorrow, and the intellect itself, are seen there as they are. The self was considered therefore as a locus of both direct presence and absolute certitude.

Godfrey of Poitiers addressed the question of a medium in Paul's vision only when he compared it to that of the Seraphim, arguing that both saw directly. He considered only the "who" category of mediators. Yet the question of whether Paul's vision was "with medium" or without became hotly contested in classroom treatments of his rapture, particularly under William of Auxerre. Shortly thereafter, it turned into a central issue encompassing the subject of heavenly vision in general. In 1241, it featured the first of ten opinions, which were condemned by bishop William of Auvergne, Chancellor Odo of Châteauroux, and all the regent masters of theology. It was forbidden to argue, the decree determined, that no one could see God's essence in itself—that is, without mediation.

The next two chapters will unfold the complicated discourse about immediate knowledge of God by demonstrating the fluidity of the concept of mediation. At the same time, they will attempt to read this discourse in the context of the tension between bookish knowledge on the one hand and personal direct experience on the other that underlay academic culture. Chapter 2's point of departure is the intriguing problem of Paul's memory on his return from his ecstasy; Chapter 3 treats the beatific vision of glorified souls.

PAUL'S RECOLLECTION AND THE COMMUNICATION OF EXPERIENCE

Augustine described Paul's vision as one without any images, similar to introspection. But when introspection ends, it is images, similes, words, and signs that make dialogue with another possible. When the prophet's vision ends and his privileged experience ceases, he must descend from the proverbial mountaintop and convey the message he received to his audience. Even before this, he must recall it himself. One of the specific traits that distinguish trance experience from spirit possession is that after the former the shaman remembers his or her celestial voyage, while in the latter case, the possessed often experience amnesia.[1] The enraptured Paul was not a prophet, but he did return from his unique experience to himself and to his people. The difficulty raised for the first time by William of Auxerre turns out therefore to be remarkably simple:[2] if Paul saw God only through his presence without any mediating images or impressions, no images could have remained in his memory upon his return to his previous state. Hence, when the vision was over he could not remember it. Paul, however, did relate his experience to the Corinthians, so he undoubtedly recalled *something*: if not what he saw, at least the fact that this rapture occurred.

How is recollection possible without images? In order to solve this new problem, William distinguishes between two kinds of cognition. "Cognition of the real thing" (*cognitio realis*), he explains, is created by encountering the real presence of a thing or by an image it emits. "Cognition of the name" or "nominal cognition" (*cognitio nominalis*), on the other hand, is not related to the real thing (*res*) at all, directly or indirectly. It is the result of a verbal explanation (*nomina exponencia rem*) or a definition (*racio*). This is how a blind man cognizes colors through a verbal description, such as "*color* is something that is known by a bodily sense." He knows what a bodily sensation is since he knows things through touch, and by way of analogy he has a faint knowledge of color. Naturally, such knowledge is inferior to the knowledge of a sighted person, yet it is still knowledge (*color* is not, say, a vegetable). Similarly, William argues that when Paul returned he had only nominal knowledge of his rapture: knowledge of the definitions of things rather than of their real essence, like the knowledge of definitions described by Aristotle.[3]

Both Roland of Cremona, an avid reader of William's *Summa Aurea*, and Riballier, the text's modern editor, claimed that no such knowledge is discussed in Aristotle's texts. While Aristotle's *Posterior Analytics* 2.10 does not treat different types of cognition, it does indeed discuss different types of definitions:

> Since a definition is said to be an account of what a thing is, it is evident that one type will be an account of what the name or a different name-like account signifies, e.g., what "triangle" signifies.[4]

The Latin translation affirmed that this is what William had in mind. James of Venice rendered this passage as follows:

> Diffinitio autem quoniam quidem dicitur ratio ipsius quid est, manifestum est quoniam aliqua quidem erit ratio ipsius quod quid significat nomen aut erit ratio altera nomina ponens, ut quid significat quid est secundum quod triangulus est.[5]

In his commentary on the *Posterior Analytics*, Ross explains that although Aristotle's first kind of definition seems formally identical to the third—namely, "thunder is noise in the clouds"—they in fact answer different questions. The first is an answer to the question "What does the name *thunder* signify?" while the third is a response to "What is the nature of this thing we know as thunder?" Concerning knowledge, the one who received the first answer now knows in the fashion of one who finds an unknown word in a book and goes to a dictionary to clarify its meaning, even though he may never have heard the sound of thunder in his life. William seems to read Aristotle here as alluding to a kind of knowledge derived from verbal description and thus something related exclusively to words, not as knowledge of the real nature of a thing.

The blind man is found in an incidental remark in the *Physics*. In the opening of his discussion of nature in book 2, Aristotle claims that there is no point in demonstrating nature's existence. As it is obvious, a demonstration would be contrary to the normal course of knowledge—that is, from the known to the unknown. Aristotle nevertheless notes that a reversal, moving from the unknown to the known, is possible and provides as an example a man blind from birth who reasons about colors. Such men necessarily use names without understanding their meaning.[6]

William considers Aristotle's methodology in the *Physics* and the *Posterior Analytics* and opines that such was the knowledge of the revelation that remained in Paul's mind upon his return from the third heaven. It was not related to anything real or to the experience itself but belonged to the realm of words and verbal approximations central to men who are blind from birth. A few years later, Roland studied William's *summa* and invested a great deal of intellectual energy in resolving the difficulty it created regarding Paul's memory of his rapture. The problem first appears immediately after his main discussion of sight through a medium or image. Roland, equipped with rich knowledge of natural philosophy, enhances William's arguments with scientific, natural materials that strengthen the connection between image and memory. At this point in the text, however, he only attempts a short, obscure solution, which rests on a distinction between memory and recollection: though Paul could recall having had an experience, he asserts, he could not remember what he had seen.[7]

Unlike William, Roland explicitly refers his readers to Aristotle's writings on memory. Let us turn with him to Aristotle's *On Memory and Recollection*. Memory in this text involves images, while recollection is unquestionably associated with images that were imprinted earlier in the soul.[8] Moreover, Aristotle associates memory with imagination, since it involves the element of time. Only accidentally is it related to thought, for mere gazing at an intellectual object is not recollection but simply knowledge. Recollection involves awareness of *time*, the prior occasion when one acquired that specific information, in addition to its content.[9] Therefore, according to Aristotle, the faculty of imagination, with which one cognizes magnitude and motion, must be involved. This does not seem to help Roland, but actually complicates things further.

Indeed, whatever Roland's first intention concerning recollection without memory, the same difficulty concerning imageless memory arises again, as if Roland had not dealt with it before, just a few passages later. Now, however, he presents it with additional thoroughness and examines at length the problems of supposing the involvement of intellectual images or forms. If a form of God were in Paul's mind, what kind of form would it have been? It could not have been an abstracted form, since God is simple, and if it were an infused form, it must have been different from God. Supposing we accept this idea in opposition to Augustine, what was the nature of this form? Was it similar to God? If not, how could it lead Paul to see God when cognition, according to all philosophers, is based on similarity? On the other hand, what similarity could there be between a creature and its creator?[10] All this puts Roland in a quandary.

> It would have been so easy, and with no shade of doubt, to say that Paul had seen God without any images, as well as all arcane things. If we could only see how he was able to recall what he has seen, it would have been a great thing, for neither authority nor pure reason allows us to say he had seen all that through images.[11]

Readers may remember that the *Summa Aurea*, in which the difficulty is raised, also suggests a solution. Yet instead of availing himself of it, Roland attacks William's solution and the idea of *cognitio nominalis* with a surprisingly emotional critique. First, he criticizes the idea that Paul possessed a definition of his vision: definitions have nothing to do with the situation as presented, and Paul's account does not resemble a definition at all. Moreover, even if he did possess the vision's definition, all he knew was the substance of the vision itself, not its content—namely, God and the occult things that he reports having seen. This is, however, an absurd claim. How can one have knowledge devoid of content? Returning to the *Posterior Analytics*, Roland rejects the idea of nominal cognition altogether and refuses to accept knowledge that is not true Aristotelian *scientia* based on prior sense perception. The blind man's cognition of colors based purely on definitions is not based on prior sense perception and therefore does not constitute knowledge at all. How can a reasonable man think that blind people have any knowledge of colors whatsoever? "I vehemently wonder that such a prudent man could say that," Roland remarks.¹² To say that Paul possessed this kind of knowledge is to say that he had none.

Roland endeavors to fashion his own solution to the problem and in fact ends up proposing three solutions. First, he argues that although during rapture no mediating images were involved, there was a different kind of medium that is not an image: created light. True, God is present in every creature *substantialiter* and *presentialiter*. Nevertheless, taking physical perception as a model, even when all veils are removed, the eye still needs a "visual spirit" or light in order to see a present object. It is exactly this light that imprinted *stigmata* of the occult things he saw. Upon his return, Paul could retrieve what he saw by using these *stigmata* or engravings and "a certain created light." These engravings or light are not considered as *media* in Roland's eyes, for they are not images in the traditional meaning of corporeal images related to the object. This must not have been, however, an entirely satisfactory solution, since Roland immediately proposes a better version of it. According to his improved second model, the original vision did not involve any signs, and the "preparing light" was not separate from the "light for vision." During the vision, light had one nature. Real vestiges of this light were only created as a result of Paul's descent. This was therefore not sight through images, but through essence proper. The medium of light serves as a sign or image but is to be considered as proper essence.

Roland finally proposes a third solution, meant for those who were not able to follow the aforementioned intricate explanation. Similarly, the process of seeing is distinguished from that of recollecting, but in a much more radical manner: after the apostle returned to his senses, God created or inspired in his mind certain images. He did not see through them during rapture, but they aided him in recalling what he had seen.¹³ The fact that Roland does not prefer this solution demonstrates his keen interest in real continuity of vision and recollection.

The author of *quaestio* 454 in MS Douai 434 presents a similar answer to that of Roland. Natural and spiritual perceptions require two media, he maintains: a *habitus* on the part of the one who sees, and an image or species of the thing seen. In the special case of Paul's vision, no *species* of that which was seen—God—was needed. On the part of the seer, however, a *habitus* was still required. This *habitus* that was conferred on Paul during his rapture, which functioned as a special sort of eyeglass for his mental eyes, remained in his mind after his return and thus enabled him to recall his vision.[14] As discussed previously, one of the questions that was treated by certain theologians beginning in the late twelfth century was whether Paul maintained his faith during this experience (his usual pair of eyeglasses, if you will), and what were the consequences of its presence, even if inactive. When the author of *quaestio* 454 addresses this question, he also provides a complete description of the situation following Paul's rapture—that is, when Paul had his faith reactivated. The light that had been infused during the rapture was subsequently joined to the light of faith, thus becoming a lesser light that could not be fully activated. Paul remembered his vision with the aid of this *habitus*, though he did not recall all that he saw. More revealing is the reason the author thought it had to be so: Paul, he adds, must have recalled for the benefit of the church.[15]

Roland's solution and that of *quaestio* 454 demonstrate a crucial development in the discourse of mediation. First and foremost, they move from a tripartite to a quadripartite model of vision. Prior to this, theologians and philosophers were accustomed to perceive the subject as an eye that receives an image of the object; but in this period, they introduce a sharp distinction within the subject—it is not enough to have an eye, for there is also a spirit of sight, a light or a kind of *habitus*, distinguished from the potency of seeing. Two "middle terms" therefore stand between the "naked" potency-subject and the object, one of each side: the image (of the object) and the light-*habitus* (of the subject, although its origin may be, as in the case of seeing God, grace coming from the object). When deprived of one of its middle terms, as in the case of Paul's imageless vision, it still retains another middle term. Usually, one would say, neither the light of the lamp nor the lenses of the eyeglasses carry in themselves the colors we see with their help. Yet in this case, in which light is identical in a certain manner to the object itself, that subjective *habitus*, which the author identifies as the light that is infused into the subject during rapture, is forced to take the semiotic, objective function of the image. It has something of the object in it. I will expand much further on this preparative light and the meaning of the shift to a quadripartite model in the next chapter. As for now, let us focus on the determination that this preparative *habitus* was introduced in order to account for communication, both to oneself and to others, both to recollect the message and to propel it beyond Paul's experiencing self to his community "for the benefit of the church."

The author of *quaestio* 454 applied his notion of a "*habitus* of rapture" that remained when Paul returned and Roland referred to a preparing *habitus*, but Hugh and Guerric deemphasize this concept. Hugh seems quite willing to deprive Paul of the content of his vision and leave him with only its substance. Despite the puzzling nature of this option, Hugh considers it akin to how we sometimes see certain things in a dream then forget them except for remembering that we had a dream and perhaps its essence. So Paul remembered that he saw ineffable words, but could not know or tell what they were when the experience was over.

No images are therefore required for the objects of Paul's vision, but Hugh nonetheless requires some residue of the dream experience itself. He calls this residue a "spirit of imitation." This is the state of the mind itself during the experience, a second-order reflection or judgment that endures beyond the fading of the experience. He employs an example of wine to demonstrate this wherein a man may remember that a wine he once drank was good without experiencing its goodness in the present. The goodness he remembers is not an image or species of the wine, but a result of the adjunct judgment, as when one "understands his own understanding."[16] In Guerric's *quaestio* on rapture, the issue of remembrance is invoked just after he addresses the problem of having faith simultaneously with rapture—that is, in direct relation to the issue of continuity.[17] Since Guerric opposes the idea of a *habitus* of rapture, such as the one embraced by the author of *quaestio* 454, remembrance presents a difficulty once again. He turns therefore to a rather inadequate, surprising solution, arguing that *during* Paul's rapture, while seeing God intellectually, Paul also saw the images in which he was to dress his vision; these images allowed for recollection on his return—a statement that seems to be hardly consistent with his view of absolute separation of the intellect.[18] Moreover, rapture becomes suspiciously similar to prophecy in that the experiencing subject receives both the intellectual content and its inferior representation, seeing them both "in the Word."

To conclude, Paul's account of his rapture presented a real problem for the masters, for this account would not be possible if Paul had not remembered his vision. Recollection is an act of both self-awareness and communication, and thus the divine presence had to become a kind of information, taking a communicable form as it did for the prophets or for Moses. As they dealt with the new problem, Paul's intellectual trance was no longer considered intimate and noncommunicative. How could its form

Table 2-1

	Medium of sight	Medium of recollection	Type of sign
William of Auxerre	–	Words	Symbol
Roland of Cremona (1)	Created light	"glyphs" (*sculptura*), stigmata	Index
Roland (2)	Created light	Vestiges created by the separation of preparatory light and light for seeing	Index
Roland (3)	Created light	Implanted images	Icon
Q. 454 in Douai 434	*Habitus* of rapture = preparatory light	The same *habitus* reduced and connected to the faith *habitus*	Index (?)
Hugh of St. Cher	–	*Spiritus immitationis*	Icon (?)
Guerric of St. Quentin		Images seen next to essence	Icon

become communicable were it not a corporeal image? The masters' solutions to these problems varied, and it may be useful to categorize them according to Charles S. Peirce's (1839–1914) classical division of signs into index, icon, and symbol.

Peirce's theory of signs is of course very complex, but his most famous, early work proves useful here. He divides signs into index (signifier tied to signified in virtue of some brute existential fact), symbol (signifier tied to signified by convention), and icon (signifier tied to signified in virtue of a similarity or a common property).[19] According to this division, we can view William's alternative as consonant with Peirce's symbol, the second in his tripartite division, as an arbitrary sign—words—whose disconnection from its signified meaning is as clear as the gulf between a flower and its definition in a dictionary. Roland's third solution suggests a similar discontinuity between real experience and the means for its later processing, but with the implanted image as an icon. Both Roland and the author of *quaestio* 454 emphasize the quadripartite model with its conception of light as preparing the mind to see God. The middle terms here function as components of a connective link that enables sustained continuity between the experiencing subject and the narrator, in our case between Paul the ecstatic and Paul the teacher. Both solutions seek an index, or even a seminal part of the signified itself, like light that is weakened but endures even after both the object and the strong light have vanished. Both writers recognized the substantial difference between image and light, with the image or the *species* belonging to the object and the *habitus* belonging to the subject. However, both also attempted to describe a capacity to transmit information relating to the object, since both were committed to demonstrating that Paul had a remembrance of *what* he had seen and not just *that* he had seen something.

The emphasis on real continuity, "some brute existential fact," echoes interestingly in Roland's use of the word *stigmata* to denote these special signs. Its source is of course Paul's own testimony in Galatians 6:17, "For I bear in my body the marks (*stigmata*) of the Lord Jesus." But in the ears of Roland and his contemporary readers it also would have evoked the *stigmata* that appeared on Francis of Assisi's body in 1224, just a couple of years before Roland wrote his text.[20] It is most revealing, therefore, that the first textual testimony of Francis's stigmata in Thomas Celano's *First Life* of 1229 describes them not as an immediate result of the vision but as a result of Francis's efforts to uncover the hidden meaning of his vision *afterward*.[21]

Like Roland, Celano shows interest in the visionary's later processing of his experience (recollection, interpretation) and furthermore endeavors to demonstrate how this processing was communicated to Francis's self and to his readers through real physical markings. This last feature fits well with McGinn's observation regarding the new mysticism that emerged these years, which introduced "a new model of contact with God, one that concentrates on visual representation and intense somatic effects that witness to the saint's immediate experience of God."[22]

On the other hand, Guerric chose icons to account for the same continuity. He casts Paul's direct experience as already comprising informative representation, images, or intelligible species available during his experience of the rapture itself. Paul was not entirely focused on meditating upon the Word intellectually, separate from any of his other mental faculties. Images—and therefore the imaginative mental faculties—were present. The obligation to report his experience was admitted into the intimate encounter with the divine. The immediate, imageless nature of Paul's trance was thus completely blurred, and the enraptured subject no longer differed from a prophet. To conclude, almost all masters sought to establish a continuity that would be based on something of the object—either an index or icon—so as to make the contents of Paul's vision communicable, even to the point of dismissing its most important characteristic—that is, its purely intellectual and imageless nature.

EXPERIENCE AND THE SELF-IMAGE OF SCHOLASTIC THEOLOGIANS

When Roland proposed his third solution, he located himself trying to figure out Paul's recollection problem between Paul's heavenly vision and the crowd of believers, all seeing in different degrees of clarity. "Do not be surprised," he says to his readers, "that we cannot *see clearly* how Paul, returning to himself, could have reasoned about what he had seen, because the human intellect, glorified then for a while, was much more powerful than we can possibly consider now."[23] Later, he notes, "we," who understand occult explanations such as the aforementioned one, still see much further than the "little" ones who cannot follow it at all and for whom this last solution was designed.

This generation of theologians was preoccupied with Paul's memory, I propose, because it implicitly engaged the tension between letters and experience in their own practice. In order to penetrate this more implicit discourse, let us return to William of Auxerre's nominal cognition and note the resemblance of this verbal "blind men's knowledge" of definitions to the knowledge produced by scholastic practice in William's era. Definitions were central to the scientific enterprise delineated by Aristotle in the *Organon* (book 6 of the *Topics* in particular) and in the demonstrative model of Euclid's *Elements*. Since the twelfth century, analyzing, correcting, and suggesting definitions had been common practice among scholastic thinkers investigating "What is x?"[24] As a matter of fact, the use of definitions became a marker of the school's methodology.

Andreas Capellanus, who played in his late twelfth-century *On Love* with the idea of love not only as the subject of experience (*experimentum*), but also of doctrine (*doctrina*), chose to open his account with a definition of the concept in order to create a quasi-scholastic style.[25] A 1240s guide for students summarized the scientific method itself as a "*modus diffinitivus divisivus*."[26] So did the authors of the *Summa Halensis*, arguing that the *modus* of science consists of *definitio*, *divisio*, and *collatio*.[27] Many theological *quaestiones* written in the 1220s and 1230s thus begin with an inquiry *quid est*, which deals with a definition or several definitions of the thing under discussion, though the extent of this practice differs according to the issue and the author. While discussions of rapture seldom revolve around definition, almost all treatises on prophecy from this period include a thorough analysis of Cassiodorus's definition, "*Divina revelatio vel inspiratio rerum eventus immobili veritate denuncians.*"[28] Each of its parts was discussed, briefly or at length, generating arguments and counterarguments. What is a *revelation* and how does it differ from *inspiration*? Who reveals and inspires? What does *an immobile truth* mean? Similarly, all treatises on faith address Paul's definition of faith in Hebrews 11:1, discussing the precise meaning of each term, the relations between its two parts, whether it is a sound Aristotelian definition or merely a description, and so on.

In the circles of Philip the Chancellor, Alexander of Hales, and John of La Rochelle, this practice was so developed that several definitions were presented, obliging an author not only to explain the peculiarity of each and the particular aspect it addressed, but also to reconcile seeming contradictions.[29] Philip the Chancellor examined several definitions in almost each of the tractates of the *Summa de Bono* (Godfrey discusses other definitions or assertions about faith as well, but does not classify them this way or another).[30] In his *Summa de anima*, John of La Rochelle brings forth no less than eleven definitions of the soul, analyzes them, and solves apparent contradictions.[31] In the tractate on formed faith found in the *Summa Halensis*, an entire *quaestio* is devoted to diverse definitions of faith before heading to the classical Pauline one.[32] Nevertheless, an intriguing feature echoing William of Auxerre's division of cognitions appears in the writing of theologians only a few years after his *Summa aurea*. Next to the investigation "according to definition" (*secundum diffinitionem*) is one "according to the thing itself" (*secundum rem*), which usually addresses questions such as whether faith is a *habitus*, whether it is a virtue, whether it is one species, etc. This innovative splitting of the investigation "What is x?" can be clearly seen in the Appendix, in which different structures of treatises on faith are compared.

This distinction is also made by Philip in his treatment of the articles of faith, by Jean of La Rochelle in the *Summa de anima*, and by Hugh of St. Cher in his *quaestio de prophetia*, as well as in many other *quaestiones*.[33]

Notably, in the treatise on formed faith in the *Summa Halensis*, an inquiry into what is faith "according to the thing itself" precedes the inquiry "according to definition." Only after settling the issues of whether faith is necessary for salvation, whether it is attained by persuasion, and whether it is a virtue, a species, or a genus, the author turns to definitions of faith. This same order occurs in several other cases as well. Definitions, therefore, played a significant role in scholastic theological inquiry. Masters used and analyzed definitions, terms, and texts in school. Nevertheless, the contemporary image of proper scientific investigation included also a growing attention to sense experience (*experientia*) as part of every investigation of reality.[34] But where is the sense experience of theology, its *cognitio realis*? Can there be such knowledge of God on earth? And does such experience have anything to do with the classroom? What was the true place of experience in theology, and how could it be imagined?

PERSONAL EXPERIENCE IN UNIVERSITY LIFE

First, let us look at school practice itself. The textual records of teaching and the statutory documents unquestionably support the common presupposition that scholastic practice centered almost exclusively on texts and reasoning. Direct experience had little if any place in it. Masters rarely turned to either their own or to others' personal experiences in order to explain, support, or illustrate their arguments in disputed *quaestiones*. Unlike in the writing of Richard of St. Victor, for instance, one does not sense that the authors know what they speak of firsthand. Nor do they admit the difficulty of writing about "sweetness I have never tasted myself," as did Herbert of Bosham (b. 1120) when he spoke about theophanies.[35]

It is possible, however, that we are facing a difference in norms of expression rather than one of practices of thought and teaching. The relation between live, actual teaching and edited texts is difficult to reconstruct. As texts are all we have, the nontextual realm largely remains a mystery. Moreover, the recourse to experience probably differed between spheres of school-life and exercises: sermons and biblical commentaries were different from disputations.[36]

The following story, told by Étienne de Bourbon, does allow us a glimpse into a live scene of a lesson involving study of personal experience. One disciple, de Bourbon tells us, asked his master why Adam ate from the forbidden tree when he could freely eat the fruit of all the other trees. The master replied that we always desire to do what is prohibited. Unsatisfied, the student said that he would not have done the same were he in Adam's place. The master entered his room, took a little bird, and put it between two salvers, then called in the disciple. Showing him all the books and other nice vessels and delicacies he had there, he said he was now going to a Mass and promised his student that he would think of a better answer. In the meantime, the disciple was welcome to walk about and do whatever he wished in the room, except move these salvers, which held something secret between them. The disciple browsed the books but kept wondering why he was allowed to touch all the other things but the salvers. When his curiosity finally led him to open them, the bird flew off. When the master returned, the student admitted he needed no further answer. "By experiencing he had already learned that the first solution was true" (*ipse experiendo dedicerat* [read: didicerat] *priorem solucionem veram esse*).[37]

We have no way of knowing to what extent tricks such as the one de Bourbon related were common and significant. Indeed, the attractiveness of the story as an *exemplum* may betray its uniqueness. Most of the intellectual play in the university, it seems, did not involve birds, but rather the desired books in the master's little paradise. Exams and lessons centered on texts and arguments, on words. Students were not instructed to look into their souls while disputing vices and virtues; local prophets were not summoned to testify in class about what they had seen in their visions.[38]

Ghost stories often provided allegedly firsthand reliable information through a different kind of experiencing subjects, those on the other world, but they usually addressed the fate of themselves or others. A later story from Thomas Aquinas's hagiography demonstrates the perceived futility of such an attempt, even when the ghost is a professional observer. One day, the ghost of Romanus, a former master of theology, appeared to Thomas. After the common establishing of Romanus's state and of his own, Thomas turned to ask Romanus two burning questions, counting on his being an eyewitness. First, he asked him whether the knowledge they both acquired in this life remains in heaven (a question that will preoccupy us in Chapter 5). "Friar Thomas, I see God; don't ask anything else about this question," was the somewhat impatient answer. Yet according to one version, Thomas kept asking questions relating directly to Romanus's experience: "*Since you see God*, tell me if you see God without a mediating species or with a certain mediating similitude?" Romanus, however, managed to find a subtle manner to turn Thomas down, replying in the words of the psalmist, "As we have heard, so we have seen in the city of the Lord of hosts, in the city of our God," and disappeared.[39]

Even Thomas failed in this direction, and it definitely did not reflect classroom practice in any way, though it does remind us that masters and students wished to have authoritative means to support their opinions other than disputations. No ecstatic experience served to authenticate or enforce one's arguments in the manner Lerner indicates regarding Rupert of Deutz, Joachim of Fiore, or Hildegard.[40] Moreover, none of these supposed occurrences were institutionalized in any way whatsoever. This, however, does not mean that there were no attempts to imagine a place for experience even in the field of theology, which, more than all other disciplines, categorically lacked direct cognition of its object, having therefore only authority and revelatory words upon which to rely.

EXPERIENCE AS A BASIS FOR TRUE KNOWLEDGE IN THEORY: TWO TRADITIONS

Theologians in the period attempted to address the problem presented by their discipline's inability to access direct cognition of its object by merging two different traditions relating to experience. From the twelfth century onward, both inside and outside of academic circles, notions of experiential-experimental knowledge appeared in two fields: natural philosophy—including medicine and occult doctrines—and Cistercian spirituality.[41] The translation of the *Posterior Analytics* introduced the Aristotelian concept of experience carrying, as Peter King has keenly distinguished, two main connotations.[42] First, experience was seen as an intermediary stage of knowing. Collection and comparison of sensual occasions of similar nature result in a partial abstraction or generalization. This, in turn, forms the basis for future abstractive, intellective knowledge. *Experientia* in this regard should be located somewhere between isolated sense impressions of particulars, on one hand, and the intellectual grasp of a universal, on the other, and as such functions as an essential part of the scientific enterprise. The second, less emphasized conception of *experientia* was as a different, separate kind of knowledge that competes with theoretical knowledge instead of serving it as a sort of temporary database. In this respect, a fresh graduate may have inferior knowledge to a skillful artisan and an astronomer may require the help of an ostensibly inferior navigator to find his way at sea. Trying to establish which is the noblest and best—*experientia*, *ars*, or *scientia*—Aristotle determines that experience is superior with regard to action, since it is closer to particulars than *scientia*. Nevertheless, as a rule, it is theoretical knowledge that is to be called "true wisdom."

The mainstream in natural philosophy accepted this hierarchy to the point of neglecting experience. But in later Greek and Arabic thought, it found its place in a group of knowledge-based fields that included medicine, optics, alchemy, and the occult, precisely because of its better position regarding particulars and its interface with practice. This tradition had led, as assessed by both older and more recent scholarship, to a growing acknowledgment of sense experience in the Latin intellectual world.[43] Lynn Thorndike, in his monumental project, was the first to systematize the multitude of references to such *scientia experimentalis* and to understand the importance of this tradition.[44] Classic medical textbooks claimed *ratio* and *experientia* as the two foundations of medical knowledge.[45] A similar approach with regard to the hidden properties of minerals, herbs, and the like, which could only be known through *experientia*, had become common, especially since the twelfth century.

Books of *experimenta* were in widespread circulation from the beginning of the thirteenth century, occupying a gray zone between medicine and magic. Figures such as Robert Grosseteste, Roger Bacon, and Albert the Great were aware of this tradition and of the role that sense experience and *scientia experimentalis* played in its image of science. They tried somewhat to integrate such knowledge into their own writings, although the precise epistemological value they attached to experience is difficult to determine.[46] All of them were part of or in contact with the Parisian school of theology of the early thirteenth century, and other contemporary theologians of the time were undoubtedly aware of these developments as well. Authority, reason, and experience were thus seen as different (variously harmonious or rival) strategies for attaining and legitimating knowledge. This notion was formulated as the explicit reflection of knowledge. The author of the treatise *De potentiis anime et obiectis* (ascribed by Callus to a master of theology active in the 1220s), for instance, defined *scientia* as a cognition attained through experiment *or* doctrine (*cognitio sumpta per viam experimenti aut doctrine*). The motive *habitus* that pertain to knowing were divided into those known by ratiocination and those "such as alchemy, through which we experience the natures of things."⁴⁷ Unlike later notions of experimentalism, the medieval concept did not always require the author-researcher to experiment himself. Many times it just meant that this fact or another was discovered thus or authenticated by someone, even if in ancient times.

Yet alchemists were not the only ones to look to experience in order to legitimate their claims and to construe experience both as a concomitant to and a possible competitor with books. The terms *experientia* and *experimentum* had an extremely important place in the writings of Bernard of Clairvaux, William of St. Thierry, and their Cistercian circles.⁴⁸ In Bernard's thought, interior *experientia* is constructed as the interior concomitant and "antipode" of words heard outside during lessons. "Your interior experience should correspond to what I speak exteriorly," he frequently remarks. "Look at the book of experience," he bids his readers. Experience authenticates, enriches, and transcends external words. It carries precious certitude with it, which he understands faith as lacking: "What they do not know from experience, let them believe," he proclaims, adding that the soul that knows by experience has a fuller and more blessed knowledge. There are cases in which understanding can follow only where experience leads. Christ himself was incarnated in order to achieve such experiential knowledge of the miseries of man ("*homo factus experimento sciret*").⁴⁹ The specific nature of experience is never truly explicated by Bernard, but it is very broad, including not only rare moments of rapture and vision, but also daily experiences that occur while reading the scriptures or praying.⁵⁰

These two traditions were associated by at least three theologians in the 1220s and 1230s. William of Auvergne, known for his broad knowledge of contemporary occult sciences,⁵¹ makes a primitive attempt at an analogy between the natural and the spiritual spheres. When discussing the difference between *scientia* and *sapientia*, so crucial to his understanding of theology, he usually refers to the traditional distinction between knowledge attained through sight alone and knowledge attained through taste. This distinction serves to distinguish the philosophical cognition of God from theological wisdom. In one case, however, *scientia* and *sapientia* are applied to the natural realm. The colors and forms of stones and plants are said to be known in a *habitus scientialis*, while their occult medicinal virtues are known through a *habitus sapientialis*.⁵² The sapient way of knowing is therefore common to theology and to the experimental lists of hidden natural properties. This aspect of experience, conceived as completing reasoned knowledge by authentication, is applied to theology only in William's discussion of rapture. Paul's rapture is an *experientia*, and such experiences are important, he remarks, since they confirm the immortality of the soul. Comparison with other disciplines is all but implicit: "In all doctrines and disciplines we are aided by the evidence and experiences of the senses; here as well (*sic et hic*)."[53]

In his attempt to fill every rubric in theology's candidature form for standard sciences, William of Auxerre drew even closer to the holistic image of science in the *Posterior Analytics*. Chapter 4 will treat his attempt to replace the notion of faith based on doctrine and authority with a notion of faith as an interior illumination analogous to that of Aristotle's immediate cognition of first principles. The articles of faith are, according to William, the first principles of the science of theology, as immediate to the illuminated mind as the principles of every strict Aristotelian science.[54] For now, it would be helpful to recall that in the last chapter of the *Posterior Analytics* Aristotle maintains that the origin of these indemonstrable principles is experience, and, as a rule, all intellectual knowledge is based on sense perception. When faith was seen as doctrinal, as "faith of hearing," no such experience could have been attested. But with this change in perception—which Chapter 4 will discuss—the way was now open. The only thing one still required to provide an experience for theology was a kind of "spiritual senses." This is precisely what Cistercian spirituality offered. As Boyd Taylor Coolman's monograph shows in detail, William was the first scholastic theologian to treat the theme of the spiritual senses, a metaphor rooted in Origen and highly developed by three Cistercians: William of St. Thierry, Bernard of Clairvaux, and Baldwin of Ford.[55] William construed the intellect as consisting of all the five spiritual senses and saw faith itself as a multisensual experience of God. The term *experientia* is not used explicitly, but it is bound up with the understanding of faith as the knowledge of principles that forms the base of the entire theological enterprise.

Roland of Cremona made this idea of *experientia* explicit, following the direction of associating spiritual experience with its equivalent sense experience in the sciences. He did this only in his treatment of Paul and with a strong connection to the distinction between philosophical and theological knowledge of God. In a rather amusing fashion, the Aristotelian model is turned against Aristotle himself when Roland speaks of the difference between the divine, grace-given gifts of understanding and wisdom on one hand and the understanding and wisdom of Aristotle (in this case it is actually the author of the *Book of Causes*) on the other:

> As there is a great difference between the cognition of he who knows the sweetness of honey he had tasted, and the cognition of he who had never tasted honey but only heard words on honey, in the same manner the understanding of Paul in which he understood God differs from the understanding in which Aristotle understood. The same is to be said of wisdom, for the understanding that Aristotle had of the creator was vain and frail, as the one he had on the angels.... The same Aristotle says that every true intellective knowledge is that which is preceded by experience. Paul had an experience of them [i.e., the angels]. Aristotle did not.[56]

The grace of faith and of wisdom is equivalent to the experimental knowledge of the senses. Paul had an experience of God; Aristotle did not. Consequently, Paul had true, intellectual knowledge of God that Aristotle lacked. Like contemporary alchemists, theologians could count on one another's experimental authority. In this angelic case, the experiential authority was none other than that of the enraptured Paul.

Roland elaborates William of Auxerre's implicit idea of *experientia* and articulates it explicitly in the prologue to his *summa*.

> Without experience one cannot obtain *ars* or *scientia*, for every intellectual cognition results from a preexisting sensitive cognition. As one who had never tasted honey would never have a true *scientia* of its flavor, and one who had never seen colors would never have a scientia of them ... in the same way he who is not well versed in the deeds of formed faith has no knowing (*agnitio*) of theology, even if he knows to speak about theology. In the same way a man blind from birth knows to speak about colors, although he has no scientia of them.[57]

Faith is essential for the true knowledge of theology, as experience is essential for any other science. It is possible to "play the game" without faith, he admits, but true knowledge of theology will not ensue, that is, in the Aristotelian sense of *scientia*, since it would not be founded on sense experience. It is at this point that our blind man reappears, the one whose mode of knowledge Roland was unable to accept as equal to that of Paul upon his return. A theologian who has not tasted the sweetness of God, Roland argues, will be like this blind man from Aristotle's *Physics*: he can speak and make definitions or complicated syllogisms about colors, but he shall never have true knowledge of them. In another place, Roland argues against William of Auxerre that knowing how to provide rational arguments for faith is *not* identical with the virtuous gifts of understanding and wisdom, for bad theologians can do that as well.[58]

These are the only explicit references I found in the corpus to faith or rapture as an experience, which is the theological equivalent of sense experience in other sciences. Perhaps this is due to the difference between the approach of William of Auxerre and Roland to theology and the approach of the rest. It may also be related to a stronger emphasis on experience as a distinct, competing road to God, rather than as an integral part of the theological road in the second manner Peter King has described, an approach closer to the coexistent models analyzed in the previous chapter.

Just such a concomitant model is implied in an anonymous *quaestio* on rapture from the 1240s. The master argues there that literate people who are perfect in their intelligence enjoy apprehension of God by reading the scriptures. Simple ones, on the other hand, who are perfect in their life, enjoy immediate apprehension of God by experience. Paul enjoyed both.[59] Experience is associated here with simple men and distinct from the knowledge attained by expert exegetes of the scriptures. Paul thus embodies the possibility of being literate and simple at the same time, as shall be discussed in Chapter 5.

BACK TO THE RECOLLECTION PROBLEM

There is more than one way to understand the interest in the problem of Paul's memory in early thirteenth-century theology. The first explanation is that of the strict historian of philosophy, and it was dealt with here only indirectly. New Aristotelian and Avicennian ideas about memory in particular and intellection in general were brought into the theological discussion, raising new concerns and also new approaches to solutions.[60] These in turn led also to the introduction of media of light into epistemological theories. Debates as to the mere possibility of an immediate vision gathered new force. New ideas regarding intelligible *species* were developed. All these issues shall be examined in detail in Chapter 3.

At the same time, this interest in Paul's memory can be viewed in the context of contemporary cultural concerns. As I have shown here, the discussion reflected a lively interest in continuity between the experiencing self and society and in the nature of their intercourse. Rapture or ecstasy is a typical noncommunicative experience: Paul heard words that could not be uttered; Francis of Assisi, as reported by Celano, was elevated many times in such a sweetness of contemplation that what he experienced transcended human senses, experiences that he did not reveal to anyone.[61] Yet the preoccupation with Paul's memory leads us to suspect that not only prophets, but ecstatic individuals, as well as knowledgeable people in general, were subject to a social demand to communicate their experiences and not keep them to themselves, a demand that will be elaborated in Chapter 6. To recall the solution of the author of *quaestio* 454 in Douai 434, Paul *had* to remember *for the sake of the church*. He could not just be enraptured and forget his vision. Intriguingly, as negotiations of the nature of the medium show, this communication was to involve more than arbitrary symbols, words, or implanted images. It needed to be of the nature of a real index such as Francis's *stigmata* or the medium of light or iconic to the point of completely transforming the enraptured subject into a prophet. There had to be real continuity between the experience and its later processing.

Last but not least, the problem of Paul's recollection and the *quaestiones de raptu* in general did not concern rapture alone; they concerned the continuum between real experience and scientific, scholastic theological activity. Contemporary theologians were familiar with the model and image of the science of their time, which included experience next to reason and authority as an essential part of the acquisition of sound knowledge and a means of legitimating claims. Much like with their colleagues the natural philosophers, experience did not find a significant place in classroom routine. Nevertheless, theologians tried to construe faith and rapture as experiences equivalent to sense experience in other disciplines, merging thereby spiritual and naturalistic perceptions. Paul's rapture figured in these attempts. With ecstatics and contemplatives on one side and natural philosophers on the other, scholastic theologians looked at themselves and wondered whether their knowledge might also be based on a certain kind of spiritual sense-experience, or whether they were themselves just blind men speaking of colors.

CHAPTER THREE
Can a soul see God or itself without intermediaries?
The self as distinct from its habits and actions
Theology between experience and observation

> Thomas Aquinas asked the ghost of Romanus again: You see God, so tell me, do you see God without an intermediary species or with a certain mediating similitude? He then replied: *As we have heard, so we have seen in the city of the Lord of hosts* [Ps 48:8] and instantly disappeared. The said doctor remained astonished at such a wonderful and unusual apparition, and amused from so calm an answer.
>
> —*Fontes vitae sancti Thomae Aquinatis notis historicis et criticis illustrati*, 119

The previous chapter followed attempts to sustain continuity between ecstatic experience and its subsequent processing by the visionary for the benefit of society. Heavenly vision seemed to pose no such problem, being an instance of continuous, intimate contact between the soul and God with no need to return to earth. Yet strong doubts regarding immediacy were voiced in several classrooms, even with regard to these heavenly visions of blessed souls. So loud were the doubts that in 1241 this issue headed the list of opinions condemned by all masters of theology.

The tension between the desire to see God's very essence and the wish to extol him as inaccessible is at least as old as the Bible. Furthermore, concepts of essence and accident are centuries-old philosophical terms and thus seem so established that they often do not prompt questions of historical contextualization in the culture of a specific period. Yet each historical phase and its culture had their own peculiarities and in each these concepts and questions resonate differently. This chapter will discuss the ambiguities that emerged from the time William of Auxerre first wondered if Paul saw God during rapture with or without a medium, along with parallel questions about the possibilities of seeing one's own soul directly, or any essence at all, for that matter. I suggest that the introduction of an academic, technical, psychological discourse affected theologians' perceptions of the soul as an indirect object. Furthermore, I look beyond the classroom to contemporary French romances, which demonstrate a similarly intense ambiguity regarding the manner in which images and *habitus* reveal an interior true self, or conversely the degree to which they might just obscure such a self completely.

PUBLIC CONDEMNATION

Few sources attest to the condemnation of ten opinions on various theological subjects that was promulgated in 1241/1243. Indeed, the very date of this event has been questioned.[1] Matthew Paris noted, with a Benedictine bias, that these opinions were professed by the chief lectors of the Dominicans and the Franciscans.[2] Most of the manuscripts that list these condemned opinions do not mention the names of those accused for adhering to them. One manuscript mentions "Brother Stephen," probably intending Stephen of Venizy, while another attributes the errors to John Pagus. The internal political context has not been sufficiently reconstructed, and perhaps such a reconstruction will remain impossible until new documents are discovered.[3]

The doctrinal aspects of the condemnation have attracted intensive scholarly attention, especially the first opinion that neither man nor angel will see the divine essence in itself ("*quod divina essentia in se nec ab homine nec ab angelo videbitur*"). It would be superfluous to summarize all of these studies at length here, but some remarks are necessary. Two scholars in particular have discussed this condemned opinion: H.-F. Dondaine and P.-M. Contenson.[4] Following Chenu, Dondaine explicated these condemnations as resulting from the conjunction of two theological traditions: the Greek tradition, which emphasized God's invisibility so that he was seen only through emanations and theophanies but never as himself; and the Western, Augustinian tradition, which perceived direct vision of God as the ultimate goal of human beings. Dondaine delineated the history of both traditions and the junctures at which they came into conflict, from the biblical authorities that were their source of inspiration, throughout the early Middle Ages, and into the twelfth century. By the 1220s, he argued, the interest in Dionysius the Areopagite, John Chrysostom, Eriugena, and other representatives of the Eastern tradition was flourishing.[5] At the same time, he observed, the interest in the subject of beatific vision increased.[6]

Until 1235, peaceful attempts were made to assimilate the diverse components of both traditions and to reconcile them. The Latin reaction emerged, Dondaine argued, due to the entrance of theologians into dialogue with recently translated texts from Greek and Arabic, particularly in relation to two principal issues. The first was the problem of knowing particulars; the other was that of infinity. Dondaine quotes William of Auvergne arguing, contra the peripatetics, that if particulars were not intelligible to the human intellect then God, being a particular, cannot be intelligible either. Hence, "if someone would have said that the intellect cannot perceive the creator without a medium, he must confess that the creator himself is imperceivable in his nature and essence."[7] In other *quaestiones* dealing with beatific vision, there appeared an argument concerning the incommensurability between the finite intellect and its infinite object, God. This gulf, he determined, necessitated a medium to bridge it.[8]

Based on Dondaine's research and the texts he published on other occasions, Contenson extended the argument concerning the dialogue with philosophy.[9] Aristotelian and Avicennian concerns extended the theological horizon to psychological and noetic questions and led to a renewal of theological discourse. Contenson asserted that Aristotelian epistemology is susceptible to two opposite interpretations, leading in turn to two corresponding opinions on the relation between understanding and the object of understanding, the "intelligible." These two opinions can be epitomized as "the soul is, in a certain manner, all that is" (*omnia quae sunt quodam modo est anima*); and "it is not the stone which is in the soul, but its *species*" (*non lapis in anima est sed species lapidis*). These two options implied two distinct understandings of the beatific vision: the soul becomes identical to what it sees—namely, God; or the soul perceives God through a *species* of God, which is not God himself (*ipse deus*), just as it apprehends a particular stone according to its species. The heresies of the Amalricians and of David of Dinant at the beginning of the century and those of 1241 represented, in his view, these two options taken to the extreme. David of Dinant, and perhaps the Amalricians, identified the known object and the knower following the first, immanent interpretation.

The opposite opinion necessitated an epistemological medium, a *species* of God, something different from God's essence. Hence, it resulted in claiming that even angels do not see God *in his essence*. This later position, argued Contenson, could easily stem from Avicennian noetics. Avicenna resists a literal understanding of Aristotle's claim that the soul becomes all things. Instead of becoming what it understands in the epistemological process, the soul acquires images or *species* of all things. The form it understands is not the reality of the thing itself, which is neither image nor species but its substantial form.[10] This applies not only to corporeal entities like stones, but to perceptions of abstract "separate forms" as well. All the soul receives are impressions, not actual forms. This happens even in the ultimate union with the first pure truth. When the soul reaches and enjoys the beauty of absolute understanding, it is transformed into a subtle representation of the cosmos, an emanation of the one truth. Thus for Avicenna, perception is never a contact or a union with the actual thing, but always the reception of an imprint. The application of this view to Christian beatific vision was easy: knowing God, the beatified soul receives an impression that emanates *from* God, which is necessarily different from God *as is* (*sicuti est*). Finally, Contenson offered a combined model for the evolution of this stream of thought: Dionysius and Erigena provided the authorities while Avicenna provided the arguments.

In 1962, however, Contenson reexamined what William of Auvergne had to say on the subject and was surprised to discover that his portrait of the heretical Avicennian theologian fit too well the reactionary author of the condemnations himself.[11] He explained this paradox through the text's ambiguity and its supposedly early date, as William's rudimentary doctrine does not yet show any knowledge of Erigenian, apophatic doctrines at this juncture.[12] Later, Trottmann also suspected that Alexander of Hales and William of Auvergne actually held a view quite similar to the one they condemned but did not pursue this issue further.[13]

The opinion condemned in 1241 and the subject of noetic vision more generally have been treated extensively attending to aspects of Eastern theological sources and Avicennian epistemology. Following the scholastic discussion of Paul's rapture and the attendant question of immediate experience, we shall pursue this subject from a somewhat different angle. The previous chapter demonstrated the flexibility of the concept of medium in treatments of Paul's recollection of his rapture, from images and similitudes of the object on one hand to the idea of a "preparing" mental disposition or *habitus* on the part of the subject on the other. This chapter will probe the ambiguity of the question of *what is to be considered a medium at all* more deeply. This ambiguity, I will demonstrate, is strongly tied to perceptions of self and self-knowledge, and in particular the question of the extent to which knowledge and the illuminating perfective part of the mind are considered integral parts of the self.

The first step in this endeavor will be to argue that in this period we witness a new threefold perception of cognitions such as rapture or faith, the three being a subject, an object, and a *habitus* of cognition between the two. This shall be demonstrated in two ways: first, by an analysis of the way treatises of faith were constructed; and second, by delving into arguments regarding the mediation of Paul's visions, the glorified souls, and the angels. I shall demonstrate that all theologians of this period agreed that interior seeing of divinity's presence is different from how one sees external objects, such as a stone. Yet even when seeing an interior, present object, there must be a certain preparation. These theologians began to stress a distinction between the "nude" potency of seeing and the additive of *habitus*-light that enables it to see. What they did not agree on was whether this *habitus* is to be considered part of the seeing self or not. The main point of conflict, therefore, was about the distinction between medium and the self (*se*).

A THREEFOLD APPROACH TO KNOWING AND THE BIRTH OF THE OBJECT

Glossing Peter Lombard's discussion of faith, Alexander of Hales observed that if you look closely, you will discern that all issues discussed by Lombard pertain to one of three components: (1) the believer ("*ex parte credentis*"), (2) the believed thing ("*ex parte crediti*"), or (3) "the medium *habitus*, which is between the believer and the believed."[14] Whether or not it was Lombard's intention, this threefold division reflects the way Alexander and his theologian colleagues constructed their own writings, rearranging different elements inherited from their masters and inserting new ones. This tendency to look at cognition as involving at least three aspects—a subject, an object, and a mediating *habitus*—is reflected remarkably well in the treatises on faith from Alexander's circle.

Although in general, all the tractates *de fide* in the decades under investigation share a more or less common lexicon of themes, problems, and arrangements similar to those in Lombard's book III, distinctions 23–24, a closer examination of their structure reveals significant differences. The tables in the Appendix show the structure of several such tractates on faith.[15] The various combinations reveal much about how the disputants' choices were simultaneously limited and infinite. Comparing them highlights the significance of their internal categorizations or "titles." Various issues concerning the cognitive *habitus* of faith were gradually organized around three main notions: quiddity, object, and subject. In Godfrey, William, and Roland, several questions were put one after the other with no apparent internal categorization. Philip, however, gives them a new title—*de credito* (that in which one believes). This category does not pertain to specific content of the articles of Christian faith, but to general concerns about the object of faith. One of the popular issues in these treatises is whether one may believe something false with a grace-given faith. Examples for such a hypothetical case involved tense and modal logics that are too complicated to even begin to explicate here. What is important for the matter at hand is that Philip relocates the question of whether one can believe a false thing to be true in grace-given faith to the first position, thus establishing truth as the principal feature of the *creditum*. Similarly, the problem that was usually phrased as "whether the article is *enuntiabile* or *res*" was reentitled "whether the *creditum* is always simple and true or can also be complex and true."

The compilers of the *Summa Halensis* took Philip's classification further. First, they categorized all treatments of faith not concerned with the specific contents of the articles under "the *habitus* of faith."[16] The investigation of that *habitus* is then divided into examining its "whatness," "act," "object," and "subject." The object of faith was that which Philip earlier called "*creditum*." The problem of "whether the same thing can be believed and known," which was discussed by Godfrey as part of his analysis of Paul's definition and which did not pertain to any specific category in William and others, was imported into this category. Divided into two, it was reentitled, "Is the object of faith apparent truth?," and "Does the object of faith include known truths?" New questions, such as the uncreated nature of the object, were introduced as well. Aside from the "object," Philip and the *Summa Halensis* compilers formed a distinct category called *subiectum fidei*, which treated "that in which the *habitus* of faith resides." As the table shows, Philip (or his editors) planned to discuss the faith of angels and that of baptized children, as well as some issues closely resembling implicit and indistinct faith. The *Summa Halensis* populated this category with inquiries about the power of the soul in which the *habitus* of faith resides and about the faith of subjects such as angels, Adam, and Christ.

The concepts "object" and "subject" are familiar to modern readers yet were not so to early thirteenth-century readers. As Lawrence Dewan has demonstrated, the Latin noun *obiectum* was an invention of these very decades.[17] Often, it was confused with *subiectum*, especially regarding knowledge. A subject could be both the content of a certain cognition, as in "the subject of 'physics' is motion," but could also denote the "thing" in which this knowledge resides, the person, or the mental potency. This confusion regarding the new term is evident in the titles and contents of the categories of the treatise on faith. *Quaestio* 530 in Douai 434, which may be earlier than Philip's *summa*, uses the title *subiectum fidei* to group together issues similar to those classified by Philip under *creditum* or *obiectum fidei*. It includes, however, also some that pertain in Philip's eyes to the *subiectum fidei*. *Quaestio* 501, a variation of this part of 530, was also entitled "on the subject of faith" ("*de subiecto fidei*") and thought it necessary to explain the term as "that is, what is believable and believable in itself" ("*scilicet, quid credibile et per se credibile*"). The common ground of its questions is the question of what fundamental articles of faith are required for individual salvation.

The diverse ordering of tractates on faith from this generation demonstrates a consolidation of two aspects of cognition: its subject, the mere power of the soul such as the intellect or the *intelligentia*; and its object, whether simple first truth or God. Regarding the former, the subject was equated with the believer and the self, while the *habitus* stood midway between this self and God.[18] In fact, this *habitus* functions as the mutable element in this tripartite scheme, while the two extremes of self and God were thought to be the fixed frame for all cognitions of the deity. When Guerric of St. Quentin addressed the exact difference between faith and beatific vision in a *quodlibet* disputation, he preferred first to define faith as not truly a vision at all, but only in the broad sense of the word.[19] But in his answer to the first objection, he admitted a general class of visions only distinguished by the mediating *habitus*. Within each genus, its species all share something in common and some thing or things that differentiate each from the others. He therefore proclaims:

In both faith and beatific vision "what is seen" is God, and "what sees" is the intellect. Hence, it is the medium that makes the difference and since the medium is the principle of vision it makes the formal and specific difference: the seer and what is seen are the matter of the vision, the former as its subject and the latter as its object. Therefore, they do not make differences within the general category of visions.[20]

THE MEDIUM INSIDE

What are the consequences of separating *habitus* from potency when addressing the problem of immediate vision? Godfrey of Poitiers was content to question whether Paul had a wayfarer's vision or that of a *comprehensor*. But when William of Auxerre discusses Paul's vision during rapture, he is not satisfied with the determination that Paul had a *comprehensor*'s vision and asks whether Paul saw with a *medium* or without one.[21] He then immediately transforms the question into an equivalent binary—namely, whether Paul saw "through image" or not. William follows the basic Augustinian position: that Paul's vision was free of images and therefore involved no medium. Like Augustine, he understood Paul's intellectual vision as an interior gaze into God's presence in the soul, an introspection that obviated the need for external images. Nevertheless, in the course of this argument, he raises several difficulties that derive from the concept of imageless vision.

One of these difficulties was Paul's recollection, as discussed in the previous chapter. Another stemmed from God's continuous presence in the soul of each person, whether enraptured or not. William contends that two "veils" hide God from our spiritual eyes: the letter and the sin. Paul declared both already removed (II Cor. 3:15–18).[22] Yet if so, then why can't we see God face-to-face right now on earth? One objection could be that a third veil of creation remained, but he dismisses this as irrelevant. Being omnipresent, God dwells in the human intellect *essentialiter* as in every other creature, and thus created beings cannot hide him. All one needs is to look inside.

To counter this argument, William neither suggests other veils nor defends the viability of these three in this world. He maintains the triad of eye, veil, and object intact and rather addresses the spiritual eye alone. Seeing God face-to-face on earth, he asserts, is impossible due to the imperfection of our intellect, a defect that must be compensated for by perfecting illumination. To support this claim, he employs the analogy of the intellect to the owl's eye that is unfit for the sunlight from Aristotle's *Metaphysics* 2.1, though without citing its source. Removal of the veils is therefore not sufficient. Light is required as well. This distinction between revelation conceived as the removal of obstacles and revelation conceived as the perfecting addition of illumination is often overlooked, but it will prove to be of major significance in the controversy over the medium.

William argues that Paul's vision was imageless, since he looked into his own soul, but another difficulty is immediately raised.[23] The model of seeing through internal presence might satisfy when applied to the special case of God's presence in the soul and of the soul's presence to itself, but an angel is neither God nor the soul. How then could Paul see angels? To solve this, William distinguishes between two kinds of images: one can see through an image emitted by the actual thing, or one can use something else as an image, as when we use images of men we have met in order to imagine what Hercules looked like. It was the latter that occurred in Paul's case. No image emitted from a real, exterior angel, but the soul looked inside and used itself as an image. Direct, imageless vision was again explained by replacing the real thing by the self. A similar solution was proposed by William for the angelic knowledge of future events in his treatment of angelic vision. Future beings have no images, either, as they are not yet existent things. The angels, therefore, do not look at images produced by the things themselves, but again, look into the mirror present within themselves. Their souls, equivalents of the divine word, are exemplars of all things, mirrors of eternity.

Yet this interior gaze into the mirror of all things, being free from external media, introduced still another problem with regard to Paul and prophecy. If the soul is the exemplar of all things, then ecstatic visionaries, prophets, and angels would be able to see *everything*.[24] One such argument in favor of angelic omniscience is found in William's Peripatetic account resting on Aristotle's theory of the intellect:

> Since the soul is able to understand all things and all things are potentially understood to or through the radiation of light . . . the soul turns from being potentially understanding to a soul understanding *in act*, and those things which were potentially understandable become understandable in act, and not only some, but all. And hence, in the light of the

eternal mirror the soul would see all things illuminated in act; the angels as well, therefore, see there all things.[25]

Since the intellect is potentially "all intelligibles" and is now illuminated and actualized, both the illuminated blessed soul and the angel will be able to see everything *in actu*.

Media, images, and figures are powerful conduits for transmitting messages, but they are also effective in controlling and filtering the flow of information, in hiding and restricting knowledge. For centuries, exegetes had emphasized the imprecision of images and media when they wished to explain how prophets like Jonah, for example, received true illumination and nevertheless misunderstood it and professed a false prophecy. Philip the Chancellor, for instance, claimed that Jonah had only seen corporeal images emitted "from the mirror" (*a speculo*)—that is, through corporeal sense. Yet he did not see "in the mirror" (*in speculo*) their meaning or their spiritual sense.[26] In an equivalent metaphor, God showed Jonah the Book of Life, which contained two possible futures: either "Nineveh will be overturned in a corporeal meaning," meaning that it will be destroyed, or "Nineveh will be overturned spiritually," meaning that the city will repent and be saved. According to Hugh of St. Cher, Jonah was allowed to read only the former contingency and thus spoke the truth according to what he had read.[27] William of Auvergne used the same images of voluntary mirror and a voluminous book with endless leaves to explain that this exemplar shows only the pages it wishes to.[28]

Is interiority free of censure? In a realm devoid of images, is control and thus censure possible? How can we preserve the directness of vision and restrict the scope of knowledge at the same time? Regarding Paul, William claimed that the mirror chooses to hide or reveal what it wishes, but he suggested no mechanism to explain how exactly this occurs. When he discussed angels, however, he broadened his conception of medium to include an internal, subjective operation of "attention":

> Two media should be distinguished, that is, "medium by which" and "medium through which." The "medium through which" is the intellect itself, because through the fact that it assimilates to God in ultimate likeness it becomes the expressed image of all things and an express mirror of all things. Hence *through its own self without a mirror and without other image*, when it wants to direct its sight on the things, it can see

them. This direction is the "medium by which" it sees them distinctly in act, and in this consists its liberty.... The angel sees therefore through two media, that is, through the mirror which is he himself... and through a "medium by which" his vision is discerned, that is, through the direction of the sight of the intellect on the thing.... In this manner the soul shall see when it shall be in glory, being entirely an intelligible mirror, as a certain philosopher says.[29]

The soul takes on a dual role, acting as both the seeing subject and the image, thus enabling William to adhere again to a vision with no "others" involved, for the assimilated self is not considered an "other." Nevertheless, the threat of omniscience on the part of a creature moves him to introduce another sort of medium that is very different from an image: the intention or concentration of the intellect's gaze on a particular thing.[30]

The need to limit omniscience is also evident in the detailed discussions of prophecy and the mirror of eternity conducted by Philip, Alexander, Hugh, and in the *Summa Duacensis*. It is not possible to treat these intricate discussions here at length, as Torrell has done in his monograph on Hugh's *de prophetia*,[31] but it is important to note that the mechanism that prohibits the prophet from seeing everything in these sources is nothing but a *habitus* of light imprinted by the mirror in the prophet's mind. As Philip puts it, "[The mirror] imprints the *habitus* of cognition, which shares the form of the exemplar as fits; through which the prophet cognizes and understands that which God wants, to the extent that God wants, and nothing else or more than that."[32] The *habitus* of light served therefore as an interior control dividing the intellect from knowing the likeness of everything present in the soul.

William of Auxerre spoke about a defective intellect that must receive a compensating light in order to see, but he did not perceive this light as a medium of any sort standing between Paul's soul and God. Others, however, considered the preparative *habitus* as such—that is, as a hindrance to immediacy. *Quaestio* 9 in the Douai 434 manuscript, discussed and published by Dondaine,[33] is perhaps the earliest systematic discussion dedicated to the medium of beatific vision. It declares itself to be the third part of a tripartite *quaestio* on beatific vision, an indication of the compiler's special interest in the issue of media.[34] Indeed, the discourse of medium changed significantly. While William of Auxerre transformed the question "with medium or not?" to "through image or not?" the author of Douai 9 does not even mention images, corporeal similitudes, or mediating creatures such as angels in his argument. All of the arguments in favor of a medium in the beatific vision relate to the necessity of introducing a light of grace to mediate between a seeing subject and the thing it sees. He is, however, well aware that it is not easy to decide what is considered as medium and what not. God is seen through medium and likeness, he finally determines, but feels obliged to clarify what he means, distinguishing therefore two senses of medium:

1. A medium that dwells between two images: the natural potency of the soul, which is a created image of God, and the divine essence itself, the image according to which the soul was created.
2. A distant medium that does not dwell in us but stands between us and the thing we see.[35]

In the state of glory, the inward presence of the object (God) in us—unlike a stone—makes the second, common kind of medium unnecessary, just as it did in the Augustinian model and for William of Auxerre. Yet this interiorization does not entirely exclude any kind of medium, he explains, for the beatified souls see through the first, interior medium.

Two senses of likeness are distinguished as well, according to the interior/exterior dichotomy:

Similarly, "seeing through likeness" has two meanings: outside and inside. We shall see through an interior likeness which shows truly the species itself, because the exemplar is seen in the very likeness in which we shall be like him; we shall not see through an exterior likeness which is not the form of the seer, but an accident or an external sign.[36]

This distinction allows the author to answer an objection that he quotes from Hugh of St. Victor's commentary on the *Celestial Hierarchy*. There, Hugh strongly opposes those who put images and simulacra "between us and our God." Where there is a likeness, it is not the actual truth, he proclaims. If we shall see through it, we shall not see the truth itself.[37] Applying the external/internal distinction, the author replies that external likeness is indeed not the truth, but an internal likeness does not necessitate the absence of the truth. This kind of likeness is not separated from the thing.

Rather, it is the very form that is imprinted in the mind by the presence of the truth.[38]

The author of *quaestio* 454 on Paul's rapture also recognizes that there are new senses of media that should be carefully distinguished from the traditional meaning of the term. In response to objections, he unfolds the term likeness (*similitudo*) into three meanings:

1. A common property of two things.
2. Something that dwells between two ends but does not inhere in either of them, like the love that connects the lover to the beloved.
3. An *idolon* of a (corporeal) thing that dwells in the eye.[39]

He excludes likeness in the first or third sense from beatific vision. There is no contradiction therefore with the traditional claim that there are no images in the beatific vision or with the negation of a common property between the created soul and its creator. A likeness of the second sense, however, definitely has a place.

John of La Rochelle makes a similar claim when he takes up the problem of mediation in the beatific state. Like William, Roland, and all other theologians, he affirms that even when there is no external mediating image, there must be a disposition in the perceiving organ in order to cognize the present object: "Although God in himself is cognizable and loveable, there must be a proper disposition of the part of the soul—not because of the imperfection of the light itself, but because of the imperfection of the soul."[40]

What all these authors assume is that God or truth is constantly present in the glorified soul, but its mere presence is not enough for the act of cognition, as the mere fact of two stones present to each other is not enough for one stone to know the other. There must be something more, a third member. This third is neither an *idolon*, such as the image of the flower impressed on the eye, nor is it a common property: it is love, a *habitus*. The Trinity is a seal that impresses a created image on the soul's wax, and this imprint is the grace that makes it similar to God in glory. Both the seal and the sealed wax are present in the soul, and yet the seal cannot be seen "as it is": we can know it only through its action upon us, through its signature in our soul.

Surprisingly, the most enthusiastic and figurative defense of the idea that presence is insufficient for cognition comes from the pen of William of

Auvergne, the very bishop who was involved in promulgating the condemnation of the ten opinions. William discusses the intellect of the blessed souls in his *De retributionibus sanctorum* (*On the Repayments of the Saints*). As we read in *De sensu* and in other books, he explains, vision is nothing but assimilation of the seeing subject to the thing seen. The same process occurs in intellectual vision: to see God is to assimilate ourselves to him according to our mind's limited capacity. Since God is an exemplar of the world, the sanctified intellect will reflect a likeness of this exemplar, as two polished mirrors facing each other directly.[41]

Is it through this image and likeness that God is seen, or perhaps only through his presence, the truth in our mind? Several arguments support sight purely through presence, but William refuses to accept this idea. For just as light can be present to blind people without them seeing it in any sense, so the divine essence is present in our souls here on earth too, but nevertheless cannot be seen. His conclusion accords therefore with that of the others: proximity and presence are insufficient for any cognition, whether internal or external. We must have an *impression* of likeness in order to perceive the object so near to us. Even a man in the middle of a fire would not feel or know it without receiving a likeness of this fire.[42]

But what if someone shall say that the immediate consequence of this position is that the saints do not see God directly, but only his image? Like the author of *quaestio* 9, William feels obliged to answer Hugh of St. Victor's position cited previously, as if he himself were an Eastern "Dionysian" in contrast to the "Western Latin reaction." He refers the reader to Aristotle's *On the Soul*. There, William argues, Aristotle explains that a picture of a lion can be looked at in two ways: as an image of something else and as a thing in its own right—namely, a drawing.[43] If it is seen as an image, the observer's mind does not remain with the drawing, but proceeds to the actual lion. It is where the thought ends that matters, not the medium. What we are said to *see* is the thing that imprinted the image on our eye, not the imprinted image itself. Every apprehension works this way: we do not see the imaginary or intelligible forms, as we do not look at *them* but at the *actual* things that imprinted them. The same happens in the state of glory. The illuminated soul looks at itself. When it stops looking at it as a soul, but instead with divine grace as a perfect image of God, it sees God. William disregards, therefore, the entire complexity of images and returns to a traditional view. Yes, there are images in each apprehension. There must be. But they do not matter, as long as we know this is what they are.

Contenson explained the apparent contradiction between William of Auvergne's views in the *De retributionibus* and the first opinion that was condemned in 1241 through reference to the time that elapsed between the former's composition and the condemnation and to William's primitive familiarity with Eriugenian thought when he formed his opinion. It is hardly plausible, however, that the learned Parisian bishop did not know in detail the book that was publicly condemned in 1225 by the archbishop of Sens, and perhaps also earlier in Paris, according to Hostiensis. The papal letter of January 23, 1225, was unambiguous about the popularity of the text.[44]

The strongest indication, perhaps, that seeing God through an interior *habitus* or disposition could be interpreted both as immediate and mediated apprehension of God's essence comes from Guerric of St. Quentin. Guyot has identified three *quaestiones* in MS Prague Univ. IV D 13 devoted to the issue of seeing the divine essence as essence in the beatific vision.[45] In the first two questions, Guerric's arguments against seeing God in essence are similar to those of *quaestio* 9, and they are applicable in principle to seeing any essence. Created intellects are receptive and therefore must receive an influence from another in order to cognize. He opens his solution with a distinction between two kinds of media as well: *medium deferens*, which is analogous to the air that exists between the eye and the seen object, and *medium disponens*, which is analogous to light.[46] God's imprint of his glory in the soul is a *medium disponens*. As in *quaestiones* 454 and 9, Guerric assigns to love the role of medium between the potency of the intellect and the visible object.[47] Love assimilates us to God. It is a "medium" only in the meaning of a bond, and it shares no common features with either of the ends it bridges. It is not, however, a likeness that is God itself, but a form emitted by him ("*forma ab ipso*") received by the rational potency.

The third question in this series was demonstrated by Dondaine and Guyot to be Guerric's retraction, written after the condemnations. Yet in spite of Guerric's corrected judgment that God's essence is indeed seen *as essence*, he still adheres to mediated vision. Once more he distinguishes between *medium deferens* and *medium disponens*; once more he claims that the beatified see through a *medium disponens*, since they must undergo some sort of preparation.[48] Again, like the author of *quaestio* 454, he argues for a medium of love and in the same breath maintains that it is a vision without a medium. The *Summa Halensis* speaks clearly and forcefully against the condemned proposition as well, but at the same time contends that God is seen by the glorified soul through the mediation of a divine influence that disposes it so it can see him in itself clearly.[49]

In fact, all theologians since William of Auxerre agreed that there must be something else besides the intellectual potency on the one hand and the present object—God, in this case—on the other. For all of them, the difference between knowledge of God now and in the afterlife was not articulated as a *removal* of veils and barriers. Rather, it was a complementary *addition* of light or disposition to an imperfect intellect. As demonstrated previously, cognition was analyzed using a threefold scheme: the subject in which it resides, the object it attempts to grasp, and the cognition itself, the *habitus* or the medium. All accepted that cognition in glory, as in any other state, requires an additional third element. This intermediary is a light of grace, which is imprinted on the soul. It is a disposition or a *habitus* that prepares the intellect to see God, making the intellect itself a perfect image of God.

This distinction between an intellect, which is a natural potency, and perfective preparation led some to hold the illuminated mind as composite of two elements, rather than a unity: either eye and light, or eye and spirit-sight. What they disagreed about was whether one should call this "immediate vision" or not—that is, whether this mediating *habitus* and assimilated self counts as a medium or an "other" that hides an essence. For William of Auxerre, Roland of Cremona, the author of 454, and, above all, for William of Auvergne, this kind of medium and likeness did not impede immediacy. But for others, it did. This is why the author of *quaestio* 454 presents the same view as found in *quaestio* 9—love as a likeness, etc.—but *his* bottom line solution is that "God is seen in the homeland in himself without any medium."[50] This is why William of Auvergne seems to maintain the opinion he condemned.

The other side of the medium question concerned defining who is "us" when we say that something stands between us and God in glory. Both Guerric and *quaestio* 9 constantly refer to the beatified subject as *potentia*. This natural, rational potency, stripped of any *habitus*, is what those who claimed disposition to be a medium considered as the self. Consequently, the disposition or *habitus* of grace or glory turned into an "other." Rather than seeing the entire illuminated soul as the likeness of its object, this position stressed its composite nature: a hyprid of potency and *habitus* of light-glory or love. Alexander of Hales articulated this idea in a *quaestio* about the cognition of blessed souls written after he had entered the Franciscan Order. When Augustine argued that nothing obtains between the mind and God, explains Alexander, he intended an already illuminated mind.[51] Those who argue that there is "something" between the seer and God during rapture or during beatific vision, presupposed, therefore, that the self is nothing more than intellective potency, whereas this "something"— that is, the cognitive disposition preparing the mind and assimilating it to God—is not the self.

INTROSPECTION AND ITS LIMITS

As shown previously, interiority was not considered devoid of media. The debate over the immediacy of ecstatic and beatific vision touched, once and again, the problem of introspection and self-perception. First and foremost, there was the novelty of taking into account God's own introspective cognition. The vision or knowledge God has of himself had been discussed for centuries. Yet up to this period, it had not been compared with beatified vision. As theologians of this age extended the parade of cognitions (see Chapter 1), they engaged it through the game of comparisons as well. The immediate result was that the beatific vision lost its supremacy to the new player—that is, God's vision of himself. Thus, Alexander of Hales deprived the saints of seeing the divine essence "in itself" in order to make room for and distinguish the peculiar vision by which God sees himself. He did not dispense with the "through image" / "through species" distinction; he just added a third part. There are three modes, he declared, and "in the first mode God alone sees the divine essence."[52] In a later question on God's self-knowledge, he affirmed that authorities who argue that no one can see God mean that no one can see God "in the form in which God knows himself."[53] Guerric of St. Quentin argued similarly that "seeing is threefold: in essence, in *specie* and in imagination. *In essence* only God sees himself; *in specie* he shall be known by the saints in the homeland; *in image* he is known now."[54] John Pagus, whose opinions were perhaps those that were condemned, also recommended in his commentary to the *Sentences* that one should understand the Eastern opinion as maintaining that the substance of God cannot be seen by anyone in the plenitude in which God himself cognizes his essence.[55] The preoccupation with "seeing the essence in itself" was therefore a logical consequence of joining God as a new "knower" of God to the group. Compared to this unique, most intimate knowledge, all others turned mediated to a certain degree.

The invocation of divine self-knowledge established new standards regarding what it means to see "an essence in itself"; but the discussion of the human soul's ability to see itself was tied to that of the beatific vision in yet another way. Regarding both issues, it was presumed that essence is not seen; only its actions were perceivable. These doubts were also raised in *quaestiones* such as "whether faith sees itself," three of which survive from this period. They represent a particular case of a more general problem: one's ability to know whether true grace dwells in one's heart or not. Many times this problem took the form of "whether man knows he has grace-given love (*caritas*)." Since faith was cognitive, it entailed a reflective aspect. One writer, William of Durham, explicitly associated cognitive faith with beatific vision.[56]

Others did so implicitly, as their arguments and citations overlapped to a certain degree with the discourse on beatific vision.[57] The author of *Quaestio* Douai 501, for instance, determined that faith is present to itself and provided a beautiful metaphor: like a line in which one point sees the end of the line, it sees itself without a medium, or rather with a medium that is faith itself.[58] William of Durham felt obliged to refine the notion of self vision in this context. He maintained that there are three kinds of self-vision: (1) seeing oneself; (2) seeing that one exists (*esse*); and (3) seeing that one is such and such (*esse tale*). Faith sees itself in the two first modes, but it does not recognize itself as grace-given faith, much like the soul that looks at itself but does not recognize it to be God's image.[59] When Guiard of Laon addressed the problem, he maintained that the traditional Augustinian claim that "faith sees itself" should be understood only as "faith sees itself *through its movements*" and not *per se*. This is equivalent, he explained, to the way potencies and virtues are known through effects: God is known through his effects and fire through the effect of heating.[60]

God-given grace cannot be recognized unequivocally as such by its receiver, and the infused, divine *habitus* is essentially different from what T. A. Graf termed "the psychological subject of grace"—that is, the human soul or the potency in which it "resides."[61] Yet what is of interest here is that grace was actually not so peculiar. In fact, the idea that one can learn about virtues and potencies—all the more so essences through actions—but not directly "in themselves" accorded well with Aristotle's methodology for the proper study of the soul, as explicated in *On the Soul*, the book William of Auvergne sent us to read. Similarly, at a certain point in his discussion of the medium of beatific vision, the author of *quaestio* 9 decided to enlarge the scope of his investigation to a "very difficult question": can any essence, whether divine or created, be known or seen "through itself" (*per se*)?[62] God cannot be seen as an essence, he determined, since the process of cognition runs in a reverse order to that of reality. In the structure of reality, essence comes first, then virtue, then the operations of that virtue. But when we cognize something, what we first see is its deeds, from which we deduce the existence of a virtue and from that the nature of an essence, *as the philosopher—that is, Aristotle—says*.[63]

In order to conjoin the potencies of the soul, Aristotle instructs readers of his *On the Soul* that the researcher must look first at its objects, then at its actions, and then deduce its virtues or potencies. Accordingly, only at the end of the investigation will we perceive the essence of a thing such as the soul.[64] We infer someone's skill at playing the flute from witnessing her play well. We cannot "see" this ability directly, only its operation. In fact, this ability is not even known directly to the flute player herself. She would know for certain that she can play only after she had truly tried to *do* so. At least two writers that discussed the soul in Paris of the 1220s–30s took this as an imperative, structuring their treatises by systematically beginning from the objects in order to deduce the different potencies of the soul.[65] Divine essence is known in a similar way, claims the author of Douai 9. Through its true and good actions, we understand that there is a virtue of truth and goodness in our soul and that this virtue is none other than the image of the Trinity.

Now William of Auvergne, the promulgator of the condemnations, agreed that we perceive both our soul and God through actions, and his similar judgment in both cases exemplifies their significant affinity. In his own *On the Soul*, he included a lengthy discussion of the opinion that the soul can be known only through its dispositions, actions, and operations, but not as it is in itself.[66] Wise people, he argued, can tell the nature of other people's souls, whether they are good or bad, wise or stupid, from their words and actions. All the more so, the wise man's own dispositions reveal his soul's nature to him. Since they reveal it faithfully, vision through these dispositions should be held as equivalent to seeing the substance in itself:

> No intelligent man doubts that the clothing of sensible accidents is a kind of cloth of the sensible substance that sustains and wears it. It is also evident, since they reveal and show it so, that when *they* are seen it is said that *it* is seen, and seeing *them* is considered as seeing *the substance itself*. This is what everybody thinks. How then it is not the same that seeing of spiritual accidents or dispositions of the human soul is held and thought of as seeing of the human substance itself?[67]

He who sees Socrates clad with a garment sees Socrates; William keeps clinging to common sense. "If someone sees a certain king under garments and splendid dress that indicate his being a king and show that he is a king, it is better to say that the king was *shown* rather than hidden or covered by them."[68] Signs, clothes, and actions are pretty good indicators for substance and essence, and therefore seeing them should be held as equivalent to seeing the essence in itself. The higher the signs' quality and the greater their quantity, the better the knowledge they transmit. This is how the soul is known to itself, he concludes: its bearer knows his soul's accidents directly, and through them he is able to know his soul's nature and substance. At least for the wise person, seeing his own psychological dispositions and acts should be held (*habebitur et reputabitur*) as seeing the substance itself (*visio ipsius substantiae*).

Note the striking similarity in word and sense between this opinion and that which was pronounced in the condemnations of 1241. The orthodox affirmation proposed against the heretical opinion was, "*Quod Deus in sua essentia vel substantia videbitur ab angelis et omnibus sanctis et videtur ab animabus glorificatis.*" Indeed, William's approach to seeing one's own soul was the same as his approach to heavenly vision. While we indeed see through signs, it should be held as seeing the essence in itself directly; yes, we see our soul through actions, but they truly indicate it, so much so that they are not to be considered as media. To sum up once more, there is no argument that both our souls and God are approachable only through their actions. The debate concerns (1) whether knowing through these signs is nevertheless to be considered equivalent to seeing essence and substance in themselves; and (2) whether perfection, assimilation, and *habitus* are "us" or an "other" distinguished from potency.

The doubt underlying disputations among early thirteenth-century Parisian theologians was whether or not our knowledge, dispositions, talents, virtues, and actions are essential components of "us." The same doubt could be turned to others around us: do we truly see their essence or just their actions and abilities? William of Auvergne's sayings should therefore be read as an answer to a genuine contemporary concern. Some believed, so it seems, that seeing a king wearing his garments should *not* be held as seeing him *in himself* and that people's behavior does not necessarily divulge their essence, even for wise men.

The immediate result was the perception that the face-to-face vision of the beatified was indirect. That was true even in the level of metaphor—looking at a person's face, some suspected, we have no direct access to his/her essence. It stops being a metaphor as we come to the fourth and final point: the soul became, in its own gaze, more fragmented, while its essence was portrayed as an inaccessible core, as alien territory. Although it was commonly accepted that looking into the soul is entirely different from looking outside it, they all found themselves using the term *medium* when relating to the former, whether to allow for recollection, control of the flow of information, or any other aim. Despite their explicit reservations, therefore, one gets the feeling that interiority and exteriority are not so different after all. As anything else, the essence of the soul and its *habitus* of virtues and knowledge are not seen by the eye of a stranger, nor are they directly approachable by their owner. The flute player must perform in order to know what she can do. There is always something in us—whether divine, grace-given, or natural—that is hidden from us.

This chapter could end here. Sometimes scholastic discourse does not lend itself to further analysis, and it is difficult to frame rigorous claims about its context. Nevertheless, I would like to suggest two potentially contemporaneous fora that resonate these dilemmas, in the hope that they will provoke a more thorough study one day.

THE IMPACT OF PSYCHOLOGY ON ITS PRACTITIONERS

The first context I suggest should be considered here is the implication of the very existence of *a* philosophical, technical discourse on the soul, regardless of its particular epistemological content discussed previously. This generation of medieval theologians was exposed to a rich philosophical and medical discourse on the soul in a flow of texts that started, slowly at first, in the late eleventh century, but it was only in the decades roughly between the 1220s and the 1240s that its influence began to be felt in Paris. They read about the vegetative soul, about passions, dispositions, and *habitus*, passive and agent intellect, and many other novel concepts. The story of this reception has been told repeatedly.[69] Yet one historical question has never been asked, to the best of my knowledge, and it is a question worth being asked, even if we never prove capable of giving it a proper answer: how did the new discourse on the soul affect its Latin receptors' approach to their own souls?

We have a vivid description of what might happen in such a situation, though from a setting slightly distant in time and place, at the Rievaulx abbey in twelfth-century Yorkshire, England. Aelred's *Dialogue on the Soul* begins with the troubled John mounting the stage. He is moved and distressed, for he has just read Augustine on the soul and checked Augustine's statements against his own feelings. *He* certainly feels that his soul is in a place—that is, in his body—but he is confused and agitated by Augustine's opposite assertion. Step by step, Aelred guides him toward harmony, not only through dictation of formal knowledge, but also by asking him to perform some introspective exercises.[70]

Unfortunately, no similar account of such a conflict survives from our later period.[71] We have no testimony of psychological notions and vocabulary that diffused into informal conversations on the streets of the Left Bank or into moments of introspection, though it is easy to imagine that they did. The servant in the medieval play *Geta* dreams that on his return home he will show off the dialectical tricks he learned in Athens, the symbolic stand-in for Paris.[72] A thirteenth-century servant could well impress his kitchen colleagues with "*habitus*," claiming to know about their soul what they have not dreamed of.

But following Greek and Arabic models, almost all the writings on the soul that survive from 1200–50 are purely scholastic in style and concerned with reconciling texts with one another instead of with one's own confused feelings. Personal experience has no place in the texts of John Blund or of the anonymous authors of the treatise composed in the 1220s on the potencies and objects of the soul. Blund proves the existence of the soul by using a *per se notum* grounded in our experience; yet it is not our own experience of the soul, but the knowledge we have acquired through our senses that certain things move voluntarily.⁷³ Richard Rufus, who taught at Paris and Oxford until 1255, employed a certain dialogue form, or at least the flavor of a lively disputation, in his theological *Sepculum animae*. His interlocutors are concerned with the correct understanding of Aristotle, its reconciliation with theological truths, and with pure reasoning and philosophical opinions.⁷⁴ Neither brought forth his own experience in the way earlier Cistercian psychological treatises did. Just as modern editors remove anecdotal sentences, so did they. In a telling insight, Henri d'Andeli, a poet close to Philip the Chancellor, remarked ironically that philosophy killed the good "I-me-mine," its great enemy.⁷⁵

The mere introduction of new texts that authoritatively presumed to tell their readers about so near an object in such difficult language could easily lead to a sense of estrangement. The new approach may have been so overwhelming, the context and style so authoritative, that it dismissed as irrelevant the informal, unarticulated experience of its avid readers. One way or another, the uncontested notion was that there is a body of formal knowledge about the soul that must be studied. Try to remember the strange experience of reading Freud or a chapter in modern psychology for the first time.

A second feature of the discourse that could contribute to fragmentation and objectification of how they perceived the soul lay in the style and method of the philosophical academic discourse itself. The method Aristotle suggested, as shown previously, dictated that in order to understand a particular ability, they must first search for acts and objects. It encouraged them to look at the soul as an unknown, non-intimate realm, basically undifferentiated from any other object of philosophy, such as the movements of animals or meteorological phenomena.

Can psychological, technical, *mediated* discussion be conceived as religious, spiritual introspection? One unique testimony supports such a view. The Franciscan John of La Rochelle wrote a treatise on the multiple division of the powers of the soul that looks like any other psychological treatise of the period. He had also written a *summa* on the subject in the same style, but prefaced it with a moving prologue, worth quoting here in full:

If you ignore yourself, most beautiful of women, go and follow after the herds of she goats etc. Rational soul, this very speech is addressed to you,

you, who are the most beautiful of women, since you are the most splendid of creatures, possessing an image and likeness of the highest beauty and elegance; if you ignore your beauty, you are compared to the irrational herds: whence *go and follow after the herds of she-goats*. For you, therefore, O soul, concerning yourself three things must be considered: namely your substance, power and activity, in which your admirable beauty exists. Give me, therefore, most loving Jesus, *the wisdom which attends upon your thrones* and *do not reject me*; but give me the wisdom that *will be with me and assist me*, that it may teach and instruct the one considering *uncovering my eyes, and I will consider the wonders* concerning my soul.[76]

John addresses his rational soul in an explicitly spiritual manner, quoting from *Song of Songs*. This rational soul is ignorant of herself, but he, the researcher who is distinguished from her at the very same time his rational soul makes the inquiry, shall reveal to her her own beauty.

John then changes his addressee and prays to Jesus for wisdom and revelation. He changes only one word in the words of the Psalmist. Instead of "the wonders of your Law," he amends the verse to "the wonders of my soul." Inspiration is sought not for deciphering the scriptures but for considering the substance, powers, and operations of one's own soul. The succeeding act of telling his ignorant soul about herself consists of highly technical, formal knowledge. The soul is looked at, therefore, through a medium. Like Paul, who knew medicine, and therefore could infer that his soul must be detached from his body as a result of enormous joy, these theologians' reflections upon their ignorant souls were mediated by books and formally acquired information. The powers of the soul were not simply accessible but hidden from the eye of its lay beholder: learned psychology was necessary to mediate the encounter.

BEYOND THE CLASSROOM: HIDING AND SEEING THE SELF IN COURTLY FRENCH ROMANCE

What is the cultural meaning of the idea that an inapproachable, fundamental essence underlies one's behavior, habits, talents, and mental and bodily clothes and cannot be told by them? Much like the subject of this chapter, we cannot see here the real souls of early thirteenth-century people.

But we may see them "through a glass darkly," looking through the feelings of their literary fictional contemporaries. John Baldwin has masterfully demonstrated this by "employing romance texts as historical sources" to reconstruct French aristocratic life through Jean Renart's works.[77] This is especially true when we employ these sources to recover contemporary moods.

An opponent may doubt such a move: the courtly self depicted by *jongleurs* and the virtuous self depicted by theologians supposedly cannot be compared. Yet the worlds of school and court were not as separate in medieval culture as some might assume. Whether in their childhood, as guests in courts, or in the streets of Paris, all masters had multiple chances to hear *jongleurs*, and many of the latter were versed with intellectual culture. More specifically in terms of geography and language close to our community, Jean Renart, author of two of the romances to be discussed later, wrote in Francien, the putative dialect of the region surrounding Paris. *Silence*, another romance to be discussed here, was written by one Master Heldris of Cornwall—a master indeed—who found it proper to introduce theological arguments about God and Adam into the Nature-Nurture debates featured in his dazzling story.[78] Heldris wrote in a mixture of Francien and Picard, and Parisian theologians could therefore easily understand them.[79] Last, medieval female mysticism has frequently been read as organized around ideals of courtly love.[80] Male theologians were exposed to these models just as well.

The dialectic of "seeing through image" was essential to the ideal of courtly love. Both narrators and audiences were fascinated by the theme of falling in love with an image rather than directly with the real person. A topos of courtly literature, contemporary texts seem to be extraordinarily preoccupied with this idea. The scene that perhaps best reflects this fascination appears in *The Song of the Shadow* (*Lai de l'ombre*) of Jean Renart. The title of the *lai* itself already hints at the centrality of the theme of reflection.[81] The male protagonist attempts to win the lady's heart with sweet talk throughout the romance and fails once and again. At the final, dramatic scene, as they sit by a well, he gives up. He tells his beloved that since she keeps refusing, he will give the ring to the woman he loves second most and throws the ring to her watery reflection in the well. The lady is so overwhelmed by this super-courtly gesture that she immediately accedes.[82] The symbolic gesture toward the reflection paves the way to the real woman.

Jean Renart's *Roman de la Rose* or *Guillaume de Dole* (to distinguish it from the more famous allegorical romance by Guillaume de Lorris and Jean de Meun), written probably between 1204 and 1228, plays further with the theme of falling in love with words and imaginary beauty. But unlike the *Shadow*, it also constantly exposes the double nature of seeing through images.[83] Surprisingly realistic, it is one of the first romances to be set in contemporary life rather than in the classical or Arthurian past. Its fictional characters speak and fight shoulder to shoulder with real thirteenth-century historical figures. The plot is launched when King Konrad hears from his *jongleur* the praises of one lady by the name of Lienor. These praises alone make him fall in love with her name and her celebrated beauty. He wishes to marry her before he has the chance to look at her. Words and signs keep the plot in motion. The king's treacherous seneschal tells the devastated king that his beloved is not a virgin. His proof is that he knows that she bears on her thigh a birthmark in the shape of a rose, a most intimate secret indeed, knowledge of which seems to be possessed by one who has seen her actual body nude. The seneschal, however, has never seen Lienor. He has fished this piece of information from her talkative mother, while seeking a way to hinder this marriage. Everybody, including Lienor's own brother who arranged the marriage, believes the accusation, its sign seeming so irrefutable. When the flesh-and-blood Lienor arrives to prove her virginity, neither the love-struck king nor the devious seneschal recognizes her. By a brilliant trick, employing pseudo-signs herself that seem certain but are false, she leads the seneschal to declare publicly that he has never seen her, proves her innocence, and marries the king. Knowledge through signs, even birthmarks on actual bodies, proves an elusive thing indeed.

When I turned to contemporary courtly literature, I hoped to find one character saying to another that the true nature of a person cannot be seen under his/her clothes or behind his/her behavior. Though I sought one or two lines, I found an entire romance. The exact date of *Silence*, a thirteenth-century romance, is uncertain, but it is assumed that the sole extant manuscript was copied for a noble lady on the occasion of her marriage, ca. 1286.[84] The main plot involves the adventures of a girl whose parents decided to raise her as a boy, because the king of England forbade women to inherit property. During her/his adventures, the audience listens to disputations between allegorical figures of "Nature" and "Nurture," as well as to Master Heldris of Cornwall's own remarks about the respective power of the two in their dialectical duality.

One remarkable feature of the story is that none of its characters, except for the girl herself, doubts the ease with which gender can be switched. This is evident already when Cador explains to his wife that he plans to "make a male of a female" (2041). Not only is this plan attainable, but it can be executed perfectly and with ease. "He will be called Silentius," decides Cador, "and if by any chance his nature is discovered, we shall change this *-us* to *-a*, and she'll be called Silentia" (2074–79). The syllable "*-us*" is not just a Latin masculine ending, but a pun on the French *us*—that is, a habit or custom. Later, when Nature and Nurture fight over the twelve-year-old Silence, the youth weighs the *us d'ome* against the *us de feme*. Clearly, a certain fundamental self is weighing here different *habitus*, assuming that it wouldn't be so difficult to change them. It is a matter of choice, and s/he indeed decides: It would not be wise "*deuser / son bon viel us et refuser / por us de feme maintenir*" ("doing away with his good old ways to take up female habits," 2629–31). At the very end of the romance, when the true nature of Silence is exposed by Merlin, no great efforts are required in order to make Silence a woman again. All Nature has to do is slightly fix the suntanned complexion of her face.

Since Silence had never seen a woman bearing arms, she wonders whether she will turn out to be a cowardly knight (2840–44). Her parents, however, express no such doubt, nor does the narrator. Throughout her/his adventures, nothing betrays her nature. Silence is raised in the woods so that her nature will not be mistakenly discovered, but the author says nothing about any difficulty posed by her female nature for training in riding, hunting, or fighting. On the contrary, he remarks that the child seemed to learn things almost by himself. Unlike Achilles, whose feminine disguise was exposed as he saw arms, Silence is not attracted to "feminine" occupations at all. He prefers to joust. Silence becomes the perfect knight, wins a tournament, and leads a cohort of French knights to victory in battle: a climax of Nurture's temporary victory over Nature, according to Heldris (5145–56). Even the lustful queen does not suspect. She presumes the young, beautiful knight rejects her since he is attracted to males. Referring to his hero/ine as a *he* throughout significant parts of the tale, Heldris helps his listeners forget this themselves. Silence, he makes clear throughout the text, could continue with this disguise forever if not for the wicked queen and Merlin. While Nature wins at the end, nothing betrays Silence. Her true nature is only discovered by Merlin the prophet.

The perfection of Silence's cover is sharpened against other instances of hidden identities. Unlike Silence, Merlin is caught when a trap is set for his nature, being seduced by the odor of cooked meat. Silence's other disguises prove less successful. While the minstrels do not see his true gender (although they live with him for several years), they quickly expose his noble status when he pretends to be the serving boy or colors his face with a certain plant juice so as to look like a lowborn (2909, 2950).

No character and no listener can see the "true," natural, gendered self of Silence under her manly *us*, not even in the midst of battle: "Whoever saw him jousting, stripped of his mantle, carrying his shield on his left arm" could not tell that he "had only the complexion, clothing, and bearing of a man" (5150–63). Her noble character, however, shines through.

We can only wonder what William of Auvergne would have thought had he been present at this tournament or just listening to this romance in the royal court where he often visited—he, who could not understand why people claim that to see the king wearing garments is not seeing the king's essence. But even without much imagination, it is evident that the problem of seeing essences was not only theological. It was part of a cultural fascination and ambivalence regarding the self and its natural and aquired *habitus* regarding notions of gender and nobility shared by masters, *jongleurs*, and courtiers.

I would go so far as to suggest that the problem of seeing essences through images reflects the self-awareness of the literary enterprise itself. The narrators of works such as *Silence* and *Guillaume de Dole* are exceptionally attentive to the intricate complexity of reality and fiction, of truth and image involved in their profession, being creators of images. Jouglet, the emperor's *jongleur* creates the lovely image of Lienor, which makes the king fall in love and sets the plot in motion. More particularly, this specific new kind of romance was innovative in its playful mixture of reality and fiction. While previous authors such as Chrétien de Trois "sought to recover the remote geography of ancient France or of classical Greece and Rome," the audiences of Jean Renart and Gerbert de Montreuil "sensed the present."[85]

Silence lives for years as a *jonglour*, a profession open to both genders. Her/his character, with its complex gender composition, is analogous to

Master Heldris's tale. She is composed of a true female nature and fictitious male *us* that hides her natural gender. Relating how her parents hide both nature and truth, the narrator equates the two. Yet if effective nurturing can improve upon nature to create the best knight, why can't the storyteller improve upon truth as well, creating a similar mixture of truth and fiction? Master Heldris seems to hint at this analogy as he sings:

> begins such a tale of adventure
> As you never heard of in any book.
> Just as it was written
> in the Latin version we read,
> we will tell it to you in French:
> I'm not saying that there isn't
> a good deal of fiction mingled with truth
> in order to improve the tale,
> but if I am any judge of things,
> I'm not putting in anything that will spoil the work,
> nor will there be any less truth in it,
> *for truth should not be silenced.*
>
> > Silence. ll. 1658–69, my italics

In the same breath, he confesses his loyalty to the Latin source and confesses mixing truth with fiction. Fiction does not damage truth but improves it, and, alluding to the name "Silence," truth is not silenced. Heldris's art thus parallels nature-nurture's ideal proportion. Like its heroine, the romance is the perfect combination of two: truth and fiction. Proximity to reality was sharpened with the rise of the realistic romance, as Jean Renart's fictional and historical characters danced with each other. Literature came closer to being an image of reality at the same time as its distance from truth was explicitly acknowledged. Above all, as Dragonetti and Zink have claimed, Romance literature began to recognize itself as such.[86]

The soul of the virtuous believer, according to Alexander of Hales, Philip the Chancellor, and the anonymous treatises on the soul, consisted of natural potencies over which grace-given *habitus* were added. This structure was not changed in heaven. There as well, natural potencies combined with *habitus* of glory. This assimilation process, therefore, was constructed upon the natural, fundamental self and, in a certain respect, apart from it, so much so as to be considered by some as always standing between the self and God. Silence's soul, as that of any other well-bred child in courtly society, is composed of good or bad, feminine or masculine nature, and a carefully built *us*. The stitches between the two layers were a matter of cultural concern both in the morning classroom in town and at the entertainments of the castle feast.

Much has been written and argued about subjectivity and the self in the Middle Ages, in its literature and spirituality in particular, and this conclusion cannot engage this discussion properly.[87] Bynum and others have noted that although interiority was indeed conceptualized in the twelfth century, it was not identical to the concept of an individual as we perceive it today—namely, a unique individual. The ideal was the same for everyone: assimilation to one model. Here, at the beginning of the thirteenth century, in university circles that were very sensitive to the spiritual tradition of the twelfth century, we see that this assimilation was somehow detached from another "self" (*se*) or subject. It is not the whole soul that is assimilated to God and upon which the seal is impressed. Assimilation itself is perceived by some as a medium, an "other" (*aliud*). The time of the "discovery of the self" was also the time of the discovery of the discoverer; of an acute awareness of the distance between the observer and her/his reflection in the looking glass.[88]

CHAPTER FOUR
Does true faith rely on anything external?
The self as an ultimate source of authority
Theology between internal and external authority

The previous chapters discussed media such as image, *species*, and light, through which information is perceived. This chapter focuses on a different sort of media that includes proofs, books, and teachers, the media that affect why we accept things to be true. We may believe a statement because it was proved to us logically and adequately, because we trust the person who said it to be a specialist, or because we saw the thing with our own eyes and we trust our own senses not to mislead us. The manner in which we receive information and turn it into a *habitus* influences greatly the degree of certitude we attach to it. Seeing through a glass darkly, we are less sure what it is that we see. Sometimes one is more certain of a fact after experiencing it directly than after hearing about it from someone else; sometimes, we prefer to believe an expert against our own intuition. Our decisions regarding whom we trust are subject to social and cultural negotiation of power and knowledge.

IMMEDIACY AND AUTHORITY

Paul's account of his rapture, in which he ascended to the third heaven, was not related in a void. His boasting in his visions and revelations adds to the other things he boasts about, while reminding his readers of his reluctance to do so. Directly following his claims to be "not at all inferior to the most eminent apostles" (II Cor. 11:5), a true apostle between false others, he strove to establish his authoritative position in a competitive climate. Similarly, the source for his distinction between seeing God enigmatically vs. face-to-face is Numbers 12:1–8, which depicts a scene between Moses, Aaron, and Miriam in which authority is questioned by inspirational claims. The three meeting points between schoolmen and ecstatic experiences to which I referred in the introduction all bear the scent of a similar struggle over the authoritative value of different forms of cognition.

So it was in the controversy over Gilbert of Poitiers' opinions, which involved logical/rational authority (Gilbert, Odo, and opponent masters), traditional or institutional authority (churchmen), and in a marginal position, prophetic authority (Hildegard). In the case of the Amalricians, whose master lost the battle over his opinion, his students turned to ecstatic legitimization and were declared heretics. Aquinas's hagiography, composed with a live memory of the harsh controversies over the master's opinions, also reaches for ecstatic authority. The reliance on ecstatic experience accords legitimacy to innovative exegesis, as Lerner has shown, and allows more flexibility in social and gender roles, as many have shown regarding Hildegard and later female mystics.[1] Supporting one's claim by saying that "I have seen it in the living light" had significant power, although, as we have seen in the case of Hildegard, it was ultimately limited. For groups such as the Amalricians, who held as the highest authority the Holy Spirit's revelation in their mind or their innate reasons, reliance on interior conviction legitimized in their eyes the undermining of social religious conventions and tradition.

Already in 1022 Orléans, in one of the first documented encounters with heretics, one chronicler put in the mouth of the heretics the following answer to the bishop: "You may spin stories in that way to those ... who believe the fictions of carnal men scribbled on animal skins. To us, however, who have the law written upon the heart by the Holy Spirit, in vain you spin out."[2]

The idea of an inborn law, written on every human being's heart, available to him or her without any need of external mediation, did not interest heretics alone. During the twelfth and early thirteenth-century revival of interest in legal theory, jurists and theologians sought to demonstrate how civil law proceeds from fundamental, natural moral precepts, the *ius naturae* or the *lex naturalis*.[3] At the same period the idea of "first principles" and axioms functioning as the fundamentals of every proper science, guided by Euclid's *Elements* and Aristotle's *Posterior Analytics*, engaged eager readers in the West. Some truths, such as "the whole is bigger than its part," were conceived as universally accepted by innate reason, having to rely on no proof or persuasion. One early thirteenth century mathematician named Jordan of Nemours, for example, attempted to apply the Euclidean model to arithmetic in an innovative manner, making a considerable effort not to rely upon geometry and to make each proposition follow the first definitions and axioms he laid down.[4]

This chapter analyzes the appeal to immediacy and the tension between inspiration and learning in contemporary treatises about faith and explores their implications for theologians' prestige, masters-student relationships, and the war on heresy. Treatises addressing faith, perhaps the most common cognition of God, often contrast immediate illumination with textual and/or ancient authority. In the absence of a direct encounter with the divine, faith represents trust in someone or something else—the community, the prelate, the Holy Scriptures: an "other" (*aliud*), a *medium*. Faith is of "things not seen" (Heb. 11:1), acquired "through hearing" (Rom. 10:17).

The *Anticlaudianus*, a late twelfth-century poem by Alan de Lille, relates how the soul on its celestial journey arrives at the gates of the realm of faith and theology and there leaves all the horses of the senses behind, save the horse of hearing.[5] Due to this reliance on authorities, faith lies somewhere between certain knowledge and mere opinion, where Hugh of St. Victor locates it.[6] The doubtful nature of hearing was emphasized in the theological treatment of Paul's ecstasy as well: while Paul confessed he "*heard* inexpressible words," his experience was pervasively related to as *vision*.

Nevertheless, as Englhardt has already pointed out, throughout the first decades of the thirteenth century a second, somewhat opposite aspect of faith was articulated.[7] The true, meritorious faith was perceived as direct adherence to the first truth *propter se*, "because of itself," as opposed to belief that relies on proofs, miracles, or authorities—the "faith of persuasion" (*fides suasa*). However, theologians articulated a vigorous claim for superior certitude based on interior illumination. This shift occupies the center of the first part of this chapter, addressing Parisian masters' different proposals regarding relations between inspirational knowledge on one hand and knowledge whose certitude depends on tradition, books, and demonstrations on the other.[8]

The tension between self—that is, the direct cognition of truths—and the dependence on another who transmits them stands not only at the heart of religious belief, but at the heart of the teaching and learning processes as well. The school environment embodied different forms of legitimizing claims, and students accepted what they were told because it accorded with their inner conviction/intuition, because they fully understood the rational arguments, and just because their admired teacher said so. Mediation is critical: most of us, after all, do not just "see" truths. In order to understand, we need someone to mediate and explain and time to digest. Teachers, on their part, do not just present or show things, pouring knowledge directly into their disciples' brains. William of Auvergne refers exactly to this active aspect of learning when he refers to the difference between prophetic vision and *scientia*. Prophets "see" and receive forms and information by passive revelation, but common human beings attain their knowledge or *ars* otherwise. Learning requires time and effort, and most of all active rather than passive reception. How else can we explain the fact that we put so much effort, he asks: "What do we sweat for? What do philosophize for?" The intellectual power, he concludes, is generative, not passive and receptive, and needs much more than mere visual attention.[9] It requires mediation, effort, and time.

Roland of Cremona inserted a charming note in his discussions of demons regarding magical techniques that promised their practitioner he would become immediately learned, providing an apt demonstration of these aspects.[10] It is told, he relates, that demons can instruct man in logic and astronomy in the shortest time if he swears to obey them. But is it really possible to become wise so quickly? Knowledge, Roland objects, can be attained either through inspiration or through learning. Since the devil and his demons cannot inspire thoughts, just corporeal images, they must speak aloud. Speaking takes time.[11] In order to engender real understanding the demon must use his voice, start from principles, and then proceed to conclusions in the right order. It does not matter how fast the master-demon speaks. The disciple needs his own time to grasp the *medietas*, or this will not be a proper *scientia*.

Medium is first and foremost a key concept in Aristotle's influential conception of the scientific syllogism and demonstrative knowledge in his *Posterior Analytics*. The length of the chain of media affects the degree of certitude and "nobility" of the knowledge one acquires. A person may simply "see" that a geometrical axiom is true; may need a moment to understand why an equilateral triangle has two equal base angles; and would usually need more time to understand a more complicated geometrical sentence, to comprehend the *media*. Even when reaching full understanding of a geometrical sentence, it will never be as clear as the first simple axioms were, which are known almost immediately.

As we shall come to assess the larger context of theologians' dealing with faith and immediacy, we shall see them address the nature of the masters' own practices, producing a body of knowledge that relies on inspirational faith, while at the same time distinguishing it clearly from others. Employing their examples of students who questioned their masters, as well as old women and forest-men who were implicated in heresy, I propose to read the masters' discourse against two broader contemporary changes in medieval society. The first are the diminishing of magisterial authority in the shift from schools to university and the increasing expectation of students not to accept things purely because they adore their master. The second shift involves the church's changing approaches to the threat heresy posed to its authority.

ILLUMINATION AS PREREQUISITE FOR LEARNING: FAITH AND *PER SE NOTA* PRINCIPLES

As seen in the Appendix, analysis of how faith is defined was an essential part of the scholastic investigation into its nature. When William of Auxerre expounds the second part of Paul's definition of faith in Heb. 11:1—evidence/argument of things not seen (*argumentum non apparentium*)—he provides two traditional explanations for the sense in which faith can be classified as an *argumentum*.[12] One of these is "evidence that convinces others." When a person expresses doubts regarding a certain article of faith, one can answer that "the ancestors, the prophets, and the apostles believed it to be so, therefore it is so."[13] Presupposing the presence of the Holy Spirit in these reverend men, their faith thus serves as evidence of its truth and as a means of persuasion.

This line of argumentation was used by King Louis IX (St. Louis) when he spoke with Joinville one day about faith. The king used to say, relates Joinville, "that we should give full credence to faith and belief even when our certainty rested only on hearsay." He then asked Joinville to the name of his father. "Simon," the latter replied. "How do you know that?" inquired the king. "I answered that I thought I could be certain of it and believe it, since my mother had been my witness," wrote Joinville. "Then," said the king, "you should believe no less firmly in all the articles of faith, of which the apostles are your witness, as you hear sung every Sunday the *Credo*."[14]

William's second explanation for *argumentum* was that the mere existence of faith "stands" or "argues" for the existence of things unseen, since faith is their effect and, through it, its cause is evident as well. Having introduced these two explanations, he went on to enumerate the problems with this definition. The first flaw that he points out is that both parts of the definition, "substance of things hoped for" and "argument of things unseen," fit hope as well as faith, thus rendering the definition insufficiently particular. In order to solve this problem, he presents a third and a fourth sense of *argumentum*, which are applicable to faith alone. Relating directly to its cognitive character, they distinguish faith from all other virtues, including hope.[15]

The third sense proposes that Paul used the word *argumentum* to express similitude: faith is *like* an *argumentum*, since the degree of certitude it produces is like that achieved by argumentative reasoning.

Englhardt has shown that the first to introduce this sense of *argumentum* was not William of Auxerre, but Peter of Corbeille (d. 1222). In Stephen Langton's commentary on Paul's Epistles, Peter is cited as comparing this to the way a syllogism leads a person—or even forces him—to agree with a conclusion he had formerly denied. Similarly, an article of faith can seem incredible to someone before he experiences faith, but the minute he does (*habita fide statim*) he assents to the article he previously denied, and it seems undeniably true in his eyes. William accepts this similitude with two minor, yet revealing changes. First, he elucidates the nature of the peculiar persuasive force of faith as an illumination of the intellect. Second, the suddenness expressed in Peter's text (*statim*) is replaced by a gradual process (*magis et magis . . . paulatim*):

> As one arrives at the knowledge of the conclusion through an argument, so one reaches step by step the perfect knowledge of the non apparent eternal good through the faith which increasingly illumines the intellect (*sicut per argumentum pervenitur in notitiam conclusionis, ita per fidem magis et magis illuminantem intellectum venitur paulatim in perfectam notitiam eternorum bonorum non apparentium*).[16]

This seemingly insignificant last nuance is noteworthy, for, as Roland's teaching demon has already taught us, time is a characteristic aspect of the distinction between learning and inspiration.

William goes one step further with regard to the certitude of faith. Proposing a fourth interpretation of *argumentum*, he turns to the *Posterior*

Analytics, drawing from it a conception of even higher and more certain cognition than demonstrative knowledge:

> The fourth sense in which faith is said to be *argumentum non apparentium* is due to the articles of faith, which are the known-of-themselves principles of faith. This is why faith disapproves their proofs. For faith, which relies upon truth alone, finds in these articles the reason why to believe in them, that is, God, as in another faculty the intellect finds in this principle "every whole is bigger than its part" the reason why it cognizes it.[17]

In the *Posterior Analytics*, Aristotle determines that pursuit of demonstrative knowledge depends necessarily on strong starting points: the *principia*. To avoid circular or infinite argumentation, these first anchors should be indemonstrable, prior, evident, certain, and immediate (ἀμεσοί). We require no medium to grasp them (71b21). This grasp is superior both to opinion (δόξα) and to demonstrative knowledge. Indeed, in the *Posterior Analytics* Aristotle calls it "undemonstrative knowledge" (ἀναπόδεικτος ἐπιστήμη) or "understanding" (νοῦς).[18] These are the very features with which William wishes to adorn faith. Faith is no longer placed between *opinio* and *scientia*, but above both. The mechanisms creating certitude or immediate acceptance of phenomena in the realms of nature and grace parallel William of Auxerre's scheme in which both kinds of principles are accepted immediately through illumination.

The comparison of faith to the *cognitio principiorum* leads to an entire model of proper science, for as William explains:

> If there were no principles in theology it would not have been an art or a science. It has therefore principles, that is, the articles of faith, although they are principles only to the faithful ... as this principle "every whole is bigger than its part" has a certain illumination of nature which illuminates the intellect, so the principle "God is the remunerator of all goods" and other articles have in themselves an illumination of grace, by which God illuminates the intellect.[19]

Grabmann calls William's account of faith as *argumentum* an "ingenious foundation" for the solution of a not-yet-articulated question, the question of whether or not theology is a *scientia*.[20] Yet William never explicitly makes a claim regarding this question or even raises it. He simply assumes it on his way to the more urgent task of positioning the articles of faith as *per se nota* principles: "If theology did not have first principles it would not be a science [it is a science]; therefore it has first principles, namely the articles of faith." At least formally, the scientific nature of theology is not questioned. Rather the implicit conviction that it is a normal science is used to fashion faith as direct, illuminated cognition.[21]

In William's view, accepting a truth only because of itself (*propter se*), rather than because of another (*propter aliud*), is one of the most important conditions for a meritorious vision. Yet aside from the Aristotelian context, this characteristic alludes also to a common theological distinction about the love of God, as seen in the opening to the *Summa Aurea*. There is love of God for the sake of temporal benefit and love for God's sake alone. In the same manner, there are two kinds of beliefs in the cognitive realm: faith that is supported by authorities or philosophical reasoning and faith for no apparent reason.[22] As a result, even prophecy is not held as meritorious by William, since the prophet believes what he has seen because of his vision, not because of its contents' inherent truthfulness.[23] This mode of "because of itself" distinguishes formed, meritorious faith from unformed faith, defining the latter as resting on rational arguments, miracles, or authority—anything other than the truth itself.

Englhardt views the new simile of Peter of Corbeille as initiating a deep revision of the conception of faith, "clarifying for the first time that true faith is not to be based on any rational reasoning, nor on the example of the fathers (*exemplum patrum*)."[24] William's introduction of the self/other dichotomy fully clarified the consequences. For the first time, this division brought reason and authority together on the side of the "other": the side of the church, of ancestors, of scriptural revelation, and even of divine authority itself.

What, then, of the mirror and the enigma of faith? William has a concept of natural faith, which is innate and different from unformed faith, which rests on rational argumentation. It is this belief that appears in several places "enigmatically through a mirror." When he wishes to distinguish natural faith from true faith, he relies on the *Posterior Analytics* once more to explain the different roles that the natural world plays in each. Natural faith leans on natural arguments and uses the world as a principle. Grace-given faith, on the other hand, uses mundane arguments only as in a mirror: it does not rely on them, but since God is not seen *in specie*, it employs the world as a kind of nod of approval, not as a proof, just as the intellect requires the senses to know a *dignitas*, while *dignitates* themselves have no proof.[25]

Nevertheless, it seems that William finds it hard to reconcile his view of faith with the higher forms of knowledge: wisdom and the beatific vision. In another *quaestio*, when required to distinguish faith from wisdom, William returns to the traditional conception of faith. Suddenly faith is compared with the knowledge one has of a wine after hearing the report of another, while wisdom is knowledge of the wine after tasting.[26] Faith again becomes the faith by hearing, relying on the words of another. Similarly, when he deals with the transition of virtues from the state of grace to the state of glory, it is only this facet of faith that is discussed. Even its designation as a vision is contested.[27] While the world is almost entirely absent from his tractate dedicated to faith, in his treatment of the transition from grace to glory, looking into the mirror of creation—a very far mirror, he stresses—becomes the central feature of faith. The mode of accepting something "because of itself" is not mentioned, nor is the illumination of the intellect or the cognition of principles.

I cannot suggest a sufficient explanation for this. Perhaps it was too difficult to think of yet another level of certitude and still maintain this model. Perhaps it is due to editorial questions from different periods of William's teaching. In the writings of William's contemporaries, the exclusion of human authority from the sphere of faith is even more conspicuous. William elegantly omits the interpretation of *argumentum* as "after the example of the fathers," but others such as Alexander of Hales and Philip the Chancellor explicitly discard it by designating it faith by persuasion (*fides suasa*), a rather weak *argumentum* and an even weaker interpretation of Paul's words.[28] Roland of Cremona, as usual, is the most scathing critic. He rejects it out of hand, arguing that to convince someone of the truth of the Trinity because "Abraham believed in it" will only lead a skeptic to reject Abraham as well: "If you say to him 'Abraham believed so,' then he who says that the Father, the Son and the Holy Spirit are not one God would say: 'if Abraham believed that he was stupid.'"[29]

The dichotomy between two forms of faith—faith "because of itself" versus faith "because of another"—was accepted by all. However, while William and Roland used the terms "unformed" and "formed" to designate the two kinds of faith, Philip, Alexander, and their circle chose other terms with which to articulate the growing gap between grace-given faith, which is all light, immediacy, and certitude on one hand, and the fragile faith that leans on authority or reason on the other.[30] The key verse for them was Romans 10:17, "faith by hearing." Following John of Damascus as quoted in the Lombardian Gloss, they foregrounded the distinction between exterior and interior hearing.[31] Since true faith is an interior illumination, the only thing that "hearing" could denote in this verse—if indeed the verse addresses the question of true faith—is an interior hearing. All the traditional characterizations of the cognition of faith as enigmatic, hesitant, or opinionated belonged now to the second, nonmeritorious faith, while interior faith remained untouched in its splendor, far beyond both opinion and knowledge.[32]

The *Summa Halensis* devotes an entire *quaestio* to discussing whether or not the virtue of faith is a result of persuasion, a *fides suasa*. After all, the scriptures are full of examples for people who believed due to something they saw or of which they heard. Their solution follows Philip's: faith derived from persuasion is entirely different from grace-given faith, although the former may serve as a primary disposition leading to the latter.[33]

The idea that hearing stands mainly for doctrine attained through verbal instruction of another is well demonstrated in the case of the salvation of the deaf. Several *quaestiones de fide* of the period query how a deaf person can be saved if faith comes through hearing. The answer is identical in all of them: doctrine, which is unavailable to those who cannot hear, is only one of four ways by which faith can come to a person. The other three are inspiration, revelation, and natural reasoning, which remain open to them and present opportunities for salvation.[34] Community and communication with human teachers are not necessary.

Like his fellow masters, William of Auvergne maintains a sharp distinction between faith dependent on persuasion (*fides suasa*) and the virtue of faith. William compared the intellect that requires proofs to someone who uses a walking stick (*baculus, fulcimentum*) and, in an even more colorful image, to a suspicious merchant who only believes his client if he gives him a deposit or security.[35] The intellect's requirement of proofs is consequently cast as contemptuous toward God, an act of pure mistrust.[36] Nevertheless, William does not present human authority, miracles, or other testimonies as walking sticks or a creditor's demand for collateral. The grouping together of all external "others"—whether reason, authority, or miracles—on the same side is thus omitted. All we are left with at the end of the discussion is the traditional opposition of faith and reason.

Roland of Cremona, Odo Rigaldi, Adam of Puteorumvilla, and an anonymous master, who might have been Guerric, also engaged with the terminology of *Posterior Analytics* as they turned to address theology's scientific status. Roland insisted on a small correction, saying that the articles of faith are not first principles, but resemble instead conclusions, while faith itself, as a light-*habitus*, plays the part of the thing that is known in and through itself.[37] Like William, he thought the idea relevant enough to raise it in the very opening of his *summa*. There, as in William's case, the scientific status of theology is not questioned but presupposed, yet it entails a series of questions.

What is the subject of theology? What does it prove and by what means? What are the things *known for themselves* that form its starting point?[38] Interestingly, Roland rejects the role of principles from holy scriptures, since it contradicts the new commitment to immediacy: one must believe the first truth because of itself. He prefers the articles of faith serve this function, from which other theological statements follow in a normal scientific, demonstrative way.[39] As in William of Auxerre's model, illumination forms the basis for scientific investigation, as the science of theology itself is built on it.

An anonymous *Quaestio de scientia divina* in manuscript Prague IV D 13 is the first we know of that raises doubts regarding theology's status as a science. The status of the articles/principles occupies a prominent place in the author's suspicion. If they are not known but believed, then theology is not a *scientia*, the objector claims, but mere faith.[40] To solve this problem, the author explains that theology is indeed a *scientia*, having all the necessary components that characterize other sciences. In the role of "things known for themselves" proper to each science, he casts the principles of the natural law rather than the articles of faith. The latter belong in his view to the category of "belief in authorities." With a surprisingly honest sobriety, he remarks that such belief forms a part of every normal science, including astronomy (believing Ptolemy, for instance). In the case of theology, it is not the authority of human savants, he hurries to say, but the authority of God.[41] The act of faith however, is a mixed one. Some statements are known as "the principles known for themselves" (*quasi per se nota, intelligit ut principia*), while others are accepted due to the authority of the church and human authorities.[42]

Odo Rigaldi faced a variation of the same objection regarding the principles in 1240. Every proper science has principles that are known without relying on any exterior source of certitude, and they form the basis for the certitude of all other conclusions. The articles of faith, it was objected, offer themselves to the intellect only with the external aid of grace. Odo replies by stating that the principles of theology are in fact those of natural law. The articles of faith, however, need no proof and in this respect are similar to the *"suppositiones"* of other sciences. According to Aristotle's *Posterior Analytics* 1.33, *suppositio* is "a belief in a proposition which is immediate and not necessary"—that is, could also be otherwise.[43] They differ nevertheless, since grace is an external "other" to the intellect-self. Odo clarifies the nature of the relationship between these two cognitive modes: cognition of the articles is faith or wisdom, while the body of knowledge that proceeds from them and from the principles of natural law is knowledge or science. Adam de Puteorumvilla (Puzzoles), a bachelor of theology who lectured the following year on the *Sentences*, accorded the articles of faith the role of *suppositiones* or *dignitates* as well.[44]

Not everyone approved the link of the certitude of faith with that of the principles to their occupation. Hugh of St. Cher, who knew the *Summa Aurea* very well, completely ignores William's third and fourth senses in his commentary. Unlike William and Roland, he does not allude to this theme at all in the prologue to his theological work. Philip the Chancellor accepted the basic analogy with the certitude of the first principles but did not refer to a science of theology or to any broader context in which the articles of faith fulfill the function of the first principles of a demonstrative science.[45] Alexander of Hales stated that faith was called *argumentum* because we believe that God is three and one "as principles, because of themselves."[46] Yet he does not specify to which science these principles belong and prefers a different analysis of the term *argumentum*.

The compilers of the *Summa Halensis* knew William's summa as well as Hugh. They chose to ignore William's fourth sense of *argumentum* and present only Peter of Corbeille's analogy—namely, that the degree of certitude in the articles is equal to that of a conclusion in a proper syllogism.[47] The question of the scientific status of theology does not arise as a subject at all.

As a matter of fact, although they accepted the analogy to the superior certitude of the knowledge of principles, Philip's circle, the *Summa fratri*

Alexandri, and William of Auvergne used the idea of such immediate cognition mainly in order to show that faith is far different from it and has a nonintellectual mechanism creating that certitude. The articles of faith, Philip explains, owe their intrinsic light of certainty to the formation of consciousness, achieved through the intellect's "captivation" by love, like a lover is captivated by earthly love:[48]

> The principle of this cognition is affection or love. As happens in vulgar love, in which someone loves another so zealously that this zeal does not permit him to believe or suspect anything sinister about the other, so also the affection one has for God, through which one believes him in everything, cannot bear anything in sense or reason which seems to contradict faith.[49]

In the same spirit, Alexander claims that the certitude of faith is not cognitive, as does the *Summa Halensis*. Rather, it is achieved through the more praiseworthy adherence of the *affectus*.[50]

William of Auvergne perhaps best represents the affective-voluntary approach. His fundamental approach maintains a strong conflict between the intellect and the objects of Christian faith. In his first argument favoring the high value and certainty of true faith, we find love again as a source of inspiration for the discourse of cognition. Both love and belief may depend either on the beloved object or on the loving subject, he explains. One can love something because it is useful and pleasant and similarly believe something because it is plausible and reasonable. In both cases, it is a property of the object that sparks love or belief. However, when one loves something bad or unpleasant, like poverty or death, the property of the object cannot be the cause. It therefore must be something within the lover himself. That love, in which the lover loves because of an interior virtue rather than the object's property, is stronger. In a similar fashion, he who believes an improbable thing to be true believes it because of some inner virtue in himself, a virtue that is not dependent on the object's plausibility at all.[51] This latter belief, he claims, enjoys more certainty than that which relies on the probability of the object of knowledge.

The painful unfitness of belief is underlined over and over again to prove the virtuousness of faith. Normal knowledge does not involve any struggle, for there is nothing difficult in accepting reasonable statements. Yet whereas plausibility pleases the intellect, improbability hurts it, and therefore accepting nonapparent truths such as those of Christianity should lead to an internal struggle. This is why, he says, faith is a *virtus*, the overcoming of a difficulty. The internal, preceding struggle of the intellect against itself is won with the aid of will and love.

Masters of theology were definitely more prone to experience such inner battles than others. William of Auvergne told King Louis IX, who disclosed it later to Jean of Joinville, of a desperate master who came to see him one day. Weeping tears, the master confessed that he could not force his heart to believe in the sacrament of the altar anymore. William verified that he felt distressed rather than pleased about this and that he was not willing to utter with his own mouth a denial of this sacrament. Afterward, he asked him if he knew that the kings of France and England were at war and that the castle of La Rochelle in Poitou lies exactly on the border of their kingdoms. He further asked the master were the king to give him the border fortress of La Rochelle to guard during the war but assigned William to Montlhéry, which lies at the peaceful heart of France, to whom should the king be more grateful at the end of war? The master answered, "La Rochelle." "Master," said the bishop, "what I am telling you is that my heart is like the castle of Montlhéry, for I have no temptation nor doubts about the sacrament of the altar. That is why I can tell you that if God is grateful to me for my firm and untroubled faith, he is four times as grateful to you for holding your heart for him in this woeful struggle."[52]

William makes extensive use of militaristic terminology in the pages of *De fide*, and it is worth noticing that the intellect's war against itself is not dissimilar to the second war it must conduct, as explained in *De bono et malo*, the war against those who use earthly arguments—that is, philosophers.[53] Being a philosophizing theologian involves in its essence a deep internal struggle. This internal war of the master of theology could not be further from William of Auxerre's peaceful, illuminated intellect, adhering to the articles of faith in which it finds the reason to believe.

As a matter of fact, William is able to provide the unbeliever with a security, a "first principle" more certain than any of the disciplines: "The first truth speaks the true." But he despises the request of the intellect for such.[54] In *De fide* as well as in *De bono et malo*, he opposes faith to the cognition of first principles that are "strongly impressed in the intellect." When something is known in itself, it is not subjected to the freedom of choice, for he who believes it or a syllogism must accept the conclusion without any hesitation. Furthermore, the superior clarity of knowing the principles over demonstrative knowledge enables William of Auvergne to lead readers of *De bono et malo* to the solution of obedience.

Having established that knowing God is the essential goal of the human intellect, he presents two ways of achieving it: by inquiry (*via inquisitionis*) and by merit (*via meriti*). The general rule is that "what is prior is more certain," the bishop determines, since the intellect is then closer to the bright light of the principles. Conclusions, therefore, are necessarily less noble and less illuminated than the propositions that lead to them. We are less certain of a geometrical sentence after following a long, exhausting proof than we are of a simple axiom. If so, William concludes, then any knowledge of God attained through demonstration will necessarily be posterior to the cognition of the principles through which it was acquired; hence, it will not be the most illustrious of all cognitions, as it should have been.[55]

Two options are left. The first is that these objects of knowledge show themselves in an intrinsic light, like the disciplinary principles or the objects of the senses. William of Auxerre chose this option to characterize the state of grace, but the bishop saves it for the state of glory as well as prelapsarian knowledge: Adam and Eve knew the articles of faith as one knows the first principles, unlike us.[56] The other option is that we should believe them through obedience of the will. The meritorious cognition of faith belongs to a world of authority, subjugation, and governance.[57]

To sum up, although the masters disagreed and were sometimes incoherent, their texts betray a deep predicament regarding the respective places of obedience, reason, and inspiration and a shared decrease of the role of human authority. Just a generation earlier, it had been entirely acceptable to contend that one believed firmly because of the "faith of the fathers"; a few decades later, it became unthinkable to gain certainty simply "because Abraham believed that was true." The masters drew inspiration for their models of direct cognition from ideals of unconditional love on the one hand and from Aristotle's concept of principles known in themselves on the other hand. None of them could resist the temptation to import Aristotelian notions into the traditional Christian scheme of knowledge (earthly faith and heavenly vision) or to his own practice. Some, like Philip and William of Auvergne, highlighted the conflict between the philosophizing, natural intellect, and the tenets of Christian faith and did not find these concepts useful for a discussion of theology at all. Gratuitous cognitive illumination and inspiration had nothing to do with learning; acts of obedience and will did. The intellect was not illumined. It struggled.

Others, William of Auxerre in particular, aimed for a more harmonious conception of inspiration and study. In order to escape the fragile basis of authority, faith was construed as an intellective illumination analogous to the natural illumination of principles. Unlike Odo, William did not think of this light as "other" or, at least, not more than the natural light of the intellect. Odo and Adam did not perceive the articles of faith in the same way but were more than willing to accord them the function of suppositions in the science of theology. All of them minimized the aspect of relying on someone's else's voice: belief "because someone says so" was no longer considered by these theologians meritorious or worthy, although it remained firm in other places, as is demonstrated in the conversation between Joinville and King Louis IX.

The Aristotelian model enabled masters both to distinguish faith from theological knowledge and to support it, in the same way as elaborate geometry differs from simple acceptance of axioms. The shift of faith from its association with authority, obedience, and externality to individual enlightenment (though still external, according to some) lay at the heart of this move. In order to make theology into a normal science, faith had to be immediate. This was, however, only one direction taken by William of Auxerre and Roland. Others would pursue another direction—that is, constructing theology as ethics—to be discussed in Chapter 6.

MAGISTERIAL AUTHORITY AND THE NASCENT UNIVERSITY

The issue of inspirational faith was so explicitly connected with some masters' attempts to define their profession that it might seem somewhat superfluous to try and contextualize it beyond that. Nonetheless, there are two small doors through which we can try to step outside the classroom and look at the changing status of authority and individuality in early thirteenth-century school and religious practices.

The first clue is that the two Williams bring up the issue of master-disciple relationship while addressing the proper relation between the intellect and the truth. William of Auxerre compares nonmeritorious belief,

belief that relies upon something, to the credulity by which one, who loves his master with deep feelings (*ex affectu*) and believes him to be the best in the faculty, when he hears something from him that in and of itself merits faith, believes this fact because his master said it was so rather than because of its truthfulness.[58] Grace-given faith is nothing like that.

William of Auvergne praises obedience and subjugation to a master in order to elucidate the nature of true faith.[59] The intellect cannot be its own teacher, he admonishes, and it is a disgrace to have teaching (*magisterium*) where learning (*discipulatum*) should have been. The intellect struggles, he contends, "to take off the things that are innate to it and put on an alien *magisterium*."[60]

Both Williams, therefore, recognize that love, power, and authority form an essential part of teaching and studying, as they can greatly influence the disciple to accept opinions not because they are true, and they were not the only ones to notice this. The *Disciplina scolarium*, a student guide that was written in the 1240s (but that allegedly speaks in the person of the sixth-century philosopher Boethius), advises one aspiring to the magistrate not to trust books and notes indiscriminately, as if they were sacred. "Boethius" relates that one Nigrio had so much confidence in his master that he had written down every word that came out of the latter's mouth. As he obtained the magisterial cathedra, all he did was read from these notes. He became as a result an "object of scorn," and the guide's advice to the ambitious master was not to be stupid and believe a teacher's words without trying to imagine later that he was mistaken.[61] Inspirational faith sees as its model this kind of student, whose love for his teacher does not stand in the way of an immediate contact with truth.

In their studies of the cultural atmosphere of pre-university medieval schools, both Stephen Jaeger and Mia Münster-Swendsen after him emphasized the importance of the affective relationship between teachers and their disciples. Proper, justified, and, not least, useful, the affective bond between master and student(s) occupied the center of pedagogical thought throughout the high Middle Ages. But more than just being a didactic strategy, it signified a cultural practice that was very much the constituting social device that bound the school milieus together in an age that did not know the institution of the university.[62] John of Salisbury, the latest of Münster-Swendsen's sources, explicitly intertwined belief with love. Following

Quintilian's seventh key to students, he notes, "They [i.e., students] listen with pleasure to those whom they love *and believe what they say*, and desire to be like them."

Both Münster-Swendsen and Jaeger end their analyses of charismatic and affective school culture before the rise of the universities by noting the gradual yet dramatic change of these elements that occurred from the end of the eleventh century through the twelfth century. The sources all telegraph a crisis of magisterial authority. Abelard is, of course, the typical audacious student of the early twelfth century that we think of in this respect. He was also the one who counseled his son Astrolabe, "Do not give your faith to the words of a beloved master."[63] Even John of Salisbury, who praised love and belief as key to learning, with all his critique of the academic position of doubting everything, still points to the fact that the opposite is just as dangerous. He mocks those who choose what to follow based on their estimation of their master. "For how can he be in doubt, who swears by the words of his master and pays attention not to what is said but to him who says it?" He who was captivated by his teacher's opinion will not be quieted with rational arguments, for everything the latter pronounced is held as trustworthy and holy [*autenticum et sacrosanctum*].[64]

Clearly, the ideal of adhering to every word coming of the mouth of an old, venerable master was eroding. It is one thing to have one admired master in a cathedral, but quite another to have many in Paris. The master's authority as an exclusive source of knowledge—indeed, the only one—was greatly reduced in the university environment, where students hopped from one master to another, comparing and judging. Armed with reason and audacity, students like Abelard embarrassed their teachers. Someone like John easily drew comparisons between the varying styles of his teachers.

While this crisis has been well documented and studied, what happened to these relationships during the first decades of the thirteenth century is difficult to reconstruct. For some reason, there are far fewer letters of the sort that flourished earlier in the schools, and consequently examples of the kind of "amatory—and even occasionally erotic—discourse between masters and students" found in the earlier sources from which Münster-Swendsen quotes extensively are rare.[65] But although the evidence is insufficient, it seems safe to assume that these relationships grew more complex with the progressive institutionalization of the Parisian schools.

The bonds holding the community were no longer only affective or loose; they "hardened" to constitute an institution. Although enrollment with one master was still the norm, both master and student were now part of a bigger system, subject to the rules of their guild. Masters were less free in determining the content of studies, the time and form of lessons, students' minimum age or educational prerequisites. These were dictated by the society of masters. The students' conduct, behavior, success, and failure did not depend on their masters alone; they were subjected to and shaped by general statutes and various officials: other masters, deans, and rectors.

The growing number of masters continued to play a role in degrading the authority and prestige of the sole master, an almost inevitable consequence of the shift from a system built on charisma to a bureaucracy. Popes Innocent III and Honorius III feared in 1207 and 1221 respectively that the multiplication of teachers was resulting in a devaluation of the profession and poverty of its practitioners.[66] Honorius also mentioned another cause, closely related to the decline of charismatic teaching and to the corrupted relationship between the chancellor and the union over licensing masters. Admitting unworthy men to the magistrate, he said, had led to a general decline of the *auctoritas magistralis*.[67]

AUTHORITY AND HERESY

A second clue may help us extend our sight beyond the school's doors to broader cultural ambiguities about trust, authority, and heresy. Again, it is William of Auxerre who leads the gaze at this direction, as the interior principles pop up in another question of his, "Whether believing against a certain article is a punishable sin."[68] As optional objections, William presents three cases in which an old, unlearned woman may unknowingly fall into the Arian error and thus jeopardize her salvation. She may hear a preacher saying that everything that the Son has is from the Father and conclude that the Father is greater than the Son; she may be so ignorant that it is simply beyond her mental capacity to understand that it is not so; or she may unknowingly follow an Arian prelate. In all these cases, the respondent could argue on her behalf that it was not her fault. But William is clear that she shall not be saved. The false authority of her prelate and her complete ignorance that led her to draw a heretical conclusion from an orthodox preacher's words would not excuse her, William explains, for she could not learn about this article from someone else anyhow. Whether learned or ignorant, she has in her speculative intellect a "known from itself" that God exists. All she has to do is to ponder the matter carefully and allow the light of truth to illuminate her. That inner, individual inspiration should guide her even when her heretic prelate deceives her. Each person has the highest prelate in his or her heart, William proceeds, whom he or she must follow.

When Roland of Cremona addresses this problem he repeats the three objections with slight variations.[69] His first is a simple man who knows how to read a little and who reads Hilary of Poitiers's assertion that the Father is greater than the Son. He either concludes that the Son is lesser than the Father or just believes Hilary straightforwardly without understanding the subtle equivocation in the use of "great." His second example is of simple folks who hear the evangelical words "my Father is greater than me," but alas, do not hear a sermon on their equality. They too could come in the Day of Judgment and say, "We were told to believe the gospel."

Like William, Roland notes the problem of false instruction, such as the believers in Hilary's time who had Arian prelates. He then proceeds to an even more complex and extreme case. Suppose a simple man was baptized, but grew up in the woods, away from human society and any religious instruction. On his return to society, he falls right into a malicious heretic's hands. The latter teaches him the Arian error by showing him the evangelical words "my father is greater than me." He, however, judges William's solution to be too cruel and suggests a simple means to save those errant souls. Such misled simple men would not sin, he suggests, if they only added to the statement they believed in "only if it accords with the Church's doctrine, or with what the prophets and apostles said." In the case of the woodsman, he cannot even add the qualifying clause "assuming that the apostles and prophets agree with that" because he knows nothing about them. Well, says Roland, he should ask other people. In case he finds no one to teach him otherwise, his "inner anointing" shall instruct him at least to add to this wrong principle a restricting clause of healthy doubt, "only if that is true." All these conditions, ironically, undermine the noble idea of unconditioned acceptance of the truth.

William and Roland set their case in the times of widespread Arianism, but their own age was also burning. At the threshold of the thirteenth century, about two centuries after the first documented instances, the church faced a throng of small and widespreading movements that challenged orthodox authority and won souls for their doctrines and participants for their rituals all over Europe. Now the topic of heresy and ecclesiastical response to its challenge, from the broader movements such as the Cathars (or "good men") and the Waldensians to local reformers and rebels, is a sea-wide topic as it organizes an extremely lively field of medieval historiography. References alone would require a book-length footnote. I would not presume to summarize the state of this warfare in the 1220s, just a bit after the pivotal decisions of 1215, still in the very midst of the Albigensian military affair and on the threshold of the first systematic inquisitions. Let us just take a look from our angle.

William's and Roland's examples of how medieval people were persuaded to adhere to nonorthodox doctrines appear in other documents as well. Individuals and groups challenged the authority and mediation of the church by relying on their own individual reason, divine inspiration, on unmediated reading of scriptures, and on the authority of information agents other than authorized church prelates and priests: "Perfect," "good men," "brothers," charismatic itinerant preachers and reformers, or even local priests who entertained heretical views.[70]

The early thirteenth century saw a dramatic escalation of the church's war against heresy. One front, though certainly not the only one, was polemical-intellectual. In order to win debates in the center of a town or village, there was a high need to train the debaters and preachers so they would know the articles of faith extremely well, master the scriptures, equip them with theological and philosophical arguments that could support their case, and, more than everything else, train them to master the art of disputation. The papacy eagerly sought to recruit university theologians to serve at this front. In 1217, Pope Honorius III addressed a letter to the masters and students residing in Paris, urging them to go to Toulouse—at the time the hottest field of battle—to teach and preach the light of truth. In 1219, he expressed his wish to extend the study of theology to form an unconquerable wall of warriors around the Catholic faith to defend it. Paris would be as David's tower with all its bulwarks. The men experienced in war with swords girded to their thighs who escort Solomon's bed in *Song of Songs* figure Parisian theologians.[71]

Naturally, the theologians embraced this as a justification for their profession and particularly for employing philosophy in their arguments, indeed, for employing arguments at all. Why are rational demonstrations and their agents needed if faith is understood as such direct adherence to the truth as shown previously, you might ask? Battling heresy was one of the three answers Godfrey of Poitiers and William of Auxerre gave in the prologues to their *summae*.[72] The anonymous commentary to the *Sentences* in Vat. Lat. 691, written by Guerric of St. Quentin, John of La Rochelle, or someone else from their circle, embraces Honorius's approach in its prologue through the very same verse drawn from *Song of Songs*: "Look! It is Solomon's carriage, escorted by sixty warriors, the noblest of Israel, all of them wearing the sword, all experienced in battle, each with his sword at his side, prepared for the terrors of the night" (3:7). The warriors, he explains, are the doctors of theology, fighting for and defending faith against heresy, armed with swords of authorities and sharp spears of arguments. Peter Lombard's *Sentences* is their armory of weapons.[73]

Robert Moore points out the close, reciprocal affinity between the educated elite and "experts" and the increasing formalization and institutionalization of persecution.[74] Theologians of this generation, such as Philip the Chancellor and Roland of Cremona, became increasingly involved in procedures of persecution and judgment of heretics and Jews.[75] Yet precisely because of their knowledge and literacy, theologians could easily find themselves on the wrong side of the battle, and sometimes did so.[76] William's and Roland's examples relate to uneducated men and women, but both knew well that heresies can issue from educated theologians as well, having the Amalricians and others in mind.

Subtleties, new ideas, and philosophical arguments created doubts within. Just like the torn, crying master whom William of Auvergne imagined sending to fight on the English-French war, Hugh of St. Cher placed the doctors in his prologue to the *Sentences* in a liminal position. Following the Pseudo-Peter of Poitiers gloss, Hugh constructed the whole introduction around the allegorical interpretation of the scene of Moses at Mount Sinai.[77] According to the holy writ, Moses posted borders around the mountain, which he argues represent the explanations of the saints and the fathers. The different approaches to these boundaries are symbolized by the figures participating in the biblical story. Moses symbolizes those who crossed the boundary and ascended to the hidden meanings of the scriptures with the help of the Holy Spirit. Hur, Aaron, and the seventy sages followed him and waited near the borders for some time but got tired and went back. Joshua, who stayed there alone, represents the eager doctors of theology who ascend right up to the borders, yet neither cross them nor turn back, standing on the border of inspiration. The *Sentences* were written for the sake of those who had grown tired on their long journey and had withdrawn to other sciences, for the sake of the people who did not even bother to exit their tents, and against those who dared to cross the boundary without being called by the Holy Spirit—namely, the heretics.

Theologians were presumed to fight, but the ground under their feet, their very position as agents of knowledge, was not as secure as that of charismatic leaders or, on the other hand, geometricians, whose clear-cut demonstrations could not be tainted with a stain of doubt. Their positions, therefore, reflect a necessarily confused attempt to engage this intricate and contradictory field of legitimacy and authority. They well recognize the strength of relying on one's proper reasoning and the "law of the heart" against the weakness of relying on prelates, hearsay, or written parchment (to use the Orléans heretics' supposed dichotomy). Yet they still have to adhere to the traditional church line, which is precisely reliance on tradition and believing "because the church believes it is so."

William's anchoring of faith and theology in a stable interior illumination of the mind occupies ground in between the two. On one hand, he establishes the base of theology in a gratuitous, intellectual illumination rather than on the weak foundation of tradition. He enforces thereby his colleagues' social position, lending them a scientific character that is vital for their authority. Their minds, further illuminated with the grace-given gift of understanding, distinguish them from the philosophers. At the same time, he presents the heretics—even simple ones—as alienated from the truth inside them. Keenly aware of this crisis of authority, he argues that any individual may entertain a certain immediate contact with interior truth; even old women are endowed with an individual speculative intellect and are therefore expected to doubt their prelates and connect to their inner truth directly. William, therefore, directly addresses the heretical crisis and emphasizes personal responsibility as opposed to that of the church, relating this to the idea of placing authority inside the individual's soul. Men raised in the woods or deaf persons remained outside the reach of both society and doctrine as well. Literacy made ignorant women not only listen to preachers and misunderstand them, but also read the gospel and interpret it by themselves. In Orléans in 1022, the heretics supposedly discarded the fictions of carnal men scribbled on animal skins in favor of the law written upon the heart by the Holy Spirit. Two hundred years after this affair, one way to win the orthodox authority back was to anchor it in this noncommunal place, the interior, natural realm as well. Persecution was thus justified by making the heretic not only disobedient, but one who fails to follow her or his heart. The heart is the only source of certitude. But it says just what the traditional church has said all along.

Roland's moves in this tricky game turned paradoxical. His idea of adding a doubting clause drains the meaning of simple adherence to the truth "for itself" and returns to traditional authority and community almost by force; even if pushed into the corner, he too admits an "internal anointing," which must direct the misled person raised in the woods to doubt. What did others do who did not follow William of Auxerre's ideas and preferred to anchor faith in the voluntary part of the soul than in the intellect proclaim? They emphasized divine authority and obedience rather than human endeavor. But no questions of theirs regarding old women or woodsmen survived to tell us how and to what they linked their thoughts on faith.

How does all this work with the enormous growth of preaching activity and the explicit aim of theology to reinforce the faith of the simple? Pretty well, in fact. For mediation is not banned; only the final source of certitude must be interior. Miracles, exemplary stories, and arguments are legitimate means of generating persuasion as a step toward inward grace, just like a student who should be able to cling to the truth "because of itself," *despite* his esteem for his teacher who had mediated it to him. The wise who know the reason the statement "God exists" is a true statement should be able to believe it "because of itself" *despite* these external reasons. Is this possible? This aspect of the mechanism of *medium* and the ambiguity that is created from the variety of media on the one hand and the emphasis on simple, individual certitude on the other occupies the center of the next chapter.

CHAPTER FIVE
What happens to old modes of cognition when new ones are introduced during trance and other transitions?
The self and its ability to manipulate parts of it during transitions
Theology between reasoned knowledge and simple faith

I don't need to believe, I know. —C. G. Jung

Paul's ecstasy was viewed as a sudden, irregular leap from an earthly cognitive state to a heavenly one and all the way back again.[1] Most of our theologians, as shown in Chapter 1, assumed that Paul still had his older *habitus* of faith during ecstasy, though inactivated, and some believed it was this residue that impeded a fully clear vision. The perception of knowledge as a fixed *habitus* posed difficulties regarding identity and selfhood, bearing not only on the apostle's experience, but also on the most fundamental and transformative process of every Christian: the transition from the state of nature to that of grace as faith is conferred and the transition from grace to glory as the blessed soul sees God face-to-face. And thus, as we look at all the questions dealing with cognitive states, we find a set of questions persistently repeated: what happens during each such transition? Is the old, less certain cognition replaced by the new one? Does it remain inactive, or does it somehow unite with the new one? These questions kept troubling the minds of theologians in later generations as well. In another version of Aquinas's life, he asks the ghost of his former colleague, Master Romanus, "What about that question on which we were frequently disputing? Do the *habitus* of the sciences, which were acquired in this life, remain in the homeland (i.e., heaven)?" The frustrating response he receives is, "Friar Thomas, I see God, and will reveal nothing else about this question."[2]

This chapter will delve into this theoretical preoccupation with cognitive transitions and the dis/continuity and hybridity of the self they imply. I shall then argue that the preoccupation with maintaining two different cognitive *habitus* within the very same soul should be read against the conflictual identity of academic scholars, vacillating between holy simplicity on the one hand and reasoned, professional knowledge on the other. The assumption that one can manipulate one's own approach so as to be simple at one hour and learned in another functioned well outside the classroom as the newly established Franciscan movement confronted the conflict between values of simplicity and of learning in the most acute manner in these very years. One specific tale by Thomas Celano about Francis will demonstrate how such a perception of the self enables one to manipulate the presentation of different parts of oneself according to the situation without being judged as a hypocrite. But first, let us listen to the theological debate itself.

THE PROBLEM OF COMPETING COGNITIONS

Suppose John read that today would be an extraordinarily rainy day. Leaving home well dressed, he confirms that it really is so. His certitude in the fact is certainly higher, now that personal experience has confirmed his original decision to believe the newspaper. But what happens to his former belief? Is it gone, being replaced by firmer knowledge? Does it remain, attached to the new knowledge? Or perhaps it is the same old cognitive *habitus*, only fortified? In short, what happens to inferior, less certain cognitions when more certain ones are acquired regarding the same object?

The biblical foundation for these discussions was located in the final words of Paul's famous speech on love in I Corinthians:

> Love never faileth (*excidit*): but whether there be prophecies, they shall fail (*evacuabuntur*); whether there be tongues, they shall cease (*cessabunt*); whether there be knowledge, it shall vanish away (*destruetur*). For we know in part.... But when that which is perfect is come, then that which is in part shall be done away (*evacuabitur*). When I was a child, I spake as a child...: but when I became a man, I put away (*evacuavi*) childish things. For now we see through a glass, darkly; but then face to face: now I know in part; but then shall I know even as also I am known. (13:8–13, King James Version)

Contrasted with *caritas*, or love, the realm of knowledge is construed by Paul as transient and changeable. Caroline Walker Bynum, who devoted several studies to notions of transformation and change in twelfth-century religious thought, noted that "change" is a deceptively simple concept. "Change" can mean the substituting of one thing for another, or it can mean that one thing alters its appearance or qualities, evolves, and grows.[3] For hundreds of years, exegetes had been trying to decipher the type of change hinted at and to determine whether it implies a total destruction of old knowledge in favor of better, new knowledge, or a perfective process of augmentation.[4] The choice of verbs—*excidit, evacuabuntur, cessabunt, destruetur*—suggests a complete disappearance of any cognition of God achieved in this life. Yet on the other hand, the metaphors of part and whole, child and adult, may imply a different sort of change, growth of the same being, rather than replacement. This basic problem was applied to other cognitive transitions by the late twelfth and early thirteenth centuries. One such instance, the problem of Paul's latent faith during his rapture, was already briefly discussed in Chapter 1. The question of unformed faith (*fides informis*) and formed faith (*fides formata*), a pair of habitus that will be later explicated, provided a second discursive context. Is unformed faith destroyed when formed faith arrives? Does it abide next to the new *habitus*, or had there been one *habitus* all along, then unformed and now formed and perfected? The discussion of this problem can be found in almost all tractates on faith and in those that addressed the "transition of virtues" (*transitus virtutum*)—that is, the question of what happens to the virtues during transitions from the state of nature to that of grace and from that of grace to glory. One master asked what happens to the *habitus* of faith during a prophetic vision;[5] another questioned whether it was wisdom evacuating and not faith, intending later to speak about the evacuation of wisdom in its turn.[6]

Last, but not least in this cluster of questions, the problem of whether the same thing can be believed and known, *idem creditum et scitum*, was a highly popular issue dealt with in contemporary treatises on faith. The Christian tradition has in its repertoire an option to attribute these two modes of cognition to two different groups of objects: probable or even possible contradictions are believed; *necessaria* are known. Thus, faith is always of "things unseen," following Hebrews 11:1. Consequently, belief in something that is indeed seen, known, and has evidence (*experimentum*) is not accorded the merit of faith at all, but is considered knowledge. Who needs to believe something when they see it right before their eyes?

As we have just seen in the previous chapter, many thought that the articles of the Christian faith just could not be grasped by natural reason alone. Nonetheless, there seems to be some overlap between the truths apprehended by faith and those based on rational or sensory evidence. All theologians agreed in those days that the notion that "God exists," for instance, was available to the mind through *both* faith and reason. Some were willing to attribute to philosophers a partial recognition of the Trinity as well, and even of the resurrection. With the growth of knowledge and the diligent work of theologians, perhaps other articles of faith would be proven as well. One option is to stick to the previous principle and argue that God's existence should not be considered an object of true Christian faith precisely *because* it can be grasped by reason. The authority most cited in this respect was Gregory's: "Faith to which human reason provides evidence has no merit" (*fides non habet meritum cui humana ratio praebet experimentum*).[7] Believing the obvious is not meritorious, and hence it does not pertain to faith. Another option, however, is to consider the possibility that the same proposition can be an object of both faith and knowledge. Aristotle, addressing a similar question about knowledge and opinion, asserted that the same statement may be an object of both. Nevertheless, it cannot be both for the same person at the same time. When a proof is provided, one does not opine anymore, one knows.[8]

Simon of Tournai, a master of theology who flourished in the last third of the twelfth century, made the same claim concerning similar objects for faith and knowledge (*scientia*). The same thing can be known by one person and believed by another, he maintained in a telling passage:

> A certain thing is knowledge to one and faith for another. Example: one learned in geometry such as Euclid knows that a line is divided into two equal parts, because he preconceives the causes of the proof. Someone simple, who knows not geometry, believes that a line is divided into two equal parts because he heard that affirmed by Euclid, who asserted that being famous in this art. *What is known by a scholar is believed by a simple man.*[9] (my italics)

While the professional, authoritative geometrician knows, the simple man acknowledges his authority and believes. Keep this in mind, for notions of authority and the positions of professionals and simple men are an important context for the discussion to follow.

This question can become even more complicated, as it did in the proceeding decades as they took up the question of whether the same thing could be known and believed by the *same* person at the same time. A third option was thus introduced to perceive change, which is perhaps not change at all: coexistence.

The two concepts of change hinted at by Paul—destruction/replacement and perfection/evolution—as well as the new proposition of coexistence can be spotted in almost every place the problem is raised, sometimes using similar *pro* and *contra* arguments and metaphors. Thus, for example, with the argument that greater light extinguishes lesser light, it could be asserted that one who has heard rational arguments forgets them as true faith is conferred upon him; that the faith of the blessed soul disappears during the beatific vision; and that the *habitus* of unformed faith surrenders its place to a new one of formed faith. The same metaphor of greater and lesser lights could serve to argue for coexistence or perfection as well. As the light of a candle does not cease to glow when the sun shines, the *habitus* of faith resides next to that of reasoned knowledge without the one destroying the other; the *habitus* of formed faith joins that of unformed faith, and they are actually the same.

The masters did not refer to abstract lights as their sole examples. Four cases of persons with a seemingly "double" cognition of the same fact were available in their repertory. The biblical person of Peter played a central role in twelfth-century theology. If faith is of "things not seen," and Peter *saw* Christ suffering, it was argued, he could not be said to *believe* it. One way to approach this problem was to suggest that Peter saw *Jesus* suffering, but believed that it was the *Son of God* suffering. This way, the objects remain distinct. One could also make elaborate analysis in the manner of epistemic logic about "*de dicto*" and "*de re*" meanings of sentences such as "Peter saw *him* suffering." This was, however, a semantic play fit for the previous generation of masters. Enthusiastic about the new psychology, the theologians of the period we are examining neglected this line of thought, as well as certain other sophisticated semantic solutions.

Peter (or sometimes John or Thomas) was the earliest example, but later sources added other figures. Another biblical figure brought forth was that of the Virgin Mary, who seemed to simultaneously both know and believe that Christ was her son and that she had an immaculate conception. In addition, we encounter two prototypical scholars suspected of having two competing cognitions, one an astronomer and the other a Christian philosopher. The first can have a reasoned knowledge of an eclipse and at the same time apprehend it with his senses. The second was led by rational argumentation to believe that there is one God and later received the grace of faith. He may now know and believe the exact same thing.

THROWING THE ARGUMENTS FROM ONE'S HEART

Godfrey of Poitiers brings up the three cases of Paul, the believing philosopher, and John the Apostle. Paul's revelatory knowledge, he determines, was not like demonstrative and sense knowledge, which annihilate faith. Regarding the philosopher who knows God exists, he proposes an interesting solution. While he indeed cannot have faith in this article, he can have the merit of faith if he "rests" in this article—that is, without referring to the natural proofs. Most of Godfrey's intellectual energies, however, are centered on the case of John, which is part of a semantic and logical discourse that characterized the preceding generation and to which we shall not enter here.

When William of Auxerre discusses the possibility that the same thing may be known and believed, he refers to the key biblical narrative of the Samaritan woman.[10] When the Samaritan woman who meets Jesus returns to her town, the evangelist relates how many of that city's inhabitants believe in him due to her words. Later, however, having Jesus staying in their town, "many more believed because of his own word; and said unto the woman: now we believe not because of thy saying: for we have heard him ourselves, and know that this is indeed the Savior of this world" (John 4:39–42). Augustine interpreted this scene as taking place in a believer's mind: first he believed his reason, and then he believed because of Christ's presence in his heart. Reason is therefore cast in the role of the mediating "other," and it becomes superfluous as a true face-to-face encounter occurs. The whole scene exemplifies an understanding of change as replacement.[11] The analogy to smaller and greater lights serves William's support of replacement: as the light of the stars ceases at dawn, the light of natural reason ceases when the sun of justification arrives. Therefore, it is impossible for a thing to be both believed and known.

This indeed shall be William's final answer, but it is the full solution that catches the eye. William classifies all cognitions of God into two groups: "natural" and "accidental." In order to explain their different degrees of certitude, he refers the reader again to concepts taken from Aristotle's *Posterior Analytics*. Knowledge acquired by natural reason is not included in the "natural" category. "Natural" here denotes "innate," rather than "naturally acquired." It is the counterpart in the pair *natural* vs. *acquired* rather than *natural* vs. *grace-given*. Moreover, formed faith is separated not only from the faith which rests on scriptural testimonies or miracles, but also from a natural, innate faith. This natural post-lapsarian cognition is slightly inferior to Adam's, but is still regarded as elementary, non-demonstrative knowledge.[12] All other non-innate cognitions, those acquired by ratiocination and those infused by grace alike, are gathered into the "accidental" group.

This classification becomes critical as William introduces a general rule for transition: one *habitus* of cognition disappears when a more direct one of the same category comes to take its place. Hence, when formed faith is infused, even though arguments, miracles, and scriptures do not disappear, they cease to create parallel *habitus* of cognitions. William is well aware of the option to argue that the *habitus* of reasoned knowledge remains inactive (*in habitu, non in actu*), but refuses to choose it. One cannot just believe *because* of these, as he had before. They do not generate faith, but rather strengthen the new grace-given *habitus*.[13] Cognitions of two different categories, on the other hand, such as knowledge of the effect and knowledge of the cause (*scientia per effectum; scientia per causam*) do not exclude each other. This is why the double cognition of the astronomer is possible.

William employs the astronomer's double cognition as a model for a different case as well when he discusses the difference between the virtue of faith and the gift of understanding, being the sixth of the seven meritorious gifts of the Holy Spirit.[14] William contends here, as he did in the question about faith, that faith in the articles is an illumination analogous to that which compels one to believe the first principles. "As the cause of cognizing the principle that 'every whole is greater than its part' lies in it and no other cause is looked for, so the believer's soul finds the cause of belief in the truth itself and looks for no other cause."[15] However, as he proceeds to the gift of understanding, there suddenly seems to be such a cause. "The gift of understanding gives the cause for those things in which faith believes," he determines. Faith differs from understanding as knowledge of the fact (*scientia quia*) differs from knowledge of the reason why (*scientia propter quid*). The gift of understanding, William concludes in the words of I Peter 3:15, is the readiness *to give an answer to every man that asks for a reason for the hope and faith that are in us*. This is the mission of the prelates.

William takes his example straight from the *Posterior Analytics* 1.13. The difference between faith and understanding, he proclaims, is analogous to that between the sciences of marine navigation and mathematical astronomy. Those who have the knowledge of navigation know that a certain star is immobile, or that other stars never set, but they do not know why it is so. Astronomers, on the other hand, know the reason and have the demonstrations. The astronomer represents the theologically trained prelate who is ready to reply and defend the truths of faith, while the sailor—that is, the simple believer—merely accepts the principles as a *scientia quia*.

Aristotle assigns these two forms of knowledge to two different sciences and subordinates one to the other, as with geometry and optics. The empirical scientists know the fact, he says, while the mathematicians know the reason why and the universals, although often they do not know some of the particulars through lack of observation. But what does this make of the astronomers-theologians?

The analogy to the astronomer reminds us of two aspects that can also be seen in the relationship between theologians and believers. First, it would be wiser to choose an experienced sailor for your next cruise than to put the smartest astronomer behind the ship's wheel. Second, on the shore, astronomers are more respected, for according to Aristotle they have the nobler form of knowledge. To draw the analogy once again, one may certainly suspect academic theologians regarding the simplicity of their faith. An old woman with firm and simple belief in her heart may seem comparable to the sailor who navigates better than the astronomer. Moreover, such a view may be seen as implicitly contradicting William's own model of the principles: professional geometers are not required to prove the axiom "the whole is greater than its part," nor would they ever find the Aristotelian "reason why" for it; if they would, they shall not accept these as axioms anymore. The only way it could work is if the gift of understanding, like the philosophical arguments, does not generate a new *habitus*—

that is, he has the reason why, but this reason is not the one that makes him accept this article. On the other hand, one should ask, do they have a nobler form of knowledge?

Godfrey thought the philosopher's arguments would not allow faith, since the latter is weaker. William maintained that the philosopher's arguments ceased to create a competing *habitus* of knowledge when faith arrived, for faith was more certain than demonstrative knowledge. But not all of the theologians of the time agreed with William, although they knew well his position. As a matter of fact, most of them used the notion of "knowledge of the fact" and "knowledge of the reason why" to argue that this Christian philosopher has indeed two *habitus*, but that those can be manipulated by the self and thus approach the same thing in two contradicting ways. As Roland of Cremona put it, "I can accept something because I know its cause or received evidence; nevertheless, I can remove this evidence from my heart and simply accept it as it is."[16] A proof or any other medium may be temporarily ignored and cast from one's mind. He takes his example for such an interior change of approach directly from the *Posterior Analytics* and its treatment of different disciplines. A specialist in one field of the arts (*artifex in sua arte*) can simply accept certain truths as principles, while another professional, such as the metaphysician, proves them by referring to exterior evidence. Roland, like the others, turns to geometry, in his case to answer the question of how philosophers can possibly believe: "But you would say: how did they [i.e., the philosophers] believe that if they had knowledge about that?" . . . Sometimes one can ponder the statement "above a given line an isosceles triangle" while relating to proofs, and then it is a knowledge of this conclusion; but sometimes [some other time?] one can look at the nature of triangle and not know the proof, or without any relation to the proving arguments, but it seems to be so, and then, he has an opinion about it."[17]

One person can accept under both modes, though not at the same moment. How can that be? Each proceeds from a different *habitus*. Roland is well aware that this might result in an inner contradiction. The counterargument doubts this trick of ignoring the medium, claiming that while an object of belief requires nothing outsides itself, an object of knowledge does, and hence, these media contradict each other. Roland dismisses William of Auxerre's scheme of natural and additional cognitions somewhat hastily, claiming that it does not contribute anything to the solution of the problem. Would not these two *habitus* contradict each other, being in the soul of one man? Roland examines in detail two Avicenna-based arguments in favor of holding two contradicting *habitus* and concludes that there is no problem in it, as long as they are not active at the same time. We may compare them to two alternating switches, which can be turned on and off. At the level of the whole, permanent, nonactive subject, they are not mutually exclusive.

Holding to the double *habitus* solution did not require a dismissal of William of Auxerre's entire scheme of replacing and nonreplacing cognitions, as in Roland's argument. All one had to do was to draw the line in a different place—that is, not between the innate and acquired parts of the mind, but between those naturally acquired and those given by grace. This was what the author of the commentary in Vat. Lat. 691 and the *Summa Halensis* did.[18] Both embraced William of Auxerre's basic scheme, proposed a dual system, and accepted the general rule. Thus, the author of Vat. Lat. 691 contends that if two cognitions belong to the same category, like faith and beatific vision, that which is less certain perishes as soon as the more certain arrives.[19] If, however, they belong to different categories and do not share the same hierarchy, the difference of certitude will not result in replacement, but in coexistence. Sense experience and demonstrative knowledge are not of the same kind and therefore can be held together in the astronomer's mind. So can faith and *scientia experimentalis*, such as those possessed by the Virgin. As one was grace-given and the other natural, the two could coexist in Mary's soul.[20] The *Summa Halensis* presents a similar classification of cognitions. Division is made according to two criteria: the psychological power (*vis animae*) in which the cognition lies and the hierarchy to which it belongs. Cognitions that do not pertain to the same psychological potency do not displace each other, and hence, intellectual understanding can peacefully reside next to the sense perception of the same fact. This is why Peter's faith, which pertains to the intellect, did not displace the cognition of Christ that he acquired by sense perception as an eyewitness.[21] Nevertheless, coexistence may also occur in the same psychological faculty if the two cognitions belong to different hierarchies—that is, when one type of cognition is not a perfect form of the other. Here too, the Aristotelian model of "knowledge of the fact" and "knowledge of the reason why" serves as an example for such a case. It accounts for the remaining of faith during Paul's rapture and in the Virgin's heart, despite the intimate experimental knowledge she had. Within the same hierarchy, when one cognition is an end (beatific vision), the other closer to it (formed faith), and there is a third even more remote (grace-given unformed faith), one *habitus* does not destroy the other. As a matter of fact, it is a process of formation and perfection of the same essential *habitus*. The gifts of understanding, wisdom, and the beatitude of purity of heart were thus redefined as more and more perfect acts of the formed, rational potency.[22]

William's text is quoted almost verbatim by the compilers of the *Summa Halensis*, but when doing so, they rename his categories as "innate" and "additional" to distinguish them from their own use of "natural," which includes acquired knowledge as well, as long as it is acquired through natural capacities. Having drawn the line between nature and grace, natural and grace-given cognitions no longer belong to the same category and thus may coexist rather than replace one another. The immediate result of this classification is that our believing philosopher may keep his old *habitus*, which relied on rational arguments. He can choose between them and decide whether to look at the reason or to adhere to the truth because of itself.[23] This solution of two, coexisting *habitus* was accepted also by Hugh of St. Cher[24] and by the anonymous Douai *quaestiones* 45, 501, and 530 (probably three *reportationes* of the same disputation *de fide*), which epitomized it by claiming that the Virgin and the converted philosopher can cognize the same fact in two different manners, just as nature and grace coexist.[25] Unfortunately, no texts of Philip the Chancellor concerning faith and knowledge survive. We have a *quaestio* entitled, "What sort of cognition does faith remove?" (*cuiusmodi cognitionem fides evacuet?*), but in all known manuscripts it is cut short before the solution.[26]

Silence, or the avoidance of an issue discussed in one's surroundings, is worth a few words as well. William of Auvergne does not conform to the discourse rules in this case, as in so many other cases, and does not relate to the problem. He seems to be so preoccupied with the idea that faith's merit lies in the war of the intellect against the counterintuitive articles of Christian faith that he leaves the problem of merit in times of peace unsettled. This lacuna protrudes even more when one reads his prologue to *De Trinitate*. Three modes of knowing God are enumerated there, with which William associates three classes of knowing subjects with three different means of knowledge. Prophets know God through revelation, which is associated with law and authority; the simple people know him through reason's obedience—that is, the meritorious virtue of faith (*virtus*). The last group is that of scholars who know God through proof and inquiry, by *ars* and *disciplina*. Theology, he contends, is directed neither to the first nor to the second group, for persuaded faith has no merit. Its only goal is to satisfy the third group of philosophers.[27] But what is the mode of the theologians themselves? William does not relate to the question of whether this profession contradicts the virtue of its practitioners or to what group they belong: is it the simple mob, the scholars, or maybe both?

PHILOSOPHERS AND OLD WOMEN

At the time that these detailed discussions about mental *habitus*, loaded with distinct theological and philosophical jargon, were held in the Parisian schools spread across town, and as the sphere of learning was rapidly changing its intellectual and institutional contours, the gap between the educated and the ignorant became increasingly evident. In his *Reason and Society in the Middle Ages*, Alexander Murray vividly paints a bitter conflict between the literate class and the ignorant peasantry. The learned, he argues, felt contempt toward the ignorant and rationalized their superiority by equating the uneducated with brute animals. The peasants, on the other hand, hated the educated clergy and directed their violent revolts at its members and the universities in particular.[28] Murray was willing to acknowledge positivity in the attitude of the learned toward the peasantry in only one sentence, noting that a few monks did respect the peasants' relation to nature and praised them as hard-working. But the truth is that their relationship was much more nuanced, especially beginning in the early thirteenth century. Indeed, Walter Map mocked the illiterate and simple Waldensians who came to Lateran III and their presumptions to preach, being so inexperienced and uneducated.[29] But almost half a century later, moralists and clergymen such as Jacques de Vitry emphasized and glorified the simple enthusiasm of men like Fulk (whom he repeatedly describes as *valde simplex*) and explicitly opposed his simplicity to the Parisian scholars' haughtiness and self-involved studies. Just a few years after Fulk, Francis of Assisi and his followers broke into the scene with force, declaring a new, idealized sense of simple life and devotion. This modification of the former antitheses of *litteratus/illitteratus* and *clericus/laicus* can be seen in the theological discourse itself.³⁰ At the end of the twelfth century the persons that featured problems of equal afterlife cognition were just "two men with unequal knowledge" or "layman and literate." A few decades later, new *quaestiones* appeared that asked whether a theologian and an old woman who have equal love for God will enjoy the same cognition in the afterlife, or whether a theologian sins more than an ignorant peasant who committed the same sin.

The previous analysis shows that theology's status as a science in the early thirteenth century was not constructed only in contrast to philosophy and other classical and legitimated sciences. It was also formed against a new understanding of faith as unconditioned and immediate adherence to the truth and against the challenge of the ideal of simplicity. The increasingly positive cultural attitude toward the simple made academic theologians wonder whether they may have lost something along the way that had escaped their philosophizing and scientific debates. The true question that lies behind all these *quaestiones* about holding faith and knowledge is where theologians stand: are they philosophers who know the reason or simple believers accepting the truth as it is, and can they reconcile the two?

In July 1228, Pope Gregory IX wrote to the theology masters of Paris to address rumors that some of them had been transgressing the borders set by the fathers by mixing philosophical reasoning in their theology. Philosophy, he warns, should be kept inferior to theology, and he demands they keep to pure and simple interpretations (*purum et simplicem intellectum*), uncontaminated by philosophical argumentation. Alongside other arguments he brings forth, he asks, "While trying to prove faith with natural reason more than necessary, don't they make it somewhat useless and empty, for *faith to which human reason supplies evidence has no merit*?"³¹(my italics). William of Auxerre, who arrived at Gregory's *curia* a few months later in the context of a different affair, could have replied with a decisive "no." So could the other theologians of his generation.³² The meritorious *habitus* of faith and reasoning do not contradict each other: the *habitus* generated by the arguments either ceases to exist, as William contended, or coexists next to faith in an inert state, as holders of the double habitus theory argued. Either way, the faith and practice of philosophizing theologians was secure.

Gregory was not the only one worried; this worry was heard in some of the classrooms as well and was tightly connected to the molding of theology's disciplinary identity. Godfrey of Poitiers hurries to declare in the very opening to his prologue, "First of all I confess that I believe there is one God *although* I know how to prove that by reasoning" [my italics], he assures the reader. "I do not rest in the first truth because of these reasons, but rather [rest] in these reasons because they accord with the first truth. For the more I believe, the more clearly I see these reasons."[33] William of Auxerre chose the issue of the immediate nature of faith—its adherence to the truth because of itself—to open his entire theological *summa*. There, however, it is not presented proudly as the noble and certain basis of the theological scientific enterprise, but on the contrary, as a potential threat. Seeing that faith proven by reason is not meritorious, doesn't the theological project deprive faith of its merit? In defense of theology, William brings the story of the Samaritan woman discussed earlier. Thanks to the replacement model, a competing *habitus* is shown to pose no danger. He who has true faith will not rely on rational arguments even in their presence but will adhere to the truth directly.[34] Theological reasoning would not jeopardize faith's merit even if all the articles of Christian truth were provable. That enables William not only to avoid demeriting faith, but to combine once again theological practice and divine illumination in one *habitus*. The greater the light of faith a person has, claims William, the easier it is for him to see rational arguments more clearly and quickly, and illumination integrates with reasoning to form one enterprise of merit and learning.[35]

Indeed, the concern over the superfluity of reasoning and loss of merit, where only simple adherence to truth is needed, appears in the earliest of three systematic *quaestiones* in which theologians reflect upon their profession. The first argument against theology's scientific nature, in the earliest known *quaestio* in which the author doubts this nature, attempts to delete the line between faith and theology. In the *quaestio de divina scientia* in codex Prague D 13 (late 1230s and early 1240s), we read that since all that is written in the divine books is accepted through faith, this *acceptio* or cognition should not be considered as *scientia*, but rather as faith or belief. Theology, therefore, is not distinguished from faith and is not a *scientia* at all.[36]

The author, however, knows he did not spend all these years for nothing and responds that if so, he who has studied has only a *habitus* of faith, which is impossible indeed, for he already had the *habitus* of faith before studying, and thus learning would result in no *habitus* or change.[37] In order to solve this puzzling similarity, the author refers to the mechanism discussed previously. Although there are things that are apparent to every intellect, he argues, the believing intellect can choose and rather rest in the divine authority regarding them and thus enjoy a true, complete faith with all merit. Nevertheless, it can also know some of these as first principles and yet others because they follow from them, as happens in every normal science.[38] The first choice is pure faith; the second is theology. The tension between study and inspiration is apparent in his next *quaestio* as well. Asking whether one who has grace-given love and consequently formed faith also knows theology, he replies that the divine can be known through experience and through knowledge, but the two differ. He who has love indeed has much evidence of divine goodness, but he knows neither the scriptures nor the arguments by which faith and morals are demonstrated.[39] Unfortunately, the author's promise to address the equally intriguing opposite question, whether it is possible to know theology without having formed faith (*si potest sciri sine fide*), remains unfulfilled.

It was still not an obligatory part of the course on the *Sentences*, but Adam de Puteorumvilla, a sententiary bachelor in the 1240s, chose to open his course with a *quaestio* about the acquisition of theology. One of the issues he discussed with his students was the possible loss of merit, and he followed William of Auxerre's approach. To Ambrose's contention that faith should be believed by fishermen rather than dialecticians, he replied that fishermen believe it with respect to merit, dialecticians and natural philosophers with respect to reason. Alluding to the Samaritan woman's story as well, he compared the articles of faith to first principles and replied that when one agrees to an article of faith because of itself rather than because of the arguments, merit is not jeopardized. Unfortunately, the summary of Adam's course survives in an awfully tiny cursive script, and his conclusion remains hardly legible. He seems to say that when theologians do refer to arguments "they are not fishermen, but teachers" (*iam non sunt quoad hoc piscatores sed doctores*). Friar Odo Regaldi, who taught and commented on the *Sentences* in the same year, repeats this notion briefly. Faith does not lose its merit if it does not actually rely upon those arguments. It is not *generated* by them, but only strengthened by them. Were it generated by arguments, they would certainly annihilate its merit.[40]

Both Odo and Adam, however, wondered what *habitus is* generated from all their studies. This *habitus* could not be faith, which was there all along anyhow, and is a product of inspiration alone. At this point, Odo follows the line of thought of Bernard of Clairvaux and the Victorines. He turns to the concept of *intelligentia*, which is nobler than any other acquired knowledge because of its subject and the mode in which it is acquired—that is, with divine help. It connotes inspiration and learning. Adam raises the idea that there are actually three *habitus* involved—faith, *scientia*, and *intelligentia*—and seems to argue that the *habitus* generated from all this trouble is a *scientia* "*secundum pietatem*." This term, distinguishing a sort of knowledge that is closer to virtue than other forms, will play a central role in the next chapter.[41]

Both models neutralize theological activity's threat of undermining its practitioners' simple adherence to faith. Both offer a mechanism in which the mind may voluntarily ignore philosophical arguments. Yet their authors did differ with regard to implied notions of harmony and conflict, as well as conceptions of grace. Godfrey of Poitiers did not assert two orders within the soul of Paul or the philosopher, although he assumed that faith and revelatory knowledge could coexist in Paul. Those like William of Auxerre, who asserted the replacement model, neutralized the threat posed by theological practice to meritorious faith by claiming that the old *habitus* completely perishes, whereas the natural reasons are allowed to remain so as to fortify the new *habitus*.[42] William, however, was the one who articulated the possibility of distinguishing two orders within the self: the natural self and the acquired self, not unlike the distinction we followed in Chapter 3. The scholar's manipulation of his mental approach is, however, much more acute when assuming two *habitus* as Roland did—that is, as the arguments generate a philosophical *habitus*, which is distinct from that of faith and can potentially be activated. This option implicitly assumes changing one's approach on occasion, rather than one decisive turn. Bynum, who studied earlier expressions of duality and hybrids in spheres other than knowledge, rightly observed that hybridism somehow negates true and complete transformation, for the option to exercise the older self remains open.[43] In our case, Paul retains inactivated faith during his ecstatic vision; the philosopher who sees the light does not forget his reasoning. Nevertheless, it exemplifies an ability to contain opposites. The hybrid embodies an intensive inner dynamic, which is going to be the subject of the next chapter.

ASTRONOMER AND SAILOR IN ONE MIND AND THE FRANCISCAN AMBIGUITY TOWARD FORMAL LEARNING

The theologian on one hand and the simple peasant or the old woman on the other were used in this discourse as stereotypes representing different groups in early thirteenth-century society. The previous analysis reveals an even more delicate moment in the process of the mutual construction of these concepts, perceiving them as parallel inner roles within one person who can choose his approach to the objects of his cognition according to his will. One could be Euclid at one moment and a *simplex* at the other. This inner mechanism could function for all theologians, but especially well in one significant context in which simplicity and learning were contrasted in the early thirteenth century: the case of the mendicants' integration into the University of Paris from 1220 onward and the clericalization process of the Franciscan order.

The mendicants' new model of religiosity contained several inner contradictions that were difficult to settle, both in the eyes of their contemporaries and in their own. Unlike common monks, the friars did not contemplate their Bible quietly in the monastery. They went to the most central and flourishing urban schools to acquire prime theological, academic education. They wished to be mediators, conveying these ideas to ever broader audiences. But at the same time, some were exposed to the danger of being carried away by the inner dynamic of learning. And thus, only a few years after they settled in Paris, competitors with the order's evident success in the university had their own reasons to contrast simplicity with learning. The Benedictine Matthew Paris felt bitterly about the Dominicans' haughty behavior toward traditional monks. Telling the readers of his *Chronica maiora* about the events of 1241/1243, in which opinions associated with Dominican masters were condemned, he could not hide his grudge. The fall of the Dominicans, he remarked, was an example of the revenge of God, "who is more pleased with the sober simplicity of a steady faith than with the most transcendent skill in theology" (*cui plus placet firmae fidei sobria simplicitas quam nimis transcendens in theologia subtilitas*).[44]

The mendicants were increasingly preoccupied with this problem themselves. Gerard of Frachet, who was in charge of writing "the life of the brothers" (*Vitae fratrum*, 1259), brings the following story to warn the brothers against losing their simplicity while chasing knowledge. A brother of the Roman Province, who was *temptatus de sciencia*, asked the Lord to give him true knowledge and show him the way to achieve knowledge of God. He then had the following vision. Before him was a book with all manner of questions of faith, at the end of which was written, "The master said here nothing, but wanted to be allowed to serve Christ in his simplicity."[45] Simplicity was, however, less valued in the Dominican order, whose properly educated founding father established a dignified place for learning from its inception. In a certain way, simplicity was even opposed to the ideals of the preachers, focusing on the individual soul rather than the souls of others. Humbert of Romans, the fifth master general of the Dominicans, explicitly expressed his discontent with the overvaluing of simplicity in his preaching guide: "Holy simplicity (*sancta simplicitas*) profits only oneself, whereas learned justice serves not just oneself but others also."[46]

The atmosphere among the Friars Minor was far more ambiguous and fiery.[47] Unlike Dominic, Francis of Assisi was uneducated. It is hard to determine, and has long been contested, whether he himself was explicitly opposed to formal learning. Rosalind Brooke saw the later process of clericalization as closely linked to learning and as opposed to Francis's original intentions: "His prohibitions and exhortations on this subject were swept aside by the current of intellectual enthusiasm that had caught hold of the progressive and thoughtful spirits of the age."[48] As Bert Roest noted, however, this historiographic account seems somewhat influenced by controversies inside the order that erupted after Francis's death. Most of the sources we have about Francis's views on scholarship and learning are the product of a community struggling over its character and direction. They were written in the midst of conflicts in which laymen and clerics, literate and illiterate, both participated as real persons and were invoked as stereotypes. This intense rivalry was projected back onto Francis's anti-intellectual approach and influenced later historiography.[49]

Whatever Francis's original approach, and even if the collision between simplicity and erudition had been present all along, it is certain that it became increasingly conflictual during the rapid development of the order and the influx of educated friars after his death and into the 1240s. The best witnesses of this change are Thomas of Celano's two *vitae* of Francis, the first of which was written in the late 1220s, while the materials for the second were gathered around 1246–47. All the sources Brooke utilizes to account for the conflict between simple and learned are noticeably drawn from Celano's later text; none is from the first. In fact, a remark in the section he devoted there to holy simplicity reveals Celano's awareness of both the change and its anticipation: "Francis sensed that times would not be long in coming when knowledge would be an occasion of ruin."[50] Later texts point in the same direction. Although Angelo Clareno's *Liber chronicarum sive tribulationum ordinis minorum* is a typical suspect for projecting fourteenth-century controversies back onto the early days of the order, it is still illuminating that the issue of simplicity appears particularly in the context of the third tribulation—that is, in the late 1240s. Love of knowledge is enumerated first among the factors leading to the misfortunes of these years.[51] Later, it relates that brother Giles of Assisi "saw that most of the brothers, having given up the obedience and the faithful following of the Rule that they had promised, had given their minds to curiosity and love of knowledge."[52] Several paragraphs praising simplicity follow immediately. Salimbene de Adam bears witness from the other side of this conflict as he complains about the dominant position and great number of lay friars during Helias's generalate. Many of them did nothing but eat and sleep, knew not one single letter, and could not hear confessions or consult. Moreover, he continues, they used simplicity to terrorize the educated friars. If a lay friar had seen or heard a young fellow speaking Latin, he used to mock him and immediately said to him, "O you miserable, do you want to dismiss holy simplicity for your knowledge of Scripture?" Young Salimbene did not remain silent. "Holy rudeness will benefit you alone, and as much as you will edify the church of Christ by living meritoriously, you will hurt it if you do not resist [its] destroyers," he used to reply back in the words of Jerome.[53]

The double *habitus* model could function in this conflictual atmosphere in several ways and might have done that somewhat better than the harmonious model proposed by William of Auxerre. First, it reflected and reconciled at the same time the inner conflict of the first mendicant masters, who embodied in their very persons what was seen as a contradiction in their social context. In this respect, one particular saying attributed to Francis in the section on simplicity is highly relevant to our discussion. According to Celano, Francis of Assisi once said that a great cleric who wants to join the order should, *in a sense (quoddam modo)*, get rid of his knowledge (*resignare, expropriare*) just like the rest of his possessions. Thus naked, he should present himself to the arms of Christ.[54] Evidently, this requirement is impossible. A rich man who wishes to become a friar minor can distribute all his money to the poor, yet this other strange form of property, knowledge, is a *habitus* of the soul that when acquired, can hardly be renounced. The ability to ignore the acquired *habitus* of knowledge, "throw the arguments," and accept the truth because of itself might serve precisely this very goal, allowing the educated to enter the order.

Second, the ability to change inner approaches, to overlook rational arguments and be simple believers, could be used to instill harmony between the educated who entered and the party of the truly simple. It is again Celano who provides us with an explicit idealization of such a use. His section on simplicity begins with a portrait of true simplicity, in which he points out that Francis demanded simplicity from *laici* and *clerici* alike, and that despite the fact that it is more difficult for the educated to be simple, they should nonetheless comply. Francis, he claims, did not perceive simplicity as a rival to wisdom, but as its sister.[55] A few lines later, Celano, who is well attuned to the currents of his time, attempts to convince his readers that Francis desired harmony of the simple and learned more than anything. Francis had outlined for his disciples, he relates, a vision he had in which many brethren, simple and learned alike, gather to listen to the sermons of two preachers, one learned and one simple. The learned friar in the story thinks it inappropriate to display his knowledge before so many men already perfect in knowledge. He fears that he will seem too curious and decides that simple talk will be more fruitful. He goes forth, therefore, clothed in a sackcloth, his head sprinkled with ashes, and delivers a short, simple exhortation. He moves his hearers so much that they reverence him as a saint. Seeing this, the simple brother thinks to himself that his learned fellow has snatched away everything *he* had planned to do. He decides, therefore, to play the role that is left and act as a wise man (*geram sapientis morem*). He chooses a few verses from the Psalms he knows as his theme, and inspired by the Holy Spirit, discusses them most eloquently and profoundly.[56]

A close reading of this intriguing story of role-switching attests to a positive approach toward manipulation of identities. Simplicity and erudition are explicitly presented as images or modes of behavior one is encouraged to wear according to the given situation.[57] The learned friar consciously chooses to present the likeness of simplicity, as he is nervous about the effect his learned persona would have. His choice to play simple turns out to be most successful. The simple friar turns in the opposite direction. Neither acts simply as who he is. This management of identities in Francis's vision is supposed to foster unity by showing that the opposing sides are not so different and that their representatives can even switch roles. Moreover, it tells Celano's readers that if the two personae can reside in one heart, peace can reside between learned and simple friars as well. I say management of identities, since neither of the fictive friars is treated by Celano as a hypocrite or a liar, although neither seems to communicate his true self. Hypocrisy is when one pretends to be what one is not. It is a mechanism similar to that of the two *habitus* that enables their role switching without hypocrisy. The first friar *does* have these two options within himself. This distinction between disguise and performance is central to the performative practice of preaching, and indeed the presence of the audience is central to the story. Celano's message is that simplicity is an image a preacher may perform in order to make his sermon more effective (*fructuosius*). The entire decision-making process in the story depends on consideration of the effect that the image of the preacher will have upon his audience.

Mendicants in general and Franciscans in particular faced allegations of hypocrisy from their very first years through the writings of William of St. Amour and Rutebeuf in the 1250s, in medieval vernacular literature (the character of *Faux-semblant* in the *Roman de la Rose* is perhaps the best known in this respect), and well into the sixteenth century.[58] But as twenty-first-century citizens of a culture that is so preoccupied with projecting images for the sake of marketing or communicating desired messages, a culture in which CVs are both true and beautified at the same time, we know that there is a very thin line between this kind of performance on one hand and hypocrisy and lying on the other. The mendicants did not fake being poor. But they fostered their poverty and used it for certain purposes. Francis's vision, as told by Celano, presents simplicity in the same manner as an image that can be manipulated in order to escape critical judgment by colleagues and move the listeners. Like a geometrician who throws the arguments from his mind when he approaches a problem in optics, the learned friar could, *in a sense*, divest his reasoned knowledge.

I would like to propose one last implication of the ability to set aside literacy in order to activate simplicity honestly. The vision described by

Celano glorifies simplicity but also could theoretically serve those many brothers who, like Salimbene, saw the early position of laymen in the order as a temporary expedient justified by the lack of educated clerics.[59] Not only could scholars defend themselves from the insult of not being simple enough, the internalization of the conflict held in itself the option to exclude truly simple men who have only rough *rusticitas* to offer. Theologically trained friars could perform both roles, but simpletons needed divine help.

THE RACE TO HEAVEN: DOES STUDY PAY OFF AT THE END?

Salimbene's lay friars mocked him for not being simple. But were there theologians who believed that their formal knowledge made them better as individuals—that is, that they would be more likely to reach heaven and enjoy better cognition there? What, after all, was their knowledge actually worth? At first, to judge from their own words, it seems not worth much in terms of individual salvation.

William of Auvergne is the only one, it seems, to concur with the view that earthly knowledge will remain in the homeland. At the end of his *De anima*, he addresses the survival of scientific knowledge attained in this life in heaven. Some may argue, he says, that all cognitions cease to exist when dying, since it is impossible to understand without any phantasms, and phantasms will be necessarily destroyed with the body. Nevertheless, he contends, knowledge that has already turned into *habitus scientialis* may definitely stay. The next objection employs the familiar light analogy: wouldn't these minor lights be destroyed by the strong splendor of glory? In reply, he separates the order of merit and salvation from that of scientific knowledge, unsurprisingly invoking the coexistence of knowledge of the fact and of the reason why. Faith, he contends, cannot exist with beatific vision—not because of the latter's stronger light, but because they are contradictory. Knowledge attained here, however, is not necessary in the state of glory. It adds nothing, and its lack will not change anything. Precisely because of its noninvolvement in the order of salvific cognitions, William of Auvergne inclines to let it remain as a decorative element, like the stars that "decorate" the sky.[60]

The different degrees of cognitive clarity and the equality of joy in heaven are discussed in the twelfth century in Peter Lombard's *Sentences* (4.49). An anonymous Parisian master later that century expanded his investigation to the issue of "two men who did not have equal cognition [on earth]."[61] An earlier master explicated the inherent social tension of the problem as he modified the very same inquiry referring to a layman (*laicus*) and a very learned man (*litteratissimus*).[62] Nevertheless, in its new formulation in William of Auxerre's *summa* the characters became even more concrete: a theologian and an old woman (*vetula*) or, in the case of Roland of Cremona, a simple peasant (*simplex rusticus*). The anonymous Parisian and Peter asserted that the two would enjoy the same amount of cognition. God would just need to add more to the less knowledgeable. William, whom we have already seen try to combine learning and grace at several points, is not firm in his opinion. First, he suggests that both the theologian and the old woman will have the same clarity of knowledge, but the theologian will enjoy more copious (*abundantius*) knowledge, since he knows how to prove and refute, which is a joy unavailable to the old woman. This is not a substantial difference, only an accidental one, yet it adds a little to the rewards of the theologian. A persistent objection follows: since the old woman will have all possible knowledge, there cannot be any difference after all. Although in the earlier forms of the issue evacuation does not arise, here it has a central role, as all the knowledge acquired by the theologian turns into nothing during the transition to the glorious state: he and the old woman both stand therefore on square one. William agrees at last, but still gives his students a way to feel that being a theologian is worth something after all. The acts of teaching and learning augment grace-given love (*caritas*) in the theologian's heart, and thus indirectly contribute to his merit.[63]

William's first idea of more copious knowledge is dismissed as ridiculous by Roland of Cremona, who arrives at the final conclusion with much more fierceness. The theologian's entire store of knowledge will cease to exist (*scientia cessabit*—he alludes once more to the Pauline vocabulary). The only way theological knowledge helps the theologian in this life is indirectly, if it leads him to act well and gives him spiritual delight.[64] Knowledge functions as a key—or not—to love. Good deeds and spiritual delight will stand at the center of Chapter 6, the last chapter.

CHAPTER SIX

Can knowledge qua knowledge be a virtue?
The self in society
Theology between theory and practice

The classroom analysis of Paul's ecstatic experience focused on his state of consciousness and mode of cognition. Yet as Chapter 1 showed, matters of love and merit were deeply and constantly engaged as well, highlighting the moral aspects of knowledge and explicitly concerned with the nature of theology. Discussing Paul's faith and/or knowledge during rapture, Godfrey of Poitiers determined that the rule that "he who knows more loves more" does not hold on earth, or at least not in practice (*in usu*). Evidently, he explained, a literate theologian does not love more than a simple old woman, although he certainly knows God better.[1]

The authors of *quaestiones* 230 and 454 in MS Douai 434 employed a similar argument in distinguishing the enraptured subject—a visitor-for-a-moment in heaven—from heaven's native citizens, as we have already seen in Chapter 1. The enraptured, they argued, experienced an imbalance of cognition and love. Only Paul's speculative intellect (or *intellectus cognitionis* in *quaestio* 230) was rectified, while beatified souls enjoy rectification of both the speculative and practical intellect (*intellectus operationis* in 230). Then, indeed, "the more I love the more I know."[2] Similarly, Alexander of Hales held that rapture does not engage the affective psychological powers. Paul's vision was thus explicitly defined as a pure intellectual cognition unmatched by the correlative amount of love. Consequently, such a vision added nothing to the visionary's merit.

The predicament created in the coupling of cognition and love, as in other formulations of knowledge and morality, has repeatedly informed the history of education. In different periods and cultural contexts, transmitting knowledge and shaping character have been and are still conceived as neatly intertwined. Schools do not only teach Latin or math; they aim to mold character, both explicitly and through an implicit or "hidden" curriculum.³ Knowledge of grammar, the natural world, or the scriptures is entwined with the knowledge of how to behave, live, dress, and talk. In the same breath, however, it has almost always been acknowledged that these two are indeed separate, albeit closely tied entities.

The central scriptural locus for early thirteenth-century discussions of purely intellectual knowledge and gifts of inspiration was the part of I Corinthians in which Paul handled the tension between ecstatic visionaries and social coherence.⁴ Let us therefore take a step backward from the verse "now enigmatically then face-to-face" (I Cor. 13) that hung over the previous chapters and zoom out to examine the broader rhetorical context of I Corinthians 12–14 in which it appears.⁵ Paul faced a spiritually boisterous community, brimming with the experiences of inspired individuals. One of these experiences involved "speaking in tongues," a form of ecstatic, unintelligible murmuring that occurs during some trances. Evidently, such diversely distributed individual gifts seemed to jeopardize the hierarchical structure and unity of the Corinthian community. Paul tackled this crisis step by step. First, he emphasized the unity and divinity of the gifts' source. Second, he made an elaborate use of the body metaphor in order to demonstrate the compatibility of individual, diverse gifts with a unified, hierarchical community. Third, he undermined the importance of such gifts and visions by contrasting them with love and communal responsibility, which he cast as superior. In the famous lines of Chapter 13, he then argued that speaking in angelic tongues, arcane knowledge, prophecy, and faith are but nothing without love.

Ultimately, Paul recognized that the same ecstasies and gifts of arcane knowledge that threatened to destabilize the Corinthian community and undermine its leaders' authority could be channeled into empowering it. Prophecy is superior to speaking in tongues, because its intelligibility edifies the church, whereas speaking in tongues lacks this communicative, pedagogical aspect (14:2–6). He then turned to augment regulation by introducing rules for organizing meetings of the congregation intended to bolster its unity, hierarchy, and internal order. His suppression of preaching by women or by inspired male members who claimed authority was an integral part of this process.

Paul's enumeration of such gifts and the attendant cluster of problems and solutions associated with them resonated forcefully over a thousand years later in early thirteenth-century university circles. This final chapter analyzes the discussions of knowledge, love, and morality, or the true and the good in light of this resonance. Unlike in the previous chapters, I will not begin with doctrine and follow its echoes outside the classroom, but instead weave the two contexts together. From the early thirteenth-century university environment we will shift to the examination of doctrine relating to gifts of knowledge independent of moral character, then to theories about the true and the good, and finally back to the Parisian community in its surrounding society.

IMBALANCE—PREVIOUS YEARS

As noted previously, in his groundbreaking study of education in cathedral schools prior to the twelfth century, Stephen Jaeger demonstrated the former's powerful association of content and method, two things that are closely related but do not necessarily overlap. In this charismatic culture that held sway in the tenth and eleventh centuries, masters taught the art of living well rather than simply book knowledge. Their principal aim being to train initiates to serve either in the religious or secular hierarchy, they focused on the material, physical, and loved presence of the master whose example was to be imitated.[6]

These two poles of intellectual and moral education exist in almost every educational institution, but their balance varies. During the twelfth century the focus shifted from manners to letters, stressing the generative and transmissive functions of masters and books over emulation of the masters' personal charisma and character. By the beginning of the thirteenth century, the age of charismatic masters had declined. Students were less attracted to Paris because of the fame of a specific master. Now they came to Paris for Paris.[7] The nature of the learning community was dramatically changed in almost all respects. Personal ties gave way to a formal system; schools became universities. Unlike the disciple of the monastic or cathedral school, the student who came to Paris in the late twelfth century spent his days in notably less supervised surroundings. As opposed to a monastic community, the multitude of masters and students in those formative years was by no means a closed, stable, and supportive community. It was competitive and fragmentary. Warlike disputations took the place of amiable dialogue and peaceful instruction. Learning was no longer conducted in closer proximity to other aspects of life. Leaving his family for the big city, our student circulated between different teachers and schools each day,[8] observed urban spectacles, and retired to his rented city room after a beer or a fight at night.[9]

But gradually, new kinds of mini-communities arose, offering a different sort of supervising environment: the *nationes* and the colleges, as well as the Parisian "houses" of several religious orders.[10] Within them and within the university as such, forms of communal and guild behavior, codes, and rites and feasts evolved. The first decades of the thirteenth century were marked by attempts to control and instill new order. The French monarchy and papal and local church authorities increased their involvement in the affairs of masters and students, who in turn struggled for their rights as an independent legal corporation. The 1215 statutes attempted to enforce, next to other regulations, communal and proper behavior. Masters of theology who wished to hold solemn lectures or sermons had to prove both their knowledge and their conduct.[11] In students' guides, which surfaced in the Paris of the 1220s and 1230s, one can discern different attempts to instruct and teach *mores* through the medium of the text, rather than or in addition to the living example.[12]

True, from the twelfth century, both philosophers and theologians kept interest in practical implications of their knowledge, and particularly in ethics,[13] from Abelard to Peter the Chanter and his circle up to the generation under our investigation, when ethics came to be studied in the Arts faculty, mostly via Aristotle, whose conceptions about the subject highly influenced proliferating theological discussions of virtue.[14] The medieval student who came to Paris learned about virtues and, among other things, about "what ought to be done." But both students and masters could easily stop short of application. The university was easily typified as a place for mere professional knowers who did not necessarily live up to what they taught, "even masters of theology!" cried Jacques de Vitry, as he described the corrupt Paris of the late twelfth century.

Perhaps the most paradigmatic expression of the appeal of the problem of knowledgeable yet immoral teachers in this period is the *Lai d'Aristote*, written in the 1230s by Henri d'Andeli, a close friend of Philip the Chancellor.[15] The *Lai* relates how Alexander the Great loses his head in his love for a dazzling Indian girl. Devoted to love, he forgets everything else, provoking discontent among his knights and barons. Aristotle, his teacher, rebukes the young king for neglecting his duties. Though he subsequently tries to avoid seeing his mistress, Alexander's efforts prove to be in vain. Love and desire are just too powerful. As he imagines her body, he feels his teacher and his knights are asking him to fight against his innermost self, and he returns to his beloved. When the young damsel hears of this, she promises to teach old Aristotle a lesson. Employing all her charms, she seduces the teacher into humiliating himself by letting her ride on his back while singing loudly. From his window, Alexander watches his teacher forget his own words. "How could you be so irrational," wails the disappointed king, "when only recently you had rebuked me about my desire to see my girl?"[16] All Aristotle can say is that Nature annihilated everything he had learned throughout the years in one brief moment. Nevertheless, he advises, the king should use the example of his teacher's humiliation to imagine how he had looked to his barons.

Masters of Ethics, and other members of the newly fashioned union, could, just like Alexander, the exemplary Aristotle's student, fall prey to desire—for love, for knowledge—and forget their duties, but they had others to remind them. Studying in Paris was a rather expensive enterprise. Rent prices alone could quickly deplete one's budget, not to mention the costs of food, books, and entertainment. Someone had to pay for all this—either wealthy parents or secular or ecclesiastical patrons. Growing sectors of medieval society invested resources in this form of education and wanted something in return. Never was the proximity between the sense of *talentum* as a coin and as talent so clear, echoing Christ's parable of the talents (Mt. 25:14–30), which tells of one who did not earn more money with the coins he received, but rather hid them in the ground. None wanted both coins and talents to be hidden. Churches and abbeys sent their people to be educated and financed their studies, but the latter used the opportunity to study more profitable disciplines such as law and medicine. In a statute from 1213, a provincial council in Paris led by Robert of Courçon forbade anyone entrusted with care for his parish to study secular sciences, "from which no good for the salvation of his flock would proceed."[17] Throughout the first decades of the thirteenth century, the papacy heavily supported the new institution of the university, but in its new, centralizing vision, Paris was to be the uncontested fountain of theological knowledge, which would water all of Christendom in its entirety. It should not turn into a swamp of stagnant water. The pure expression of this ideal is found in Jacques de Vitry's *Western History*. His protagonist, a simple illiterate priest named

Fulk, comes to Paris to study, but remains unaffected by its charms. In contrast to the masters and scholars who enjoy debating among themselves, he takes every opportunity to return to his flock and pour the knowledge he has drawn from the fountain into the souls of his listeners. Soon after completing his studies, he goes out preaching.

The popes of the early thirteenth century, following the incentive of Innocent III, used this general imperative to use knowledge and talent to buttress specific interests as well. In 1218, Honorius III recommended Mathew de Scotia for an extra chair in theology, stating that "such talent should not be wasted and hidden, when it can be expressed for the benefit of the public."[18] Gregory IX followed the same line in his letters recommending Michael Scot to Stephen Langton in 1224 and 1227.[19] Though ultimately in vain, he asked Emperor Frederick II to employ his divine gifts of knowledge in loftier pursuits. In 1228, Gregory IX encouraged the masters of theology not to apply philosophy to their teaching, for they often do so to take pride in their knowledge rather than to contribute to their auditors' progress (*ad ostentationem scientie, non profectum aliquem auditorum*). They fail to supply the vivifying water of knowledge to their thirsty listeners.[20]

The challenge of channeling knowledge to others was warmly embraced by both Dominicans and Franciscans. Mulcahey has already demonstrated this amply regarding Dominicans,[21] and Franciscans followed the same path. Their Pre-Narbonnian constitutions of 1239, as well as the constitutions of 1260, recommended accepting only learned novices.[22] The latter added the following reason for this restriction: "Since God called us not only for the salvation of our souls but also to the edification of others . . . no one will be admitted to our order except he who is a cleric who is well instructed in grammar and logic."[23] Salimbene, as noted in the previous chapter, answered those who mocked him for not being simple enough by saying that holy rudeness will benefit them alone, while his learning will benefit society. This dynamic, social image of knowledge diverged from the masters' pursuit of knowledge for its own sake or for the glory of their names within the university, for which the preachers were fond of rebuking them. At the same time, it diverged from monastic images and practices of learning. The apostolic shift of ideals toward worldly engagement during the twelfth and thirteenth centuries, the clearest expression of which (among many others) was the success of the mendicants, shaped ideals of learning afresh. The stress was now laid on society's needs rather than on the individual's experience of meditative, delighted learning in the context of private contemplation.

A story by Gerard of Frachet about one German friar illustrates this point beautifully. The friar's devotion was so great, Gerard relates, that during one vision Christ let him "taste such marvelous and surpassing sweetness from each of his sacred wounds, that thenceforth all worldly joys and pleasures became bitter as gall to him." One Saturday the Virgin appeared to him and endowed him with those very virtues for which he used to petition her daily. As a result, he put aside all study and other pursuits and gave himself up entirely to prayer, in which he experienced singular delight.[24] Yet while the friar's fervent devotion, prayer, sweetness, and delight could make for a very fine story, it does not end here. The friars' fellow Dominicans noted his conduct and accused him of making himself unfit for the duties of the order by not applying himself to study. Whereupon our brother asked the Lord "to turn some of that sweetness into knowledge (*quod partem illius dulcedinis in scientiam commutaret*), so that he might benefit the souls of others for the glory of His name." His plea was indeed granted, and his scanty store of learning was so increased that he preached fluently in German and Latin and was endowed with a rare understanding.[25] Mendicant friars, therefore, as well as secular masters, were deeply engaged with the social obligations of the knowledgeable in a time of change. All these concerns shall be clearly heard in the masters' discussions of rapture, prophecy, faith, and other cognitive states. Let us therefore step back into the classroom to listen.

THE GIFT OF PROPHECY AND THE SEPARATION OF GRACE AND MERIT

What questions were university theologians accustomed to asking themselves and their students about the phenomenon of prophecy? The main interest at the beginning of the century lay in the tension between the truth value of prophetic predictions and the free will of God to change his mind. Cassiodorus's definition of prophecy was frequently discussed as well.[26] From the 1220s onward, however, Parisian masters of theology introduced a new question to their repertoire: is prophecy a *virtus*? In the double, philosophical-theological arena of the time, this question had two meanings: (1) which of Aristotle's two species of psychological *habi-*

tus is prophecy, *scientia* or *virtus*; and (2) given the specific theological meaning of virtue, whether or not prophecy was a grace-given, *meritorious* virtue that makes its beholder a good person meriting eternal life.

William of Auxerre's *Summa aurea* contains the first systematic discussion of this question.[27] A *habitus* is a virtue, he pondered, only if the actions that proceed from it are meritorious. Some would argue, therefore, that announcing prophetic messages and warning the people to repent are meritorious acts, and therefore prophecy would constitute a virtue. William, however, points out that one must distinguish between the proper actions of the *habitus* at stake and actions that are related to it but do not pertain to its essence. The proper act of justice, for instance, is to give what should be given to whom it should be given, at the correct place, time, and for the correct reason. Justice, in and of itself, is meritorious, and therefore a virtue. The proper act of prophecy, however, is reduced by William to "clearly seeing something put before one's eyes." What the prophet *does* in response to his vision is a different matter. The question should be, therefore, whether knowing-seeing is a meritorious act in itself. William considers and ultimately rejects several criteria for judging an act as meritorious. Perhaps a virtue is present only in the face of some sort of struggle and requires the overcoming of a difficulty? This was a common criterion in the theology of the period. William of Auvergne, for instance, based the virtuousness of faith on the struggle of the intellect to agree, against its natural inclination, to the contradictory truths of Christianity. This struggle is what made faith a virtue in *his* eyes. William of Auxerre is also cognizant of the view that claims everything by which one is elevated above himself is a virtue. A prophet cannot attain arcane knowledge all by himself. Isaiah's prophecy about the Virgin, for instance, transcends the intellect of both men and angels and therefore requires that the prophet be elevated a certain degree above himself (*supra se*). But William ultimately chose a different path. His solution introduces a distinction between two kinds of seeing that focuses on the parallel distinctions of true vs. good and their respective sites in the soul.

According to the Aristotelian and Avicennian traditions as understood at this time, virtues belonged to the practical intellect and were directed toward the good as their object, while pure cognitions aimed at the truth and resided in the speculative intellect. Visions divide accordingly:

There are two kinds of visions, for there is a vision of adherence, and a vision not of adherence. A vision of adherence stands still in the apprehension of truth, lies in the speculative intellect, and is therefore not a virtue. A vision not of adherence lies in the practical intellect and transfers from apprehension of the true to delight in the good, and is therefore a virtue. Prophetic vision is of the first kind rather than the second, and is therefore not a virtue.[28]

Alexander of Hales expresses a similar view when engaging the problematic relation between prophetic vision and the moral conduct of the prophet. Virtues, it was commonly assumed, could not reside with sin in the same soul, and he therefore asked whether prophecy could exist in man's heart along with sin. Consider, for instance, the passage in I Samuel 16 where the spirit of the Lord leaves Saul and a malign spirit, sin, takes its place. Was the spirit of prophecy, the illumination of his intellect to see future events, removed?[29] And if so, does it not prove that prophecy is necessarily dependent upon moral conduct?

In response, Alexander splits prophetic illumination into two kinds, similar to the two kinds of vision suggested by William of Auxerre. The first one is a virtue that enlightens a man in a way that enables him to see a truth by reaching the intellect through the affective part of the soul. This cannot be sustained in a sinner's heart. The other kind of prophetic illumination reaches the intellect in a purely intellectual manner. It may dwell in a sinner, although sin still obscures vision a little.[30] Intriguingly, in spite of its relative independence from the moral condition of the person its subject, the latter kind of illumination retains ethical value: it is given to a person *for the benefit of others*. Alexander cannot think of a better example for this special kind of grace than the gift of preaching: when given to a bad man, he can still provide evidence that might strengthen the faith in the minds of his good listeners.[31]

In his own *On Prophecy*, Philip the Chancellor addressed the same problematics. Along with the author of an anonymous *quaestio* on prophecy in codex Douai 434 (q. 540), Philip split the problem into two separate questions: whether prophecy is a gift (*donum*) and whether it is a virtue. Prophecy is considered a divine gift, Philip argues, "particularly because it is not possible for man of himself" ("*maxime quia non est possibile homini ex se*").[32]

This is the reason prophecy was included among the gifts enumerated in I Cor. 12. Only after clarifying that prophecy is indeed a divine gift do Philip and the author of Douai 540 address the question of whether it constitutes a virtue. Like William, the author of Douai 540 argues that admonishing the people and encouraging them with promises are meritorious acts.[33] Like William, he quickly positions these acts as pruned from the essence of prophecy. Even if it were said that the acts of speech and announcement pertain to the motive part of the soul, these are only conditions through which knowledge is mediated outward, not the essence of prophecy itself, which is entirely cognitive.

One counterargument refers to the soul's division, claiming that prophecy does not dwell in the motive parts of the soul and therefore is not a virtue. Thus reduced to its cognitive element, prophecy is excluded from being meritorious in itself, although it remains a divine gift elevating one beyond oneself. Moreover, Philip argues that certain gifts reside only in saints and good people, and *nonetheless* are not virtues (that is, they are not the gifts that *make* their subjects good).[34] This notion, that extensional overlap does not necessarily entail a causal relation, intensifies the detachment from moral concern. Even when there seems to be a correlation between the moral state of the subject and the gift conferred upon him or her, it is not perceived as satisfying proof of their interdependence. That being said, both Alexander and Philip assign a place for a special kind of prophecy that is a virtue nevertheless, a *"prophetia secundum pietatem."*

The discourse over prophecy as virtue in the 1220s and 1230s pivoted not on criteria of difficulty or of supernatural provenance, but on the distinction between goodness and truth and thus established a basis for distinguishing the supernatural element from individual salvation. A development similar to that found in the *quaestiones* on prophecy occurs in treatments of the theological issue addressed as "unformed faith."[35]

The designation "unformed" originates in the Aristotelian principle that form, unlike subject or matter, is that which gives a particular nature and essence to a thing. But its specific denotation when qualifying "faith" differed. William of Auxerre and Roland of Cremona used "unformed faith" to denote faith that is acquired through doctrine or reason, which they contrasted with "formed faith," which is grace-given and meritorious. Philip the Chancellor and Alexander of Hales, however, utilized the term "unformed faith" to denote a *habitus* of faith that is indeed infused by grace, but that nevertheless does not make its beholder worthy of eternal life, for it requires further perfection. When Philip and Alexander tackled the issue of unformed faith, they split the question "whether unformed faith is a light" from that of "whether it is a virtue," just as they did with regard to prophecy.[36] Since the articles of the Christian faith cannot be grasped naturally, unformed faith must be a gift from God, a form of illumination. Even the intellect of a sinner must be elevated above itself to grasp objects such as the Trinity. Nevertheless, unformed faith is not a perfect meritorious virtue, since it lacks "movement toward the truth as delighting," the truth being its first form, as well as additional movement directed toward the highest good, its ultimate perfection.[37] Thus, for the first time in systematic theology, the "super-self" element was clearly separated from individual salvation,[38] as the preliminary cognitive *above-oneself* stage was from the next stages of formation, delight, and merit.[39]

THE BIRTH OF A NEW CATEGORY: NONGRATIFYING GIFTS

The theme of knowledge unaccompanied by love and moral virtuousness had come to occupy a prominent place in the articulation of a new category of grace. This emergent conceptualization is beautifully illustrated in the choices theologians made as to where to locate the *quaestio de prophetia* in larger theological gatherings. Like few other issues, prophecy did not have a definite place in the meta-narrative arc of deity-creation-fall-salvation, nor in any other scheme available to contemporary theologians. Many a time it was not included at all. The *summa* of Robert of Courçon (1204–8), for instance, contains no such question, nor does the *summa* of Praepositinus of Cremona. Alexander of Nequam mentions the wrong prophecies of Isaiah and Ezekiel in his *speculum*, but his promise to discuss it later at length remains unfulfilled.[40]

When a *De prophetia* was included, it was often in the context of God's foreknowledge and predestination. Master Martin, writing at the turn of the thirteenth century, as well as the author of the summa *Ne transgrediaris* (1200–1206?), which was attributed to Gerardus Novariensis, chose to posit it next to questions on divine knowledge.[41] In two collections of Stephen Langton's questions, *De prophetia* was copied after discussions of predestination.[42] Godfrey of Poitiers placed his at the end of the second book, together with other *quaestiones* loosely related to issues of predestination as well.[43]

Unlike his predecessors, William of Auxerre posited *On Prophecy* as part of his general treatment of angels, following a treatise on angelic cognition. The reason for this novel approach, he explained, was that prophets see what they see in the mirror of eternity, as angels do.[44] Herbert of Auxerre, the anonymous author of the *Summa Basiliensis*, and John of Treviso followed him,[45] and this juxtaposition of different sorts of cognitions appears also in random collections of *quaestiones*.[46] Roland of Cremona, who usually follows the order of the *Summa Aurea*, chose differently and placed this topic in the second book, after the creation of Adam and Eve, since this was the first prophecy about Christ and the church, and, therefore, an account on prophecy is needed.[47]

Contrary to this multiplicity of options available at the time, Philip the Chancellor decided to locate his *On Prophecy* under a new category. Organizing his *summa* around the theme of "the good," he divided the part dealing with "the good of grace" into two sections and entitled the first with a rather new term: *gratia gratis data non gratum faciens*—grace that is freely given, but that does not make its receiver worthy of eternal life and of God (henceforth NGF). Philip traces this category to Paul in I Cor. 12, arguing that it encompasses the other gifts mentioned there as well.[48]

However, as we immediately learn, the other gifts all seem to have prior designations. Some will be discussed in treatises about meritorious virtues with which they share common features; others, like the gift of performing miracles, were already discussed by Philip in the treatise on angels. It remains, therefore, to discuss prophecy alone.[49] A new category was born, but it was not yet strong enough to gather its parts from their former locations.[50]

Philip's choice is intriguing, as a pure structural consideration would not require creating a new category for just one issue. Grace could be divided into other subdivisions, as Philip himself divided it earlier in his *summa* and as earlier theologians had done.[51] Furthermore, he draws the dividing line between nongratifying grace and gratifying grace very similarly to the line differentiating pure cognition from virtue. In fact, this borderline even passes *within* certain virtues. Faith and wisdom, for instance, are meritorious, but when viewed as cognitions alone, they belong to the category of nongratifying grace.[52]

A few years later, the *Summa Halensis* offered a more systematized and lengthy account with a separate general treatise that precedes the discussion of each gift. It comprises such questions as whether there is such a thing as nongratifying grace (NGF) at all and, if there is, what is its nature? Its first arguments testify to the inherent problem of the new concept. If a gift of the Holy Spirit must be followed by the Holy Spirit itself, the counter-argument goes, the man who has them both is worthy, and therefore every grace is gratifying grace.[53]

The solution asks the reader to distinguish between two kinds of spirit: "a spirit of truth" (*spiritus veritatis*) and "a spirit of adoption" (*spiritus adoptionis*).[54] The latter makes its beholder a worthy son of God, while the former just makes him a participant in God's knowledge. This spirit of truth is the one that is active in bad people's prophecies and in NGF in general. The Holy Spirit can be the source of certain gifts or be the gift itself. But God is present in man only in the second case. This distinction between presence and representation is drawn by John of La Rochelle as well in his treatment of NGF gifts in his commentary on I Corinthians. He interprets Paul as distinguishing the two forms of grace, noting that gratifying grace makes the Holy Spirit present in man *in reality*, while nongratifying grace is *a manifestation* of the spirit alone.[55]

The *Summa Halensis* provides a carefully formulated definition for this new concept and analyzes each of its parts: an NGF gift is, we are told, "a gift infused to a rational nature without merits in itself, preparing man for his own salvation or for the edification of another."[56] It differs from a gratifying gift as a form differs from a perfecting form (both with regard to the individual), or as a gift given to an individual for himself differs from a gift that is given to him for the sake of another.[57] They divide into:

1. Gifts given to a person for his own benefit, but that are preparatory and therefore not gratifying in and of themselves (unformed faith, for instance).
2. Gifts given to man for the benefit of the church or of his fellow man. These are the gifts enumerated in I Cor. 12, and they are divided into teaching the sentence of truth; confirming truth and explaining truth
3. Gifts given to man for the honor of God.[58]

The following pages fail, however, to make good on this promise for the two last groups. Both of them are crowded together under the category "the graces of speech" (*De gratiis sermonis*). This includes the following: whether the gifts of speaking wisdom, knowledge, and faith should be counted as one gift; whether these gifts are given to bad people as well; whether the gift of preaching—a new gift pops up!—is superior to the gift of prophecy; and last, whether grace of speech is sufficient to edify listeners. All other gifts enumerated in I Cor. 12 and promised to be discussed in the beginning have disappeared.

The absence of a *quaestio de prophetia* from the *Summa Halensis* is particularly striking, since such a question by Alexander was certainly accessible to the *Summa*'s authors and editors. Prophets are mentioned only in comparison with preachers. Although superior in their mode of their revelation, they are inferior when it comes to communicating messages. They aim to tell the truth, whereas preachers aim to save souls. Truth and its specific uses are shown again as prominent characteristics of the discourse.

To conclude, toward the end of the twelfth century, theologians proposed and discussed diverse taxonomies of grace. According to Artur Landgraf, the great scholar of early scholasticism, around the middle of the twelfth century, the concept of grace was rigidly defined. Grace was understood as that which makes the subject worthy of eternal life—that is, *faciens gratum*. However, a concept of grace that is not justifying but only "helps," "facilitates," "prepares," "excites," and the like was emerging at the beginning of the thirteenth century in the writings of Stephen Langton and William of Auxerre.[59]

Landgraf pointed out a few of the problems that led to the general broadening of the concept of grace, among them the question of children's faith, the good deeds of sinners, and servile fear. As demonstrated previously, the theme of knowledge unaccompanied by love and moral virtue plays a dominant role in the articulation of the new category.[60] Prophecy and unformed faith were the typical forms of NGF grace.[61] Both represented cognition that cannot be attained solely by the natural capacities of their subject and that can reside in bad and good people. The spirit active in the NGF is characterized as the "spirit of truth."

This conceptualization has many contextual facets that merit discussion, but one should be noted up front that regards the spirit of truth. In the introduction, we noted how the Amalricians blended scholarly doctrines and norms of behavior with revelatory ones. At the same time, they represent an extreme case of contemporary preoccupation with the moral consequences of knowledge described previously. God, the students of master Amaury argued, is present in everything that exists. According to Garnerius of Rochefort in his *Contra Amaurianos*, they concluded that he who *knows* God works within him cannot sin: "God works all in everything; henceforth they infer: therefore, both good and bad things; therefore, he who knows that God works everything in everything cannot sin."[62]

Knowledge of that truth alone could therefore purify man of sin. Moreover, true knowledge is identical with salvation. There were no paradise and hell like those painted on church doors. Hell was ignorance; paradise equaled knowledge of truth.[63] "If anyone was 'in the spirit,' they said, there would be no sin in him even if he were to commit fornication or to be fouled by any other filthiness," reported Caesar of Heisterbach.[64] Since knowledge of truth was the presence of the Holy Spirit, they, as true knowers, were immune from sin. The separation of knowledge from presence in the theorization of NGF, although the Amalrician heresy is nowhere explicitly mentioned, cuts off this line of thought that bound together presence, knowledge, and immunity from sin. The "spirit of truth" can be separated from the essence of the Holy Spirit and be given as a mere manifestation. In *this* gift of knowing the truth, God is not present, and it has no moral consequences on its beholder.

ANNOUNCING THE TRUTH FOR THE BENEFIT OF OTHERS: GIFTS AND PREACHING

The fashioning of the concept of *charismata* or of inspirational gifts meshed well with the new currents in both preaching and teaching. Alexander of Hales, as noted earlier, referred to the gift of preaching as an example of a nongratifying gift. Commenting on I Cor. 12, his Franciscan fellow master John of La Rochelle contended that all these gifts are aspects of the gift of preaching. After all, preaching requires not only one, but several gifts: to know what one preaches about, to be able to persuade, to be able to delight one's audience, and so on.[65]

The "gift" element was not always that explicit. Morenzoni, who examined preaching manuals in the genre of *Artes praedicandi*, noted that although the idea that divine grace participates in the sermon is a very old one, it received proper theoretical attention only in the second half of the thirteenth century. The first guides, written in the second half of the twelfth century, and even that of Thomas Chobham, which was written no later than 1227, viewed preaching purely as an *ars* with teachable rules, offered tips for approaching different audiences, and provided model sermons.[66]

One who knew his theology or one who had learned the rhetorical technique of preaching could do just as well, especially when preaching aids became increasingly available. According to Morenzoni, it was only Humbert of the Romans in the 1260s who first admitted in a guide that another mysterious ingredient must be involved, something that no book could teach. Other arts, he reflected openly, are acquired through frequent training and practice: we become guitar players through playing guitar. The grace of preaching is, however, due to a special gift of God.[67] The particular gift of preaching was distinct from other intellectual talents. A beautiful example for this distinction is found in a rather long note of Salimbene de Adam about William of Auxerre's talents. William, tells Salimbene, was known for his great "grace of disputing" (*magnam gratiam disputandi*). No one could vanquish this great logician and theologian in disputation. Yet when he was required to preach, he found nothing to say.[68]

This observation paves the way for Salimbene to devote a rather long excursus to "the distinction the Apostle made when he said 'to some the speech of wisdom was given through the spirit,'" the very verse with which this chapter began and that according to Philip described the category of NGF. Salimbene comments at length on each verse, providing biblical and modern examples, underlining the unequal yet harmonious distribution of gifts among human beings.

This growing consideration of the special charisma of preaching can partly be explained by the emergence of a new kind of charismatic preaching in the late twelfth–early thirteenth-century stage, or rather, from a Weberian point of view, new forms of interactions between audiences and preachers. Jacques de Vitry provides a vivid, detailed description of such a relationship, noting the enormous impact of Fulk of Neuilly's preaching and the almost hysterical behavior of his auditors. When Fulk left Paris to preach in the country to kings and simple men alike, he had to get new clothes almost every day, for they were torn away by enthusiastic listeners who were lurking in his way to serve as relics of a living preacher-saint. In order not to be suffocated by the crowd, he had to use a stick to defend himself.[69]

Francis of Assisi is an even more classical example for medievalists of a purely charismatic leader and preacher, and these are only the most familiar cases. The conceptualization of charisma and particularly of the gift of speech is the scholarly response to these new modes of interaction between leaders and preachers and their respective flocks.

This is, however, only a partial explanation. Charismatic preachers, authorized and unauthorized alike, had been wandering through Western Europe for at least a century already. While the dimensions of this phenomenon and the awareness of it definitely grew over this period, we should also turn our gaze to charisma's rival, formal learning. In his above-mentioned *Western History*, Jacques de Vitry makes considerable effort to contrast Fulk, his hero, with his Parisian fellow schoolmen. The authority and grace of Fulk's words were so great, he stated, that although Parisian masters and disciples wanted to record his addresses, when they attempted to do so his words lost their force. They tasted different in the mouths of others and did not achieve the same results.[70] Thomas Celano told a similar story about St. Francis. One erudite and eloquent physician had testified that while he was able to remember others' sermons word for word, St. Francis's words fled from his mind. Even when he did commit some of them to his memory, they did not seem to him like those that had sprung from Francis's lips.[71]

This very sharp contrast between the erudite and the gifted made charisma shine that much brighter: in fact, they were co-conceptualized. Furthermore, it was not until the church (the papacy, in particular) wished to embrace charisma and apostolic fervor on its own terms—that is, combined with proper education and subject to its control—that this mysterious element was defined. Fulk *did* go to Paris and only then moved onward: both parts of his exemplary trail were mutually dependent and equally important.

Reciprocity, sociologist Marcel Mauss argued, is one of the fundamental principles of gift-giving. Following this principle, Jonathan Parry argued that the notion of "pure gifts" has subversive potential, for it seems to renounce the mechanism of reciprocity and its implied aspect of interdependence.[72] Whether the medieval perception of gift-giving conforms to these rules has yet to be established.[73] Yet, if reciprocity is a central obligation of gift-giving, then what happens in our case is that the subversive potential of gifts-talents (whether because they are unequally distributed or because they are freely given) is treated by *negating*, within the narrow realm of the interaction between God and humans, this interdependence. Rather, a multi-participant play is performed. Endowed subjects should not reciprocate with a counter-gift, nor should they do anything to facilitate reception in the first place. They should pass it onward to their fellows. In the conceptualization of NGF, as gifts not gratifying their receivers but given for the sake of another, the radical, antisocial, and individualistic power of charisma is transformed.

One problem remained with regard to the ideal of using talents and gifts for the sake of others: unauthorized talented people who were not of the ecclesiastical hierarchy and who skipped over the preparative study of theology. The case of the Franciscans in the next decades would demonstrate the delicacy and perhaps impossibility of the embrace of charismatic movements and how tempting yet difficult it is to infuse institutional hierarchy with enthusiasm. And so, at the same time that ecclesiastical authorities encouraged their clergy to go and preach, ambivalently embracing the enthusiastic mendicants, they tried to limit the participation of unauthorized men and women who shared the very same idea of employing their talent for the sake of others.

The distinction between pure and affective knowledge, which opened this chapter, proved useful in this respect as well. In a university sermon to scholars, Gauthier of Chateau-Thierry, chancellor of the university from 1246 to 1249 and a master of theology, repudiated prelates who not only neglected their preaching duties but refrained from inviting others to preach as well. At the same time, in an extensive *quaestio* he devoted to the office of preaching, he directed his energies to explain why those who do not come from the official ecclesiastical ranks but are eager to save others' souls should not be allowed to do so.[74]

Among the pro and contra positions regarding women's and laymen's preaching and those considered "unsent" in general, arguments such as "anyone who has the talent of knowledge and eloquence must multiply it to save their friends, even if the prelate forbids" also circulated.[75] Gauthier had to reconcile his conviction that talent must be used on one hand with the prohibition of preaching by talented lay men women on the other. His intriguing solution was to accept heartily the principle and declare that anybody who has the talent of knowledge and eloquence should certainly use it. In the same breath, however, he restricted this preaching to the private domestic sphere, to the correction of children and close friends. Preaching in public remained the prerogative of official clergymen. Were not women prophets in biblical times? And if prophets, why not preachers as well? Gauthier distinguishes between two kinds of prophecy: the announcement of truth and the announcement of truth *secundum pietatem*, which is accompanied by proper interpretation. Whereas the first might be found in both good and bad persons of both sexes, the latter can reside only in good *men*.[76] The move depicted in I Corinthians 12–14, from the demarcation of charismatic gifts to the emphasis on love and communicability and all the way to regulation and exclusion, had now been completed.

TRUTH AND GOODNESS, KNOWLEDGE AND LOVE

But can knowledge be a virtue nevertheless? The potential blurring of the distinction between possessing truth and goodness emerges in a wide array of theoretical disputations dealing with topics such as the distinction between *scientia* and *virtus* and the idea that the intellect delights in truth. This vast topic exceeds the scope of this book, but a brief overview of two clusters of issues in particular can provide a taste of its relevance to the story:

1. How can knowledge be a virtue?
2. What is the proper relation between the true and the good?

Knowledge and virtue were considered two species of the general category of *habitus*. Nothing could, in principle, be both. The first embedded information; the second directed deeds. The first made one knowledgeable, the other made one a good person. This dichotomy was also embedded in the structure of the soul: following Aristotle and Avicenna, *scientiae* were thought to reside in the speculative intellect, while virtues in the practical, although this view was frequently debated. Some theological virtues, however, presumably contained a cognitive element, such as faith, prudence, and the gratifying gifts of understanding and wisdom.

All the masters who discussed these virtues addressed this difficulty, and in their writings one suggestion is considered once and again. Whereas sciences such as geometry are clearly not virtues, "knowledge of what ought to be done" may be considered a virtue, for it is necessary in order to *do* the right thing. Yet as they discussed cognitive virtues such as prudence, most of them rejected this line, quoting Aristotle's contention that "knowledge contributes little or nothing to virtue."

William of Auxerre's first concern in the treatise he devoted to prudence was to explain to his students that prudence has nothing in common with the science of morals (*scientia moralis*) found in the books of Solomon or in Aristotle's *Ethics*. In this first chapter, entitled "Whether prudence is identical to knowledge" (*utrum prudentia sit idem quod scientia*), he determines that the cases of faith, understanding, and wisdom, being cognition and virtue at the same time, are rather exceptional. As a rule, such hybrid combination is impossible. People wrongly identify the virtue of prudence with some form of ethical knowledge, but the truth is that reason has two functions: *judging* that something should be done and *commanding* to do it. The first function cannot be considered a virtue, for many people know what should be done but fail to do it. The virtue of prudence is not a counselor (*consiliarius*), but rather a commander (*imperans*).[77] It is true that if a person needs to do something, he has to know what to do, but one is not praised or blamed because one did not *know*, but because one did not *do*.[78] William repeats this notion as he discusses the gift of *scientia*. No cognition is a virtue (save faith, understanding, and wisdom), since knowing does not necessarily entail acting: a servant may know his master's will without acting upon it. Virtue, on the other hand, necessarily leads to action, and therefore the virtue of *scientia* presupposes knowledge, but is not identical to it. Like prudence, it is governing (*regitiva*)—that is, commanding in its nature.[79]

Philip firmly denies this line of argument as well. Both in his general account of virtue and in his treatment of prudence, he addresses Aristotle's dictum that "knowledge contributes little or nothing to virtue." Indeed, there are sciences that do not relate to virtue in any way, and others that would help us to act virtuously in direct manner or that produce an indirect effect. The latter are, for instance, knowing good and bad in an abstract manner or the knowledge of the wonders of this world, which may incite one to the love of the creator. Yet the bottom line remains firm. This is not the *virtue* of prudence.[80] Although certain kinds of knowledge can dispose or lead to good conduct, they are never its cause, for a cause must be necessary.[81] Like William of Auxerre, he clearly acknowledges the deep frustration in recognizing the gap between reading a cookbook and mastering cooking. Even the knowledge of theology does not necessarily lead to just life, remarks Roland of Cremona as he examines Augustine's definition of virtue.[82] William of Auvergne is the only one who claims forcefully that the knowledge of living well is indeed virtuous. But he too confesses that virtue cannot be engendered in the apprehensive power, but only in the imperative power, for someone who is more knowledgeable in ethics is not necessarily a better person.[83]

A different strategy was to claim that the supposedly cognitive virtues indeed combine both cognitive and affective elements, but only the latter designates them virtues. Their psychological "location" in the potencies of the soul was divided accordingly—they were either in a speculative intellect that "stretches" toward the practical one or in the faculty of free choice that was already conceived as mixing the two elements. This strategy is manifest in Philip's treatments of virtue in general, of faith, and of prudence. When asked which virtue is "more" virtuous, one that is mixed with cognition, such as faith or prudence, or one that is a pure *affectio*, Philip replies that a virtue is determined as such by the aspect of affection.[84] Faith and prudence, therefore, should not be defined in the genus *cognitio* or *scientia* at all. These solutions responded to a more fundamental "threat" for such sharp distinctions, which is evident in various questions on the virtuousness of faith, prudence, and their like, as well as in direct questions on goodness and truth.

"Good," "movement," "desire," "satisfaction," "fruition," "delight," "happiness": these and other concepts create a conceptual web that organizes the ethical sphere and defines it. At the beginning of the thirteenth century, we see a lively negotiation of the boundaries of this ethical realm, rooted in Aristotle's *Physics* and *Ethics*, as well as in Avicenna's philosophy. Scott McDonald has shown that from the 1220s on, the very specific sense of "good" as identical to "goal" and "perfection" gained force. Under the influence of Aristotelian and Islamic thought, "the good" was perceived as the perfection of any particular being's development toward the full actualization of its natural potential. Anything in which perfection, satiation, or rest is found was, accordingly, a "good."[85]

The striving for the good hence became a generic formula that could be applied to every movement of a being toward an end, toward its actualization. The concept of good, together with a complete structure of perceptions and concepts, moved beyond its traditional context of political and personal conduct into the world of nature. One could say that a stone "desires" to reach the ground. A neat expression of the partial identification of truth, goodness, and being was the emerging theory of transcendentals, a philosophical matter that would be further developed over the next centuries.[86] From the 1220s, our masters conducted a systematic investigation of those transcendent predicates that can be applied to every Aristotelian category. The first steps were taken in William of Auxerre's *Summa Aurea* and were followed by a more systematic articulation in Philip the Chancellor's *Summa de Bono*. For the first time, these medieval masters systematically discussed identity and difference between goodness, being, truth, and later beauty and oneness, building up a cluster of authoritative arguments for each position.[87] In favor of the proposition that being, truth, and goodness are the same, for instance, was God's repeated contention that "it was good" in the process of his creation; Augustine's claim that "all things that are, are good,"[88] or Aristotle's contention that "the true is identical with the good, but it is called 'true' insofar as it is without any action, and 'good' when it leads to action" ("with action").[89]

Part of the appeal of this identification was its association with the intellectual war against Cathar doctrines, which was far from ending. Proving that "everything that is, is good," was an enormously powerful refutation of dualistic arguments. But it could also lead to confusion. In the transcendental questions, as well as in many others by William of Auxerre, questions in which he addressed the relation between the true and the good, fruition, the hierarchy of virtues, and other matters. In treating these matters, William applied ethical terminology such as love, appetite, good, movement, and delight to the cognitive realm. As said previously, he regarded faith, understanding, and wisdom as exceptional, being cognitions that are nevertheless also virtues. When he explains this, he turns to the "ethical formula." God, the first truth, satisfies the intellect's appetite and therefore it is a "good"; the intellect moves toward truth as an end that it fully enjoys and in which it finds rest.

In William's endeavor to establish pure cognition as delightful, the beautiful becomes a key concept. One argument that recurs in his different attempts to argue for virtuous cognition is that seeing a beautiful, corporeal object affords genuine sensual delight to the eye, and therefore spiritual beauty delights the spiritual eye, the intellect, as well. The first argument brought forth in support of the virtuousness of the gift of understanding contends that Augustine was wrong when saying that understanding is without delight (*intellectus esse sine delectatione*), for there is genuine delight in a vision of a beautiful meadow and hence all the more so in the vision of God. Since we see God in the intellect, there is delight in the intellect.[90] A similar argument is presented in his treatise on the order of virtues, where he identifies the first truth with the first beauty. Corporeal sight delights in corporeal beauty, and therefore all the more so spiritual sight, understanding, delights in the highest spiritual beauty through faith. Faith delights, therefore, in the first truth or the first beauty and loves it. Hence, it is essentially *a* love, although perhaps not the meritorious, general love that is *caritas*.[91]

As the scope of what William construes as the ethical broadens its application, positing the intellect in the ethical formula threatened the distinction between the good and the true and, respectively, between the virtues of *faith* and *caritas*. See, for instance, the second argument in the *quaestio* concerning the difference between the good and the true (*que sit differentia inter bonum et verum*):

> It is agreed that "he who has the rest has the motion towards the rest" [Aristotle, *Physica* 6.8]. But movement towards rest is desire ... the first truth, therefore, inasmuch as it is a first truth, is that which quiets (*quietativa*) the desire. Therefore, inasmuch as it is the first truth it is a good. Therefore, love of the first truth *inasmuch as it is the first truth* is love of the first or highest good. But love of the highest good is nothing else but *caritas*.[92]

William attempts to resolve this problem in various complicated ways that are beyond the scope of the present discussion, but what is important to establish is his promotion of the idea of the intellect's delight. He cares to give faith, *as a cognition*, its own status of a virtue without the "help" of the virtue of love (*caritas*). He nevertheless limits it only to the virtues faith, understanding, and wisdom and is very careful to appoint love and the superior good their own sphere.[93]

William of Auvergne wrote extensively on the problem of knowledge as virtue in *De virtutibus, De fide, De bono et malo*, and *De anima*. He discusses in depth the relation between the true and the good, as well as diverse aspects of the "ethical formula."[94] Knowledge in general is delightful, he claims on several occasions. A firm contention is threaded through *De bono et malo* that the hunger for truth is innate and natural to the human soul.[95] Like William of Auxerre, he brings forth Aristotle's *incipit* of the *Metaphysics* in order to support the existence of intellectual desire: all men naturally desire knowledge. Intellectual power is a faculty encompassing all ethical aspects of obedience, desire, merit, and delight, he contends. He is nevertheless well aware of the problem of losing the distinction between virtues and cognitions. After long discussions on the possibility of cognitive virtue, he concludes that the will motivates in general all sorts of perfections but *knows* in a particular way, whereas the intellect apprehends in general and *motivates* in particular—that is, regarding its own perfection. Intellectual virtues are therefore not only apprehensive but mobile and motive as well.

At the end of *De bono et malo*, William faces the challenge of explaining how prudence can be both apprehension and affection. It must be so, he argues, for if this were not the case, there would be no desire or delight in it. Undoubtedly, our cognitive power moves, desires, and rests in its delightful end (*delectabitur igitur vis apprehensiva nostra in scientia et erit scientia delectabilis et concupiscibilis*). Arguments regarding pleasure identical to those proposed by William of Auxerre follow one after the other. Corporeal beauty pleases the exterior eye, and therefore spiritual beauty pleases the spiritual eye of the intellect; delight is caused by the conjunction of two corresponding things.[96]

Philip the Chancellor chooses the ethical realm to be the organizing principle of his major theological composition, the *Summa de bono*.[97] Its parts bear titles accordingly, such as "the good of nature which is not reduced by sin"; "the good of grace"; and perhaps a section on "the good of glory" was intended as well. Between the prologue and the first section, Philip placed a group of questions that became known as "the first tractate on transcendentals" in the history of Western philosophy.[98] As McDonald has demonstrated, Philip gathered the questions about the relations of being, goodness, and truth, which were found in William of Auxerre, reorganized them, and put them not only before the virtues, but before his entire work. Issues that are relevant to our concern, such as those raised in this context by William of Auxerre, do not hold a considerable place here. Among the arguments in favor of the difference between the good and the true, Philip mentions the respective distinction of faith and *caritas* briefly,[99] but the solution focuses on other aspects of truth. In the argumentative part of the *questio de ordinatione veri ad bonum* appear arguments such as "the intellect desires the true as pleasing but nothing desires the good as true,"[100] but they play no role in the solution.

Philip was well aware of the danger posed by configuring cognition in the ethical formula, which might lead to the complete disappearance of the distinction between knowledge and virtues. One might make the following argument, he reflects: the end of virtue is the good, and there are various goods, one for each power (the rational, irascible, and desiring); faith moves believers to the true, but this true is also a good—that is, the good of the rational power. This, he notes, would lead to the false conclusion that knowledge is a virtue.[101]

Here, as in other places, Philip appeals very little if at all to intellectual delight, though he does not deny to the intellect its proper ethical realm. The intellect, he agrees, moves toward its particular good (*quoddam bonum*), but not toward the highest good or *the good* as such.[102] He proposes therefore a double movement. Faith moves toward the truth as its own good in a first formation, which changes it from unformed faith into formed faith. Then love (*caritas*) assigns it a second form or perfection by drawing it further toward the highest good. The ethical sphere now includes the "little ethic" within it but is certainly not equal to it.

THEOLOGY AS ETHICS?

I have flown swiftly here over intense, long, and intricate texts dealing with diverse issues of virtues cognition and knowledge. They are worth a book of their own. Here my main interest is to demonstrate that there was a very lively discussion in which our masters tried to explain to their students the balance between the intellect's desire for the truth and the "bigger realm" of supreme goodness. Two metaphors that were raised in this discourse will lead us back to the historical context with which we started: that of the counselor and the king and that of rest and motion.

In the kingdom of the soul, William of Auvergne asserted, the will is given the role of the emperor, while the intellect serves as its humble counselor.[103] In the *De anima*, he refines the metaphor. The counselor lends his advice in general but is autonomous regarding all acts intended to achieve his proper perfection and end: "It is manifest that studying, disputing, thinking, listening to teachers, inspecting books and pondering on reality itself are all movements which undoubtedly help it [the intellect] to acquire the perfection which is knowledge."[104]

William's allusion to the situation of university masters is unmistakable. By 1200, the community of teachers and students in Paris, as in other places, was negotiating its independent position as a legitimate social institution. The story of its legal, sometimes violent struggle during the first decades of the thirteenth century during which our theologians work has been told many times.[105] In the temporal kingdom of earthly society, they were consolidating their position as advisers to both the clerical and secular governors. Yet at the same time, they fought for the autonomy and independence of their internal sphere, of "movement" toward proper intellectual perfection.

The second and more powerful metaphor employed throughout these discussions is that of rest (in truth) and movement (toward the good); it reflects the same tension between the internal intellectual sphere and the world outside, as "remaining in the truth" remarkably resembles the situation of "remaining in Paris." Studies in the schools had an aspect of detachment from the path or course of life and from traditional frameworks of control. Administrative procedures were established to allow this dispensation of duties, such as orders to allow studying clerks to keep their benefices and be considered as present when they were actually not in duty anywhere near their chapter, or the recurring permissions from prelates and abbots to leave the monastic life for a while to attend school.[106] Such dispensations and special privileges were granted also by the early Dominican rules, permitting excellent students to retire from the regular course of daily duties in order to pursue their studies.[107]

Nonetheless, these dispensations had their limits, and the university, unlike the convent, was not considered a place for life nor studies a permanent occupation. As noted in the beginning of this chapter, monks and prelates were expected to return to their communities after a certain period or to serve in further functions in the church or their order's administration.[108] Others were encouraged to leave in order to spread the vivifying salvific word. It was this contrast that served Jacques de Vitry's objective to encourage those masters who had no love in their hearts, who were wholly focused on their own affairs, as well as those students who would stay in Paris for years without returning to their families or religious communities, to move and not to rest in the knowledge of the truth.

The strong relevance of the truth-goodness issue for theologians' self-definition is evident in the way several masters wished to present theology as ethically superior to other sciences and cognitions and thereby distinguish themselves from the enraptured, such as Paul, or from a certain kind of prophet who only saw the truth. Yes, it cannot necessitate the movement toward the good like a gratifying virtue can, but it is aimed to do the best cognition can. Theology, they argued, was a practical, affective science, a doctrine of truth *secundum pietatem* entirely engaged with merit. Its aim was not to make its beholders knowledgeable, but just. It thus encompassed the double movement mentioned previously. This was the spirit of the earliest known *quaestio* to address the end of theology (*De fine theologie*) systematically. The text in codex Douai 434 is attributed to a certain Master Willermus, whose identity is uncertain, and to whom three additional *quaestiones* in this codex are attributed. As Sileo, who edited and studied the *quaestio* observed, the text is barely organized, being perhaps a hasty *reportatio* of a live disputation or a preliminary draft, certainly not a finished product.[109]

What *is* the proper, essential end of theology? Several options are discussed, among them "fear" and "God." A short digression follows, after which the author proposes that the proper end of theology is to make man just and perfect. Next comes a series of arguments and solutions revolving around the idea that truth or its contemplation is the end of theology, rather than the just (*iustitia*), followed by a second series of arguments addressing the idea that its end is beatitude.

Every cognition tends to the truth. The least one should do, therefore, is to add truth as an equal, second end of theology. Truth would stand for the contemplative aspect of theology, while justification would stand for its operative aspect. In reply, the author (or the respondent) refines his statement. He argues that, as a matter of fact, theology has two ends: one proximate and proper, which is cognition, and a more remote one, which is living according to what has been cognized (*vivere secundum cognitum*). Theology begins in the cognitive faculty but is then perfected in the operative (*initium habet in cognitiva, perfectionem in operativa*). Our already familiar distinction between purely intellectual truth and truth *secundum pietatem* is now raised, marking the proper end of theology as the latter. Throughout the discussion philosophical ethics serves as an explicit model. We do not pursue the knowledge of ethics, Aristotle argued, in order to become wise, but in order to become good (*ut boni fiamus*). In a similar manner, the author concludes, we study superior ethics—namely, theology—in order to be just (*ut justi fiamus*). He will argue later that wishing to teach theology for the sake of enjoying knowledge is mere curiosity, whereas the proper aim is to edify the church.[110]

The next solution suggests an intriguing parallel in divine cognition. God knows things in two manners. Both bad and good things are known through simple knowledge. Nevertheless, there is also a "knowledge of appropriation and experience" (*scientia appropriationis et experientiae*), by which God knows good things only.[111] This latter kind of knowledge is the end of theology. Another round of arguments begins, adding the delight element over that of leading to operation: theology does not move toward cognition alone, but toward delight in the cognized thing. Simple contemplation of God as an object of cognition is not its end, but rather contemplation of God as an object of desire. Theology, therefore, is perfected in the *affectus* and not in the intellect. The Franciscan Odo Rigaldi expresses a similar view.[112]

Construing theology as ethics and the confusion regarding the potential of remaining in the truth characterizes the expectations contemporary theologians had from the course of studies and from themselves. First, in response to the destabilized image of teaching by word and example (*verbo et exemplo*) by wondering whether they were purely agents of academic knowledge or, unlike masters of other disciplines perhaps, must live up to what they teach. The relevant texts that survive address this issue together with that of preaching. Alexander of Hales determined that reading or lecturing (*legere*) accords with the intellect and the imagination; teaching (*docere*) with the pure, or speculative intellect; and preaching (*praedicare*) with the practical intellect or the *affectus*. The more perfect and worthy the activity is, the higher the required degree of purity. Anyone can lecture, but in order to truly teach (*docere*) teachers must be of pure intellect. Nevertheless, teachers who teach the truth of piety—that is, theology masters—should maintain purity of life as well.[113]

A short question in MS Vat. Lat. 782 debates whether sinners may teach as well. Preaching, one argument runs, is aimed at communicating life and hence must be done by one who is spiritually alive; teaching doctrine, however, relates to knowledge, and therefore its only condition is that it should be conducted by the knowledgeable, regardless of his conduct. However, the master who decided this debate thought otherwise. Teachers can hardly use theology's theoretical aspect alone, he claims, just as Aristotle's *Ethics* is not meant just to be known but to make its knower good.¹¹⁴ Since theology has to do with both knowing and doing, a teacher in a state of sin should not teach.¹¹⁵

The anonymous author of the questions *De fine actionum spiritualium* in BnF Lat. 3804A supported this view. Preaching is aimed at deeds, whereas teaching (*docere*) is aimed at obtaining the truth of the deed (*veritas operis*). Therefore, sin stains the reliability of both the preacher and the teacher: they shall not be believed. Yet he too reveals that other theologians did not judge the teacher and the preacher equally. Teachers, they argued, transmit pure knowledge. While the preacher's moral appearance is essential for his credibility, the teacher's credibility depends on his being knowledgeable and truth-speaking; what he actually does is irrelevant.¹¹⁶

John Pagus's introduction to his commentary on the *Sentences* is a rare testimony we possess of addressing students about this issue. In the first day of his lecture on the *Sentences*, John invited the present students in a quite uncustomary fashion, to pray with him to God to remove their sins and purify their minds:

> The investigation or wisdom of the Holy Scriptures belongs only to minds purified from the blemish of sin. How can men stained through sin presume to explain the Holy Scriptures when the wisdom of the Holy Scripture does not reside in them? Let us therefore call God, who is the only one to remove sin and purify our minds: purge our minds.¹¹⁷

TRUTH AND GOODNESS INSIDE THEOLOGICAL PRACTICE

Finally, the model of truth-goodness was applied also within the field of theology itself, as systematic theology, represented in the study of the Lombard's *Sentences* and the writing of *quaestiones* and *summae*, took the inferior but independent position of "truth," while the Bible and the style of writing associated with it were placed in the superior affective position. Willermus suggested that there are two ends for theology, according to its speculative and operative aims: truth and justification. The author of the *quaestio de divina scientia* in Prague IV D 13 preserves this line of thought when he discusses the unity of the subject of this science, keeping to this unity even when it is argued that one part of the science of theology should be in the speculative intellect and the other in the active, and thus theology cannot be one *habitus* in the soul, nor can it be one doctrine.[118] But the clearest application of this hybridity of theology to the different methods of its practitioners lies in a contemporary *quaestio* whose subject is "scientia religionis catholicae."[119] It deals with many of the subjects discussed earlier, but its most interesting part occurs toward the end.

Theology has two parts. The true forms the object of the first part, while the beatifying good is the object of the second, teaching what causes happiness in this world and afterward. These two parts correspond perfectly to the pair intellect and *affectus*, for they teach respectively both what illuminates the intellect and what moves the *affectus* to love and acquisition of the beatifying good.[120] The sixth subquestion keeps investigating these two poles, adding speculative and active intellects to the discussion and an intriguing new dimension of matching styles of theological writing and matching textbooks. *Exempla*, figures, fables, promises, and threats incite wonder, fears, and other emotions, and therefore the second part of the Catholic science uses the biblical narrative with its full, literal, and spiritual dimensions. The intellect, on the other hand, is moved by syllogistic arguments and demonstrations, for which the book of *Sentences* is most fit. The whole dual scheme can be summed as shown in Table 6-1.

A similar correspondence of styles and intellects is stated by Philip in the prologue to the *Summa de bono*. Starting with verses from Job and Ecclesiastics about gold and silver, he constructs a dual space made of parallel couples: wisdom and understanding, *caritas* and faith, and the practical and speculative intellects. Theology is then divided accordingly: the perfection of the practical intellect belongs to the *sapientia morum*, while the perfection of the speculative intellect relates to the *intelligentia questionum*.[121] Having said that, Philip focuses on the origins of silver alone. The entire

Table 6-1

Verum credibile	Bonum beatificans
Intellectus	Affectus
Speculative intellect	Practical intellect
Illuminating for knowing the truth	Motivating the *affectus* to love and acquisition of beatifying good
The *Sentences*	The Bible
Arguments, syllogisms	Narrative, exempla

summa that follows this introduction belongs, the reader must conclude, to the silver part and to the perfection of the speculative intellect.[122]

The flourishment of systematic theology and the new independence and prestige accorded to study of the *Sentences* in particular during this very period was deeply connected with the set of distinctions discussed in this chapter as well.[123]

Indeed, most introductions to systematic works on theology say very little concerning goodness, delight, or perfection of the soul. William of Auvergne holds to the idea that knowledge is a perfection of the soul and in the middle of his *De Trinitate* argues that true philosophizing aims for the light of belief and truth as well as the sweetness of goodness.[124] Yet, he does not mention it in the introductions to his treatises. The prologue of *De Trinitate* focuses on the end of satisfying philosophers and fighting heretics; his prologue to the second part of *De universo* contends that the goal of his *magisterium* is glorifying God, but mere knowledge of the creator does not perfect the soul: religious cult is the true perfecting beauty.[125]

In reply to a question regarding the benefit of theology for the theologian, Roland of Cremona replies that theological knowledge increases the probability of acting in the right manner in this life and that it also affords delight.[126] But this feature of theology as an ethics or as delightful knowledge is not developed in the prologue at all. He declares the purpose of his writing to be double: "to help simple people a little and drive away idleness (*repellere otium*)."[127]

Many masters, mostly Dominicans, were focused on providing useful, easily navigated works. Hugh of St. Cher aims his arrows straight at the laziness of his readers in the introduction to his commentary on the *Sentences* (parts of which were analyzed in Chapter 4).[128] In his view, the *Sentences* were both a shield against the heretics and, quite explicitly, a short substitute for the Bible in an era in which there was no time for unlimited meditation of the biblical text itself or for delight. In the same spirit, the *Filia Magistri* (1232–45), an abridgment of the *Sentences* that borrows heavily from Hugh and William of Auxerre,[129] openly declares its aversion to long-windedness, the "mother of disgust," and appeals to those who delight in brevity.[130] Perfection of the soul, be it intellective or affective, is not even mentioned. The commentary in Vat. Lat. 691 also remains silent regarding aspects of perfection and delight. Its favorite context of theology is battling heresy, rather than "perfection of souls."

SUMMARY AND EPILOGUE

The anonymous fourteenth-century text *Sister Katherine* (*Schwester Kathrei*) depicts a spiritually intense relationship between a passionate nun and her learned confessor. Although he begins as her instructor, at a certain point in the plot the two switch roles and he becomes eager to listen to her. Nevertheless, he attempts to convince her—insists even—that his learning makes him at least an equally emphatic listener, if not superior, although both recognize his "knowing" is nothing like "living."

> He wins her consent through love, and she speaks with him about mysteries and deep things such as the universal experience of divine truth, so that he says: "Realize that this is foreign to all people. Were I not so learned a priest that I had myself read this about divine wisdom, it would also be foreign to me."
>
> She says: "I'm sorry about that. I wish you had learned it with your life!"
>
> He says: "I tell you that I have learned so much of it that I know it just as well as I know that I said mass today. But I will admit to you it grieves me that I did not learn it through life."
>
> She says: "Pray for me."[1]

Both learned and mystic subjects in the period indeed had much about which to speak. Each in his or her way cognized divine matters: God's essence, the Trinity, angels, Christ, the virtues. Their special epistemic status granted their words authority, which was essential in these times of harsh ecclesiastical war on heresy. The special knowledge both possessed might and did lead some of them into the fray. What they "saw" and said could buttress orthodox doctrines; it could also undermine them. Yet despite their similar claims to privileged knowledge, theologians and visionaries differed in the ways in which they spoke, in their epistemological foundations, and above all in their social positions.

This book has delved into this intricate world of knowledge and power during the formative stage of the University of Paris, through the lens of the theological discourse regarding ecstatic experience. This discourse represents an intriguing interface between the institutional-rational mentality associated with the schoolmen and the mental experience of rapture. It followed inquiries about the body-soul relationship during trance and the possibility of complete separation of the intellect; about the specific state of consciousness enjoyed by the enraptured; about whether the aftermath was marked by memory or oblivion; and about the merit of the experience and the information it claimed to transmit.

In the course of this research, I was determined not to write a standard account of "medieval theories of rapture." Rather, I wanted to know what troubled and interested these theologians as they approached this phenomenon as a window on their concerns about the knowing subject and about their own activities as producers of knowledge. I hoped to follow the thin threads binding scholastic theology and epistemology to the early thirteenth-century world in which the men who molded it lived: their classrooms and the emerging university, but also the broader world of visionaries, popes, friars, heretics, charismatic preachers, *jongleurs*, knights, and ladies. It is not easy to demonstrate such echoes through conventional forms of academic rigor, but I hope that even the reader who remains unpersuaded by the argument will have found its suggestions and questions thought-provoking.

This discourse, I have argued, was part of a delicate boundary-work by which the new masters of theology explicated for themselves what they shared and did not share with ecstatic agents of knowledge, as well as how they differed from philosophers and believers. According to the Aristotelian schemes of thought, they constructed within their analyses of rapture a general category—genus—of "visions," which hosted different cognitions of God yet that all held God as their object while differing from each other. Although theologians did not always explicitly include themselves within this group, they used the distinctions between believers, the enraptured, prophets, angels, and others when discussing their own mode of apprehending God, thus both marking an alliance with these others and simultaneously distinguishing themselves. In this process of categorization, the masters appointed themselves as those who draw the lines, situating all others as their objects of analysis. They were the observers, making use of rational, philosophical tools and approach. At the same time, like Paul, whose first/third person account of his rapture brightly illustrates the duality of both experiencing and observing, they were subjects, elaborating the practice of reflecting upon their own occupation in distinctive *quaestiones* on theology (Chapter 1). By insisting on a real continuity between Paul's rapture and his later observations—indeed, his entire later theological knowledge—they echoed the role of spiritual experience in theology. Marginalizing the place of institutional authority and giving more importance to inspiration, they could claim that true theology was itself based on genuine inspiration. At the same time, theology was also distinct—as distinct as the elaborate science of geometry is from mere recognition of axioms (Chapters 2, 4). Through their complex treatment of questions of rivaling *habitus* of cognitions, they were able to claim that they did not lose this inspiration, since they were able either to harmonize professional knowledge with true simplicity, like that enjoyed by simple believers and ecstatics, or to switch between the two when needed (Chapter 5). Finally, their distinction between pure, speculative knowledge, such as that of Paul when enraptured, and affective knowledge allowed them to construct themselves as the best suited and most authoritative among all other agents of knowledge to spread the Word of God. Prophets and the enraptured were assigned to the private sphere and designated as only "visionaries" holding pure knowledge. Despite their privileged sight, preachers and masters of theology could correctly interpret their visions and thus publicly communicate their salvific water of knowledge to the general society (Chapter 6).

INTEGRATION OF SPIRITUAL AND SCIENTIFIC ELEMENTS

The theories discussed here were a product of unique interactions—they are always unique—between readers and books. The theologians sought their way between struggles of all sorts over their position: between local chapter, bishop, and chancellor, the papacy, the city, the French monarchy, knights, monks, and parents. With this concern, they approached newly discovered and exciting materials from Aristotle, Avicenna, and others and revived interest in centuries-old Pauline, patristic, and twelfth-century themes. Two models of religious life, the contemplative-monastic and the secular or apostolic, are reflected in their diverse discussions of rapture and other modes of cognizing the divine. At the same time, we cannot imagine these discussions without the immense influence of Aristotelian notions learned through the *Analytics*, *Physics*, and *Ethics* and without Avicenna's psychological theories. Each chapter, I hope, has shown this magical fusion of contemporary concerns about spirituality with new terminology and ideas. William of Auxerre constructed sophisticated analogies with Aristotelian conceptions such as *experientia*, first principles, and "knowledge of the reason why." He introduced for the first time into scholastic theology spiritual themes such as the spiritual senses or wedding gifts of the soul and a stress on illumination, pleasure, and delight. Next to allusions to Avicennian epistemologies throughout the discourse, love (toward women and God alike) was once and again a source of analogies to explain trance or faith. The establishment of a systematic discussion about beauty included elements from Cistercian and Victorine thought with Avicennian and Aristotelian elements as well.[2] This in itself is an act of identity-making: setting themselves between philosophers and mystics, they embraced ideas from both the new science and twelfth-century monastic spirituality.[3]

The intense interest in the soul presents a similar case for spirituality and science-making, as I have argued in Chapter 3. In the twelfth century, the vast majority of religious treatises on the soul came from Victorine and Cistercian circles, with the interesting exceptions of Gundissalinus. At the turn of the century, we see philosophers such as John Blund and perhaps David of Dinant intrigued by this subject, but unfortunately, we lack sufficient evidence for this phase, as few materials survive from the arts faculty in these years. Clearly, however, the soul was a hot subject for several competing disciplines, from natural philosophy, metaphysics, and physics to medicine and theology.

From the beginning of the thirteenth century, especially from 1220 onward, we see a significant burst of interest in psychology in the faculty of theology. William of Auvergne, Philip the Chancellor, Alexander of Hales, John of la Rochelle, and others wrote their own *De anima*s. The teachings of Hugh of St. Victor, Bernard of Clairvaux, and especially the *De spiritu et anima* of Alcher of Clairvaux are richly present in these treatises side to side with references to Aristotle. And although their tone is not similar to that of their predecessors, we still have John's prologue to his *Summa de Anima*, which opens with a verse from Song of Songs and a prayer requesting the wisdom to inquire into his soul, its potencies, and its acts.

The Aristotelian corpus provided powerful images of what constructed fields of knowledge may look like. While some looked to the *Posterior Analytics* and the *Physics* on science, others favored modeling theology as ethics. Unlike sterile theoretical sciences, it was about "what should be done" and was studied not for one to know the good, but for one to become good and just. It embodied the ideals of harmonious letters and manners, teaching *verbo et exemplo*, which were so important in monastic learning and spirituality of the previous centuries. Both these lines respond to the urgent need to justify what it was that they were doing and its worth to medieval society to their fellows in the other faculties and above all to themselves. Whether demonstrating that theological knowledge has a firm ground in illumination or insisting upon its edifying mission, they attempted to defend themselves from philosophers who questioned the scientific nature of their craft, old devout women who seemed to possess superior knowledge of God, or popes who suspected their philosophical innovations and urged them not to spend their efforts on Parisian disputations.

The figure of Paul served as a focal point of this integrative approach. Recently Colleen Shantz attempted to present a holistic view of Paul that combines and harmonizes his ecstasies with the better known and favored aspects of his figure as a rationalostic theologian. The premise of her book, she wrote, is "that ecstasy is actually a significant feature of Paul's life and impetus to his thought and thus it seems necessary to account for its absence in the usual journeys through the letters."[4] She opposed what she termed "the cultural bias against ecstasy . . . a pervasive tendency in modernity to value the rational over all other forms of knowing."[5] The scholastic discourse is not present in her study, but some aspects are remarkably similar. The binding together of ecstatic experience and rationalistic thought in the figure of Paul, the theologian and the preacher; the attempt to apply contemporary neurological insights to understand his experience;[6] the doubts as to whether we can try to do so regarding another's experience; the renewed interest in his confusion; the gap—and the bridges—between rationalism or "cognicentrism" and ecstasy. More than anything, I believe, it shows the relevance of medieval exegesis to that of modern times.

SELF AND TRANSFORMATION

To discuss trance is to discuss the possibility of transformation. The issues of body, memory, immediacy, and transition discussed throughout the book reveal a complex perception of the soul and the self. This perception consists of a fundamental natural platform of potencies—constructed increasingly as *the* self—to which different, sometimes contradictory *habitus* of cognition are loosely attached. These *habitus* stand between the self and its objects of cognition in the exterior world, but also between the soul and itself. They mediate every act of cognition and experience (Chapters 2, 3), and may be manipulated and changed according to the situation (Chapter 5). This structure embodies both significant stability and diverse options for change.

In Chapter 1, I mention Bynum's and Douglas's attempts, along with those of others, to relate society's dominant perception of trance (possible/impossible; positive/negative) to its social structure, whether rigid or loose, stratified or dynamic. The colorful picture that arises from this very specific, small, elite group of theologians tells us more about them than about anyone else. Clearly, we cannot take this microhistory on its own as evidence for nonscholarly, early thirteenth-century perceptions of self, change, or social roles. Yet, I would suggest that this structure of the self, as well as the deep preoccupation with transformation in general and in its multiple, modular manifestations, were both an influential and influenced part of a broader preoccupation with ideas of fashioning the self. This preoccupation focused on tensions between natural and acquirable traits of character as well as the roles of gender and social status that are evident in contemporary courtly literature. It calls for a further analysis of the theological, philosophical, and literary discourse of nature in all its manifestations, particularly those of grace on the one hand and natural/acquired social status as natural noble character on the other.

INTERNAL DIFFERENCES IN THE COMMUNITY

Although coming from different nations and schools, the masters' very long period of training proved to be successful in establishing a common language among them. I would like to use this epilogue, however, to enumerate the peculiarities within the community. Bishop William of Auvergne, as was evident from Chapter 1 onward, was a provocative outsider to the Parisian scholastic discourse. While he treats many of the same issues discussed by his colleagues and uses a rather similar vocabulary and "library" of sources that he knows well, he does not conform to the rules of the university discourse. He writes no tractates on "prophecy" or "rapture" like the rest, uses a very loose form of disputation mixed with other styles of writing, is rarely quoted by others, and rarely refers to former or contemporary masters. In general, he does not seem to count himself among the school doctors and disciples.[7]

William of Auxerre is undoubtedly the most influential of the group. Surprisingly, however, many of his views and ideas were shown to be rejected or appropriated only to a limited degree by the theologians examined here. His intriguing perceptions concerning theology or the delight in intellectual activity are especially noteworthy for their poor reception. Roland of Cremona follows William of Auxerre closely in terms of order of discussion and choice of issues, but is a particularly harsh, somtimes unwise critic of many of William's views, although he appropriates many others. He enriches the latter's discussion with new arguments, taken from medical and philosophical sources, but they do not usually lead to any breakthroughs in his solutions. While Hugh of St. Cher's commentary on the *Sentences* is close to William of Auxerre's *Summa aurea*, often presenting a range of views without choosing one, his *quaestiones* found at Douai 434 share with Philip the Chancellor and Alexander most of the same discursive features and views.

Dominican masters were just consolidating their intellectual community in this period. Can we discern any distinctive "Dominican" methods or views? I found no typical tendency with respect to style. As to views, the most typical example may be found in Chapter 1, whereby Roland, Hugh, and Guerric, in opposition to almost all others, contend that the intellect can be entirely separate from the body while remaining in the body, thus allowing pure abstraction and clear, angelic-like vision here on earth. All of them treated the problem of Paul's self-ignorance and exhibited far less interest in matters of *habitus*, *status*, and *caritas* than did Alexander and several anonymous *quaestiones de raptu* and *de prophetia* in Douai 434. Prophecy and rapture were treated by them almost as *non-habitus*, having less to do with the continuous identity of the cognizer. Although familiar with the category of non-gratifying gifts, they did not develop it. In addition, it seems that they were more interested in the useful and instrumental aspect of theological knowledge than in aspects of individual perfection of the rational soul. In this respect, they conform well to papal and Dominican policies of education.

It became gradually evident, throughout the research, that Alexander of Hales and Philip the Chancellor share the vast majority of discursive features and views in common. This affinity has already been noted by scholars, though it cannot be grounded in historical sources, save perhaps their relation to the Franciscans: in the year Philip died and chose to be buried among them, Alexander had already joined them. His doctrines from the time he was a secular master, as Philip's ideas, were appropriated into the *Summa Halensis* and into later Franciscan theology in general.

Among the most prominent features they share are a preoccupation with matters of *status*, a tripartite approach to the soul, and an emphasis on cognition as a rather fixed *habitus* residing in a specific power of the soul that casts true transformation as always partial. Along with the *Summa Duacensis*, several anonymous *quaestiones* in Douai 434, and John of La Rochelle, both Alexander and Philip are particularly interested in the application of the binary "purely cognitive vs. affective knowledge." This includes a clear formulation of non-gratifying gifts, a strong notion of a prophecy "*secundum pietatem*," a claim for priority of *caritas* over faith, and the marginalization of the idea that there is proper delectation or merit-value in cognition alone.

The year 1245 marks the end of a period. By the end of that year, all our protagonists had passed away, clearing the way for their students who would develop high scholasticism: Albert the Great, Bonaventure, and Thomas Aquinas. The social, political, and spiritual sphere of the university and beyond would enter a new phase as well, introducing new conflicts and convergences between spirituality and learning. The strands excavated here would mature into the schools of thought called by some "Aristotelian" and "Augustinian." The impact of the philosophers would be felt much more heavily, and the tensions between mendicants and the university regarding monkhood, friarhood, and teaching would escalate in the *querelles universitaires*, mixed with claims for prophetic knowledge in the image of the eternal gospel, accusations in heresy within and outside the university, by and toward theologians and with bitter conflicts of legitimacy of agency of knowledge.

Modern academic culture is very distant from its medieval predecessor. And yet, those of us who live in and beyond the classroom—that is, all of us—might recognize many of the tensions delineated in this book. There remains a constant tension between academy and "life," between formal knowledge and all other kinds; the hidden nuances of self-knowledge and ignorance mediated by literature; a constant feeling that something would always stand between the observer and the world and hinder direct contact with reality, obscured by veils of words, conceptions, and prejudices. Both professors and students feel the search for proper balance between spiritual delight and the pressure to prove productive and useful to society.

Researchers may not be modern shamans, but they too ascend to the heavens of the esoteric knowledge of physics, of biology, or of medieval theology, then return to communicate what they have seen. It takes much effort to immerse oneself in a world so wonderfully different from ours. It takes a different sort of effort to communicate it when returning to our own time and culture. Like Paul and other enraptured subjects, all we have at the end of this spiritual journey is mere words with which to convey things seen. It is my hope that I have managed to relate at least something of both use and delight.

APPENDIX

The following is a comparison of the structure of several *quaestiones* on faith discussed in the book. The structure of *quaestiones* is a fascinating issue in itself, especially its rapid development in the early thirteenth century, from a very simple structure to a multi-hierarchical one. Intriguing in itself is the fact that often, due to incomplete processes of editing and circulation, the prospectus placed at the beginning does not accurately match the actual order and content of the text.[1] Something about the variations of Hugh's commentary can be found in the minute survey of its manuscript tradition in Faes de Mottoni, "Les manuscrits du commentaire des Sentences de Hugues de Saint-Cher." An issue proclaimed in the initial prospectus but that did not appear in the actual text is denoted here in brackets, except in the case of Philip's tractate, in which the plan was so different from the actual text that it was easier to present in two separate columns. Where the text includes numbering (*ad primum, secundo queritur*, etc.) these are designated by Arabic numerals. Where no such clear numbering was apparent, the table follows internal textual links as far as possible.[2]

Table A-1

William of Auxerre	Roland of Cremona	Hugh of St. Cher
	1. Etymology of *fides*, its various senses; "Why are we called 'sons of God' by faith rather than by love?"; "Why did the Apostle say *Iustus ex fide vivit* rather than *Iustus ex caritate vivit?*"	
1. What is faith? Heb. 11:1 2. Is faith a virtue? 3. Is faith one species or a genus? 4. Is the same thing known and doubted/believed? 5. Implicit and explicit faith 6. Distinct and indistinct faith	2. What is faith? Heb. 11:1 3. Is faith virtue or knowledge? 4. Is faith one species or genus? 5. Is the same thing known and believed? 6. Implicit and explicit faith 7. Philosophers' and gentiles' faith: in what should they believe in order to be saved? 8. Distinct and indistinct faith	1. What is faith? Heb. 11:1 –Is faith first among virtues? 2. Is faith a virtue? 3. Is faith one species or genus? 4. Are unformed and formed faith one and the same? Do natural gifts transform into grace-given gifts? 5. Is the same thing known and believed? 6. The ancients' faith 7. Implicit and explicit faith
7. <u>Articles of faith</u>: a separate list of contents in the text 1. What is an article + etymology? [2]. Is it an enuntiabile or res?[a] [2. The number of articles] 3. Can a false thing be believed in faith the virtue? 4. Can man believe the contradiction of an article without a sin?	9. <u>Articles of faith</u>: a separate list of contents 1. Etymology of 2 *articulus* 2. What is an article? 3. Is it an *enuntiabile* or *res*? [4. The number of articles] 5. Can a false thing be believed in faith the virtue?	8. <u>Articles of faith</u>: –What is an article? –Is it enuntiabile or res? –number of articles 9. Can a false thing be believed in faith the virtue? [Whether faith is displaced by perfect vision.] *Instead*: The equality of virtues

Douai 530	Philip the Chancellor (plan)	Philip the Chancellor (actual discussion)	Summa Halensis
What is faith? *Secundum rationem* –Heb. 11:1 Other definitions –*Secundum rem* (principle of what cognition; what sort of habitus; matters relevant to "is faith a virtue") What kind of similitude of divine mind is it	What is faith? –Heb. 11:1 –Other definitions –Different senses of *fides* The act of faith Difference between *intellectus fidei* and other *intellectus*[b] Does faith have many species?	What is faith? –Heb. 11:1 –Other definitions –Different senses of faith (leading to "is faith virtue") Is faith a genus? Unformed and formed faiths (a series of questions) Act of faith	Is faith the habitus? What is faith? 1. *Secundum rem*: a. Is it necessary for salvation? b. Is it acquired? c. Is it a virtue? d. Is it a species or a genus? 2. *Secundum definitionem*: a. Other definitions b. Heb. 11:1 The act of faith
De subiecto fidei 1. Interpretation of two verses regarding faith 2. Is faith "of" one God, omnipotent one God or the trinity? How will a deaf be saved?; implicit faith 3. Of what faith is (cuius est fides) –Is faith "of" temporal or eternal?; sensible or intelligible? –Is the same thing be known and believed? –Is faith of the particular, the universal or intermediaries? (4.?) In which power of the soul does faith lie?	De credito –What does it need to be a credendum? –Is it just the true? –Is it just? necessary true? –Is it incomplex or complex? –Is it under any sort of complexity? –What does an article have to be? –What are the articles and number of articles? –Comparison of symbola –Difference between creditum and cognitum secundum alios modos cognoscendi The subject in that faith is –Can it be in angels?	What is *creditum*? *(articulus secundum rem)*: –What is "to believe"? –Is it just the true? –Is it just necessary true? –Is it incomplex or complex? –Is it under any sort of complexity? What is an article? *secundum diffinitionem* –Is "God exists" an article of faith? –Creeds What cognition does faith remove?	De obiecto fidei a. Can it be false or only true b. Is it only apparent true? c. Is it only known true? d. Contingent or necessary true? e. Complex or incomplex? f. Created or uncreated? The subject of faith a. In which power of the soul faith dwells b. In angels before confirmation c. In Adam before the fall d. passion In Christ before the Faith's effects Certitudo

(continued)

Table A-1 (*continued*)

William of Auxerre	Roland of Cremona	Hugh of St. Cher
5. In which moment a man is considered first as a believer?	Without numbers ("it is used to ask these questions):	
[not mentioned in the general list: Cognitio dei + separate list of contents]	–Can a man believe contradiction of an article without a sin?	
1. faith of philosop hers and heretics 2. faith of Jews 3. Faith of disciples	–In that moment he is supposed to believe. –Faith of philosophers –Faith of Jews number of articles –What does "faith of hearing" mean?	

[a] This question does not appear in the list of contents as a separate question but is considered in its place as Chapter 2 (219). Since the issue of the number of the articles of faith does appear in the contents but is absent, the numbering remains the same.

[b] The tractate on faith in Münster 257, dated to the 1240s, was planned to include such question as well: "Que differencia inter intellectum fidei et quosdam alios intellectus"; Franz Pelster, "Literaturgeschichtliches zur Pariser theologischen Schule aus den Jahren 1230 bis 1256," Scholastik 5 (1930): 51. Perhaps these were close to the form of questiones "De intellectu" such as that of William of Durham mentioned in Chapter 3 and quaestio 12 in Douai BM 434.

Douai 530	Philip the Chancellor (plan)	Philip the Chancellor (actual discussion)	Summa Halensis
(5.?) Does every *creditum* about Christ involve contradiction? (6.?) Does faith see itself? [The variation in q. 501 has in its prospectus here a question about Augustine's categorization of virtues].	–In children? –Is it in children in sacrament or in habitu? –In habitu or in actu? –Can it be in idolatry adults and in believers of one God who do not believe all articles? Implicit and explicit faith distinct and indistinct faith Formed and unformed faith: Is it the same habitu?; does unformed faith remain when formed faith arrives?; are they identical in substance?; Does faith displace all other cognitions? The priority of faith		a. progress b. (*profectus*) Comparison with other virtues II fides quod creditur—the articles

ACKNOWLEDGMENTS

This book is about a community of knowledge agents; it could not be written without such communities, institutions, and the people that constitute them. The history department of Tel-Aviv University in the first decade of the 2000s, Ron Barkai, Aviad Kleinberg, and Gadi Algazi, in particular, opened my eyes to the richness of medieval European culture. Later, the strong community of the Cohn Institute for the History and Philosophy of Sciences and Ideas, Rivka Feldhay and Snait Gissis in particular, constituted a unique home, a greenhouse and constant inspiration for stimulating thinking about intellectual history, creativity, and interdisciplinarity.

One day during my early undergraduate years I noticed an ad in campus inviting students to a lecture about scholastic theology. The lecturer was a charismatic candidate for teaching who instantly caught my attention. The next semester I registered for all the classes this new professor offered, as all of them miraculously touched the topics I was most interested in then. Yossi Schwartz quickly became the most significant figure in my academic life. He introduced me to the difficult world of scholasticism and to endless other breathtaking intellectual landscapes and provided steady and generous support during a long journey of professional and personal growth.

It is not an easy task to write on medieval Christian theology in Israel. Ittai Weinryb, Oded Rabinovitch, Daniel Hershenzon, Haim Mahlev, Merav Haklai, and Lilach Assaf helped me with materials needed for my research and constituted a supportive peer community. Prof. Gilbert Dahan helped me to find my Paris libraries; Prof. Marcia Colish suggested valuable bibliography. I thank all the members of Martin-Grabmann-Institut in LMU Munich, in particular Frau Susanne Kaup, for their extraordinary hospitality and generosity regarding the use of the microfilm collection and the library.

Ideas have matured in new communities that provided novel perspectives and precious time. With the aid of the Rothschild fellowship I enjoyed a fruitful stay at the IRHT-CNRS with Dominique Poirel; later, I was fortunate to join the Minerva Institute in Tel Aviv University and then spend time at the Open University under Iris Shagrir's supervision. Final writing was done at the Hebrew University, whose warm and encouraging history department has kindly accepted me into its lines.

I was most fortunate to have by my side Yael Arbel, with her attentive reading and stimulating questions, and Ori Weisberg, who edited the first English manuscript and proved to be not only a sensitive editor, but a true reader. Without the kind and perceptive Lydia Schumacher, this project might not have seen the light of day. I heartily thank Franklin Harkins, Mary Erler, and Will Cerbone of Fordham University Press, who believed in the book, and to Eric Newman, Aldene Fredenburg, and others of the production phase who made this book a fact in print. It has been a pleasure to work with you.

An uncompromised premise of this study was that one should examine intellectual activity looking outside the classrooms' windows. I owe more than I can express here to Udi Wahrsager, my life partner, for constant support, patience, and illuminating questions; to him, to my dear parents, Sima and the late Shalom Even-Ezra; and to Dina and the late Shmuel Wahrsager for their help in providing the time needed for research. I wish Shalom and Shmuel could have seen this book. Without the love and joy I have for all of you and for my sweetest Dor and Yaara, it would all be for nothing.

NOTES

INTRODUCTION

1. Lewis Carroll, *Alice's Adventures in Wonderland* (1865; repr. Chicago: VolumeOne, 1998), 1:19-20.

2. Literature on the rise of the medieval university is vast. I would name here only a few selected works: Gaines Post, "Alexander III, the *Licentia Docendi* and the Rise of the Universities," in *C. H. Haskins Anniversary Essays*, ed. John I. La Monte and Charles H. Taylor (Boston: Houghton Mifflin, 1929), 255-77; Hastings Rashdall, *The Universities of Europe in the Middle Ages*, 3 vols. (Oxford: Oxford University Press, 1936); Stephen C. Ferruolo, *The Origins of the University: The Schools of Paris and Their Critics, 1100-1215* (Stanford, Calif.: Stanford University Press, 1985); Olga Weijers, *Terminologie des universités au XIIIe siècle* (Rome: Ateneo, 1987); Hilde de Ridder-Symoens, ed., *A History of the University in Europe*, vol. 1 (Cambridge: Cambridge University Press, 1992); Jacques Verger, *Les universités françaises au Moyen Age* (Leiden and New York: Brill, 1995); John Van Engen, ed., *Learning Institutionalized: Teaching in the Medieval University* (Notre Dame, Ind.: University of Notre Dame Press, 2000); William J. Courtenay, Jürgen Miethke, and David B. Priest, eds., *Universities and Schooling in Medieval Society* (Leiden and Boston: Brill, 2000).

3. See, among others: Paul Zumthor, *Merlin le prophète: Un thème de la littérature polémique de l'historiographie et des romans* (Lausanne: Payot, 1943); Richard Trachsler, ed., *Moult obscures paroles: Études sur la prophétie médiévale* (Paris: Presses de l'Université Paris-Sorbonne, 2007).

4. Gerald of Wales reports of such shaman-like practice in his *Itinerarium Kambriae et Descrpitio Kambriae* 1.16, ed. James F. Dimock, in *Giraldi Cambrensis opera* (London: Rolls Series, 1868), 6:194-95.

5. Bernard McGinn, *The Flowering of Mysticism: Men and Women in the New Mysticism*, vol. 3 of *The Presence of God: A History of Western Christian Mysticism*. (New York: Crossroad, 1998), 29 and passim.

6. Paolo Nardi, "Relations with Authority," in De Ridder-Symoens, *History of the University in Europe*, 77-106; Alan E. Bernstein, "Magisterium and License: Corporate Autonomy against Papal Authority in the Medieval University of Paris," *Viator* 9 (1978): 291-308.

7. Post, Kimon Giocarinis, and Robert Kay, "The Medieval Heritage of a Humanistic Ideal: 'Scientia donum dei est, unde vendi non potest,'" *Traditio* 11 (1955): 195-234. The opinions on whether teaching philosophy too is a spiritual matter varied. See William of Auxerre, *Summa aurea* [SA] 3.49.2.5 ("De venditione scientie"), ed. Jean Ribaillier, in *Spicilegium Bonaventurianum* (Paris: Grottaferrata, 1980-87), 3:962-66; Roland of Cremona, *Summa Magistri Rolandi*

Cremonensis O. P. Liber Tercius [SR] 3, Editio princeps, ed. Alois Cortesi (Bergamo: Monumenta Bergomensia, 1962), 1253–56.

8. Roland of Cremona, SR 3, 1253–56: "Laycus posset docere theologiam, si esset consuetudo in ecclesia."

9. On this affair, see Constant J. Mews, "Hildegard and the Schools," in *Hildegard of Bingen in the Context of Her Thought and Art*, ed. Charles Burnett and Peter Dronke (London: Warburg Institute, 1998), 101–3; A. Stover, "Hildegard, the Schools and Their Critics," in *A Companion to Hildegard of Bingen*, ed. Beverly Kienzle, George Ferzoco, and Debra Stoudt (Leiden: Brill, 2011), 115–19.

10. Hildegard of Bingen, Letters 40–40r, in *Hildegardis Bingensis epistolarium, pars prima*, ed. Lieven Van Acker, CCCM 91, no. 1 (Turnhout: Brepols, 1991), 102–5. English translation follows *The Letters of Hildegard of Bingen*, trans. Joseph L. Baird and Radd K. Ehrman (New York: Oxford University Press, 1994), 1:109–12. On the problem of dating, see Stover, "Hildegard, the Schools and Their Critics," 116–17.

11. Cf. Isa 24:16: "Et dixi: Secretum meum mihi, secretum meum mihi. Vae mihi! praevaricantes praevaricati sunt, et praevaricatione transgressorum praevaricati sunt" (Vulgate version).

12. John Marenbon, "Gilbert of Poitiers," in *A Companion to Philosophy in the Middle Ages*, ed. Jorge J. E. Gracia and Timothy B. Noone (Malden, Mass.: Blackwell, 2003), 264–66.

13. Stover, "Hildegard, the Schools and Their Critics," 119–20.

14. Ibid., 117.

15. Hildegard of Bingen, *Acta Inquisitionis de virtutibus et miraculis sanctae Hildegardis*, ed. Charles Daremberg and F. A. Reuss, PL 197:138A. Bruno's testimony is part of the typical "circumstances" section in the canonization inquiry records. An error in the PL misleads scholars to believe that the text claims that Hildegard herself went to Paris, a clearly unlikely event, as Mews remarks. Nevertheless, the text speaks about *Bruno* going there, which is quite likely. It is difficult to assess when the entire affair took place. The petition for canonization was made between 1226 and 1228. Bruno does not name the bishop but does tell that this bishop had as a master William of Auxerre, which fits these dates. Bruno's testimony was corroborated by two other learned witnesses. For an English translation, see *Jutta and Hildegard: The Biographical Sources*, trans., introduction Anna Silvas (University Park: Pennsylvania State University Press, 1998), 268–69, 271–72.

16. Paris, BnF Lat. 14726. On William of Auxerre's *quaestiones* there, see Spencer E. Young, "Paris BNF MS Lat. 14726—Peter Bar, Stephen Berout and Master G.: A New Witness to William of Auxerre?," *Bulletin de Philosophie Médiévale* 50 (2008): 53–82.

17. All relevant sources for the Amalrician case were recently gathered as appendices to the new critical edition of Garnerius of Rochefort, *Contra Amauricianos*, ed. Paolo Lucentini, CCCM 232 (Brepols: Turnhout, 2010).

See also Nathalie Gorochov, *Naissance de l'université: Les écoles de Paris d'Innocent III à Thomas d'Aquin (v. 1200–v. 1245)* (Paris: Champion, 2012), 184–93; J. M. M. H. Thijssen, "Master Amalric and the Amalricians: Inquisitorial Procedure and the Supression of Heresy in the University of Paris," *Speculum* 71, no. 1 (1996): 43–65, and the dated but still valuable Catherine-Germaine Capelle, *Autour du décret de 1210 III: Amaury de Bène* (Paris: Vrin, 1932).

18. "In omnibus facultatibus in quibus studebat aliis contrarius inveniebatur"; Garnerius of Rochefort, *Contra Amauricianos*, Appendix XI, 73.

19. Ibid., Appendix IX, 67–68.

20. Caesar of Heisterbach takes the trouble of detailing all their names, noting with precision the involvement of each in theological studies (ibid., Appendix XIV, 79). The prime lesson of the story for the young novice is that even literate people might fall into heresy. While Caesar says that Bernard was the only one who did not study theology, the chronicler of Lyon names both Garin and Bernard as masters (ibid., 73). Perhaps he was only a master of arts. Robert of Auxerre describes them briefly as "scioli litterarum" (ibid., 60).

21. Caesar of Heisterbach and the *Chronica regia Coloniensis* use the exact same wording: "Quandoque uultu eleuato se spiritu in celum raptum simulabat et postea aliqua que se uidisse dicebat in conuenticulis eorum enarrabat" (ibid., Appendix XII, 75; Appendix XIV, 81).

22. "Stephanus, presbyter of Celle, 'confessed . . . that hell is not a place but the ignorance of truth; heaven is the cognition of truth'" (fragments from the interrogation, Appendix III, 56); cf. *Contra Amaurianos*, Appendix III, 16.

23. *Fragmentum Viconiense, Contra Amaurianos*, Appendix V, 60.

24. For the current state of the problem, see *Contra Amaurianos*, Appendix V, lviii–lx.

25. On Thomas's canonization and the legends presented here, see James A. Weisheipel, *Friar Thomas d'Aquino: His Life, Thought and Work* (Oxford: Blackwell, 1973), 343–49; Edmund Colledge, "The Legend of St. Thomas Aquinas," in *St. Thomas Aquinas 1274–1974: Commemorative Studies* (Toronto: Pontifical Institute of Mediaeval Studies, 1974), 1:13–28.

26. Tocco, in *Fontes vitae sancti Thomae Aquinatis notis historicis et criticis illustrati*, ed. Domenicus Prümmer and M. H. Laurent (Toulouse: Saint Maximin, 1912), 346.

27. Calo, in *Fontes*, 36; Tocco, in ibid., 104–5.

28. "Cum ab eodem intellectu divino subjecta omnium scienciarum prodeant a quo divine sapiencie veritates emanant"; Gui, in *Fontes*, 218.

29. Calo, in *Fontes*, 31.

30. Calo, in *Fontes*, 37 (Calo); Tocco, in ibid., 104.

31. Gui, in *Fontes*, 184, following a series of other instances of rapture. There might be an apologetic aspect here as well, seeing that Nicholas of Lyre found Thomas's literal interpretation of 8:4 so disturbing that he doubted the authenticity of Thomas's authorship for the entire commentary; Hyacinthe-François

Dondaine and Léon Reid, "Introduction," in Thomas Aquinas, *Expositio super Isaiam ad litteram*, Editio Leonina 28 (Rome: Editori di San Tommaso, 1974), 3–4.

32. Calo, in *Fontes*, 42; Tocco, in ibid., 116–17; Gui, in ibid., 191.

33. Tocco, in *Fontes*, 125–26.

34. Gui, in *Fontes*, 190.

35. Calo, in *Fontes*, 38ff; Tocco, in ibid., 108ff; Gui, in ibid., 189ff.

36. "Quia talia vidi, quod ea que scripsi et docui modica mihi videntur, et ex hoc spero in deo, quod sicut doctrine mee sic erit cito finis et vite mee"; Calo, in *Fontes*, 43–44. Cf. Tocco, in ibid., 120; Gui, in ibid., 193.

37. Tocco lists several prefigurations from the Old Testament, among which he compares Thomas with Moses seeing God, and adds, "Quorum magnitudine intellecta et scripta despiceret prae illorum excellentia quae vidisset; sicut circa finem imposuit, admiranti de eius raptu socio, revelavit"; Tocco, in *Fontes*, 82–83.

38. "Bene sicut in hac vita homo vivens in corpore potest scire. Sed volo, ut mecum venias, et ducam te ad locum ubi clariorem habebis de omnibus intellectum. Et videbatur ipsum per cappam accipere et ducere extra scolas"; Calo, in *Fontes.*, 49; Tocco, in ibid., 134; Gui, in ibid., 208.

39. Bernard Gui, quoting from the booklet read by the "Bequini," writes, "Circa finem sui [i.e., Olivi's] transitus, post sacram inunctionem receptam ... dixit totam scientiam suam per infusionem recepisse a Deo, et Parisius in ecclesia hora tertia subito se fuisse illuminatum a Domino Jhesu Christo"; Gui, *Manuel de l'inquisiteur*, ed., trans. Guillaume Mollat and Georges Drioux (Paris: Champion, 1926), 1:192. On Peter John Olivi in this respect, see: David Burr, *The Persecution of Peter Olivi* (Philadelphia: American Philosophical Society, 1976); Burr, "Olivi on Marriage: The Conservative as Prophet," *Journal of Mediaeval and Renaissance Studies* 2 (1972): 183–204; Burr, "Olivi on Prophecy," *Cristianesimo nella Storia* 17, no. 2 (1996): 369–91; and Burr, "Did the Beguins Understand Olivi?," in *Pierre de Jean Olivi (1248–1298): Pensée scolastique, dissidence spirituelle et société; Actes du colloque de Narbonne (mars 1998)*, ed. Alain Boureau and Sylvain Piron (Paris: Vrin, 1999), 309–18; as well as Catherine König-Pralong, *Le bon usage des saviors: Scolastique, philosophie et politique culturelle* (Paris: Vrin, 2011).

40. Paraphrasing Gorochov, *Naissance de l'université*, 20, who reviews this approach in the last decades; cf. Étienne Anheim and Sylvain Piron, "Le travail intellectuel au Moyen Âge: Institutions et circulations," *Revue de synthèse* 129, no. 4 (2008): 481–84, and the response of Olga Weijers, "Quelque réflexions sur le travail intellectuel au Moyen Âge: Àpropos d'un numéro récent de la *Revue de synthèse*," *Bulletin de philosophie médiévale* 51 (2009): 221–28.

41. On the psychology of faith from the twelfth century to William of Auxerre, William of Auvergne, and Philip the Chancellor, see Georg Englhardt, *Die Entwicklung der dogmatischen Glaubenspsychologie in der mittelalterlichen Scholastik vom Abaelardstreit (um 1140) bis zu Philipp dem Kanzler (gest. 1236)*

(Münster in Westfalen: Aschendorff, 1933); Riccardo Saccenti, *Conservare la retta volontà: L'atto morale nelle dottrine di Filippo il Cancelliere e Ugo di Saint-Cher (1225–1235)* (Bologna: Il Mulino, 2013). On the doctrine of beatific vision, see Nikolaus Wicki, *Die Lehre von der himmlischen Seligkeit in der mittelalterlichen Scholastik von Petrus Lombardus bis Thomas von Aquin* (Freiburg, Switzerland: Universitätsverlag, 1954), and Christian Trottmann, *La vision béatifique: Des disputes scolastiques à sa définition par Benoît XII* (Rome: École française de Rome, 1995). On prophecy, see Bruno Decker, *Die Entwicklung der Lehre von der prophetischen Offenbarung* (Breslau: Müller and Seiffert, 1940); Marianne Schlosser, *Lucerna in caliginoso loco: Aspekte des Prophetie-Begriffes in der scholastischen Theologie* (Paderborn: Schöningh, 2000); Jean-Pierre Torrell, *Théorie de la prophétie et philosophie de la connaissance aux environs de 1230: La contribution d'Hugues de Saint-Cher (Ms. Douai 434, Question 481)* (Leuven: Spicilegium Sacrum Lovaniense, 1977); Torrell, *Recherches sur la théorie de la prophétie au moyen âge, XIIe-XIVe siécles: Études et textes* (Fribourg: Éditions Universitaires Fribourg Suisse, 1992). Barbara Faes de Mottoni has conducted research on William of Auxerre and Roland of Cremona's theories of rapture and contemplation in *Figure e motivi della contemplazione nelle teologie medievali* (Florence: SISMEL, Edizioni del Galluzzo, 2007). She has also edited Hugh of St. Cher's question on rapture in "Il ms. Douai Bibliothéque Municipale 434/II e la questio N. 480 De raptu," *AHDLMA* 73, no. 1 (2006): 165–201.

42. Jean Lave and Étienne Wenger, *Situated Learning: Legitimate Peripheral Participation* (Cambridge and New York: Cambridge University Press, 1991). For further development of the concept, see Wenger, *Communities of Practice: Learning, Meaning, and Identity* (Cambridge and New York: Cambridge University Press, 1998).

43. John W. Baldwin, *Masters, Princes, and Merchants: The Social Views of Peter the Chanter and His Circle* (Princeton: Princeton University Press, 1970). Hester Gelber's study of the Oxford Dominicans in the first half of the fourteenth century, a group designated by her as a "conversational community," is another example; Gelber, *It Could Have Been Otherwise: Contingency and Necessity in Dominican Theology at Oxford, 1300–1350* (Leiden and Boston: Brill, 2004).

44. This was already noted in Post's classic article "Parisian Masters as a Corporation, 1200–1246," *Speculum* 9 (1934): 421–45.

45. Baldwin, "Masters at Paris from 1179 to 1215: A Social Perspective," in *Renaissance and Renewal in the Twelfth Century*, ed. Robert L. Benson and Giles Constable, with Carol D. Lanham (Cambridge, Mass.: Harvard University Press, 1982), 158.

46. Gorochov, *Naissance*; Gorochov, "The Self-image of the Masters of Theology at the University of Paris in the Late Thirteenth and Early Fourteenth Centuries," *Journal of Ecclesiastical History* 46 (1995): 398–431; Young, *Scholarly Community at the Early University of Paris: Theologians, Education and Society*,

1215–1248 (Cambridge: Cambridge University Press, 2014). Ian Wei takes a longer period as his subject in his *Intellectual Culture in Medieval Paris* (Cambridge: Cambridge University Press, 2012). On the relative neglect of this particular generation until very recently, see Young, *Scholarly Community*, 9–11.

47. For a comprehensive list, see Young, *Scholarly Community*, Appendix, 212–31. For a thorough discussion of their profile, origin, and update bibliography on each, see Gorochov, *Naissance*. Both works ameliorate the list made by Palémon Glorieux, *Répertoire des maîtres en théologie de Paris au XIIIe siècle* (Paris: Vrin, 1933).

48. A full description and analysis of the first two volumes is in Glorieux, "Les 572 Questions du manuscrit de Douai 434," *RTAM* 10 (1938): 123–52, 225–67. He also identified a bulk of *quaestiones* that formed a part of an incomplete *summa de bono*, and edited them as the *Summa Duacensis*, dating around 1230; *La "Summa Duacensis" (Douai 434), texte critique avec une introduction et des tables*, ed. Palémon Glorieux, Textes philosophiques du moyen âge 2 (Paris: Vrin, 1955). On the date of the entire collection and the identity of its compiler, magister G, see the aforementioned article, as well as Victorin Doucet, "A travers le manuscrit 434 de Douai," *Antonianum* 27 (1952): 531–80. A recent codicological description of all three volumes including a list of all *quaestiones* edited and published by now and a bibliography up to 1995 is in Riccardo Quinto, "Il codice 434 di Douai, Stefano Langton e Nicola di Tournai," *Sacris Erudiri* 36 (1996): 233–361.

49. Albert Fries believed it to be Guerric's, but Landgraf and Lottin disagreed. Many years after that undecided dispute, Bougerol claimed it is more likely to belong to John of La Rochelle or at least to the Parisian Franciscan school; Fries, "De commentario Guerrici de S. Quintino in libros sententiarum," *Archivum Fratrum Praedicatorum* 5 (1935): 326–41; Jacques Guy Bougerol, "La glose sur les *Sentences* du manuscrit Vat. Lat. 691," *Antonianum* 55 (1980): 108–73. For further references and a summary of the dispute over the authorship, see Torrell's introduction to the life and works of Guerric of St. Quentin, in *Guerric of Saint-Quentin: Quaestiones de quolibet*, ed. Walter H. Principe and Jonathan Glenn Black (Toronto: Pontifical Institute of Mediaeval Studies, 2002), 6–9.

50. Robert Pasnau, *Theories of Cognition in the Later Middle Ages* (New York: Cambridge University Press, 1997); Steven P. Marrone, *The Light of Thy Countenance: Science and Knowledge of God in the Thirteenth Century* (Leiden and Boston: Brill, 2001).

51. On Aristotelian reception in this generation, see Young, *Scholarly Community*, 16–17, and the secondary literature he cites there. Both Decker, *Die Entwicklung*, and Schlosser, *Lucerna in caliginoso loco*, follow a "reception" line of argumentation and explanation, pointing to the effect Augustine's and Avicenna's doctrines among others had on theories of prophecy. The same line is taken by Magdalena Bieniak, *The Soul-Body Problem at Paris, ca. 1200–1250: Hugh of St. Cher and His Contemporaries*, Ancient and Medieval Philosophy Series 1.42

(Leuven: Leuven University Press, 2010), and by Thomas Pitour, *Wilhelm von Auvergnes Psychologie: Von der Rezeption des aristotelischen Hylemorphismus zur Reformulierung der Imago-Dei-Lehre Augustins* (Paderborn: Ferdinand Schöningh, 2011).

52. Baldwin, *Masters, Princes*, and Wei, *Intellectual Culture in Medieval Paris* (especially Part 2) are great examples for this kind of contextualization in the framework of the medieval university of Paris.

53. See, besides the two works cited previously, Baldwin, "Masters at Paris"; Gorochov, "Self-Image"; and König-Pralong, *Le bon usage de savoirs*.

54. Schlosser, *Lucerna in caliginoso*, explicitly avoids the context of the theories on prophecies in most of her book (she declares so in page 1), but nevertheless demonstrates the importance of the prophet concept to the mendicants (Chapter 4.3) and investigates interrelationship between concepts of pseudo-prophets and the secular-mendicant conflict (5.3.2).

55. Thomas F. Gieryn, "Boundary-Work and the Demarcation of Science from Non-Science: Strains and Interests in Professional Ideologies of Scientists," *American Sociological Review* 48, no. 6. (1983): 781–95.

56. To this we may add the revival of interest in the philosophical concept of truth, to which Marrone devoted his important *William of Auvergne and Robert Grosseteste: New Ideas of Truth in the Early Thirteenth Century* (Princeton: Princeton University Press, 1983).

57. Erwin Panofsky's influential thesis on the relationship between Gothic architecture and scholasticism was translated to French by Pierre Bourdieu, who had also added a text of his own in which he developed his idea of *habitus*; Bourdieu, "Postface" for Erwin Panofski, *Architecture gothique et pensée scolastique* (Paris: Les Editions de Minuit, 1967), 133–67.

58. On Aristotle's theory of *habitus*, see especially Thomas Kiefer, *Aristotle's Theory of Knowledge*, Chap. 2 (London: Continuum, 2007). On the medieval term and the twelfth century background, see Englhardt, *Die Entwicklung der dogmatischen Glaubenspsychologie*, chapter 2.2; Cary J. Nederman, "Nature, Ethics, and the Doctrine of 'Habitus': Aristotelian Moral Psychology in the Twelfth Century," *Traditio* 45 (1989–90), and Marcia L. Colish, "*Habitus* Revisited: A Reply to Cary Nederman," *Traditio* 48 (1993): 77–92.

59. Nederman, "Nature, Ethics, and The Doctrine of '*Habitus*,'" 90.

60. Aristotle, *Nicomachean Ethics* I.x.1100b2. Cf. "Differt autem habitus affectione quod permanentior et diuturnior est. . . . Non videtur facile posse moveri neque facile permutari. . . . Similiter autem et in aliis, nisi forte in his quoque contingit per temporis longitudinem in naturam cuiusque translata et insanabilis vel difficile mobilis, quam iam quilibet habitudinem vocet"; Aristotle, *Categories* VIII 8b28-29a4, in *Categoriae vel Praedicamenta: Translatio Boethii, Editio Composite, Translatio Guillelmi de Moerbeka, Lemmata e Simplicii commentario decerpta, Pseudo-Augustini Paraphrasis Themistiana*, Aristoteles Latinus 1, ed. Minio Paluello (Bruges and Paris: Desclée De Brouwer, 1961), 23–24.

61. Bernard McGinn, review of *Vision und Visionliteratur in Mittelalter* (Stuttgart: Anton Hiersemann, 1981), by Peter Dinzelbacher, *Speculum* 59, no. 1 (Jan. 1984): 138–40.

62. See the translator's notes in the introduction to Silvas, *Jutta and Hildegard: The Biographical Sources*, 129.

63. Torrell, *Théorie de la prophétie*, 11.

1. WHY WAS PAUL IGNORANT OF HIS OWN STATE, AND HOW DO VARIOUS MODES OF COGNIZING GOD DIFFER?

1. For contemporary commentary on this passage see, among others: James D. Tabor, *Things Unutterable: Paul's Ascent to Paradise in Its Greco-Roman, Judaic and Early Christian Contexts*, Studies in Judaism (Lanham, Md.: University Press of America, 1986); Allan Segal, *Paul the Convert: The Apostolate and Apostasy of Saul the Pharisee* (New Haven, Conn.: Yale University Press, 1990), 34–71; Colleen Shantz, *Paul in Ecstasy: The Neurobiology of the Apostle's Life and Thought* (Cambridge: Cambridge University Press, 2009), Chapter 2; for further bibliography, see Shantz, *Paul in Ecstasy*, notes, 77–78.

2. For a summary and discussion of contemporary exegesis of the use of third person here, see Shantz, *Paul in Ecstasy*, 39–42, 44–45.

3. Erica Bourguignon, "Introduction: A Framework for the Comparative Study of Altered States of Consciousness," in *Religion, Altered States of Consciousness and Social Change*, ed. Erica Bourguignon (Columbus: Ohio State University Press, 1973), 5–9, surveys and criticizes classifications presented by Ronald Fischer and Arnold Ludwig (1968); another classification from the point of view of psychiatry was suggested by Carl Bell, "States of Consciousness," *Journal of the National Medical Association* 72, no. 4 (1980): 331–34, where he treats trance and rapture separately (the latter characterized by its highly positive feeling), as well as dreams, hypnotic states, etc. For modern questionnaires and evaluation tools, see Carl Bell et al., "Altered States of Consciousness Profile: An Afro-Centric Intrapsychic Evaluation Tool," *Journal of the National Medical Association* 77, no. 9 (1985): 715–28; Erich Studerus, Alex Gamma, and Franz X. Vollenweider, "Psychometric Evaluation of the Altered States of Consciousness Rating Scale (OSV)," *PLoS One* 5, no. 8 (2010), doi:10.1371/journal.pone.0012412. On the difficulty to distinguish contemplatives, visionaries, mystics, and prophets from a historian's point of view, see Bernard McGinn, *The Growth of Mysticism: Gregory the Great through the 12th Century*, vol. 2 of *The Presence of God: A History of Western Christian Mysticism* (New York: Crossroad, 1994), 324–26.

4. Questionnaires such as those devised in the articles cited previously include, among factors such as the dose of the inducing drug, his or her description of the experience. Studerus et al., "Psychometric Evaluation," specifies that "subjects were asked to describe their experience/were instructed to retrospectively rate their whole experience."

5. Mary Douglas, *Natural Symbols, Explorations in Cosmology* (New York: Pantheon, 1970), 65–84; Carolyn Walker Bynum, "Monsters, Medians, and Marvelous Mixtures: Hybrids in the Spirituality of Bernard of Clairvaux," in *Metamorphosis and Identity* (New York: Zone, 2001), 113–62.

6. Codex Douai BM 434 contains an anonymous "*quaestio* de subiecto teologie" and a "de fine teologie," attributed to magister Willermus (see also Chapter 6); Codex Prague, Univ. IV D 13 contains an anonymous *quaestio* "de scientia divina"; Codex Paris, BnF Lat. 15652, dated by Chenu to ca. 1240 and by Glorieux to the years 1242–47, contains similar questions; for description and study, see Marie-Dominique Chenu, "Maîtres et bacheliers de l'Université de Paris v. 1240: Description du manuscrit Paris, Bibl. Nat. lat. 15652," *Études d'Histoire Littéraire et Doctrinale du XIIIe Siècle* 1 (1932): 11–39; Palémon Glorieux, "Les années 1242–1247 à la Faculté de Théologie de Paris," *RTAM* 29 (1962): 234–49. The introduction of such questions in the beginning of the yearly course on the *Sentences* is clearly set by Adam of Puteorumvilla (fol. 89r) and Odo Rigaldi in this manuscript, but not by other bachelors. It seems, therefore, not to be a commonly accepted practice in these years. For editions and further discussion, see Leonardo Sileo, *Teoria della scienza theologica: Quaestio de scientia theologiae di Odo Rigaldi e altri testi inedita (1230–1250)*, 2 vols. (Rome: Pontificium Athenaeum Antonianum, 1984). A general overview of the beginnings of the reflective discussion in theology and other chapters in its history can be found there, as well as in Martin Grabmann, *Die theologische Erkenntnis und Einleitungslehre des hl. Thomas von Aquin* (Freiburg, Switzerland: Paulus-verlag, 1948); Chenu, *La théologie comme science au XIIIe siècle* (Paris: Vrin, 1957), and Christian Trottmann, *Théologie et noétique au XIIIe siècle: À la recherche d'un statut* (Paris: Vrin, 1999).

7. "Et cum sit cognitio per gratiam fidei, per gratiam donorum intellectus et sapientiae, per gratiam prophetiae, per gratiam raptus, hic tantummodo quaeremus de medio cognoscendi"; Alexander of Hales, *Summa theologica seu sic ab origine dicta "Summa Fratris Alexandri"* [SH], tractatus introductorius, ed. Bernardini Klumper, Victorin Doucet, and the Quaracchi Fathers (Rome: Collegii S. Bonaventurae, 1924), 1:32.

8. Augustine, *De genesi ad litteram libri duodecim* 12.1, ed. Joseph Zycha, Corpus Scriptorum Ecclesiasticorum Latinorum 28 (Prague: Tempsky, 1894), 379.

9. For contemporary approaches to the problem of Paul's repeated uncertainty and the extremely different solutions offered in modern times, see Shantz, *Paul in Ecstasy*, 90–94.

10. Augustine, *De genesi ad litteram* 12.3, 382–83.

11. Ibid., 12.5, 385–86.

12. Ibid., 12.6, 387.

13. Ibid., 12.28, 422.

14. "Quo enim alio modo ipse intellectus nisi intelligendo conspicitur? Ita et charitas, gaudium, pax, longanimitas, benignitas, bonitas, fides, mansuetudo,

continentia, et caetera hujusmodi, quibus propinquatur Deo, et ipse Deus, ex quo omnia, per quem omnia, in quo omnia"; ibid., 12.24, 416. The theme of reflective thought and self perception is a central theme of Augustinian thought, developed much further in *De trinitate, confessiones*, and other texts.

15. Nikolaus Wicki, *Die Lehre von der himmlischen Seligkeit in der mittelalterlichen Scholastik von Petrus Lombardus bis Thomas von Aquin* (Freiburg, Switzerland: Universitätsverlag, 1954), 162.

16. For a survey of 1970s and 1980s scholarship about "three-ness," see Bynum, "Monsters, Medians, and Marvelous Mixtures," 114.

17. "Mira societas carnis et animae, spiritus vitae et limi terrae. . . . Plenum fuit miraculo, quod tam diversa et tam divisa ab invicem, ad invicem potuerunt conjungi. Nec minus mirabile fuit quod limo nostro Deus se ipsum conjunxit, ut sibi invicem unirentur Deus et limus, tanta sublimitas, tanta vilitas. . . . Mirabilis fuit conjunctio prima, mirabilis et secunda, nec minus mirabilis erit tertia, cum homo et angelus et Deus, unus erit spiritus"; Alcher of Clairvaux (Pseudo-Augustine), *De spiritu et anima liber unus*, 14, PL 40:790. On this interesting text, see Frances Carmel Regan, *A Study of the "Liber de spiritu et Anima": Its Doctrine, Sources, and Historical Significance* (Toronto: University of Toronto Press, 1948); Bernard McGinn, ed., *Three Treatises on Man: Cistercian Anthropology* (Kalamazoo, Mich.: Cistercian Publishers, 1977).

18. See, for example, the opening words of Hugh of St. Victor, *De unione corporis et spiritus*: "Quod natum est ex carne caro est, et quod natum est ex spiritu spiritus est. Si nihil inter spiritum et corpus medium esset, neque spiritus cum corpore, neque corpus cum spiritu convenire potuisset"; PL 177:285.

19. James J. Bono, "Medical Spirits and the Medieval Language of Life," *Traditio* 40 (1984): 105.

20. Hugh of St. Victor, *De unione corporis et animae*, PL 77:285.

21. Bono, "Medical Spirits and the Medieval Language of Life," 100.

22. Ibid., 103 ff.

23. "Est enim mens in summo, anima in imo, spiritus in medio"; Nikolaus M. Häring, "Gilbert of Poitiers, Author of *the De Discretione animae, spiritus et mentis* commonly attributed to Achard of Saint Victor," *Mediaeval Studies* 22, no. 1 (1960): 181.

24. Jacques Le Goff, *The Birth of Purgatory* (Chicago: University of Chicago Press, 1984).

25. Caroline Walker Bynum, "Metamorphosis, or Gerald and the Werewolf," in *Metamorphosis and Identity* (New York: Zone, 2001), 77–111. For the earlier work, see Bynum, *The Resurrection of the Body in Western Christianity, 200–1336* (New York: Columbia University Press, 1995).

26. "Dicendum ergo quod anima Pauli separata fuit secundum potentiam, non secundum essentiam. Et bene scivit suam animam non esse separatam secundum essentiam nec secundum actum. Quod ergo dubitavit et dixit *nescio*

deus scit, dicendum quod ipse nescivit secundum scientiam que ortum habet in sensu. Sed scivit scientia revelationis a deo"; Douai, BM 434 I, fol. 102ra.

27. Nathalie Gorochov, *Naissance de l'université: Les écoles de Paris d'Innocent III à Thomas d'Aquin (v. 1200–v. 1245)* (Paris: Champion, 2012), 67.

28. PaulAnciaux, "La date de composition de la Somme de Godefroid de Poitiers," *RTAM* 16 (1949): 165–66; Gorochov, *Naissance*, 325.

29. This Dionysian-based interpretation was first introduced by Bruno the Carthusian (St. Bruno, 1030–1101) in his commentary on II Corinthians 12, PL 153:273–74.

30. "Sed quomodo potuit scire illa summa secreta, quin sciverit an esset rapta in corpore an extra, quod longe minus est. Dico quod aliquis sciret facere magnum sermonem in teologia, non tamen sciret dicere alfabetum"; Avranches, BM 121 f. 86va.

31. Walter Map, *De nugiis Curialium: Courtiers' Trifles* 1.31, ed., trans. M. R. James, rev. C. N. L. Brooke and R. A. B. Mynors (Oxford: Clarendon, 1983), 124–25. The issue of literacy in the Waldensians is of course more complicated than the way Map describes them here. On this issue, see Peter Biller and Anne Hudson, eds., *Heresy and Literacy* (Cambridge: Cambridge University Press, 1994), and Chapter 4 of this volume.

32. See Chapter 5.

33. "Nos scimus quod si apostolus videt media[stina] visione, non fuit anima extra corpus, si comprehensiva fuit extra corpus. Hoc scimus nos, similiter apostolus"; Avranches, BM 121, f. 86va.

34. For a summary of the known detail on William of Auxerre, see the multiple references in Gorochov, *Naissance*, and Spencer E. Young, *Scholarly Community at the Early University of Paris: Theologians, Education and Society, 1215–1248* (Cambridge: Cambridge University Press, 2014).

35. Salimbene de Adam, *Cronica*, ed. Giuseppe Scalia, CCCM 125–25A (Turnhout: Brepols, 1998), 1:322. William of Auxerre is the only one mentioned by name in Bruno's testimony about the examination of Hildegard's texts. He was sent to the pope by the Capetian house as their messenger in the affairs with England and stayed there during the great strike of 1230 to promote the university's case.

36. The *Summa aurea*, probably edited by William himself from earlier, separate *quaestiones*, had at least two separate versions: a longer one, which Ribaillier estimated to be the earlier, and a shorter one; Ribaillier, "Prolegomena," in SA, 5:16ff.

37. Ibid.

38. SA 3.37.2, 3:701.

39. For a fuller discussion of the mirror of eternity, see Marianne Schlosser, *Lucerna in caliginoso loco: Aspekte des Prophetie-Begriffes in der scholastischen Theologie* (Paderborn: Schöningh, 2000), 104–13, as well as Chapter 2 of this volume.

40. Wicki differentiates between William of Auxerre and his predecessors in that while the latter classified *visio mediastina* as essentially different from the *comprehensor*'s vision, William makes clarity an accidental distinction; Wicki, *Die Lehre von der himmlischen Seligkeit*, 167. He offers therefore a bipartite, hierarchical classification (1; 2.1; 2.2) instead of a three-part model (1; 2; 3).

41. SA 3.37.4, 3:702. Chapter 2 will address further the problem of memory and oblivion.

42. Alexander of Hales, *De raptu Pauli*, *Quaestiones disputatae "Antequam esset frater* [QDA] q. 68, ed. Quarracchi Fathers, Bibliotheca Franciscana scholastica medii aevi, t. 19–21 (Quaracchi, Florence: Collegii S. Bonaventurae, 1960), 3:1345–63.

43. Ibid., 3:1354–56.

44. Ibid., 3:1348–49.

45. Gerard of Frachet, the hagiographer of the Dominican community, relates the story of his conversion, which made a great impact, saving thereby the Bologna settlement, which was on the threshold of being closed and its members dispersed; Gerard de Frachet, *Vitae Fratrum Ordinis Praedicatorum*, ed. Benedict M. Reichert, Monumenta Ordinis Pradicatorum Historica 1 (Louvain: Charpentier and Schoonjas, 1896), 25–27. The only systematic study of Roland remained Ephrem Filthaut, *Roland von Cremona, O.P., und die anfänge der scholastik im Predigerorden: Ein beitrag zur geistesgeschichte der älteren dominikaner* (Vechta: Albertus-Magnus-Verlag der Dominikaner, 1936). On the question of whether Roland taught medicine in Bologna, see pp. 14–19. Notes 35–36 on page 16 provide valuable lists of occurrences of citations from Galen, Hippocrates, Constantinus, and Johaninus, and of implicit references to medical sources.

46. "In illa visione sic assumpta fuit anima ut nullo modo carne impediretur, quoniam corpus potest ita vegetari quod nullo modo anima erit intenta corpori secundum quod ipsa intelligit"; Roland of Cremona, SR, 3.337, 988.

47. Ibid., 989.

48. Ibid., 1002.

49. "Hoc non potest dici, quoniam Paulus fuit peritissimus in arte medicinali, similiter in arte naturali"; ibid., 1003.

50. Ibid., 1004.

51. Stephen de Bourbon tells two different stories about the moment Guerric decided to leave philosophy and enter the order; Stephen de Bourbon, *Tractatus de diversis materiis*, extracts published by Albert Lecoy de La Marche, in *Anecdotes historiques, légendes et apologues, tirés du recueil inédit d'Etienne de Bourbon* (Paris: Henri Loones, 1877), 222, 346.

52. See Jean-Pierre Torrell's introduction, in Guerric of St. Quentin, *Guerric of Saint-Quentin: Quaestiones de quolibet*, ed. Walter H. Principe and Jonathan Glenn Black (Toronto: Pontifical Institute of Mediaeval Studies, 2002), 3–4.

53. Paris, BnF Lat. 15604, fols. 60ra–61ra.

54. A full description of the manuscript is provided in Bertrand-G. Guyot, "Quaestiones Guerrici, Alexandri et aliorum magistrorum Parisiensium (Praha, Univ. IV. D. 13)," *Archivum Fratrum Praedicatorum* 32 (1962): 5–125. This *quaestio* is in fols. 58r–58v.

55. "Raptus ergo dicitur ad tercium celum, ut uideret illo modo quo cheraphi (sic!) uident. Ex quo patet quod non uidit mediastina uisione. Quod etiam patet quia non est status medius inter statum comprehensoris et uiatoris, quare nec cognicio media"; Paris, BnF Lat. 15604, fol. 60vb.

56. For a general account of the group's ideas about soul-body relationship, see Magdalena Bieniak, *The Soul-Body Problem at Paris, ca. 1200–1250: Hugh of St. Cher and His Contemporaries*, Ancient and Medieval Philosophy Series 1.42 (Leuven: Leuven University Press, 2010), particularly section 1.1. Although it does not relate to the issue of rapture as a case for these theories or to the vital spirit in their theories, it provides a full account of their sources and views as expressed in questions on the soul. Various aspects are dealt in the different parts of Odon Lottin, *Psychologie et morale aux XIIe et XIIIe siècles*, 6 vols. (Gembloux: Duculot, 1949–60).

57. "Ad quod potest dici quod spiritus vitalis medium est inter animam et corpus tenens animam in corpore. Qui spiritus est a corpore supercelesti: si enim anima est a domino inmediate et corpus a natura inferiori est inmediate, videtur quod spiritus qui est medium sit a tam media scilicet a corpore supercelesti. Si enim esset a natura inferiori iam cederet in extremum et sic non esset medium"; Paris, BnF Lat. 15604, fol. 60vb.

58. Alexander's name appears twice; Prague, Univ. IV D 13, fol. 58rb.

59. "Actus corruptionis oppositum uisioni perfecte, sed non ipsa corruptio siue corruptionis habitus. Unde oportuit ab actu corruptionis, sed non oportuit quod fieret ab actu corruptionis fuit a corruptione"; Ibid.

60. "Contra. Comparat uisionem uisioni. Non ergo habetur differentias ad ea que caritatis sunt uel ardoris." And later in the response: "Non fuit ibi comparatio quantum ad uisionis immeditionem, quia hoc est commune omnibus angelis, sed quantum ad lympiditatem. Similiter non fuit comparatio quantum ad ardorem, quia penes hoc non accipitur differentia uisionis"; ibid., fol. 58vb.

61. On Hugh of St. Cher, see in particular the papers collected in Gilbert Dahan, Pierre-Marie Gy, and Louis-Jacques Bataillon, eds., *Hugues De Saint-Cher (†1263): Bibliste et Théologien; Actes du colloque "Hugues de Saint-Cher, OP, bibliste et théologien" Paris, Centre d'études du Saulchoir, 13–15 mars 2000* (Turnhout: Brepols, 2004). The *quaestio* was edited by Barbara Faes de Mottoni in Hugh of St. Cher, "Il ms. Douai Bibliothèque Municipale 434/ii e la questio N. 480 de raptu," *AHDLMA* 73, no. 1 (2006): 165–201.

62. Faes de Mottoni, ed., "Il ms. Douai," 196. In his commentary to the II Cor. 12, Hugh seems to side with the intermediary vision, but in the *quaestio* he already adapts the aforementioned solution; ibid., 183.

63. Paris, BnF Lat. 15602, f. 172v: "Et dicunt quod si hoc fuit, habuit visionem comprehensoris; si autem anima fuit in corpore, habuit quandam visionem mediastinam inter visionem comprehensoris et viatoris. Quod non putamus, immo utroque nisi visionem comprehensoris."

64. This finding slightly differs from Wicki, *Die Lehre von der himmlischen Seligkeit*, 166, who claims that the *visio mediastina* solution was rejected in this period.

65. William of Auvergne, *De anima*, *Guilielmi Alverni Opera Omnia* [GOO] (Paris, 1674), 2:193.

66. Jacques de Vitry, *The Life of Marie d'Oignies by Jacques de Vitry*, trans. Margot H. King, introduction and notes Margot H. King and Miriam Marsolais (Toronto, Ontario: Peregrina, 1993), 38.

67. Marshall E. Crossnoe, "Education and the Care of Souls: Pope Gregory IX, the Order of St. Victor and the University of Paris in 1237," *Mediaeval Studies* 61 (1999): 137–72; Catherine Guyon, *Les écoliers du Christ: L'ordre canonial du Val des écoliers 1201–1539* (Saint-Étienne: Presses Universitaires de Saint-Étienne, 1998).

68. William of Auvergne, *De anima*, GOO 2:191.

69. See Introduction.

70. Alexander of Hales, *De raptu Pauli*, QDA 3:1359.

71. *Glossa Ordinaria*, PL 113:89, quoted for instance in *quaestio* 230, Douai BM 434 I f. 101vb.

72. Alexander of Hales, *Glossa in quatuor libros Sententiarum Petri Lombardi* [GS], d. 23, ed. the Quaracchi Fathers, Bibliotheca Franciscana scholastica medii aevi (Quaracchi, Florence: Collegii S. Bonaventurae, 1952), 2:205; cf. ibid., d. 29, 2:276.

73. "Differt autem visio in raptu a visione quae est glorificatorum, quod haec visio est secundum modum cognitivae; illa vero secundum modum cognitivae et operativae, quia ibi idem erit videre quod habere.... In raptu autem est videre tantum"; ibid., d. 29, 2:279.

74. Cf. Schlosser, *Lucerna in caliginoso loco*, 113–26.

75. Alexander of Hales, *De prophetia*; QDA, q. 18, 1:302–3.

76. "Si enim essent hae visiones in diversis potentiis animae, tunc facile esset assignare differentiam earum!"; Ibid., 1:303.

77. This idea of cooperation also enables each to find a place for the four gifts that Paul contrasts with "speaking in tongues" in I Corinthians 14:6. If the intellect cooperates with the cogitative faculty, it is "agnitio," and if not, it is revelation. If it cooperates with the interpretative faculty, it can be either prophecy in the broad sense of the word, or teaching; ibid., 1:303–4.

78. This is a classical *quaestio de raptu*, although its point of departure is Adam's sleep. According to Glorieux, it is a part of a series of questions by magister G (questions 202–33). Q. 260, which is a duplication of part of it, is included in another group of G's questions; Glorieux, "Les 572 Questions du

manuscrit de Douai 434," *RTAM* 10 (1938): 264–65. On the debate over the identity of G, see Riccardo Quinto, "Il codice 454 di Douai, Stefano Langton e Nicola di Tournai," *Sacris Erudiri* 36 (1996): 233–361.

79. Douai BM 434 I, fol. 101va–102ra.

80. "Primi non sunt rapti, similiter nec secundi, quia eorum cognitio est in natura. Tercii sunt rapti, quia eorum est supra naturam"; ibid. fol. 102ra.

81. "In diffinitione raptus li 'preter naturam' refertur ad id quod eleuatur uel rapitur. Cum autem dicitur 'fides eleuerat etc.,' li 'preter naturam' refertur ad id ad quod sit elevatio"; Prague, Univ. IV D 13, fol. 58rb.

82. "Solutio. In nobis est operationis intellectus et cognitionis, et glorificati uident utroque intellectu. Sed rapti tantum uident potentia cognitiua. Unde uidere glorificatorum est eis idem quod habere, sed non uidere raptorum. . . . Sed Adam sopitus uidit intellectuali uisione, et uidit quod habuit, sed non ut habuit nec per quod habuit id est uidit ut anima glorificata"; Douai BM 434 I, fol. 102ra.

83. "Item queritur an vidit facie ad faciem. Si sic, ergo per speciem, ergo erat comprehensor. Sed dicendum quod duobus modis dicitur videre facie ad faciem quia potest esse quod sit reciproca visio nostra et dei. Et sic vidit facie ad faciem, aut ita ut glorificati vident tanquam ibi essent tactus spiritualis. Sic non vidit apostolus"; ibid.

84. "Que differentia inter cognicionem anime glorificate et eius qui rapitur? *Item* que differentia inter cognitionem angelorum et raptum pauli? *Item* que est differentia inter cognicionem anime Christi que omnia cognouit et raptum, seu cognicionem que est in raptu? *Item* que differentia inter uisionem prophetarum et raptum? *Item* que inter uisionem in extasi ade et raptu? *Item* que differentia est inter uisionem Moysi et Iacob, qui viderunt Deum facie ad faciem et raptum? *Item* que differentia inter visionem de quo loquitur Glossa II ad Corinthos 12 circa finem, ubi dicitur, *hoc est tercium celum scilicet visio qua deus uidetur facie ad faciem et hoc est si dici potest paradisus paradisorum*, et inter illam uisionem de qua dicitur I ad Corinthos xii u*idemus nunc per speciem, tunc autem facie ad faciem*"; Douai BM 434 II, fol. 95va.

85. Ibid., fol. 95vb.

86. "Aliter autem est in raptu, quoniam in raptu est uiolenta abstractio extra statum suum. Unde sic diffinitur raptus: est mutatio status preter naturam in statum distantem uel quasi distantem a se, iuxta uim dominantis nature per gratiam, per uim intelligibilem"; ibid., fol. 95va. Cf. the definition given in Alexander's Gloss on the *Sentences*: "Raptus est mutatio preter naturam in situm vel quasi situm ualde distantem secundum uim dominantis naturae"; Alexander of Hales, GS II d. 29, 2:277.

87. Ibid.

88. "Visio autem pauli in raptu fuit secundum rectitudinem speculatiui intellectus, et propter hoc caritas non fuit tamta in paulo quamta eius cognicio. . . . Alia est rectitudo aspectionis secundum practicum intellectum. . . . Hec rectitudo aspectus completa erit in patria"; Douai BM 434 I, fol. 96ra.

89. "Ad aliud dicendum quod uisio Pauli mediastina dicitur, et bene. Bene quedam communicat que pertinent ad statum vie, quedam que ad statum patrie. Ad statum uie ex parte corporis pertinet carnis corruptiblitas que erat in ipso, et fides ex parte anime. . . . Similiter ad statum uie [*read:* patrie] pertinet uisio aperta que est in speculo. . . . Ergo eadem caritas habuit . . . in raptu, licet in raptu fuerit feruentior motus caritatis. Quia ergo non mansit in raptu status uniformis, sed sicut dictum est fuit quidam medius status siue mediastina uisio, non ualet argumentatio prius facta, quanto crescit cognitio tanto crescit dilectio. Bene enim sequeretur si esset status uniformis"; ibid.

90. Riccardo Quinto claimed that *quaestiones* 338–81 belong to Langton's school; Quinto, "Il codice 454 di Douai, Stefano Langton e Nicola di Tournai," 239.

91. " Nota quod vii sunt gradus, sed tres hic distinguuntur"; Douai BM 434 II, fol. 12vb.

92. "Et differt uisio Pauli a uisione glorificatorum quia glorificata <anima?> <uidit> quod est in se et <uidit> in se ipsam speciem. Unde uidens est in se et per quod <videt> et in quo videt et quod videt, et ita uidet quod habet in se ut sumatur 'quod' et nominaliter et adverbialiter. Cumque uiator non videt quod habet in se, deum habet in se et non uidet"; ibid., fol. 13ra (words put in <> are my suggestions). The beatified soul sees the divine light both as the medium and as the object and is aware of seeing it.

93. "Item de differentia contemplatiuorum . . . uisio autem contemplantis ad quid est extenditur sursum et est intellectus. Non uidet quod habet nec quod in se habet licet in eo sit"; ibid.

94. "De uisione actiui, nota quod uidet per opera"; ibid.

95. " In omnibus hiis sit unus presentius alio. Presentius uidet contemplatiuus quam actiuus, plus propheta, plus Christus. Possum dicere 'ego uideo solummodo per se.' Hic primus modus quia in se habet lumen et lux a sole. Item lucem uideo in se. Item uideo colorem quod habet naturam lucis per se et hoc uariis modis. Item uideo per speculum hic duplex lumen. Item uideo per lunam hic lineas respectu uisionis et reflexus respectu solis uideo. Etiam per candelam, per carbunculum . . . et cornu noctue"; ibid.

96. "Item Romanos 1 *Inuisibilia dei a creatura per ea que facta sunt intellecta conspiciuntur,* ibi Glossa: 'Tria genera uisionis in Scripturis inueniuntur: corporalis, spiritualis, intellectualis. De tercio genere est hec uisio quam hic commemorat apostolus.' Ergo philosophi cognouerunt Deum intellectuali uisione. Ergo fuerunt rapti usque ad tercium celum sicut paulus. Item angeli uident deum, paulus in raptu uidet deum, philosophi per creaturas uiderunt deum, sancti per contemplationem uident deum. Item omnes fideles secundum fidem uident deum. Item prophete uiderunt deum. Quam differentiam inter omnes istas uisiones?"; Hugh of St. Victor, "Il ms. Douai Bibliothéque Municipale 434/II e la questio N. 480 *De raptu,*" 193. For the parallel paragraph in Hugh's commentary, see ibid., 182. For the text of the gloss, see Peter Lombard, *Collectanea in omnes epistolas divi Pauli apostoli, Glossa in Ep. ad Rom.*, 1:20, PL 191:1328.

97. Hugh of St. Victor, "Il ms. Douai Bibliothéque Municipale 434/II e la questio N. 480 *De raptu*," 198–99.

98. Bourguignon, "Introduction," 5.

99. On William of Auvergne, see Franco Morenzoni and Jean-Yves Tilliette, eds., *Autour de Guillaume d'Auvergne, [mort en] 1249: Texte imprimé* (Turnhout: Brepols, 2005). A partial description of William of Auvergne's dealing with rapture is provided in Faes de Mottoni, "Guglielmo d'Alvernia e l'anima rapita," in ibid., 55–74.

100. William of Auvergne, *De anima*, GOO 2:191–93. Cf. William of Auvergne, *De retributionibus sanctorum*, GOO 1:315.

101. Alexander of Hales, *De visione vel cognitione Dei in patria, De cognitione Dei activa et passiva*, Bologna Univ. 2554, fols. 86va–90rb; Doucet, "Prolegomena," SH, 4:178.

102. Schlosser devoted Chapter 4 in her *Lucerna in caliginoso loco* to the similarities and dissimilarities scholastic theologians found between exegetes and theologians and prophecy but did not wish to interpret the existence of this comparison further.

103. Roland of Cremona, SR 337, 999.

104. Quoted in McGinn, *The Growth of Mysticism*, 333.

105. Caesar of Heisterbach, *Caesarius Heiserbacencis monachi ordinis Cisterciensis Dialogus miraculorum* 8.1, ed. Joseph Strange (Cologne: Heberle, 1851), 2:82–83.

106. Ibid., 8.4, 2:85.

107. See, for instance, Thomas's treatment of the problem of natural prophecy and natural disposition for prophecy in his *Quaestio de prophetia*, articles 3–4 (Disputed Questions on Truth).

2. HOW COULD PAUL REMEMBER HIS RAPTURE?

1. Erica Bourguingnon, "Introduction: A Framework for the Comparative Study of Altered States of Consciousness," in *Religion, Altered States of Consciousness and Social Change*, ed. Erica Bourguignon (Columbus: Ohio State University Press, 1973), 12–13.

2. William of Auxerre, *Summa aurea* [SA] 3.37.3, ed. Jean Ribaillier, in *Spicilegium Bonaventurianum* (Paris: Grottaferrata, 1986), 3:706–8.

Richard of St. Victor addresses the subject of memories from rapture and ecstatical experiences several times, noting the varieties of cases in which some can and some cannot recall what they have seen on their return to themselves, Richard of St. Victor, *The Twelve Patriarchs: The Mystical Ark, Book Three of the Trinity* 4:23, 5:1, trans., introduction Grover A. Zinn (New-York: Paulist, 1979), 306, 309–12. As noted in the end of the previous chapter, however, his work is almost absent from this academic discourse.

3. William of Auxerre, SA 3.37.3, 3:708.

4. "ὁρισμὸς δ'ἐπειδὴ λέγεται εἶναι λόγος τοῦ τί ἐστι, φανερὸν ὅτι ὁ μέν τις ἔσται λόγος τοῦ τί σημαίνει τὸ ὄνομα ἢ λόγος ἕτερος ὀνοματώδης, οἷον τί

σημαίνει [τί ἐστι] τρίγωνον"; Aristotle, *Posterior Analytics* 2.10, 93b30. The Greek might also be read as if the "or" is not between *onoma* and *logos heteros*, but between both *logoi*,—of "what the name signifies," and another, "nominal."

5. Aristotle, *Analytica Posteriora*, ed. Laurentius Minio-Paluello and Bernardus G. Dod, Aristoteles Latinus IV 1–4 (Bruges: Desclée de Brouwer, 1954), 83. John of Toledo chose "*verbum alterum pro nomine positum*" (ibid., 167), and Gerard of Cremona "*sermo positus vice nominis, sicut sermo exponens nomen*" (ibid., 261). William of Moerbecke had later rendered the old translation of "*ratio altera nomina ponens*" simply as "*ratio altera nominalis*" (ibid., 329).

6. Aristotle, *Physics* 2.1, 193a5–9. I thank Dr. Orna Harari for this reference. The Latin translator rendered this passage as follows: "Demonstrare autem manifesta per inmanifesta non possibile iudicare est propter ipsum et non propter ipsum cognitum. Quod autem contingat hoc pati, non inmanifestum est; sillogizabit enim utique aliquis cum natus sit cecus de coloribus; quare necesse est huiusmodi de nominibus inesse rationem, nichil autem intelligere"; Aristotle, Physica, *Translatio vetus*, ed. Fernand Bossier and Jozef Brams, Aristoteles Latinus VII, 1 (Leiden and New York: Brill, 1990), 45.

7. "Ad hoc dicimus quod non potuit illud reducere ad memoriam; tamen potuit illud ad reminiscentiam, quoniam potuit de illa reminisci. Intellectus enim potest reminisci, quamvis non possit memorari"; Roland of Cremona, *Summa Magistri Rolandi Cremonensis O.P. Liber Tercius* [SR] 3, Editio princeps, ed. Alois Cortesi (Bergamo: Monumenta Bergomensia, 1962), 992.

8. Aristotle, *On Memory* 451a15: "Quid igitur est memoria et memorari dictum est, quoniam fantasmatis est sicut ymaginis et cuius fantasma habitus est, et cuius partium que sunt in nobis, quia primi sensibilis quod tempore sentimus." The Latin translation of Jacobus Venetus is taken from the draft edition of Silvia Donati in the *Aristoteles Latinus Database*, Brepols, http://www.brepols.net/Pages/ShowProduct. aspx?prod_id=IS-9782503511108-1, accessed December 2015. A future edition for the Aristoteles Latinus series (14:1–2) is being prepared by David Bloch.

9. Aristotle, *On Memory* 449b9–23.

10. Roland of Cremona, SR 3.340, 994.

11. "Facile esset, et absque aliqua dubitatione, dicere quod Paulus vidisset Deum sine aliquibus ymaginibus, et illa archana, si solum possemus videre quomodo potuit recolere que vidisset, magnum esset. Nec auctoritates nec ipsa ratio patitur ut dicamus quod viderit illa per ymaginem"; ibid.

12. Ibid., 996.

13. Ibid., 993, 996–97.

14. "Quomodo rediens ad statum suum potuit recordari eorum que uidit in raptu. Solutio. In uisione naturali et prophetica spiritualis habitus necessarius est, et preter habitum necessaria est species qua mediante procedit cognitio. Sed in illo speculo eternitatis nulla species est necessaria. Ex parte tamen uidentis

fuit habitus, scilicet ex parte pauli, et ita non fuit simile de hac uisione et aliis"; Hugh of St. Cher, Douai, BM 434 II, f. 96ra.

15. "Illud enim lumen infusum in raptu, post raptum coniectum fuit fidei, et factum est minus lumen, et ideo in actum suum exire non potuit. Dicendum ergo quod secundum illum habitum fuit recordatio uisorum in raptu et forsitam non plena omnium nec obstat de sompniantibus qui eorum que uiderunt non recordantur quondam. Cum ergo illorum fit ex communi sensu qui plenus est formis, nec possunt recordari quoniam non fit impressio in sensu singulari. Paulum autem fuit recordari propter utilitatem ecclessie"; ibid.

16. Hugh of St. Cher, *De raptu*, ed. Barbara Faes de Mottoni, "Il ms. Douai Bibliothéque Municipale 434/II e la questio N. 480 *De raptu*," *AHDLMA* 73, no. 1 (2006): 200–201.

17. Guerric of St. Quentin, "Quarto, an fides mansit in illo raptu; Quinto, quomodo habuit memoriam eorum que uidit in illo raptu"; MS Prague, Univ. IV D 13, f. 58ra.

18. "Si obicitur quomodo induitur illa uisio ymaginibus, respondeo: in uerbo ubi illa uidit uidit que illa induere talibus, talibus et talibus ymaginibus, et uidit ibi ymagines quibus debuit induere uisa et uidendo induit. Unde cum ymagines uidit in primo non oportuit quod per conuersionem ad ipsas auerteretur adeo"; ibid., f. 58vb.

19. Charles S. Peirce, *The Writings of Charles S. Peirce: A Chronological Edition*, ed. Max H. Fisch (Bloomington: Indiana University Press, 1982), 2:53–54.

20. Roland wrote his *Summa* only after he left Paris to Toulouse—that is, in the mid 1230s; Odon Lottin, "Roland de Crémone et Hugues de Saint-Cher," *RTAM* 12 (1940): 136–43.

21. "[Francis] wondered anxiously what this vision could mean, and his soul was uneasy as it searched for understanding. And as his understanding sought in vain for an explanation and his heart was filled with perplexity at the great novelty of this vision, the marks of nails began to appear in his hands and feet, just as he had seen them slightly earlier in the crucified man above him"; Thomas Celano, *Vita Prima, Vita Secunda, et Tractatus de Miraculis* 2.3:94, in *Analecta Franciscana* (Rome: Quaracchi, 1926–41), 10:72. Hereafter David Burr's translation, *Medieval Sourcebook*, at http://www.fordham.edu/halsall/source/stfran-lives.html.

22. Bernard McGinn, *The Flowering of Mysticism: Men and Women in the New Mysticism*, vol. 3 of *The Presence of God: A History of Western Christian Mysticism* (New York: Crossroad, 1998), 38.

23. "Nec mireris si non aperte possumus videre qualiter Paulus potuit, cum ad se rediit, de his que vidit ratiocinari, quoniam intellectus humanus, qui fuit tunc ad tempus glorificatus, maioris virtutis fuit quam possimus ad presens considerari"; Roland of Cremona, SR 3, ed. Cortesi, 997.

24. On twelfth-century instruction in the art of defining, see John of Salisbury, *Metalogicon: The Metalogicon of John of Salisbury; A Twelfth-Century*

Defense of the Verbal and Logical Arts of the Trivium 2.6, trans., introduction, and notes Daniel McGarry (Gloucester, Mass.: Peter Smith, 1971), 85.

25. The introduction poses the question "What is love?" in a scholastic manner. It is followed by the definition "Love is an inborn suffering...," which is then analyzed into its parts; Andreas Capellanus, *De Amore: Andreas Capellanus on Love* 1.1, ed., trans. Patrick G. Walsh (London: Duckworth, 1982), 32–33.

26. Claude Lafleur, ed., in collaboration with Joanne Carrier, *Le "Guide de l'étudiant" d'un maître anonyme de la faculté des arts de Paris au XIIIe siècle*, Édition critique provisoire du ms. Barcelona, Arxiu de la Corona d'Aragó, Ripoll 109, ff. 134ra–58va (Québec: Université Laval, 1992), 57n86.

27. Alexander of Hales, *Summa theologica seu sic ab origine dicta "Summa Fratris Alexandri"* [SH] 1, Tractatus introductorius, ed. Bernardini Klumper, Victorin Doucet. and the Quaracchi Fathers (Rome: Collegii S. Bonaventurae, 1924), 1:8.

28. Cassiodorus, *Expositio Psalmorum*, Prologue, ed. M. Adriaen, CCSL 97–98 (Turnhout: Brepols, 1958), 1:7.

29. See also William J. Conlan, "The Definition of Faith according to a Question of MS. Assisi 138: Study and edition of Text," in *Essays in Honour of Anton Charles Pegis*, ed. J. Reginald O'Donnell (Toronto: Pontifical Institute of Mediaeval Studies, 1974), 17–69.

30. Philip the Chancellor, *Philippi Cancellarii Summa de bono* [SB], ed. Nikolaus Wicki, 2 vols. (Bern: Francke, 1985), passim.

31. Jean de la Rochelle, *Summa de anima*, ed. Jacques Guy Bougerol, Textes philosophiques du moyen âge XIX (Paris: Vrin, 1995), 52–62 ("quid sit anima secundum diffinicionem").

32. Alexander of Hales, SH 3.3.2.1.5, 1:1072.

33. Cf. Philip the Chancellor, SB, 2:618; Jean-Pierre Torrell, *Théorie de la prophétie et philosophie de la connaissance aux environs de 1230: La contribution d'Hugues de Saint-Cher (Ms. Douai 434, Question 481)* (Leuven: Spicilegium Sacrum Lovaniense, 1977), 3.

34. On the multiple meanings of *experientia* and *experimentum*, their overlap and distinction throughout the Middle Ages, see the discussion held in John E. Murdoch and Edith D. Sylla, eds., *The Cultural Context of Medieval Learning: Proceedings of the First International Colloquium on Philosophy, Science and Theology in the Middle Ages*, September 1973 (Dordrecht: Reidel, 1975), 265–68. Different studies of this vocabulary since antiquity through Galileo to Hegel are gathered in Marco Veneziani, ed., *Experientia: X Colloquio internazionale Roma 4–6 gennaio 2001* (Florence: Olschki, 2002). More on *experientia* and *experimentum* to come.

35. "Unde et infelix ego luteam domum inhabitans, de tam suavi tam excellentie manifestationis dulcedine quod ego non gustavi, aliis eructare non possum. Verumtamen de hoc manifestationis genere ab aliis instructus accepi

ego phamas has animae omnino a terrenis suspensae et aeternorum desiderio adeo inflammatae"; Herbert of Bosham, *Liber melorum*, PL 190:1369.

36. Examples from students' life in biblical commentaries were used by John Baldwin as windows into their world in *Masters, Princes and Merchants: The Social Views of Peter the Chanter and His Circle* (Princeton: Princeton University Press, 1970), but in questions they are rarely found. Sermons are naturally richer in exempla. Nevertheless, in order to understand better their authoritative value, there is a need of qualitative and quantitative assessment of such references to experiences in such texts.

37. Stephen de Bourbon, *Tractatus de diversis materiis*, ed. Albert Lecoy de La Marche, in *Anecdotes Historiques, légendes et apologues, tirés du recueil inédit d'Etienne de Bourbon* (Paris: Henri Loones, 1877), 251–52. The source of this story, according to de Bourbon, is a sermon of Nicholas de Flavigny, a master of theology active in the 1220s.

38. Ecstasy itself, as I shall show, was regarded as a source of information about the nature of the soul, but the information, that is "what" the visionaries saw had no place. This may also be the way Hugh of St. Victor's words on the subject to which Ian P. Wei referred (*Intellectual Culture in Medieval Paris* [Cambridge: Cambridge University Press, 2012], 119) should be read.

39. Tocco, in *Fontes vitae sancti Thomae Aquinatis notis historicis et criticis illustrati*, ed. Domenicus Prümmer and M. H. Laurent (Toulouse: Saint Maximin, 1912), 119.

40. Robert Lerner, "Ecstatic Dissent," *Speculum* 67, no. 1 (1992): 33–57.

41. See Jacqueline Hamesse, "Experientia/experimentum dans les lexiques médiévaux et dans les textes philosophiques antérieurs au 14e-siècle," in *Experientia: X Colloquio internazionale, Roma, 4–6 gennaio 2001*, ed. Marco Veneziani (Florence: Olschki, 2002), 77–90. As she points out, the history of *experimentum* in the medical discourse is yet to be written. In their introduction to the volume *Expertus sum*, Draelants and Bénatouïl point out that the medieval concept of *experientia* was used not only in the natural context but with regard to spiritual phenomena and creatures as well; Thomas Bénatouïl and Isabelle Draelants, eds., *Expertus sum: L'expérience par les sens dans la philosophie naturelle médiévale* (Florence: SISMEL Edizioni del Galuzzo, 2011), 6. All three parts of the volume, however, focus on natural philosophy, the occult, and medicine.

42. Peter King, "Two Conceptions of Experience," *Medieval Philosophy and Theology* 11, no. 2 (2003): 203–26.

43. Two collections of articles were devoted to the medieval concept of experience in recent years: Alexander Fidora and Matthias Lutz-Bachmann, eds., *Erfahrung und Beweis: Die Wissenschaften von der Natur im 13. und 14. Jahrhundert / Experience and Demonstration: The Sciences of Nature in the 13th and 14th Centuries* (Berlin: Akademie Verlag, 2006), and Bénatouïl and Draelants, *Expertus sum*. On Grosseteste, see Alistair Cameron Crombie, *Robert Grosseteste*

and the Origins of Experimental Science, 1100–1700 (Oxford: Clarendon, 1953), which provoked a lively debate after its publication. A summary of its main points can be found at Crombie, "Grosseteste's Position in the History of Science," in *Robert Grosseteste: Scholar and Bishop*, ed. Daniel A. P. Callus (Oxford: Clarendon, 1955), 98–120. Peter King's article, cited previously, refers to William of Ockham in this respect as well. On Roger Bacon and optics with regard to this issue, see Nicholas W. Fisher and Sabetai Unguru, "Experimental Science and Mathematics in Roger Bacon's Thought," *Traditio* 27 (1971): 353–78; Unguru, "Experiment in Medieval Optics," in *Physics, Cosmology and Astronomy 1300–1700: Tension and Accommodation*, ed. Sabetai Unguru (Dordrecht: Kluwer Academic, 1991), 163–81; Klaus Hedwig, "Roger Bacon's *Scientia experimentalis*," in *Philosophen des Mittelalters*, ed. Theo Kobush (Darmstadt: Primus, 2000), 140–51; and Jeremiah Hackett, "Experientia, experimentum and Perception of Objects in Space: Roger Bacon," in *Raum und Raumvorstellungen im Mittelalter*, ed. Jan Aersten and Andreas Speer (Berlin: Walter de Gruyter, 1998), 101–20.

44. Lynn Thorndike, *A History of Magic and Experimental Science*, 8 vols. (New York: Columbia University Press, 1923).

45. Bénatouïl and Draelants, *Expertus sum*, 4.

46. See in particular Draelants, "Expérience et autorités dans la philosophie naturelle d'Albert le Grand," in Bénatouïl and Draelants, *Expertus sum*, 89–122, where the exact meaning and value of statements such as *"expertus sum"* are carefully examined.

47. "Quidam est ut sciamus ratiocinari, et quidam est ut sciamus rerum naturas, sicut est alkimia, per ipsam enim experimentamur nos de naturis rerum"; Daniel A. Callus, "The Powers of the Soul: An Early Unpublished Text," *RTAM* 19 (1952): 160.

48. On Bernard's extensive use of the verb *experiri*, see Brian Stock, "Some Observations on Bernard of Clairvaux," in *The Cultural Context of Medieval Learning: Proceedings of the First International Colloquium on Philosophy, Science and Theology in the Middle Ages, September 1973*, 223–25 (Dordrecht: Reidel, 1975), 223–25; Kilian McDonnell, "Spirit and Experience in Bernard of Clairvaux," *Theological Studies* 58 (1997): 3–18.

49. Stock, "Some Observations," 223.

50. Ibid. On Bernard's "book of experience," Augustine's opposition between word and experience, and the change from mysticism of sensual experience to mysticism of non-experience, see also Bernard McGinn, "The Language of Inner Experience in Christian Mysticism," *Spiritus* 1, no. 2 (2001): 156–71.

51. Thorndike, *A History of Magic and Experimental Science*, 2:338–71; Antonella Sannino, "Guillaume d'Auvergne e i *libri experimentorum*," in Bénatouïl and Draelants, *Expertus sum*, 67–88.

52. William of Auvergne, *De anima*, in *Guilielmi Alverni Opera Omnia* [GOO] (Paris, 1674), 2:99. William does not relate to the problem of Paul's recollection at all.

53. "Respondeo in hoc quia quemadmodum in omnibus doctrinis et disciplinis adiuvamur testimoniis et experientia sensuum, sic et hic: a sensu enim animarum quibus istae irradiationes fiunt ostenditur certitudo immortalitatis earum"; ibid., 194.

54. William of Auxerre, SA 3.12.1, 3:199.

55. Boyd Taylor Coolman, *Knowing God by Experience: The Spiritual Senses in the Theology of William of Auxerre* (Washington, D.C.: The Catholic University of America Press, 2004).

56. "Sicut est differentia magna inter cognitionem illius qui cognoscit dulcedinem mellis qui gustavit, et cognitionem illius qui numquam gustavit aliquam dulcedinem sed tantum audivit verba de dulcedine, ita differt intellectus Pauli quo intelligebat creatorem, ab illo intellectu quo intelligebat Aristoteles; similiter dicendum est de sapientia, Unde quem habuit Aristoteles de creatore fuit vanus et non solidus, et quem habuit de angelis; unde et nullum [multum] herravit in sermone de angelis in libro de pura bonitate. Unde idem Aristoteles dicit quod omnis vera scientia intellectiva fit ita quod precedat experientia; in Paulo fuit experientia illorum, non in Aristotele"; Roland of Cremona, SR 3, 921.

57. "Sine experientia enim non habetur ars vel scientia, et omnis intellecta cognitio ex preexistenti cognitione sensitiva fit Sicut enim qui nunquam gustavit mel, nunquam habet veridicam scientiam de sapore eius, et qui nunquam vidit colores, nunquam habet scientia eorum, quia pereunte uno sensu perit et demonstratio, ita qui non est exercitatus in operibus fidei formate, theologie agnitionem non habet, et tamen scit loqui de theologia. Similiter et cecus natus scit loqui de coloribus, et tamen scientiam eorum non habet"; Roland of Cremona, SR, Prologue, ed. Giuseppe Cremascoli, *Studi Medievali* 16 (1975): 867.

58. Roland of Cremona, SR 3.315, 921.

59. "Dicendum ergo quod non uidet immediate nisi perfectus. Sed perfectus potest esse aliquis uel ex parte intelligentie, ita quod non ex parte uite licet sit bonus. Et talis potest habere uisionem immediatam, tamen potest exercitari in scripturis, et talis uisio est per medium auditus, non gustus uel uisus . . . et hoc est uisio litteratorum. Aliquando est perfectus in uita set simplex in intelligencia. Et talis potest uenire ad immediatam uisionem que est per medium experientie. Et sic multi simplices sapiunt plus quam sapientes et habent certitudinem experientie. Et horum est non raptus proprie. . . . Aliquando est perfectus ad utrumque et talium est proprie raptus"; Padova, Pontificia Bibliotheca Antoniana 152, f. 158ra–rb.

60. On the Augustinian and Avicennian traditions on memory and their assimilation, see Magdalena Bieniak, *The Soul-Body Problem at Paris, ca. 1200–1250: Hugh of St. Cher and His Contemporaries*, Ancient and Medieval Philosophy Series 1.42 (Leuven: Leuven University Press, 2010), Chapter 2.3.

61. Celano, *Vita Prima, Vita Secunda, et Tractatus de Miraculis*, part 2, 64:98, *Analecta Franciscana* 10:188.

3. CAN A SOUL SEE GOD OR ITSELF WITHOUT INTERMEDIARIES?

1. *Chartularium Universitatis Parisiensis* [CUP] I, no. 128, ed. Heinrich Denifle, Emile Chatelain, Charles Samaran, and Émile A. van Moé (Brussells: Culture et civilisation, 1964), 1:170–72, dates to 1241; reprint of Paris: Delalain, 1889–91. Victorin Doucet proposed a later date in "La date des condamnations Parisiennes dites de 1241: Faut-il corriger le cartulaire de l'Université?," in *Mélanges Auguste Pelzer: Études d'histoire littéraire et doctrinale de la scolastique médiévale offertes à Monseigneur Auguste Pelzer à l'occasion de son soixante-dixième anniversaire* (Louvain: Bibliothèque de l'Université Bureaux du "Recueil," 1947), 183–93, and a year later Franz Pelster addressed the issue in "Die Pariser Verurteilung von 1241: Eine Frage der Datierung," *Archivum Fratrum Praedicatorum* 18 (1948): 405–17. Jürgen Miethke believes there were two condemnations, one "internal" among the masters, and a more ceremonial procedure in 1244; Miethke, "Papst, Ortsbichof und Universität in den Pariser Theologenprozessen des 13. Jahrhunderts," in *Die Auseinandersetzungen an der pariser Universität im XIII Jahrhundert*, ed. Albert Zimmermann (Berlin: De Gruyter, 1976), 63. A summary of present knowledge about this condemnation and its date is provided in William J. Courtenay, "Dominicans and Suspect Opinion in the Thirteenth Century: The Cases of Stephen of Venizy, Peter of Tarentaise, and the Articles of 1270 and 1271," *Vivarium* 32 (1994): 186–95, as well as Nathalie Gorochov, *Naissance de l'université: Les écoles de Paris d'Innocent III à Thomas d'Aquin (v. 1200–v. 1245)* (Paris: Champion, 2012), 526–40.

2. His report of the condemnations (referred by him to 1243) follows lengthy complaints on the Preachers and Minorites and their haughty behavior; Matthew Paris, *Chronica maiora: Matthew Paris's English History 1235–1273*, trans. John Allan Giles (New York: AMS, 1968), 1:476.

3. There are indications that ten years before, Pagus had attracted hostility from the circles of William of Auvergne and the royal court. In his epistle of May 6, 1231, Pope Gregory IX implores Louis IX to welcome William of Auxerre, Godfrey of Poitiers, and *Magister Johannes Pagius*, and not to believe false rumors about their fidelity to him (CUP I, no. 90, p. 145). Miethke believes too that existing sources are not sufficient to understand this condemnation and suspects that Odo of Chateauroux had a significant role; Miethke, "Papst, Ortsbichof und Universität in den Pariser Theologenprozessen des 13. Jahrhunderts," 66.

4. Hyacinthe-François Dondaine, "L'objet et le 'medium' de la vision béatifique chez les théologiens du XIIIe siècle," *RTAM* 19 (1952): 60–130; P. M. de Contenson, "Avicennisme latin et vision de Dieu au début du XIIIe siècle," *AHDLMA* 26 (1959): 29–97; Contenson, "La théologie de la vision de Dieu au début du XIIIe siècle: Le *De retributionibus sanctorum* de Guillaume d'Auvergne et la condamnation de 1241," *RSPT* 46 (1962): 409–44. More recently Christian Trottmann published a monumental monograph on the issue of beatific vision in which he includes a long discussion of the 1241 condemnations and subse-

quent developments of this problematics; Trottmann, *La vision béatifique: Des disputes scolastiques à sa définition par Benoît XII* (Rome: École française de Rome, 1995), 175 ff.

5. The lively interest in Eriugena in the 1220s is attested by Honorius III's order to burn every copy of the book—"idem liber, sicut accepimus, in nonnullis monasteriis et aliis locis habetur, et nonnulli cluastrales et viri scholastici . . . se studiosius occupant dicti libri"; CUP I, no. 50, p. 107.

6. Dondaine, "L'objet et le 'medium' de la vision béatifique chez les théologiens du XIIIe siècle," 60.

7. Ibid., 92.

8. Ibid., 94ff. On the concept of infinity, see also Anne Ashley Davenport, *Measure of a Different Greatness: The Intensive Infinite, 1250–1650* (Leiden and Boston: Brill, 1999); Antoine Côté, *L'infinité divine dans la théologie médiévale, 1220–1255* (Paris: Vrin, 2002).

9. Contenson, "Avicennisme latin et vision de Dieu au début du XIIIe siècle."

10. Ibid., 46.

11. Contenson, "La théologie de la vision de Dieu."

12. Ibid., 440 ff.

13. Trottmann, *La vision béatifique*, 185–87.

14. "Nota quod omnes dubitationes incidentes circa fidem aut incidunt ex parte credentis, aut ex parte crediti, aut ex parte medii habitus qui est inter credentem et creditum, ut patere potest subtiliter inspicienti"; Alexander of Hales, *Glossa in quatuor libros Sententiarum Petri Lombardi* [GS] 3 d., ed. the Quaracchi Fathers, Bibliotheca Franciscana scholastica medii aevi, t. 12–15 (Quaracchi, Florence: Collegii S. Bonaventurae, 1954), 3:262.

15. For William, see the prospectus he provided at the beginning of William of Auxerre, *Summa aurea* [SA] 3.12, ed. Jean Ribaillier, in *Spicilegium Bonaventurianum* (Paris: Grottaferrata, 1986, 3:196, as well as the body of the text; For Roland of Cremona, see the list of contents provided at the beginning of Roland of Cremona, *Summa Magistri Rolandi Cremonensis O.P. Liber Tercius* [SR] 3, Editio princeps, ed. Alois Cortesi (Bergamo: Monumenta Bergomensia, 1962), 287. The text has no numbered division, but "consequenter queritur" and the like that accord with the general prospectus. Hugh of St. Cher presents in the commentary the order of Peter Lombard's questions and then heads to another series of questions arranged differently: "Accedamus ad questiones fidei, et hic possunt queri x in universo"; Padova Univ. 853, fol. 93ra. Philip's plan is in Philip the Chancellor, *Philippi Cancellarii Summa de bono* [SB], ed. Nikolaus Wicki (Bern: Francke, 1985), 2:561–62. The plan of the *Summa Halensis* was reconstructed according to Alexander of Hales, *Summa theologica seu sic ab origine dicta "Summa Fratris Alexandri"* [SH] 3.3.2, ed. Bernardini Klumper, Victorin Doucet, and the Quaracchi Fathers (Rome: Collegii S. Bonaventurae), 2:1062ff.

16. Perhaps one can detect an earlier stage in this evolution in William of Auxerre by his perception of "faith" principally as a habitus rather than as

"Christian faith" in general, encompassing all theological material. Berndt suggests, "Guillaume d'Auxerre . . . ne connaît la fides que comme la principle des vertus théologales. Cependant, il intègre dans son traité de la fois un chapitre sur les articuli fidei et sur la question de la conaissance de dieu"; Rainer Berndt, "La théologie comme système du monde: Sur l'évolution des sommes théologiques de Hughes de Saint-Victor à Saint Thomas d'Aquin," *RSPT* 78, no. 4 (1994): 571, n. 72.

17. *RSPT* 78, no. 4 (1994): Dewan, "'*Obiectum*': Notes on the Invention of a Word," *AHDLMA* 48 (1981): 37–96.

18. I do not expound here on the manner in which this process reflects the views of Philip and the *Summa Halensis* about the nature of this *obiectum*, for this would require a separate analysis of the discussions about the nature of *enuntiabilia* and its twelfth-century nominalist and realist background. In all the questions in the category of *obiectum fidei*, both Philip and the *Summa Halensis* take the position that the articles of faith are "*res*" rather than statements or *enuntiabilia*. They insist that the object of faith is the first truth, which is simple, necessary, and uncreated, purified of any aspect of time, complexity or language. Articles of faith such as "Christ suffered" are complex only when viewed from the cognizer's point of view. "Real" articles are eternal and identical at all times. I believe one of the reasons for propounding this view was the attempt to constitute a continuity and identity between the object of faith and of beatific vision. The interested reader may consult Chenu's pioneering essay "Grammaire et théologie," in Marie-Dominique Chenu, *La théologie au douzième siècle* (Paris: Vrin, 1957), Chap. 4, as well as Iwakuma Yukio, "*Enuntiabilia* in Twelfth-Century Logic and Theology," in *Vestigia, imagines, verba: Semiotics and Logic in Medieval Theological Texts*, ed. Costantino Marmo (Turnhout: Brepols, 1997), and Harm Goris, "Tense Logic in 13th-Century Theology," *Vivarium* 39 (2001): 161–84.

19. Following William of Auxerre (SA 3.42.2, 3:805). In this tractate, which regards the transition from faith to beatific vision, William boldly claims that medium is not a *differens* at all—seeing a white thing through a mirror and seeing it directly are not different *in specie*. Yet, in other places he does treat faith as vision. On these two options, see also Chap. 4.

20. "In visione fidei et speciei, quod videtur Deus est, videns intellectus. Unde medium differt et ideo, cum medium sit ratio visionis, facit formalem et specificam differentiam. Videns enim et quod videtur sunt materia visionis, hoc sicut obiectum, illud sicut subiectum, et ideo non faciunt differre visionem secundum speciem"; *Guerric of Saint-Quentin*, Quodlibet 2, "Utrum visio fidei differat secundum speciem a visione patriae," in *Guerric of Saint-Quentin: Quaestiones de quolibet*, ed. Walter H. Principe and Jonathan Glenn Black, introduction Jean-Pierre Torrell (Toronto: Pontifical Institute of Mediaeval Studies, 2002), 198.

21. William of Auxerre, SA 3.37.3, 3:704.

22. Ibid., 3:705.
23. William of Auxerre, SA 3.37.3, 3:707.
24. Ibid., 2.6.4, 2:136.
25. "Cum anima sit potens intelligere omnia et omnia sint potentialiter intelligibilia ei per irradiationem lucis … de potentia intelligente fiet actu intelligens, et que potentia erant intelligibilia, fient actu intellecta, et non quedam solum sed omnia; et ita in lumine speculi eterni videbit anima omnia actu illuminata; ergo et angelus ibi videt omnia"; William of Auxerre, SA 2.6.2, quest. 2, 2:132.
26. Philip the Chancellor, SB, 2:513.
27. Jean-Pierre Torrell, *Théorie de la prophétie et philosophie de la connaissance aux environs de 1230: La contribution d'Hugues de Saint-Cher (Ms. Douai 434, Question 481)* (Leuven: Spicilegium Sacrum Lovaniense, 1977), 10. On the voluntary character of the mirror, again equated with a book, see also William of Auvergne: "Et huiusmodi exemplum licet incogitabilis dissimilitudinis est liber innumerabilium foliorum sive voluminum, quem qui tenet in manu et apertit et ostendit inspectori quodcumque vult ex foliis vel voluminibus, exempli gratia versum unum vel plura vel forte dimidium"; *De anima, Guilielmi Alverni Opera Omnia* [GOO] (Paris, 1674), 2:212. For metaphors of mirror and book regarding the intellect, see 2:215.
28. William of Auvergne, *De anima*, GOO 2:212.
29. "Angeli vident res existentes in proprio genere per medium. Sed distinguendum est duplex medium, videlicet medium quo et medium per quod. Medium per quod ipse est intellectus, quia per hoc quod assimilatur Deo ultima assimilatione est expressa ymago omnium et expressum speculum omnium. Unde per se ipsum sine speculo et sine alia ymagine, quando vult dirigere aciem supra res ipsas, potest eas videre, et ipsa directio est medium quo eas videt distincte actu, et in hoc consistit libertas eius. … Videt ergo angelus per duplex medium, scilicet per speculum quod ipse est, licet universale, et per medium quo discernitur eius visio, id est per directionem aciei intellectus super rem … et hoc modo videbit anima quando erit in gloria, dum erit plene speculum intelligibile, sicut dicit quidam philosophus"; William of Auxerre, SA 2.6.4, 2:137. Although Robert of Melun had already described the divine word as a mirror, the term "speculum eternitatis" appears for the first time in this period; Marianne Schlosser, *Lucerna in caliginoso loco: Aspekte des Prophetie-Begriffes in der scholastischen Theologie* (Paderborn: Schöningh, 2000), 104–13.
30. A similar argument asserts that angels cannot see simultaneously everything *in actu*. See, for instance, the anonymous author of *quaestio* 337 in Douai BM 434 who likens it to the latent knowledge of geometry: "Angeli creati sunt perfecti quantum ad potenciam et habitum, non quantum ad actum. Sicut qui didicit geometriam habet habitum ad ea que sunt geometrie, non tamen actum habet omnium singularium, licet habeat habitum uniuersalem ad omnia que sunt geometrie, et ita in angelo, ut potencia exeat in actum exigitur ordinatio

dei uel voluntas"; Douai BM 434 II, fol. 11va. William of Auxerre prefers to name this mechanism an *acies*.

31. Torrell, *Théorie de la prophétie*.

32. "Similiter et [speculum] imprimit cognitionis habitum quantum expedit ipsi exemplari conformem, per quod cognoscit et intelligit propheta id quod Deus vult et quantum Deus vult et non aliud nec amplius"; Philip the Chancellor, SB, 2:513. Cf. Hugh of St. Cher, in Torrell, *Théorie de la prophétie*, 30.

33. Dondaine, "L'objet et le 'medium' de la vision béatifique chez les théologiens du XIIIe siècle," 106–17.

34. Quaestio no. 9 is identical with no. 531 in the same collection, except that in its first appearance it is presented with this prologue: "Cum supra de Dei visione in gloria determinaverimus secundum modum rei vise in natura divina vel humana et secundum modum rei videntis angeli vel hominis, restat hic ut de natura medii per quod vidimus aliqua secundum potestatem nostram probabilia determinemus"; ibid., 107.

35. Ibid., 108.

36. Ibid.

37. Hugh of St. Victor, *Commentariorium in Hierarchiam Coelestem S. Dionysii*, PL 175:954–55. The critical edition is *Hugonis de Sancto Victore Super Ierarchiam Dionysii* II.1, ed. Dominic Poirel, CCCM 178 (Turnhout: Brepols, 2015), 443–44.

38. Dondaine, "L'objet et le 'medium' de la vision béatifique chez les théologiens du XIIIe siècle," 111.

39. "Ad illud: *similes ei erimus*, dicimus quod est triplex similitudo. Quandoque dicitur similitudo quando aliqua sunt similia in hoc quod habent aliquam communem qualitatem que est in illis. Talis non est similitudo in patria inter deum et animam. Item dicitur similitudo quantum ad aliquid quod est inter utrumque extremorum, et non est in utroque per inherentiam. Et hec similitudo erit in patria, et erit amor coniungens amantem cum amato. Et erit hic (?) amor in anima ut subiecto, in deo ut in causa, et ita non erit in utroque per inherentiam. Erit tamen in utroque, sed in anima tantum per inherentiam, in deo per causam. Tercio modo dicitur similitudo idolum rei ex re visa relictum in oculo. Hec similitudo non erit in patria, quoniam si esset ibi infinita occurerent ydola, quoniam unum prout est sapientia, alium prout bonitas et sic de aliis"; Douai BM 434 I, fol. 96va.

40. "Ad aliud quod obicit de luce corporali dicendum quod, licet immediate se faciat in oculo, non mediante altero extrinseco, tamen nihilominus exigitur debita dispositio in organo ad hoc quod fiat in eo. Similiter dico quod oportet ex parte illa. Licet enim Deus seipso sit cognoscibilis et amabilis, tamen oportet esse debitam dispositionem a parte anime et hoc non est ex impotentia ipsius lucis, sed magis ex impotentia anime"; Toulouse, Bib. Mun. 737 f. 156vb. See also Nikolaus Wicki, *Die Lehre von der himmlischen Seligkeit in der mittelalterlichen*

Scholastik von Petrus Lombardus bis Thomas von Aquin (Freiburg, Switzerland: Universitätsverlag, 1954), 77, no. 61.

41. William of Auvergne, *De retributionibus*, GOO 1:317.

42. "Non ergo sola veritatis sue presentia illam cognoscimus, sed sua irradiatione super animas nostras ... non presentia essentialis aut propinquitas perficit cognitionem, sed impressio similitudinis"; ibid, 318.

43. "Si quis autem dicat quia juxta hoc quod dicimus non deus ipse videbitur ab anima humana in patria sed imago ejus, quam diximus, licet Arist. ad hoc respondisse in libro suo de anima, ubi dicit quod imago leonis picta duobus modis considerari potest, videlicet, ut imago leonis et ut res"; ibid. An analogy for a picture is made in Aristotle, *De memoria* 450b20, but I found no lions there. William of Durham, a contemporary master who left only few works, employs the same distinction between an image of the lion as a thing in itself and as an image of something else his *quaestio de intellectu*: "Sed anima infidelis qualiter concipit, hoc est uidere in pictura leonis quam aspiciens puer terretur, si adultus non. Ita est de anima so accipiat simpliciter similitudinem dei non mouetur. Si ut similitudinem dei, mouebitur. Sic igitur patet quod eadem est similitudo et tamen sic accepta mouet, et sic non mouet"; Douai BM 434 II, fol. 164ra. The soul that sees itself just as a soul, rather than as God's image, would not be motivated by what it sees, whereas the soul that does see the image as image of something else—God—is.

44. CUP I, no. 50 pp. 106–7. Hostiensis's testimony is quoted there, p. 107, n. 1.

45. For a description of the manuscript's content, see Bertrand-Georges Guyot, "Quaestiones Guerrici, Alexandri et aliorum magistrorum Parisiensium (Prague, Univ. IV. D. 13)," *Archivum Fratrum Praedicatorum* 32 (1962): 5–125. These *quaestiones* were pubished in Hyacinthe-François Dondaine and Guyot, "Guerric de Saint-Quentin et la condamnation de 1241," *RSPT* 44 (1960): 225–42.

46. "Solutio. Secundum Anselmum in omni visione tria sunt: videns, visum et medium. Unde videbimus in patria per medium non deferens ut modo est aer, sed disponens ut lux est"; Dondaine and Guyot, "Guerric de Saint-Quentin et la condamnation de 1241," 237.

47. Ibid., 237. The discussion that follows concerns the controversial role of love in cognition. Trottmann interprets Guerric's contention that love is the medium as a retreat to a twelfth-century mystic of love in order to avoid the consequences of an Avicennian noetic medium, in "Psycho-somatique de la vision béatifique selon Guerric de saint-Quentin," *RSPT* 78 (1994): 220.

48. Trottmann, "Psycho-somatique," 240–41.

49. Alexander of Hales, SH 2.4.3.4, 2:769.

50. Douai BM 434 II, fol. 96va. Dondaine has already noted that questions 454 and 9 do not truly contradict each other, since the first negates an intermediary between the soul and God while the latter affirms a subjective medium that enables the soul to see God. He, however, did not develop this distinction

further; Dondaine, "L'objet et le 'medium' de la vision béatifique chez les théologiens du XIIIe siècle," 85.

51. "Dicendum quod uerum est quod nulla est creatura que existat tanquam media inter deum et mentem. Tamen est aliqua illuminatio procedens ab deo illuminans mentem ad hoc ut possit peruenire ad cognicionem dei, et cum dicit Augustinus quod *inter mentem et deum* etcetera. accepit mentem illuminatam illa informatione aut dono"; Alexander of Hales, *Quaestio de uisione vel cognitione dei*, Bologna, Univ. 2554, fol. 88ra. On the attribution of this question to Alexander of Hales, see François-Marie Henquinet, "Les questions inédits d'Alexandre de Halès sur les fins dernières," *RTAM* 10 (1938): 72–74.

52. "Primo modo videt solus Deus essentiam divinam"; Alexander, quoted in Dondaine, "L'objet et le 'medium' de la vision béatifique chez les théologiens du XIIIe siècle," 79.

53. "Concedimus quod deus est cognoscibilis ab anima humana. Ad primum obiectum in contrarium, dicendum quod illa auctoritas sic habet intelligi . . . quod lux inaccesibilis ab anima eo modo quo est accesibilis a se ipsa, quo enim modo cognoscit deus se ipsum"; Bologna, Univ. 2554, fol. 87ra.

54. "Triplex est videre: in essentia, in specie, in imaginatione. In essentia solus Deus videt seipsum; in specie cognoscetur a sanctis in patria; in imaginatione modo cognoscitur"; Dondaine and Guyot, "Guerric de Saint-Quentin et la condamnation de 1241," 231. This opinion is attributed to *quidam* in the question on seeing divine essence in Vat. Lat. 691, fol. 62va, edited in Côté, *L'infinité divine dans la théologie médiévale, 1220–1255*, 222–24.

55. John Pagus, commentary on the Sentences 4, d. 49, edited in Johannes Gründel, "Die Sentenzenglosse des Johannes Pagus (circa 1243–1245) in Padua, Bibl. Ant. 139," *Münchener theologische Zeitschrift* 9, no. 3 (1958): 178.

56. Asking "how does faith or *intellectus* see itself?," William of Durham refers first to the traditional contention that "faith sees itself" and to the presence of faith to itself. One of the counterarguments, however, leads to a lengthy, interesting discussion on seeing the divine essence "*in se*," including the familiar arsenal of arguments such as the proportion of finite and infinite, divine simplicity, etc.; Douai BM 434 II, fol. 164rb–va (following original pagination).

57. The sub-question entitled, "Does faith see itself?" occurs in the *quaestio de fide* of Guiard de Laon (no. 500 in Douai 434), in the two parallel *quaestiones de fide* nos. 45 and 501 (though not in their counterpart variation in 530) and in William of Durham's *quaestio de intellectu* (no. 520).

58. "Solutio. Exemplum: si intelligamus lineam habentem potentiam aut naturam lucis, et lux terminatur ad punctum, et ille punctus esset lux habens in se potentiam cognoscitivam, tunc dicerem ille punctus potest uidere lineam istam, aut finitam aut infinitam. Dico ergo quod in quantum uidet fides est principium, sed uidetur in quantum finis linee. In fide est natura luminis, unde signatum est lumen uultus, et habet in se naturam cognoscitiuam. Fides est habitus et perfectio potentie, et sic fides est actiuum (sic!), in quantum uidet,

in quantum uidetur passiuua [sic!]"; Douai BM 434 II, fol. 300b (following Glorieux's pagination): *La "Summa Duacensis" (Douai 434), texte critique avec une introduction et des tables*, ed. Palémon Glorieux, Textes philosophiques du moyen âge 2 (Paris: Vrin, 1955). In *quaestio* 45 this simile appears as well, in a slightly different place and wording; Douai BM 434 I, fol. 46vb.

59. Douai BM 434 II, fol. 164va.

60. "Ad obiecta ergo respondendum, quod sicut potentie et virtutes cognoscuntur per effectus, sic fides humana modo per motum, et sic per sui motus presentiam, sicut humano modo intelligo deum ut agentem, et moventem, et sicut ignem ut calefacientem"; Douai BM 434 II, fol. 299a (following Glorieux's pagination).

61. Thomas Graf, *De subiecto psychico gratiae et virtutum secundum doctrinam scholasticorum usque ad medium saeculum* XIV, Pars 1/1, *De subiecto virtutum cardinalium* (Rome: Herder, 1934).

62. Dondaine, "L'objet et le 'medium' de la vision béatifique chez les théologiens du XIIIe siècle," 108–9.

63. "Prior est essentia quam uirtus, et uirtus quam operatio; in cognitione autem e conuerso: actus enim primi et priores sunt potentiis secundum rationem, ut dicit Philosophus, et finis primus in ratione"; ibid., 110.

64. Aristotle, *On the Soul* 415a17–18; cf. Aristotle, *Metaphysics* 1049b4. It was not difficult to combine this Aristotelian reverse order of investigation with a similar triad taken from Pseudo Dionysius that included essence as well: essence, virtue and operation (essentia; virtus; operatio), Ps. Dionysius, *De coelestia Hierarchia*, c. 11 (for the Latin, see John Scotus Eriugena, *Iohannis Scoti Eriugenae Expositiones in Ierarchiam Coelestem*, ed. Jeanne Barbet (Turnhout: Brepols, 1975), 160.

65. "The Powers of the Soul: An Early Unpublished Text," *RTAM* 19 (1952): 147. Cf. R. A. Gauthier, "Le Traité *De anima et potenciis eius* d'un maître ès Arts (vers 1225)," *RSPT* 66 (1985): 31ff. Both quote Aristotle, *De anima* 415a17–18.

66. William of Auvergne, *De anima*, GOO 2:102.

67. "Nulli intelligenti dubium est quin accidentium sensibilium circumvestitio velut quedam vestis sit substantiae sensibilis sustinentis et portantis illam. Manifestum etiam est quoniam adeo indicant et ostendunt illam ut visis illis dicatur videri, et quoniam visio illorum sive illius, visio ipsius substantiae habeatur, et ab omnibus reputetur. Quomodo igitur non similiter visio accidentium spiritualium seu dispositionum animae humanae visio ipsius substantiae non habebitur et reputabitur et non dicetur?"; ibid., 2:103.

68. "Si sub vestibus et ornatu videret quis regem aliquem quibus rex esse indicaretur et quae regem illum ostenderent, magis diceret regem sibi ostendi per illa, quam abscondi vel operiri"; ibid.

69. See, in particular, the important work of Dag Nikolaus Hasse, *Avicenna's De Anima in the Latin West: The Formation of a Peripatetic Philosophy of the Soul, 1160–1300* (London: Warburg Institute, 2000).

70. Aelred of Rievaulx, *Dialogus de Anima*, in *Aelredi Rievallensis Opera omnia*, ed. Anselm Hoste and Charles H. Talbot. CCCM (Turnhout: Brepols, 1971), 1:685–754.

71. Wei recognized this interesting shift between the twelfth century, abounding with colorful biographic and autobiographical accounts of scholars, and the thirteenth century, in which there were none. But I do not completely agree with the reasons he provides for this shift; Ian P. Wei, "From Twelfth-Century Schools to Thirteenth-Century Universities: The Disappearance of Biographical and Autobiographical Representations of Scholars," *Speculum* 86, no. 1 (2011): 42–78.

72. *Geta*, in *Three Latin Comedies*, ed. Keith A. Bate (Toronto: Pontifical Institute of Mediaeval Studies, 1976), 15–34.

73. John Blund, *Iohannes Blund Tractatus de Anima*, ed. Daniel A. Callus and Richard. W. Hunt, Auctores Britannici Medii Aevi 2 (London: Oxford University Press, 1970), 1: "Nos videmus quod quedam sunt que moventur voluntarie, unde ab hoc quod a sensu habemus, possumus ostendere quod anima est."

74. Matthew Etchemendy and Rega Wood, "Speculum animae: Richard Rufus on Perception and Cognition," *Franciscan Studies* 69, no. 1 (2011): 53–115.

75. Henri D'Andeli, "La bataille des sept arts," in *Les Dits d'Henri d'Andeli*, ed., trans. Alain Corbellari (Paris: Champion, 2003), 70.

76. "*Si ignoras te, o pulcherrima mulierum, uade et abi post greges caprarum* etc. Tibi, anima racionalis, proponitur uerbum istud, que es mulierum pulcherrima, quia omnium creaturarum speciosissima, tenens ymaginem et similitudinem summe pulchritudinis et decoris; hanc tuam si ignoras pulchritudinem, irracionabilibus gregibus compararis: unde *uade et abi post greges caprarum*. Tibi ergo, anima, de te ipsa consideranda sunt tria: substancia uidelicet tua, uirtus et operacio, in quibus consistit tua admirabilis pulchritudo. Da michi ergo, amantissime Ihesu, *sedium tuarum assistricem sapienciam et noli me reprobare*; sed da michi sapienciam que *mecum sit et mecum laboret*, considerantem doceat et instruat, reuelans *oculos meos, et considerabo mirabilia* de anima mea"; John of La Rochelle, *Summa de anima*, ed. Jacques Guy Bougerol, Textes philosophiques du moyen âge XIX (Paris: Vrin, 1995), 47.

77. John Baldwin, *Aristocratic Life in Medieval France: The Romances of Jean Renart and Gerbert de Montreuil, 1190–1230* (Baltimore and London: The John Hopkins University Press, 2000).

78. Heldris of Cornwall, *Silence: A Thirteenth-Century French Romance*, ed., trans., with introduction and notes Sarah Roche-Mahdi (East Lansing, Mich.: Colleagues, 1992), lines 5995–6090.

79. Ibid., 3.

80. See, among others, J. Reynaert, "Hadewijch: Mystic Poetry and Courtly Love," in *Medieval Dutch Literature in Its European Context*, ed. Erik Kooper (Cambridge University Press, 1994), 208–25, and Meredith Minister, *Trinitarian Theology and Power Relations. God Embodied* (New York: Palgrave Macmillan, 2014), particularly Chap. 3 on Mechtild of Magdeburg.

81. Jehan [Jean] Renart, *Le lai de l'ombre*, trans., introduction Adrian P. Tudor, ed. Alan Hindley and Brian J. Levy, *Liverpool Online Series*, critical editions of French texts 8 (2004), https://www.liverpool.ac.uk/media/livacuk/modern-languages-and-cultures/liverpoolonline/ombre.pdf.

82. Ibid., lines 864–940.

83. Jean Renart, *The Romance of the Rose or Guillaume de Dole*, trans. Patricia Terry and Nancy Vine Durling (Philadelphia: University of Pennsylvania Press, 1993). Misleading appearance is a key element in the development of the plot of Jean Renart's earliest romance, *L'Escoufle*, as well; ibid, 3.

84. Sarah Roche-Mahdi, Introduction to Heldris of Cornwall, *Silence*, xxiii. A full, up-to-date bibliography on *Silence* is available at Arlima database, http://www.arlima.net/eh/heldris_de_cornouailles.html.

85. Baldwin, *Aristocratic Life*, 13.

86. Roger Dragonetti, *Le mirage des sources: L'art du faux dans le roman médiéval* (Paris: Seuil, 1987); Michel Zink, *The Invention of Literary Subjectivity*, trans. Davis Sices (Baltimore: John Hopkins University Press, 1999).

87. For a survey of relevant research up to 1980, see Caroline Walker Bynum, Chap. 3, "Did the Twelfth Century Discover the Individual?," in *Jesus as Mother: Studies in the Spirituality of the High Middle Ages* (Berkeley and Los Angeles: University of California Press, 1982).

88. The mirror metaphor that is so dominant in the discourse of cognizing God is powerful in this respect as well. Mirrors both allow one to see oneself and create a distance between one's true self and one's reflection. According to Donald Maddox, medieval French literature since the late twelfth century favored scenes in which a hero learns crucial facts about himself through meeting a person or seeing an object at a significant moment of the narrative. He named this widespread motif the "specular encounter" in Maddox, *Fictions of Identity in Medieval France* (Cambridge and New York: Cambridge University Press, 2000).

4. DOES TRUE FAITH RELY ON ANYTHING EXTERNAL?

1. Robert E. Lerner, "Ecstatic Dissent," *Speculum* 67, no. 1 (1992): 33–57.

2. Paul of Chartres's account, following Walter L. Wakefield and Austin P. Evans, trans. and eds., *Heresies of the High Middle Ages: Selected Sources* (New York: Columbia University Press, 1991), 81, who translate from *Vetus Aganon* vi.iii, ed. Benjamin Edmé-Charles Guérard, in *Cartulaire de l'abbaye de Saint-Pe're de Chartres* (Paris, 1840).

3. For a short preview of the medieval concept of natural law, see Kenneth Pennington, "Natural Law," in *Dictionary of the Middle Ages: Supplement 1* (New York: Charles Scribners Sons–Thompson-Gale, 2004), 417–20. See also Odon Lottin, *Le Droit Naturel chez saint Thomas et ses prédécesseurs* (Bruges: Bayert, 1931); Rudolf Weigand, *Die Naturrechtslehre der Legisten und Dekretisten von Irnerius bis Accursius und von Gratian bis Johannes Teutonicus* (Munich: Max

Hueber, 1967); Anthony J. Lisska, *Aquinas's Theory of Natural Law: An Analytic Reconstruction* (Oxford: Clarendon, 1996); Robert A. Greene, "Instinct of Nature: Natural Law, Synderesis, and the Moral Sense," *Journal of the History of Ideas* 58, no. 2 (1997): 173–98; Brian Tierney, *The Idea of Natural Rights: Studies on Natural Rights, Natural Law and Church Law 1150–1625* (Atlanta: Scholars Press, 1997); Pennington, "Lex naturalis and Ius naturale," *Jurist* 68 (2008): 569–91.

4. On this innovative approach of Jordanus Nemorarius, see Leo Corry, "Geometry and Arithmetic in the Medieval Traditions of Euclid's *Elements*: A View from Book II," *Archive for History of Exact Sciences* 67, no. 6 (2013): 684.

5. Alan de Lille, *Anticlaudianus: Texte critique avec une introduction et des tables*, book 5, ll. 258–61, ed. Robert Bossuat (Paris: Vrin, 1955), 131.

6. Hugh of St. Victor, *De Sacramentis*, PL 176:330.

7. Georg Englhardt, *Die Entwicklung der dogmatischen Glaubenspsychologie in der mittelalterlichen Scholastik vom Abaelardstreit (um 1140) bis zu Philipp dem Kanzler (gest. 1236)* (Münster in Westfalen: Aschendorff, 1933), Chap. 2.

8. For background on the developments analyzed in this section see ibid., Chap. 1.

9. William of Auvergne, *De anima*, *Guilielmi Alverni Opera Omnia* [GOO] (Paris, 1674), 2:122. See also pp. 205 and 221, in which he rejects the perception of learning as passive seeing and assimilates it to reading a book. Mere "reading" without creating a *habitus* of understanding within the soul is insufficient.

10. The most famous of contemporary guides to these techniques was the *Ars Notoriae*, on which see Julien Véronèse, *"L'Ars notoria" au Moyen Âge: Introduction et édition critique* (Florence: SISMEL, Edizioni del Galluzzo, 2007).

11. "De demonibus dicitur quod subito possunt et ualde cito instruere hominem in aliqua scientia, et quod possent in breuissimo tempore docere loycam vel astronomiam"; Roland of Cremona, *Summa Magistri Rolandi Cremonensis O.P. Liber Tercius* [SR], lib. 2, Vat. Lat. 729, fol. 87ra, and Mazarine 795, fol. 29va.

12. William of Auxerre, *Summa aurea* [SA] 3.12.1, ed. Jean Ribaillier, in *Spicilegium Bonaventurianum* (Paris: Grottaferrata, 1986), 3:197–99.

13. Cf. this anonymous twelfth-century variation: "If anyone asks wherefrom you know of the virginal birth . . . I have no other *argumentum* except that I believe without any doubt that prophets and others who spoke through the Holy Spirit and whom God would not deceive in any way, said this, since he spoke in them and did miracles." (Si quis quaereret: unde scis partum virginis . . . non habeo aliud *argumentum* nisi quod indubitanter credo illud, quod prophetae et alii qui per spiritum sanctum sunt locuti, inde dixerunt, quos deus nullo modo falleret, cum in eis loqueretur et miracula faceret etc.); Englhardt, *Die Entwicklung der dogmatischen Glaubenspsychologie*, 402.

14. Jean de Joinville, *Vie de St. Louis*, 1.45, translated in *The Life of St. Louis by John of Joinville*, trans. René Hague (London and New York: Sheed and Ward, 1955), 34–35.

15. The first part is not superfluous: despite being common to faith and hope, it distinguishes formed faith from unformed faith.

16. "Sicut enim syllogismus inducit aliquem et quodammodo cogit ad concedendam conclusionem, quam prius negabat, sic si aliquis articulus videbatur alicui incredibilis ante fidem, habita fide statim concedebat, quod prius negabat, et liquebit ei esse verum. et ita dicitur fides *argumentum* per simile, quia probat." The text was published by Englhardt in *Die Entwicklung der dogmatischen Glaubenspsychologie*, 424. His analysis of the text and of Peter of Corbeille's role is in pages 115–23.

17. "Quarto modo dicitur fides *argumentum non apparentium* propter articulos fidei, qui sunt principia fidei per se nota. Unde fides sive fidelis respuit eorum probationes. Fides enim, quia soli veritati innititur, in ipsis articulis invenit causam quare credit eis, scilicet Deum, sicut in alia facultate intellectus in hoc principio 'omne totum est maius sua parte,' causam invenit per quam cognoscit illud"; William of Auxerre, SA 3.12.1, 3:199.

18. In 76a16–22 it is called "undemonstrative knowledge," but later (88b30) Aristotle gives the faculty that grasps the principles the name νοῦς and distinguishes it from ἐπιστήμη, which is here identified solely with demonstrative cognition.

19. "Quoniam si in theologia non essent principia, non esset ars vel scientia. Habet ergo principia, scilicet articulos, qui tamen solis fidelibus sunt principia ... sicut enim hoc principium 'omne totum est maius sua parte' habet aliquantam illuminationem per modum nature illuminantis intellectum, ita hoc principium 'Deus est remunaerator omnium bonorum' et alii articuli habent in se illuminationem per modum gratie, qua deus illuminat intellectum"; William of Auxerre, SA 3.12.1, 3:199.

20. Martin Grabmann, *Die theologische Erkenntnis- und Einleitungslehre des hl. Thomas von Aquin* (Freiburg, Switzerland: Paulusverlag, 1948), 187.

21. This scheme connects William with the Porretan School, which proclaimed "maxims" or axioms for each science, including theology. No such explicit claim for separate illumination of grace was articulated, however. Thus, Alan de Lille opens his *Regule Celestis Iuris* with the words "omnis scientia suis nititur regulis." He enumerates a series of sciences and their respective maxims and then claims that *Supercelestis vero scientia i.e. theologia suis non fraudatur maximis*; de Lille, *Regule Celestis Iuris*, ed. Nikolaus M. Häring, in "Magistri Regule Celestis Iuris," in *AHDLMA* 48 (1981): 121–22. The first axioms in Alan's model are indemonstrable, too: at the minute one understands them, one affirms them. Nevertheless, Alan does not claim that any special, grace-given light is needed for that, although intense training in theology, pure mind, and wisdom are required: "Iste propositiones [i.e., theologorum] quanto intelligentiam habent altiorem tanto magis peritum exigunt auditorem.... Hae enim propositiones in peritiori sinu theologie absconduntur et solis sapientibus collocuntur; ibid., 123. The propositions that follow, however, seem to be philosophically comprehensible.

For other interesting references to theology as a science with its own principles with regard to Gilbert of Poitiers's commentary on Boethius's *De Trinitate*, see John Marenbon, "Gilbert of Poitiers and the Porretans on Mathematics in the Division of Sciences," in *"Scientia" und Disciplina": Wissentheorie und Wissenschaftspraxis im 12. und 13. Jahrhundert*, ed. Reiner Berndt et al. (Berlin: Akademie Verlag, 2002), 37–69.

22. "*Fides est substantia rerum sperandarum, argumentum non aparentium. Sicut enim vera dilectione diligitur Deus propter seipsum super omnia, ita fide acqiescitur prime veritati super omnia propter se*"; William of Auxerre, SA 1, Prologue, 1:15.

23. Ibid., 2.8.1, 2:145.

24. Englhardt, *Die Entwicklung der dogmatischen Glaubenspsychologie*, 118.

25. William of Auxerre, SA 3.12.7, 3:217.

26. Ibid., 3.34.2, 3:650.

27. "*Quia essentia fidei est speculum et enigma*"; ibid., 3.42.2, 3:80; "*Fides non est proprie visio dei, sed est quedam cognitio vel coniecturatio . . . cum ergo non videatur Deus visione fidei aut per propriam speciem sue speciei aut per suam ipsius presenciam, patet quod fides non est proprie visio*"; ibid., 805; cf. 814 as well.

28. Alexander of Hales mentions this interpretation briefly, stating that the fact that the ancient fathers believed so or that "God said so" is not an *argumentum*, but rather a remote disposition for believing; *De definitione fidei data ab Apostolo*, q. 38, *Quaestiones disputatae "Antequam esset frater* [QDA], ed. Quaracchi Fathers, Bibliotheca Franciscana scholastica medii aevi, t. 19–21 (Quaracchi, Florence: Collegii S. Bonaventurae, 1960), 2:670. Philip rejects this interpretation as well, while raising another objection: the ancient ancestors did not have any ancestors of their own, and hence this sense of *argumentum* could not be valid in their case; Philip the Chancellor, *Philippi Cancellarii Summa de bono* [SB], ed. Nikolaus Wicki (Bern: Francke, 1985), 2:567. The author of Vat. Lat. 691 repeats that opposition (fol. 108r), and so does the *Summa Halensis*, in *Summa theologica seu sic ab origine dicta "Summa Fratris Alexandri"* [SH], ed. Bernardini Klumper, Victorin Doucet, and the Quaracchi Fathers (Rome: Collegii S. Bonaventurae, 1928), 2:1075.

29. "*Cum autem tu dicis illi: 'Abraam credidit hoc,' ille, qui dicit quod non sunt Pater et Filius et Spiritus unus Deus, dicet: 'si Abraam credidit, stultus fuit'*"; Roland of Cremona, SR 3.97, 292.

30. See Chapter 6.

31. Peter Lombard, *Collectanea in omnes epistolas divi Pauli apostoli*, PL 191:1479.

32. Cf. Philip the Chancellor, SB, 2:575.

33. Alexander of Hales, *Summa theologica seu sic ab origine dicta "Summa Fratris Alexandri"* [SH], 3.2.1.2, 2:1065–67.

34. Alexander of Hales, *Glossa in quatuor libros Sententiarum Petri Lombardi* [GS], ed. the Quaracchi Fathers, Bibliotheca Franciscana scholastica medii aevi,

t. 12–15 (Quaracchi, Florence: Collegii S. Bonaventurae, 1954), 3:264; Q. 501 in Douai, BM 434 II, fol. 300a, following Glorieux's pagination (*La "Summa Duacensis," (Douai 434), texte critique avec une introduction et des tables*. ed. Palémon Glorieux, Textes philosophiques du moyen âge 2 (Paris: Vrin, 1955), and its equivalents in *quaestiones* 45 and 530.

35. "Sicut venditor incredulus, qui emptori non aliter credit, nisi pignus, vel cautionem sive securitatem det ipsi, et probatio sive suasio, ut pignus est, et cautio securitatis, sine qua non credit huiusmodi intellectus ... exactio pignoris aut alterius cautionis non est nisi ex parvitate seu debilitate credulitatis, aut ex defectu ipsius; quare manifestum est intellectum exactorem huiusmodi pignoris et securitatum videlicet probationum ... esse credulitate infirmum aut incredulum"; William of Auvergne, *De fide*, GOO 1:5.

36. "The faithless bears the name Burgundio, and William claims that this guarantee or deposit is not only parallel to the first principles of other sciences, but is the most evident of them all"; see William of Auvergne, *De bono et malo*, ed. J. Reginald O'Donnell, "Tractatus Magistri Guillelmi Alvernensis *De bono et malo*," *Mediaeval Studies* 8 (1946): 284.

37. Roland of Cremona, SR 3.97, 294.

38. "Constat, cum sit scientia, quod habet subiectum de quo agit ... si habeat subiectum et habet ea que probat de illo subiecto et ea per que probat"; Roland of Cremona, SR, Prologue, ed. Giuseppe Cremascoli, *Studi Medievali* 16 (1975): 864.

39. "Non insunt fides et articuli per modum artis et complexionis, sed per modum assertionis quam facit fides in anima ... Sed alie conclusiones exeunt ab articulis per modum scientie vel artis"; ibid., 865–66.

40. "Item in scientiis duo sunt, quedam per se nota ut principia quorum acceptio dicitur intellectus et ex hiis per se notis sequuntur alia ut conclusiones, et dicuntur scita que ex per se nota veniunt in noticiam. Hoc non est in theologia, cuius prima sunt articuli, qui non noscuntur nisi per fidem. Ergo que sequuntur ex hiis non sunt scita, sed credita"; Prague, Univ. IV D 13, fol. 79rb.

41. "Primo quod simpliciter scientia est, non tamen omnia que in ea sunt scita, sicut est in aliis scientiis. Quedam sunt principia per se nota, ut principia legis naturalis ... quedam in quibus creditur, non tamen maiorum, sed ipsius dei auctoritati, ut articuli fidei. ... Et hoc patet quod habet quicquid necesse est ad scientiam, et plus quia in illis principiis in quibus credulitas est necessaria ut in astronomia terram esse sphericam"; ibid., fol. 79va.

42. "Alia est acceptio [fidei], que in quibusdam, ut in articulis credit quasi per se nota intelligit, ut principia alia scit per principia. In aliis tamquam maiorum narrationibus, maioribus credit et ecclesie auctoritati"; ibid.

43. Aristotle, *Posterior Analytics* 1.33, 89a4, in *The Complete Works of Aristotle*, ed., trans. Jonathan Barnes (Princeton: Princeton University Press, 1984).

44. Solution to the seventh question, "Quis habitus per eam [i.e., theologiam] acquiritur," which begins, "Circa septimum: Fides ex inspiracione, non ergo ex habitu"; BnF Lat. 15652, fol. 89rb. On the relationship between Adam and Odo

Rigaldi, see Englhardt, "Adam de Puteorumvilla, un maître proche d'Odon Rigaud: Sa psychologie de la foi," *RTAM* 8 (1936): 61–78. For the dating of both lectures, see Nathalie Gorochov, *Naissance*, 483.

45. Philip the Chancellor, SB, 2:572–73.

46. Alexander of Hales, *De definitione fidei data ab Apostolo*, q. 38 [QDA], 2:670.

47. Alexander of Hales, SH 3.2.1, 2:1077.

48. "Nec tamen est motus fidei secundum ratiocinationem, ut dixi, sed secundum affectionem, quod non est in argumento logico"; Philip the Chancellor, SB, 571.

49. "Cognitionis huius est principium affectio sive amor. Et est sicut contingit in amore vulgari quod plerumque tanto amore aliquis zelat alium, quod ipse zelus non permittit ipsum credere vel suspiciari de illo aliquid sinistrum, ita affectio quam habet quis ad deum per quam in omnibus ei credit, non sustinet aliquid sive in sensu sive in ratione quod videatur fidei repugnare"; ibid, 576.

50. Ibid., 669; Alexander of Hales, SH 3.2.1, 2:1064.

51. William of Auvergne, *De fide*, *Guilielmi Alverni Opera Omnia* [GOO] (Paris, 1674), 1:2–3.

52. Jean de Joinville, *Vie de St. Louis* 1.46; English translation from *The Life of St. Louis*, 34–35.

The exemplum was translated into modern French in Jacques Berlioz, "La voix de l'évêque: Guillaume d'Auvergne dans les exempla (xiiie–xive siècle)," in *Autour de Guillaume d'Auvergne [mort en] 1249*, ed. Franco Morenzoni and Jean-Yves Tilliette (Turnhout: Brepols, 2005), 23. The war he referred to ended in 1242 in Louis IX's victory, thus placing the scene before that year.

53. William of Auvergne, *De bono et malo*, 293.

54. Ibid., 284.

55. Ibid., 281–82.

56. Ibid., 277. "Natural" for William of Auvergne usually denotes "in the state of innocence"; cf. *De virtutibus*, GOO 1:24. Asking what the natural cognition of Adam and Eve was, whether it is similar to sensual perception, the understanding of first principles, understanding through demonstration or any other cognition, he determines that it was similar to that of the principles and was impressed even deeper in the mind.

57. "Hoc autem non potest esse nisi secundum duos modos, quorum alter est ut sua luciditate eidem illucescant, quemadmodum disciplinalia principia aut sensibilia, quae se gratis nobis ostendunt, aut sicut credita ei ex oboedientia, scilicet eo quod scilicet iussa sit ab illo imperatore universali credere illa"; William of Auvergne, *De bono et malo*, 283.

58. "Sic est de credulitate qua quis diligens magistrum suum ex affectu et credens ipsum esse summum in facultate sua, cum audit ab eo aliquid quod per se est dignum fide, magis credit illi rei propter hoc quod magister suus dicit eam quam propter ipsius rei veritatem"; William of Auxerre, SA 2.7.1, 2:145.

59. "Jam igitur manifestum est non aliam viam veniendi humanae naturae ad finem suum ultimum et gloriam atque perfectionem suam ultimam nisi per oboedientiam, qualem quidem determinavimus. Hoc autem est qua Deo vivitur, qua ipsa tota vita alieno magisterio et voluntati tota traditur, hoc est dominio, magisterio et volunatati, hoc est nihil contra Dei magisterium sentire"; William of Auvergne, *De bono et malo*, 287–88.

60. Ibid., 288, 292 et passim.

61. "Stulciusque est magistratus oracionibus omnino confidere, sed primo est credendum donec videatur quid senciat, postea fingendum est eundem in docendo erasse"; Ps. Boethius, *Disciplina scolarium* 5.3–4, ed. Olga Weijers (Leiden and Cologne: Brill, 1976), 120–21.

62. Mia Münster-Swendsen, "The Model of Scholastic Mastery in Northern Europe c. 970–1200," in *Teaching and Learning in Northern Europe 1000–1200*, ed. Sally N. Vaughn and Jay Rubenstein (Turnhout: Brepols, 2003), 306–42.

63. Ibid., 328.

64. "Quid enim dubitat qui iuratus in uerba magistri non quid sed a quo quid dicatur attendit? . . . nec rationibus adquiescit quem doctoris captiuauit opinio. Quicquid enim ille protulit, autenticum et sacrosanctum est"; John of Salisbury, *Policraticus, sive de nugis curialium et vestigiisphilosophorum* 7.9, ed. Clement C. I. Webb (Frankfurt am Main: Minerva, 1965), 122–23.

65. Ian P. Wei, "From Twelfth-Century Schools to Thirteenth-Century Universities: The Disappearance of Biographical and Autobiographical Representations of Scholars," *Speculum* 86, no. 1 (2011): 42–78.

66. *Chartularium Universitatis Parisiensis* [CUP] I, no. 5, p. 65, ed. Heinrich Denifle, Emile Chatelain, Charles Samaran, and Émile A. van Moé (Brussells: Culture et civilisation, 1964).

67. "Ad docendum non solum in aliis facultatibus set etiam in theologia interdum repulsis dignis admittuntur indigni et adeo excrescit numerus magistrorum, ut tum pro numerositate tum pro insufficientia eorundem vilescat auctoritas magistralis"; CUP I, no. 41, p. 99.

68. William of Auxerre, SA 3.12.6.4, 3:229–31.

69. Roland of Cremona, SR 3.108, 36–40.

70. A typical image of a charismatic itinerant preacher emerges from the accounts about Henri Le-Mans. Lambert le Begue is a good example of a radical reforming leader who was accused in heresy, while the colorful person of Pierre Clergue from the village Montaillou, whose portrait is painted in Ladourie's *Montaillou*, comes to mind as well; Emanuel Le Roi Ladourie, *Montaillou: Village occitan, de 1294 à 1324* (Paris: Gallimard, 1975).

71. CUP I, no. 25, p. 83; no. 32, p. 92.

72. Avranches 121 f. 2ra: "Secunda causa est defensio fidei propter hereticos"; William of Auxerre, SA, Prologue, 1:16: "Secunda ratio est defensio fidei contra hereticos."

73. Vat. Lat. 691, fol. 1r. The correspondence between this image of theology's role and papal agenda is clearly seen, therefore, for this exact verse with the same interpretation was used in 1219 by Honorius III to explain his interest in supporting theology studies; CUP I, no. 32, p. 92.

74. Robert I. Moore, *The Formation of a Persecuting Society: Authority and Deviance in Western Europe 950–1250*, 2nd ed. (Malden, Mass.: Blackwell, 2007), 131–34.

75. David A. Trail, "Philip the Chancellor and the Heresy Inquisition in Northern France, 1235–1236," *Viator* 37 (2006): 241–54. Roland had left his new chair of theology to preach against the heretics in Toulouse and Italy; Pierre Bonassie and Gérard Pradalié, eds., *La capitulation de Raymond VII et la fondation de l'université de Toulouse, 1229–1979: Un anniversaire en question* (Toulouse: Université Toulouse-Le Mirail, 1979), 59–60.

76. For the complicated role of literacy in the origin and spread of heresy, see especially the articles collected in Peter Biller and Anne Hudson, eds., *Heresy and Literacy* (Cambridge: Cambridge University Press, 1994), as well as in Biller and Barrie Dobson, eds., *The Medieval Church: Universities, Heresy and the Religious Life: Essays in Honour of Gordon Leff* (Suffolk, UK, and Rochester, N.Y.: Boydell, 1999).

77. For a translation and commentary on the introduction to Pseudo-Peter of Poitiers' Gloss, see Philipp W. Rosemann, *The Story of a Great Medieval Book: Peter Lombard's Sentences* (Toronto: University of Toronto Press, 2007), 43–51, esp. 49.

5. WHAT HAPPENS TO OLD MODES OF COGNITION WHEN NEW ONES ARE INTRODUCED DURING TRANCE AND OTHER TRANSITIONS?

1. The epigraph is from Carl Gustav Jung, "The Face to Face Interview," in *C. G. Jung Speaking: Interviews and Encounters*, ed. William McGuire and R. F. C. Hull (Princeton: Bollingen Paperbacks, 1977), 428.

2. "Quaero: quid est, de illa quaestione, quam frequenter disputavimus? Utrum habitus scientiarum in hac vita acquisiti maneant in patria? At ille respondit: Frater Thoma, ego video Deum, et nihil aliud de hac quaestione petatis"; *Fontes vitae sancti Thomae Aquinatis notis historicis et criticis illustrati*, ed. Domenicus Prümmer and M. H. Laurent (Toulouse: Saint Maximin, 1912), 119.

3. Caroline Walker Bynum, *Metamorphosis and Identity* (New York: Zone, 2001), 19.

4. The authority most cited for this view is Ambrose: "Qui enim fieri potest ut lingua humana omne complectatur quod Dei est? Ideo destruetur imperfectio nostra, non id quod verum est evacuabitur, sed dum additur imperfectio quod deest, destruetur. Destructio enim imperfectionis est, quando id quod Imperfectum est impletur in verum"; In epistolam b. Pauli ad Corinthios primam, PL 17:253. Cf. Hatto of Vercelli (d. 961), PL 134:388.

5. Jean-Pierre Torrell, *Théorie de la prophétie et philosophie de la connaissance aux environs de 1230: La contribution d'Hugues de Saint-Cher (Ms. Douai 434, Question 481)* (Leuven: Spicilegium Sacrum Lovaniense, 1977), 31.

6. Quaestiones 498–99, Douai MB 434 II, fols. 297–98, according to Glorieux's pagination (*La "Summa Duacensis" [Douai 434], texte critique avec une introduction et des tables*, ed. Palémon Glorieux, Textes philosophiques du moyen âge 2 [Paris: Vrin, 1955]).

7. Gregory the Great, *Homelia* 26.1, PL 76:1197.

8. Aristotle, *Posterior Analytics* 88b30–89b6. Cf. also 71b5 that it is possible for a person to know something in one sense and not know it in another sense.

9. "Alicui est aliquid scientia, quod alii est fides: verbi gratia. Doctus in geometriciis ut euclides scit lineam per aequalia dividi, necessarias enim causas probationis praeconcipit. Simplex vero aliquis expers geometricae, quia tamen hoc audit affirmari ab Euclide lineam per aequalia dividi credit, quia notus in arte hoc asserit. Quod ergo a docto scitur, a simplice creditur"; Georg Englhardt, *Die Entwicklung der dogmatischen Glaubenspsychologie in der mittelalterlichen Scholastik vom Abaelardstreit (um 1140) bis zu Philipp dem Kanzler (gest. 1236)* (Münster in Westfalen: Aschendorff, 1933), 404.

The reference is to Euclid's *Elements*, proposition 1.10.

10. William of Auxerre, *Summa aurea* [SA] 3.12.4; ed. Jean Ribaillier, in *Spicilegium Bonaventurianum* (Paris: Grottaferrata, 1986), 3:207–8.

11. Augustine, *In Ioannem* 15.18. Cf. also PL 114:372.

12. Regarding this natural cognition, see William of Auxerre, SA 3.12.7, 3:216.

13. Ibid., 3.12.4, 3:208.

14. Ibid., 3.34.1 ("quid sit intellectus et quid sapientia"), 3:650.

15. "Sicut enim in hoc principio 'omne totum maius est sua parte' invenitur causa sue cognitionis nec alia causa queritur, ita anima fidelis in ipsa prima veritate que creditur invenit causam fidei nec aliam causam querit"; ibid.

16. Roland of Cremona, *Summa Magistri Rolandi Cremonensis O.P. Liber Tercius* [SR] 3.100, Editio princeps, ed. Alois Cortesi (Bergamo: Monumenta Bergomensia, 1962), 307.

17. Ibid.

18. "Visio sensitiua est incercior cognicione fidei. Visio intellectualis cercior. Visio autem cercior euacuat fidem, non autem incercior euacuat eam, et ita cum fide potest manere cognicio sensitiua"; Vat. Lat. 691, fol. 108r, left bottom corner.

19. "Quedam est cognicio, que est eiusdem generis cum alia, et est una ordinata ad aliam cum se habent fides et uisio, et tunc incercior excluditur per cerciorem. Similiter cum fides sit eiusdem generis cum fide informi cum utraque est in genere gratuitorum et informis ordinetur ad fidem formatam, patet quod adueniente formalis fides excluditur"; ibid.

20. "Item est aliqua cognicio que non est eiusdem generis cum alia nec est ordinata ad aliam, et sic cum una est cercior alia patet quod incercior non excluditur per cerciorem. Immo manet cum ea. Sic sunt fides et scientia experimentalis.

Non enim sunt eiusdem generis quia una naturalis, alia gratuita, nec est una ordinata ad alteram sicut imperfectio ad perfectio. Similiter scientia experimentalis adveniente demonstratiua"; ibid.

21. Alexander of Hales, *Summa theologica seu sic ab origine dicta "Summa Fratris Alexandri"* [SH] 3.2.1, ed. Bernardini Klumper, Victorin Doucet. and the Quaracchi Fathers (Rome: Collegii S. Bonaventurae, 1924–48), 2:1090.

22. About the systematization of virtues-gifts-beatitudes into a triad of more perfect acts of the same potency, see Odon Lottin, "Les dons du Saint-Esprit chez les théologiens depuis Pierre Lombard jusqu'à S. Thomas d'Aquin," in *Psychologie et Morale aux XIIe et XIIIe Siècles* (Gembloux: Duculot, 1949), 1:456.

23. Alexander of Hales, SH 3.2.1, 2:1092.

24. Hugh of St. Cher extensively quotes William's solution for the problem of knowing and believing the same thing in his commentary on the Lombard's *Sentences*. Nevertheless, he asserts that the converted philosopher does not lose his former cognition, but only its use, comparing him to someone who holds a burning candle when the sun rises; Padova, Univ. 853, f. 95rb.

25. Douai, BM 434 I f. 46va; II f. 300b.

26. Philip the Chancellor, *Philippi Cancellarii Summa de bono* [SB], ed. Nikolaus Wicki (Bern: Francke, 1985), 2:647.

27. William of Auvergne, *De Trinitate*, ed. Bruno Switalski (Toronto: Pontifical Institute of Mediaeval Studies, 1976), 15–16.

28. Alexander Murray, *Reason and Society in the Middle Ages* (Oxford: Clarendon, 1978).

29. Walter Map, *De nugis curialium* 1.31, ed., trans. M. R. James, revised C. N. L. Brooke and R. A. B. Mynors (Oxford: Clarendon, 1983), 60–61.

30. Concerning the pairs *laicus:clericus* and *litteratus:illiteratus*, the change in their meaning, and occasional interchangeability, see Michael T. Clanchy, "Literate and Illiterate: Hearing and Seeing," in *From Memory to Written Record: England 1066–1307* (Oxford: Blackwell, 1993), 177–79.

31. "Et dum fidem conantur plus debito ratione astruere naturali, none illam reddunt quodammodo inutilem et inanem, quoniam fides non habet meritum, cui humana ratio prebet experimentum?"; *Chartularium Universitatis Parisiensis* [CUP] I, no. 59, pp. 114–15, ed. Heinrich Denifle, Emile Chatelain, Charles Samaran, and Émile A. van Moé (Brussells: Culture et civilisation, 1964).

32. William of Auxerre arrived at the papal curia as a messenger of the French crown regarding the highly tense relationship with England. His presence there turned out to be crucial also to university affairs, as the crisis broke out a few months earlier. In May 10, 1230, Gregory asked the masters and students to send representatives on behalf of the university to the curia, "although we thought that master W[illermus] should remain here for this purpose"; CUP I, no. 74, pp. 132–33; no. 75, p. 134.

33. "In primis ergo confiteor me credere unum deum esse, licet rationes habeam ad probandum, non enim acquiesco prime veritate propter illas rationes,

set potius adquiesco illis rationibus quia consentiunt prime veritati. Quia quanto magis credo, tanto magis clarius illas rationes inspicio. Fides enim mentes illuminat ad videnedum res divinas"; Avranches, BM 121 fol. 2ra. This part does not appear in the abridged version of Godfrey's prologue in Paris, BnF Lat. 3143.

34. William of Auxerre, SA, Prologus, 1:16.

35. Ibid.

36. "Ad primum sunt rationes, quod non sit scientia, quia fides, vel acceptio fidei non est scientia, vel acceptio scientie, sed omnia que sunt in divinis libris accipiunt per fidem, ut quod abraham genuit ysaac, creditur, non scitur, et sic de aliis. Ergo hec acceptio vel cognitio non est scientie, nec scientia, sed fides vel credulitas"; Prague IV D 13, fol. 79rb.

37. Ibid., fol. 79va.

38. "Acceptio una que tota est fidei, et tota habet meritum, ut cum apertum sit 'hoc non facias alii' omni intellectui, tamen fidelis intellectus vult acquiescere spiritualiter divine auctoritati in hoc. Alia est acceptio, que in quibusdam ut in articulis credit quasi per se nota intelligit ut principia alia scit per principia, in aliis tamquam maiorum narrationibus, maioribus credit et ecclesie auctoritati"; ibid.

39. "Multa divine bonitatis indicia, tamen talis propter hoc non scit libros divinos et rationes quibus ostenditur fides et mores, et alia"; ibid., fol. 80rb.

40. Odo Rigaldi, Prologue to his *Lectura super Sententias*, in Leonardo Sileo, *Teoria della scienza theologica: Quaestio de scientia theologiae di Odo Rigaldi e altri testi inedita (1230–1250)* (Rome: Pontificium Athenaeum Antonianum, 1984) 2:89.

41. Paris, BnF Lat. 15652, f. 32r.

42. The scheme implies that innate knowledge of "God exists" coexists with other cognitions of the same fact, but William does not present this as an explicit coexistence.

43. Caroline Walker Bynum, "Monsters, Medians, and Marvelous Mixtures: Hybrids in the Spirituality of Bernard of Clairvaux," in *Metamorphosis and Identity* (New York: Zone, 2001).

44. Matthew Paris, *Chronica majora*, ed. Henry Richard Luard (London: Longman, 1872), 4.281; English translation from *Matthew Paris's English History 1235–1273*, trans. John Allan Giles (New York: AMS, 1968), 1:476. A nonexhaustive survey of Paris's use of *simplicitas* throughout the chronicle shows that it is almost always used in a positive sense. It is attributed particularly to kings, queens, or Englishmen in general, and appears mainly in the combination "circumvenire simplicitatem," meaning deceiving and abusing one's naivety. When he speaks about the peasant revolt in France in the year 1251 he says the message of their leader was that with their simplicity and humility the pastors will conquer the Holy Land. This simplicity was, however, quite hostile to the clergy: when in Orléans, they attacked clergymen, particularly the schoolmen and their books. Doing that, however, their naivety was proven false. Queen

Blanche, according to Paris, realized later that they were mere deceivers; Paris, *Chronica maiora: Matthew Paris's English History*, 5.247–51.

45. Gerard of Frachet, *Vitae Fratrum Ordinis Praedicatorum* 5.20.5, ed. Benedict M. Reichert, Monumenta Ordinis Pradicatorum Historica 1 (Louvain: Charpentier and Schoonjas, 1896), 209.

46. Humbert de Romanis, *De eruditione praedicatorum* 21, quoted in Lester K. Little, *Religious Poverty and the Profit Economy in Medieval Europe* (Ithaca, N.Y.: Cornell University Press, 1978), 184.

47. Regarding preaching, inspiration, and the conflict over learning in the Franciscan order in this context, see Bert Roest, *A History of Franciscan Education (c. 1210–1517)* (Leiden: Brill, 2000), 276; Achim Wesjohann, "'Simplicitas' als franziskanisches Ideal und die Prozess der Institutionalisierung des Minoritenordens," in *Die Bettelorden im Aufbau: Beiträge zu Institutionalizierungsprozessen im mittelalterichen Religiosentum*, edited by Gert Melville and Jörg Oberste (Münster: LIT, 1999), 107–67; Neslihan Şenocak, *The Poor and the Perfect: The Rise of Learning in the Franciscan Order, 1 209–1310* (Ithaca, N.Y.: Cornell University Press, 2012), esp. from 99.

48. Rosalind B. Brooke, *Early Franciscan Government; Elias to Bonaventure* (Cambridge: Cambridge University Press, 1959), 86. On the clericalization of the Franciscan order in its first decades, see also Lawrence Landini, *The Causes of the Clericalization of the Order of Friars Minor 1209–1260 in the Light of the Early Franciscan Sources* (Chicago: Pontifica Universitas Gregoriana, 1968), and Michael Robson and Jens Röhrkasten, eds., *Franciscan Organization in the Mendicant Context: Formal and Informal Structures of the Friars' Lives and Ministry in the Middle Ages* (Berlin: LIT, 2010).

49. Roest, *History of Franciscan Education*, 1–3; see in particular n. 1.

50. "Praeodorabatur etiam tempora non longe ventura, in quibus occasionem ruinae fore scientiam sciret, spiritus vero fulcimentum spiritualibus intendisse"; Thomas Celano, *Vita Prima, Vita Secunda, et Tractatus de Miraculis* 147:195, in *Analecta Franciscana* (Rome: Quaracchi, 1926–41), 10:242.

51. Angelo Clareno, *Liber chronicarum sive tribulationum ordinis minorum di frate Angelo Clareno*, ed. Giovanni Boccali, introduction Felice Accrocca, Italian trans. Marino Bigaroni (Perugia: Santa Maria degli Angeli, 1999), 332. For the English translation, see Clareno, *A Chronicle or History of the Seven Tribulations of the Order of Brothers Minor*, ed. and trans. David Burr and E. Randolph Daniel (St. Bonaventure, N.Y.: Franciscan Institute, 2005), 96–100.

52. Clareno, *Liber*, 360; *Chronicle*, 95–96.

53. Salimbene de Adam, *Cronica*, ed. Giuseppe Scalia, CCCM 125–25A, 1:150 (Turnhout: Brepols, 1998). Allusion is to Hieronymus, *Ad Paulinum Ep. 53*, 3 (272).

54. "Dixit aliquando magnum clericum etiam scientiae quodammodo resignare debere, cum veniret ad Ordinem, ut tali expropriatus possessione, nudum se offerret brachiis Crucifixi"; Celano, *Vita Prima, Vita Secunda* 10:146, 241.

55. Ibid., 189, 238.

56. Ibid., 144:191, 239-40.

57. The expression "*gerere imaginem*" or *morem* appears earlier this section as Francis advises a man who excels in education (*litteratura praecellet*) to wear the image of pious simplicity.

58. Guy Geltner, "*Faux Semblants*: Antifraternalism Reconsidered in Jean de Meun and Chaucer," *Studies in Philology* 101, no. 4 (2004): 357-80; Geltner, "William of Saint-Amour's *De periculis novissimorum temporum*: A False Start to Medieval Antifraternalism?," in *Critics and Defenders of Franciscan Life*, ed. Michael F. Cusato and Guy Geltner (Leiden: Brill, 2009), 129.

59. David Burr, *The Spiritual Franciscans: From Protest to Persecution in the Century after Saint Francis* (University Park: Pennsylvania State University Press, 2001), 16.

60. William of Auvergne, *De anima, Guilielmi Alverni Opera Omnia* [GOO] (Paris, 1674), 2: 222.

61. British Library (Previously BM), Royal 9 E XII, 3vb-4ra, "Posito quod aliqui duo decedunt in pari caritate sed dispari cognitione."

62. Nikolaus Wicki, *Die Lehre von der himmlischen Seligkeit in der mittelalterlichen Scholastik von Petrus Lombardus bis Thomas von Aquin* (Fribourg, Switzerland: Universitätsverlag, 1954), 21, n. 11. Peter Capua's question begins: "Queritur de cognitione, an omnium cognitio sit equalis. . . . Item utrum tantum sciat laicus quantum litteratissimus parem habens caritatem cum illo? Item decedant duo in pari caritate, sed dispari cognitione."

63. William of Auxerre, SA 3.15.1.2, 3:283-4.

64. Roland of Cremona, SR 3.141, 417-19.

6. CAN KNOWLEDGE QUA KNOWLEDGE BE A VIRTUE?

1. Avranches BM 121, f. 86rb: "Auctoritas ista *que magis cognoscit magis diligit* [cf. Lombardus, *Sententiae* II d. 9] dicta est de comprehensoribus. Ibi enim qui magis cognoscit, id est, qui maiorem habet scientiam Domini, maiorem habet caritatem. . . . De usu enim non est uerum, sicut patet in literato et uetula: magis enim cognoscit literatus quam uetula, non tamen magis diligit."

2. Douai, BM 434 II, fol. 96rb.

3. On the concept of "hidden curriculum," see Henry A. Giroux and David E. Purpel, eds., *The Hidden Curriculum and Moral Education: Deception or Discovery?* Berkeley, Calif.: McCutchan, 1983.

4. This was also Rudolf Sohm's—and following him, Max Weber's—inspiration for their own perceptions of charisma. Weber's writings on charisma were gathered in *Max Weber on Charisma and Institution Building: Selected Papers*, ed. Shmuel N. Eisenstadt (Chicago: University of Chicago Press, 1968). A good account of Sohm's theory of charisma and its influence on Weber is Peter Haley, "Rudolph Sohm on Charisma," *Journal of Religion* 60, no. 2 (1980): 185-97.

5. For contemporary commentary on this biblical section, see the comprehensive bibliography cited in Colleen Shantz, *Paul in Ecstasy: The Neurobiology of the Apostle's Life and Thought* (Cambridge: Cambridge University Press, 2009), Chap. 4.

6. C. Stephen Jaeger, *The Envy of Angels: Cathedral Schools and Social Ideas in Medieval Europe, 950–1200* (Philadelphia: University of Pennsylvania Press, 1994), 3.

7. Mia Münster-Swendsen, "Medieval 'Virtuosity': Classroom Practice and the Transfer of Charismatic Power in Medieval Scholarly Culture c. 1000–1230," in *Negotiating Heritage: Memories of the Middle Ages*, ed. Mette B. Bruun and Stephanie Glaser (Turnhout: Brepols, 2008), 43–63.

8. The statutes of 1215 determine that "nullus sit scolaris Parisius, qui certum magistrum non habeat," indicating thereby that there were certainly such students at the time; *Chartularium Universitatis Parisiensis* [CUP] I, no. 20, p. 79, ed. Heinrich Denifle, Emile Chatelain, Charles Samaran, and Émile A. van Moé (Brussels: Culture et civilisation, 1964).

9. For a short portrait of the undisciplined student (*scolaris discolus*), see Ps. Boethius, *De Disciplina Scolarium* 2.3, ed. Olga Weijers (Leiden and Cologne: Brill, 1976), 99. Many other sources are discussed by Stephen C. Ferruolo, *The Origins of the University: The Schools of Paris and Their Critics, 1100–1215* (Stanford, Calif.: Stanford University Press, 1985). For a fictional yet vivid depiction, see Umberto Eco, *Baudolino*, trans. William Weaver (New York: Harcourt, 2002), esp. Chaps. 6–8.

10. On the housing crisis in the early thirteenth century, see Bertrand Durbin, "La crise du lodgement des étudiants à Paris au XIIème siècle" (Ph.D. diss., Paris: Université Panthéon-Assas, 2005). On the evolution of the college in Paris, see especially Alexander Gieysztor, "Management and Resources," in *A History of the University in Europe*, ed. Hilde de Ridder-Symoens (Cambridge: Cambridge University Press, 1992), 1:116–19.

11. "Nullus recipiatur Parisius ad lectiones sollempnes vel ad predicationes, nisi probate vite fuerit et scientie"; CUP I, no. 20, p, 79. The statutes of 1231 describe a discrete procedure of examining the life and conduct of a candidate as well; CUP I, no.79, p. 137.

12. Charles H. Haskins, *Studies in Mediaeval Culture* (New York: Ungar, 1929), 79–92. John of Garland, an English grammar teacher living in Paris, wrote, next to other grammatical and pedagogical works, a guide that had the explicit aim to promote *curialitas* and to cast away *rusticitas* from the disciples' life; Garland, *Morale Scolarium of John of Garland (Johannes de Garlandia)*, ed., introduction Louis John Paetow (Berkeley: University of California Press, 1927), 188, 397, and passim.

13. On political theory, see Jürgen Miethke, "Practical Intentions of Scholasticism: The Example of Political Theory," in *Universities and Schooling in Medieval Society*, ed. William J. Courtenay and Jürgen Miethke (Leiden, Boston, and Cologne: Brill, 2000), 211–28.

14. On the teaching of ethics in the faculty of arts, see Réné A. Gauthier, "Le cours sur l'Ethica Nova d'un maître ès Arts (1235–1240)," *AHDLMA* 42 (1975): 71–141; Georg Wieland, *Ethica, scientia practica: Die Anfänge der philosophischen Ethik im 13. Jahrhundert* (Münster and Bonn: Aschendorff, 1981); Valeria A. Buffon, "Happiness and Knowledge in Some Masters of Arts before 1250: An Analysis of Some Commentaries on the Book I of Nicomachean Ethics," *Patristica et Medievalia* 25 (2004): 111–15; David Luscombe, "Ethics in the Early Thirteenth Century," in *Albertus Magnus und die Anfänge der Aristoteles-Rezeption im lateinischen Mittelalter: Von Richardus Rufus bis zu Franciscus de Mayronis* (Münster: Aschendorff, 2005), 657–83; Buffon, "The Structure of the Soul, Intellectual Virtues, and the Ethical Ideal of Masters of Arts in Early Commentaries on the *Nichomachean Ethics*," in *Virtue Ethics in the Middle Ages: Commentaries on Aristotle's Nicomachean Ethics, 1200–1500*, ed. István Pieter Bejczy (Leiden and Boston: Brill, 2008), 13–30. Although Aristotle's *Ethics* was known only partly, it seems that at least Roland of Cremona knew also the sixth book; see *Summa Magistri Rolandi Cremonensis O.P. Liber Tercius* [SR], ed. Alois Cortesi (Bergamo: Monumenta Bergomensia, 1962), 266.

15. Henri d'Andeli, *Les dits d'Henri D'Andeli: Suivis de deux versions du Mariage des septs Arts*, ed., trans. Alain Corbellari (Paris: Champion, 2003), 75–87. On the topos of the seduced Aristotle, see Susan L. Smith, "Tales of the Mounted Aristotle," in *The Power of Women: A Topos in Medieval Art and Literature* (Philadelphia: University of Pennsylvania Press, 1985), 66–74. Jacques de Vitry's version of the story appears there as well.

16. D'Andeli, *Les dits*, 85 (my translation).

17. CUP I, no. 19, pp. 77–78.

18. CUP I, no. 27, p. 85.

19. CUP I, no. 48, p.105. Cf. I, no. 54, p.110.

20. CUP I, no. 59, p. 115.

21. Marian Michel Mulchahey, *"First the Bow Is Bent in Study . . . ," Dominican Education Before 1350* (Toronto: Pontifical Institute of Mediaeval Studies, 1998).

22. The constitutions of 1239 were compiled under Albert of Pisa, forming the legislative basis for those of the 1260s compiled under Bonaventure. The fragments that survived from this early legislative corpus are discussed by several articles of Cenci, and were published in Cenci, "De fratrum minorum constitutionibus praenarbonensibus," 50–95.

23. "[No. I.3] Et, quia non solum propter nostram salutem vocavit nos deus, verum etiam propter aliorum aedificationem per exempla, consilia et salubria hortamenta; ordinavimus quod nullus recipiatur in ordine nostro nisi sit talis clericus qui sit competenter instructus in gramatica vel logica"; ibid., 75. The Pre-Narbonian constitutions lack the reasoning clause, beginning with "nullus recipiatur" and enumerate in addition also medicine, canon and civil law, and theology.

24. Gerard of Frachet, *Vitae Fratrum Ordinis Praedicatorum* 5.5, ed. Benedict M. Reichert, Monumenta Ordinis Pradicatorum Historica 1 (Louvain: Charpentier and Schoonjas, 1896), 160.

25. Ibid., 161.

26. Cassiodorus, "Prophetia est inspiratio vel revelatio divina rerum eventus immobili veritate pronunciat (or: *denuncians* in several manuscripts)"; *Prologus super Psalmos*, CCL 97.7.

27. William of Auxerre, *Summa aurea* [SA] 2.7.1, ed. Jean Ribaillier, in *Spicilegium Bonaventurianum* (Paris: Grottaferrata, 1980–87), 1:143.

28. "Duplex est visio. Est enim visio adherentie et est visio non adherentie. Visio enim adherentie est que stat in apprehensione veri et est in speculativo intellectu; et ideo ipsa non est virtus. Visio autem non adherentie que est in intellectu practico et transsit ab apprehensione veri usque ad delectationem boni, virtus est. Visio autem prophetie primi generis erat, non secundi; et ideo virtus non erat"; William of Auxerre, SA 2.7.1, 1:145.

29. Alexander of Hales, *De prophetia*, Quaestiones disputatae *"Antequam esset frater"* [QDA], q. 18, ed. Quaracchi Fathers, Bibliotheca Franciscana scholastica medii aevi, t. 19–21 (Quaracchi, Florence: Collegii S. Bonaventurae, 1960), 1:332.

30. Ibid., 1:333.

31. "Sicut gratia praedicandi datur alicui malo aliquando, non propter se, sed propter alios, quia quando adversarii testimoniis suis confirmant fidem, multo maior est confirmatio bonorum in bono et boni firmiores redduntur"; ibid.

32. Philip the Chancellor, *Philippi Cancellarii Summa de bono* [SB], ed. Nikolaus Wicki (Bern: Francke, 1985), 2:506.

33. Jean-Pierre Torrell, "La question 540 (*De Prophetia*) du Manuscrit de Douai 434," *Antonianum* 49 (1974): 522.

34. Philip the Chancellor, SB, 2:508.

35. A great account of the evolution of the idea of unformed and formed faith, as well as the subtle discussions over the role of caritas in faith's formation as a virtue, is in Georg Englhardt, *Die Entwicklung der dogmatischen Glaubenspsychologie in der mittelalterlichen Scholastik vom Abaelardstreit (um 1140) bis zu Philipp dem Kanzler (gest. 1236)* (Münster in Westfalen: Aschendorff, 1933), Chap. 2.3.

36. See Alexander's *Glossa*, where he enumerates his questions in this order: "Utrum fides informis sit donum dei; deinde utrum sit virtus; tertium utrum sit in cognitiva vel in operativa; quarto utrum fit virtus adveniente caritate; quinto utrum sit idem habitus cum fide formata"; Alexander of Hales, *Glossa in quatuor libros Sententiarum Petri Lombardi* [GS], lib. III, ed. the Quaracchi, Bibliotheca Franciscana scholastica medii aevi, t. 12–15 (Florence: Collegii S. Bonaventurae, 1954), 3:265. Cf. Alexander's question *De fide informi*, QDA 2:673.

37. Philip the Chancellor, SB, 2:599.

38. This is another aspect of the general systematization of the concepts of natural and supernatural that occurred in early thirteenth-century theology. For

other aspects, see Robert Bartlett, *The Natural and the Supernatural in the Middle Ages* (Cambridge: Cambridge University Press, 1998), especially Chap. 1.

39. I preferred using here the somewhat cumbersome yet emic expression *super se* rather than the more familiar "supernatural," since the expressions *contra naturam, preter naturam*, and *supra naturam* are not used in this specific context.

40. Jean-Pierre Torrell, *Théorie de la prophétie et philosophie de la connaissance aux environs de 1230: La contribution d'Hugues de Saint-Cher (Ms. Douai 434, Question 481)* (Leuven: Spicilegium Sacrum Lovaniense, 1977), 118–19.

41. On Martin, see Richard Heinzmann, *Die "Compilatio quaestionum theologiae secundum Magistrum Martinum"* (Munich: Hueber, 1964), 9.

For the "Ne transgrediaris," see Vat. Lat. 10754, fol. 28rb–31rb.

42. Paris, BnF Lat. 16385, fols. 53a–54b, and Cambridge, St. John's College 57, fols. 288c–290a. In the summa, however, *On Prophecy* is placed at the end of the first book. See George Lacombe, "The Questiones of Cardinal Stephen Langton: Part II," *New Scholasticism* 3 (1929): 134, as well as Riccardo Quinto's survey of manuscripts in *Doctor Nominatissimus: Stefano Langton (1228) e la tradizione delle sue opere*, Beiträge zur Geschichte der Philosophie und Theologie des Mittelalters 39 (Münster: Aschendorff, 1994), 183–84 and 159, 162.

43. Brugge, Stadtbibliothek 220, fols. 99va–101rb.

44. William of Auxerre, SA 2.7.2, 2:142.

45. Torrell, *Théorie de la prophétie*, 268.

46. In codex Douai BM 434, see questions 337–38 (cognition of angels and rapture), as well as 480–81 (rapture and prophecy). A juxtaposition similar to the latter is found also in one of the manuscripts of Alexander's early *quaestiones*, Toulouse, BM 737, fols.102c–4b; 104b–8a, according to the description of manuscript's contents provided in the prolegomena to Alexander of Hales's *Quaestiones* QDA 1:13*.

47. Paris, Mazarine 795, fol. 35vb.

48. Philip the Chancellor, SB, 2:489.

49. Ibid. Cf. the *Summa Douacensis*, where the "bonum gratie in homine" section is divided into nongratifying and gratifying grace, the quotation from I Cor. 12 is brought forth, and an apology follows, regarding the absence of all other issues pertaining to this class as they were already discussed in other places; *La "Summa Duacensis" (Douai 434): Texte critique avec une introduction et des tables*, ed. Palémon Glorieux, Textes philosophiques du moyen âge 2 (Paris: Vrin, 1955), 123–24.

50. This term is not found in Stephen Langton, as far as I was able to check, except for a comment in the margin of Paris, BnF, Lat. 16385, fol. 53r, noting that "prophetia est donum gratuitum non gratum faciens." It can however be a later addition.

51. See, for instance, the chapter "De gratia in generali: De diversis acceptionibus gratie et eius rationibus"; Philip the Chancellor, SB, 1:355ff.

52. Ibid., 2:530, 2:758.

53. Alexander of Hales, *Summa Halensis*, in *Summa theologica seu sic ab origine dicta "Summa Fratris Alexandri"* [SH] 3.1.2.1, ed. Bernardini Klumper, Victorin Doucet, and the Quaracchi Fathers (Rome: Collegii S. Bonaventurae, 1928), 2:1023.

54. "The spirit of adoption" is positioned against that of servitude in Rom. 8:15. For "the spirit of truth," see John 16:13.

55. "Duplex differentia: prima est quod gratia gratum faciens facit habere spiritum sanctum, et si non habetur. Gratia enim gratum faciens ponit spiritum in re. Gratia vero gratis data ponit spiritum sanctum in manifestatione siue ostensione"; Paris, BnF Lat. 15602, fol.112ra. Cf. the discussion of divine presence in the soul in SH 1.1.2.3.3, 1:83: "dona gratis data sunt sicut dispositiones quae animam ad hoc disponunt, sicut est prophetia, scientia et huiusmodi: nec tamen anima adhuc est templum dei."

56. "Donum infusum rationali naturae sine meritis quantum in se est, disponens ad salutem propriam vel aedificationem alterius"; SH 3.3.1.2, 2:1025.

57. Ibid., 2:1026.

58. Ibid., 2:1027.

59. Artur M. Landgraf, "Die Erkenntnis der helfenden Gnade in der Frühscholastik," in *Dogmengeschichte der Frühscholastik* (Regensburg: Pustet, 1952), 1:52–62.

60. An indexical survey of Alexander of Hales's Gloss to the *Sentences* confirms this observation. Almost all instances of the distinction *gratum / non gratum faciens* occur in a context of knowledge devoid of moral aspects, such as the merit of a prophet who has no love in his heart or the circumstances under which wisdom and sin can reside next to each other. In principle every grace is "freely given," *gratis data*. Yet sometimes NGF is called in short *gratia gratis data*, as opposed to *gratia gratum faciens*; see Alexander of Hales, *Glossa* lib. 1, dist. 16, 18, GS 1:164–65, 182.

61. For earlier distinctions between gifts "with the spirit" (*cum spiritu*) and "by the spirit," see Alan de Lille's text, quoted in Odon Lottin, *Psychologie et morale aux XIIe et XIIIe siècles* (Gembloux: Duculot, 1949), 1:333. Praepositinus of Cremona presents the same distinction dealing with the difference between the Holy Spirit and the spirit of prophecy, bringing the case of a prophet who sins; Todi, Lat. 65, fol.25rb.

62. "Deus operatur omnia in omnibus; unde inferunt: ergo tam bona quam mala. Ergo qui cognoscit deum in se omnia operari, peccare non potest"; Garnerius of Rochefort, *Contra Amaurianos*, ed. Paolo Lucentini, CCCM 232 (Brepols: Turnhout, 2010), 12.

63. Ibid., 15, as well as almost all other descriptions of the Amalrician errors.

64. Ibid., 80; cf. 15.

65. Guerric of St. Quentin, his Dominican contemporary and colleague, pays little attention if at all to preaching or to NGF grace in his commentary on the

same verses; Paris, BnF Lat. 15604, fols. 41v–42r. He distinguishes gifts necessary for salvation from gifts that are not and characterizes the latter as given for the benefit of the church, but neither develops these ideas nor connects them with preaching.

66. Franco Morenzoni, "Parole du prédicateur et inspiration divine d'après les artes praedicandi," in La Parole du prédicateur Ve–XVe siècle, ed. Rosa Maria Dessi and Michel Lauwers (Nice: Collection du centre d'études médiévales, 1997), 271–310. See in this respect also Carla Casagrande, "Le calame du Saint-Esprit: Grâce et rhétorique dans la prédication au XIIIe siècle," in La parole du prédicateur, Ve–XVe siècle, ed. Rosa Maria Dessi and Michel Lauwers (Nice: Presses Universitaires de Nice, 1997), 235–54.

67. Quoted in Morenzoni, "Parole du prédicateur et inspiration divine," 282.

68. Salimbene de Adam, Cronica, ed. Giuseppe Scalia, CCCM 125–25A (Turnhout: Brepols, 1998–99), 1:322.

69. Jacques de Vitry, The Historia Occidentalis of Jacques de Vitry: A Critical Edition, ed. John Frederick Hinnebusch, Spicilegium Friburgense 17 (Fribourg: University Press, 1972), 97.

70. Ibid., 100.

71. Thomas Celano, Vita Prima, Vita Secunda, et Tractatus de Miraculis, 73.10, in Analecta Franciscana (Rome: Quaracchi, 1926–41), 10:193–94.

72. Jonathan Parry, "Mauss, Dumont and the Distinction between Status and Power," in Marcel Mauss, A Centenary Tribute, ed. Wendy James and N. J. Allen (New York: Berghahn, 1998), 166–67, cited by Gadi Algazi, "Doing Things with Gifts," in Negotiating the Gift: Pre-modern Figurations of Exchange, ed. Gadi Algazi, Valentin Groebner, and Bernhard Jussen (Göttingen: Vandenhoeck and Ruprecht, 2003), 16.

73. An all-applicability should not be assumed a priori. In a preliminary study about the semantic field of gift, Bernhard Jussen claimed that in religious discourse the model of gift and counter-gift rarely existed, against his expectations. The common model until the twelfth century, he argues, was "more like a contract," based on the reciprocity of opus-remuneratio; Bernhard Jussen, "Religious Discourses of the Gift in the Middle Ages: Semantic Evidences (Second to Twelfth Centuries)," in Negotiating the Gift, 189.

74. Ayelet Even-Ezra, "The Questio de officio predicacionis of Gauthier de Château Thierry: A Critical Edition," AHDLMA 81 (2014): 385–462.

75. Ibid., 421, 440, 444, 447.

76. Ibid., 402, 405. Cf. Alexander de Hales, De officio praedicationis, QDA, 1: 520.

77. William of Auxerre, SA 3.20.1, 3:388–389.

78. Ibid., 3:391.

79. Ibid., 3.33.3 (3:634, 639, 644, 647). Cf. the discussion of prudence in 3:380ff.

80. Philip the Chancellor, SB, 2:761–62

81. Ibid., 2:541.

82. Roland of Cremona, SR 3.85, 257.

83. "Non qui magis opinatur aut scit in eis quae virtutum sunt, magis bonus aut virtuosus est, hoc autem ex necessitate sequeretur"; William of Auvergne, *De virtutibus, Guilielmi Alverni Opera Omnia* [GOO] (Paris, 1674), 1:111.

84. "Esse virtutis ex parte affectionis determinatur"; Philip the Chancellor, SB, 2:538–39. Cf. 2:758.

85. MacDonald usefully distinguishes between two separate ways to think about the relationship between goodness and being in the Western tradition, the ways combined to different degrees in many authors from Plato and Aristotle on. He terms the first the "participation" or "creation" approach, in which all forms and beings are seen as emanating from the good and returning to it. Through Augustine, Boethius, and Pseudo-Dionysius, this approach was dominant until the early thirteenth century, when the second approach—the "nature" approach—became influential; Scott MacDonald, ed., *Being and Goodness: The Concept of the Good in Metaphysics and Philosophical Theology* (Ithaca, N.Y.: Cornell University Press, 1991), Introduction, as well as MacDonald, "Goodness as Transcendental: The Early Thirteenth-Century Recovery of an Aristotelian Idea," *Topoi* 11 (1992): 177–80.

86. Two long bibliographic lists on the medieval theory of transcendentals up to 1999 are provided in Jan Aertsen, "The Medieval Doctrine of the Transcendentals: The Current State of Research," *Bulletin de philosophie médiévale* 33 (1966): 130–47, and Aertsen, "The Medieval Doctrine of the Transcendentals: New Literature," *Bulletin de philosophie médiévale* 41 (1999): 107–21.

87. On beauty as transcendental, see, among the articles cited previously, Henri Pouillon's old work, "La beauté, propriété transcendantale chez les scolastiques (1220–1270)," *AHDLMA* 15 (1946): 293–305.

88. Augustine, *De diversis quaestionibus octoginta tribus liber*, q. 24, ed. Almut Mutzenbacher, CCSL 44a (Turnhout: Brepols, 1975), 29.

89. "Idem est verum quod bonum; sed verum dicitur in quantum est sine actu, bonum in quantum est cum actu"; William of Auxerre, SA 3.10.4, 3:153. Cf. Aristotle's *De anima* 431b10–11. James of Venice's translation reads (according to Ribaillier's note), "Et omnino in actione et sine autem actu verum et falsum in eodem genere est bono et malo."

90. Ibid., 3.34.2, 3:651. On William of Auxerre's aesthetics, see also Boyd Taylor Coolman, *Knowing God by Experience: The Spiritual Senses in the Theology of William of Auxerre* (Washington, D.C.: The Catholic University of America Press, 2004), 162–83.

91. Cf. William's third argument in the *quaestio quid frui*: "Delectatio est in visione pulchri sensibilis; ergo delectatio est in visione pulchri intelligibilis; ergo intellectus habet delectationem suam in fine suo et perfectione; sed perfectio intellectus est fides; fide igitur delectatur intellectus in deo, et sic fide fruimur Deo"; William of Auxerre, SA 3.36.1, 3:685.

92. "Item, constat quod 'cuius est quies, eius est motus ad quietem' [Aristotle, *Physica* 6.8]. Sed motus ad quietem est desiderium . . . ergo prima veritas, in quantum est prima veritas est quietativa desiderii; ergo in quantum est prima veritas est bonum; ergo amor prime veritatis, in quantum est prima veritas, est amor primi sive sumi boni; sed amor summi boni nichil aliud est quam caritas"; Ibid., 3.10.4, 3:150.

93. One of William's intriguing ideas to explain faith being a cognitive virtue is his original application of Avicenna's concept of *estimatio* to this subject. It exceeds the framework of this study, but a brief treatment is provided in Coolman, *Knowing God by Experience*, 125–28. Cf. the contributions of Magdalena Bieniak and Riccardo Saccenti in Marco Forlivesi, Riccardo Quinto, and Silvana Vecchio, eds., *"Fides virtus": The Virtue of Faith from the Twelfth to the Early Sixteenth Century* (Münster: Aschendorff, 2014).

94. William of Auvergne, "Tractatus Magistri Guillelmi Alvernensis *De bono et malo*," ed. J. Reginald O'Donnell, *Mediaeval Studies* 8 (1946): 247–49. The transcendental discussions focus on goodness and being, but the true returns around page 277.

95. Ibid., 325.

96. Ibid., 297.

97. The *Summa Douacensis* shares this organizing principle, according to Glorieux's reconstruction; *La "Summa Duacensis"* (Douai 434), 7–8. An earlier attempt to organize a theological comprehensive work around an ethical principle is Radulfus Ardens's *Speculum Universale*, which begins with the problem "What is Scientia," proceeds to "What is ethics," ethic's parts and virtue's definition, then to various theological issues; *Speculum Universale* I–V, ed. Claudia Heinmann and Stephan Herst, CCCM 241 (Tournhout: Brepols, 2011).

98. Pouillon, "Le premier traité des propriétés transcendentals, La 'Summa de bono' du Chancellier Phillipe," *Revue néoscolastique de philosophie* 42 (1939): 40–77.

99. "Item verum est fidei, bonum autem caritatis aut spei . . . ergo per hoc constat verum et bonum differre, quare et habere aliam definitionem"; Philip the Chancellor, SB, 1:9.

100. Ibid., 1:17.

101. "Sed contra. Secundum hoc videretur quod scientia esset virtus, nam secundum scientiam tendit intellectus in suum delectabile et ita in bonum sibi, et omne tendens in bonum simpliciter aut in bonum sibi, huic est virtus, Ergo *scientia est virtus*"; Philip the Chancellor, SB, 2:588.

102. Ibid.

103. An elaborate version of this metaphor is provided in page 122 of William of Auvergne, *De virtutibus*. The will is the king; the exterior senses are his emissaries or informants; common sense, imagination, and memory are the king's treasure chests or libraries; the intellect is his counselor, while reason is the judge.

104. "Manifestum autem est quod studere, disputare, cogitare, doctores audire, libros inspicere et in rebus ipsis meditari motus sunt quos non est dubium esse ei adminicula ad acquisitionem perfectionis quae scientia est"; William of Auvergne, *De anima*, GOO 2:98 (the metaphor of the counselor appearing in pages 95–96).

105. The most recent being Nathalie Gorochov, *Naissance de l'université: Les écoles de Paris d'Innocent III à Thomas d'Aquin (v. 1200–v. 1245)* (Paris: Champion, 2012), and Ian P. Wei, *Intellectual Culture in Medieval Paris* (Cambridge: Cambridge University Press, 2012).

106. Cf. CUP I no. 4, p. 63; I, no. 19, p. 77; I, no. 32, p. 91.

107. Ibid., I, no. 57, p. 113. Mulchahey points out many other privileges for excellent students throughout her monograph *"First the Bow Is Bent in Study . . ."*

108. In his study of careers of masters of theology, Avi-Yonah sees the decades under investigation in this dissertation as a turning point in this respect. In the two decades of 1201–20, he observed, there is an increase in the number of secular masters of theology who leave the university to pursue their career outside it. This process reached its peak in the decade of 1221–30, as out of seventeen known masters, only four had what he terms "inter-university" careers. Out of these four, he claims, "only William of Auxerre, the well known theologian, can be said to have truly chosen the university." Thirteen left, out of which eight became bishops, one an archbishop, and two cardinals. Later, however, he discerns a sharp decrease in the number of those who leave and a matching increase in the number of those who choose to continue teaching, and the numbers are more or less equal. From 1230 onward, there is also a sharp decrease in the number of secular masters appointed to high ecclesiastical functions; Reuven Avi-Yonah, "Career Trends of Parisian Masters of Theology, 1200–1320," *History of Universities* 6 (1986): 50–51. Young, however, criticizes Avi-Yonah's arguments; Spencer E. Young, *Scholarly Community at the Early University of Paris: Theologians, Education and Society, 1215–1248* (Cambridge: Cambridge University Press, 2014), 66–70.

109. Leonardo Sileo, *Teoria della scienza theologica: Quaestio de scientia theologiae di Odo Rigaldi e altri testi inedita (1230–1250)* (Rome: Pontificium Athenaeum Antonianum, 1984), 2:73.

110. Cf. Young, *Scholarly Community*, 37.

111. This is an important aspect of the distinction between pure neutral knowledge and "active" moral knowledge, which could not receive proper attention in this study. One of the solutions to the dualist position was to distinguish within the divine knowledge between neutral divine knowledge, by which God knows both good and bad things, and a creative, *experiential* knowledge, by which God knows only the good things.

112. According to Rigaldi, theology is both theoretical and practical. Nevertheless, he determines it to be entirely practical, for it has one ultimate end, to which everything is ordained: the good and the deed. Theology does not stand in

truth (*sistit in vero*) and therefore concerns both the intellect and the *affectus*; Sileo, *Teoria della scienza theologica*, 42, 47, 49–51.

113. Alexander de Hales, *De officio praedicationis*, QDA 2:523.

114. Aristotle, *Ethica vetus*, in *Ethica Nicomachea: Translatio Roberti Grosseteste Lincoliensis*, ed. René A. Gauthier, Aristoteles Latinus XXVI, 3. (Leiden and Brussells: Brill, 1972), 7.

115. Vat. Lat. 782, fol. 136ra. For an extended discussion, see Even-Ezra, "'Qui predicat magister est': Preaching and Teaching in Paris according to Gualterus de Castro Theodorici (d. 1249)," in *Les débuts de l'enseignement universitaire à Paris (1200–1245 environ)*, ed. Olga Weijers and Jacques Verger (Tournhout: Brepols, 2013), 349–57.

116. Paris, BnF Lat. 3804A, fol. 108rb.

117. "Perscrutatio sive sapientia sacrae scripturae non est nisi mentium purgatarum a labe peccati: quomodo homines immundi per peccatum praesumunt exponere Sacram Scripturam cum sapientia sacrae scripturae in eis non habitet. Igitur invocandus est deus, cuius solius est peccata dimittere et mentes purgare: purget mentes nostras"; transcribed in G. Abate and G. Luisetto, *Codici e manoscritti della Biblioteca Antoniana*, col catalogo delle miniature, ed. F. Avril, F. d'Arcais, and G. Mariani Canova. (Vicenza: Neri Pozza, 1975), 176.

118. Prague IV D 13, fol. 80rb.

119. The text was edited in Jeanne Bignamie-Odier, "Le manuscrit Vatican Latin 2186," *AHDLMA* 11 (1937): 133–66.

120. "Scientia pietatis docet et ea per que illuminatur intelligens ad cognitiones veritatis credibilium et operabilium, et ea per que movetur affectus ad amorem et aquisitionem boni beatificantis et genera eius que exiguntur ad hec"; ibid., 147.

121. Philip the Chancellor, SB, Prologue, 1:4.

122. A rare example of direct application of these ideas of different styles for different parts of the soul and different aims of the writer is found in William of Auvergne's *De Virtutibus*. William declares already at the beginning that he is about to investigate the next issues in two ways. The way of proofs should create in the reader certitude about these questions. Later, he promises, he shall talk about the same subjects in a different, enjoyable manner, in order to create in the reader the affective knowledge, and he does so remarkably; William of Auvergne, *De virtutibus*, GOO, 1:102, 119. On the *via probationis* vs. *via narrationum*, see also William of Auvergne, "Tractatus secundus Guillelmi Alvernensis *De bono et malo*," ed. J. Reginald O'Donnell, *Mediaeval Studies* 16 (1954): 220.

123. Alexander is presumed to have introduced the *Sentences* into the formal curriculum of theological training, although it had been available from at least the days of Lombard's direct disciples. The evidence we have for this development is very scattered and insufficient, but I am inclined to accept Rosemann's interpretation that Alexander's novelty was that he was the first master who based his "ordinary" morning lectures upon the *Sentences* rather than upon

scriptures and did not leave them to the afternoon "cursory" exercises. This move, however, was controversial, as Rosemann shows: when a similar move was made at the University of Oxford in the 1240s, Robert Grosseteste protested vigorously; the masters appealed to the curia, and Rome sided with them. In both Paris and Oxford, the *Sentences* became a standard textbook, yet the work of the bachelor; Philipp W. Rosemann, *The Story of a Great Medieval Book: Peter Lombard's Sentences* (Toronto: University of Toronto Press, 2007), 60–61.

124. William of Auvergne, *De Trinitate* 26, ed. Bruno Switalski (Toronto: Pontifical Institute of Mediaeval Studies, 1976), 150–52.

125. Ibid., 16. For a thorough account of William's understanding of his own project, see Roland J. Teske, "William of Auvergne on Philosophy as *divinalis* and *sapientialis*," in *Was ist Philosophie im Mittelalter? / Qu'est-ce que la philosophie au moyen age? / What Is Philosophy in the Middle Ages?: Akten Der 10. Internationale Kongress für Mittelalterliche Philosophie vom 25. bis 30. August 1997 in Erfurt in Kurzfassungen*, ed. Jan A. Aersten and Andreas Speer (Berlin and New York: Walter de Gruyter, 1998), 475–81. Relevant quotations from the *De universo* are there; see 477–78.

126. Roland of Cremona, SR lib. 3.141, 418–19.

127. Giuseppe Cremascoli, "La 'Summa' di Rolando di Cremona, Il testo del prologo," *Studi Medievali* 16 (1975): 860.

128. Hugh's commentary has two prologues, designated by Faes de Mottoni as "Prologue I" (a discussion about divine attributes) and "Prologue II," which is a true prologue that is found in thirteen manuscripts; Barbara Faes de Mottoni, "Les manuscrits du commentaire des Sentences de Hugues de Saint-Cher," in *Hugues De Saint-Cher (†1263): Bibliste et theologien; Actes du colloque "Hugues de Saint-Cher, O.P., bibliste et théologien," Paris, Centre d'études du Saulchoir, 13–15 mars 2000* (Turnhout: Brepols, 2004), 280. I refer here to Prologue II, following MS Padova, Univ. 853.

129. Heinrich Weisweiler, "Théologiens de l'entourage d'Hugues de Saint-Cher," *RTAM* 8 (1936): 389–407; Franklin Harkins, "*Filiae Magistri*: Peter Lomard's Sentences and Medieval Theological Education 'On the Ground,'" in *Medieval Commentaries on the Sentences of Peter Lombard*, ed. Philipp W. Rosemann (Leiden: Brill, 2015), 26–78.

130. Rosemann, *Story of a Great Medieval Book*, 33–37.

SUMMARY AND EPILOGUE

1. The English translation of *Schwester Kathrei* follows Elvira Borgstädt's translation in Bernard McGinn ed., *Meister Eckhart, Teacher and Preacher*, Classics of Western Spirituality (N.Y.: Paulist Press, 1986), 350.

2. For how Beauty had become a subject for systematic thought in this period and about Victorine and Cistercian antecedents, see Wladyslaw Tatarkiewicz, *History of Aesthetics* (The Hague: Mouton, 1970–74), 1:3, 1.213, Umberto Eco, *The Aesthetics of Thomas Aquinas*, trans. Hugh Bredin (Cambridge, Mass.: Harvard

University Press, 1988), 4, 19; and Edgar de Bruyne, Introduction, in *Études d'esthétique médiévale*, 3 vols. (Brugge: De Tempel, 1946). Extracts from the early thirteenth century are provided in de Bruyne from 3:72 onward.

3. I use here "monastic" and "scholastic" as ideal types in the same way Jean Leclercq did in *The Love of Learning and the Desire for God: A Study of Monastic Culture*, trans. Catharine Misrahi (New York: Fordham University Press, 1974), although clearly these worlds actively interacted. It seems, however, that more emphasis was put on the way scholastic ideas and texts can be found in works such as the *Hortus deliciarum* than the other way around.

4. Colleen Shantz, *Paul in Ecstasy: The Neurobiology of the Apostle's Life and Thought* (Cambridge: Cambridge University Press, 2009), 13.

5. Ibid. Chapter 1 expounds on this bias.

6. Ibid., Chapter 2, esp. 87ff.

7. Cf. "De hoc vero quod apud scholasticos doctores atque scholares usualiter dicitur quod tres sunt dotes ... manifestum est sermonem huiusmodi plus habere rhetoricae quam exploratae veritatis"; *De retributionibus sanctorum*, GOO 1:327–28; *De virtutibus*, ibid., 1:168.

APPENDIX

1. On the editing process and the structure of the *Summa Aurea*, see William of Auxerre [SA], ed. Jean Ribaillier, in *Spicilegium Bonaventurianum* (Paris: Grottaferrata, 1987, 5:30–32, as well as Ayelet Even-Ezra, "Schemata as Maps and Editing Tools in Early Thirteenth-Century Scholasticism," *Manuscripta* 61, no. 1 (2017): 21–71.

2. Five *quaestiones* in Douai BM 434 I and II are *de fide*: q. 28 (continued forty pages later as no. 129), 45, 500 (attributed to Guiard of Laon), 501, and 530. The *quaestiones* 45, 501, and the last part of 530 present an intriguing philological challenge, as they are remarkably close in content, though different in wording and internal numbering (the same issue is, for instance, a "tertium membrum" in 501, and a "septimo queritur" in 45). They may be different student reports of the same disputation.

BIBLIOGRAPHY

ABBREVIATIONS

AHDLMA	Archives d'histoire doctrinale et littéraire du Moyen Âge
CCCM	Corpus Christianorum Continuatio Mediaevalis
CCL	Corpus Christianorum Latinorum
CUP	*Chartularium Universitatis Parisiensis*
GA	Alexander of Hales, *Glossa in quatuor libros Sententiarum Petri Lombardi*
GOO	William of Auvergne, *Guilielmi Alverni Opera Omnia.* 2 vols.
PL	*Patrologia Latina*
QDA	Alexander of Hales, *Quaestiones disputatae "Antequam esset frater"*
RSPT	*Revue des sciences philosophiques et théologiques*
RTAM	*Recherches de théologie ancienne et médiévale*
SA	William of Auxerre, *Summa aurea*
SB	Philip the Chancellor, *Summa de bono*
SH	Alexander of Hales, *Summa Halensis*, published as *Summa theologica seu sic ab origine dicta "Summa Fratris Alexandri"*
SR	The summa or "liber questionum" of Roland of Cremona, either in specified manuscripts or in Aloyso Cortesi, ed., *Summa Magistri Rolandi Cremonensis O. P. Liber Tercius*

MANUSCRIPTS

Assisi, Bibliotheca Communale 415
Avranches, Bibliothèque Municipale 121
Bologna, Università 2554
Brugge, Stadtbibliothek 220
Cambridge, St. John's College 57
Douai, Bibliothèque Municipale 434 vols. I and II
London, British Library (Previously BM), Royal 9 E XII
Padova, Università, 853
Padova, Pontifica Bibliotheca Antoniana 152
Paris, Bibliothèque Nationale Lat. 3143
Paris, Bibliothèque Nationale Lat. 3804A
Paris, Bibliothèque Nationale Lat. 14526
Paris, Bibliothèque Nationale Lat. 14726
Paris, Bibliothèque Nationale Lat. 15602
Paris, Bibliothèque Nationale Lat. 15604
Paris, Bibliothèque Nationale Lat. 15652

Paris, Bibliothèque Nationale Lat. 16385
Paris, Mazarine 795
Prague, University Library IV D 13
Todi, Bibliothèque Municipale, Lat. 65
Toulouse, Bibliothèque Municipale 737
Vatican, Vat. Lat. 691
Vatican, Vat. Lat. 782
Vatican, Vat. Lat. 10754
Vatican, Barb. Lat.729

PRIMARY EDITED SOURCES

Aelred of Riveaux. *Dialogus De Anima*. In *Aelredi Rievallensis Opera omnia*, edited by Anselm Hoste and Charles H. Talbot. CCCM 1, 1: 685–754. Turnhout: Brepols, 1971–2005.

Alan de Lille. *Anticlaudianus: Texte critique avec une introduction et des tables.* Edited by Robert Bossuat. Paris: Vrin, 1955.

———. *De virtutibus et vitiis*. Edited by Odon Lottin. In "Le traité d'Alain de Lille sur les Vertus, les Vices et les Dons du Saint-Esprit." *Psychologie et morale aux XIIe et XIIIe siècles*, 5:45–92. Gembloux: Duculot, 1960.

———. *Regule Celestis Iuris*. Edited by Nikolaus M. Häring. "Magistri Alani Regule Celestis Iuris." *AHDLMA* 48 (1981): 97–226.

Alcher of Clairvaux (Pseudo-Augustine). *De spiritu et anima liber unus*. PL 40, cols. 779–832.

Alexander of Hales. [=GS] *Glossa in quatuor libros Sententiarum Petri Lombardi*. Edited by the Quaracchi Fathers. Bibliotheca Franciscana scholastica medii aevi, t. 12–15, 4 vols. Quaracchi, Florence: Collegii S. Bonaventurae, 1951, 1952, 1954, 1957.

———. [=QDA] *Quaestiones disputatae "Antequam esset frater."* Edited by the Quarracchi Fathers. Bibliotheca Franciscana scholastica medii aevi, t. 19–21. 3 vols. Quaracchi, Florence: Collegii S. Bonaventurae, 1960.

———. [=SH] *Summa theologica seu sic ab origine dicta "Summa Fratris Alexandri."* Edited by Bernardini Klumper, Victorin Doucet, and the Quarracchi Fathers, 4 vols. Rome: Collegii S. Bonaventurae, 1924–48.

Angelo Clareno. *A Chronicle or History of the Seven Tribulations of the Order of Brothers Minor*. Edited and translated by David Burr and E. Randolph Daniel. St. Bonaventure, N.Y.: Franciscan Institute, 2005.

———. *Liber chronicarum sive tribulationum ordinis minorum di frate Angelo Clareno*. Edited by Giovanni Boccali, with introduction by Felice Accrocca and Italian translation by Marino Bigaroni. Perugia: Santa Maria degli Angeli, 1999.

Aristotle. *Analytica Posteriora*. Edited by Laurentius Minio-Paluello and Bernardus G. Dod. Aristoteles Latinus IV 1–4. Bruges: Desclée de Brouwer, 1954.

---. *Analytica Posteriora: Aristotle's Prior and Posterior Analytics*. A revised text with introduction and commentary by William. D. Ross. Oxford: Clarendon, 1965.

---. *Categoriae vel Praedicamenta Translatio Boethii, Editio Composite, Translatio Guillelmi de Moerbeka, Lemmata e Simplicii commentario decerpta, Pseudo-Augustini Paraphrasis Themistiana*. Edited by Laurentius Minio-Paluello. Aristoteles Latinus I.1–5. Bruges and Paris: Desclée de Brouwer, 1961.

---. *The Complete Works of Aristotle*. Edited by Jonathan Barnes. Various translators. Princeton: Princeton University Press, 1984.

---. *Ethica Nicomachea: Translatio Roberti Grosseteste Lincoliensis*. Edited by René A. Gauthier. Aristoteles Latinus XXVI, 3. Leiden and Brussells: Brill, 1972.

---. *Ethica Nicomachea: Translatio antiquissima libr. II–III sive "Ethica Vetus" et Translationis antiquioris quae supersunt sive "Ethica Nova," "Hoferiana," "Borghesiana."* Edited by René A. Gauthier. Aristoteles Latinus XXVI, 2. Leiden and Brussells: Brill, 1972.

---. *Physica, Translatio vetus*. Edited by Fernand Bossier and Jozef Brams. Aristoteles Latinus VII, 1. Leiden and New York: Brill, 1990.

Aristoteles Latinus Database, Brepols. http://www.brepols.net/Pages /ShowProduct. aspx?prod_id=IS-9782503511108-1. Accessed December 2015.

Atto of Vercelli. *Expositio in epistolas Beati Pauli*. PL 134, cols. 125–834.

Augustine. *De diversis quaestionibus octoginta tribus liber*. Edited by Almut Mutzenbecher. CCSL 44a. Turnhout: Brepols, 1975.

---. *De genesi ad litteram libri duodecim*. Edited by Joseph Zycha. Corpus Scriptorum Ecclesiasticorum Latinorum 28. Prague: Tempsky, 1894.

Avicenna Latinus. *Liber de anima seu Sextus de naturalibus*. Edited by Simone Van Riet. Introduction by Gerald Verbeke. Louvain and Leiden: Peeters and Brill, vol. 1 (lib. I–III) 1972; vol. 2 (lib. IV–V), 1968.

Bernard Gui. *Manuel de l'inquisiteur*. Edited and translated by Guillaume Mollat and Georges Drioux. 2 vols. Paris: Champion, 1926.

Blund, John. *Iohannes Blund Tractatus de Anima*. Edited by Daniel A. Callus and Richard. W. Hunt. Auctores Britannici Medii Aevi 2. London: Oxford University Press, 1970.

Boethius (Ps.). *De disciplina scolarium*. Edited by Olga Weijers. Leiden and Cologne: Brill, 1976.

Bourbon, Stephen de. *Tractatus de diversis materiis*. Extracts published by Albert Lecoy de La Marche. In *Anecdotes historiques, légendes et apologues, tirés du recueil inédit d'Etienne de Bourbon*. Paris: Henri Loones, 1877.

Bruno the Carthusian. *Divi Brunonis expositio in epistolas Pauli*. PL 153, cols. 11–567.

Caesarius of Heisterbach. *Caesarius Heiserbacencis monachi ordinis Cisterciensis Dialogus miraculorum*. Edited by Joseph Strange. 2 vols. Cologne: Heberle, 1851.

Capellanus, Andreas. *De Amore: Andreas Capellanus on Love*. Edited and translated by Patrick G. Walsh. London: Duckworth, 1982.

Cassiodorus. *Expositio Psalmorum*. Edited by M. Adriaen. 2 vols. CCSL 97–98. Turnhout: Brepols, 1958.

Chartularium Universitatis Parisiensis. [=CUP] Edited by Heinrich Denifle, Emile Chatelain, Charles Samaran, and Émile A. van Moé. 4 vols. Brussells: Culture et civilisation, 1964. Reprint of: Paris: Ex typis fratrum Delalain, 1889–1891.

Chrétien de Troyes. *Erec et Enide: Edition critique d'aprés le manuscrit B.N. Fr. 1376*. Translation, presentation, and notes by Jean-Marie Fritz. Paris: Livres de poche, 1992.

Cours sur l'Ethica Nova. Edited by René A. Gauthier. "Le cours sur l'Ethica Nova d'un maître ès Arts (1235–1240)." *AHDLMA* 42 (1975): 71–141.

d'Andeli, Henri. *Les dits d'Henri d'Andeli: Suivis de deux versions du Mariage des Sept arts*. Edited and translated by Alain Corbellari. Paris: Champion, 2003.

De anima et potenciis eius. Edited by René A. Gauthier. "Le Traité *De anima et potenciis eius* d'un maître ès Arts (vers 1225)." *RSPT* 66 (1985): 27–54.

De potentiis animae et obiectis. Edited by Daniel A. Callus. "The Powers of the Soul: An Early Unpublished Text." *RTAM* 19 (1952): 131–70.

De prophetia (Douai 540). Jean-Pierre Torrell. "La question 540 (*De Prophetia*) du Manuscrit de Douai 434." *Antonianum* 49 (1974): 499–526. Reprinted in Jean-Pierre Torrell, *Recherches sur la théorie de la prophétie au moyen âge, XIIe-XIVe siécles: Études et textes*. Fribourg: Editions Universitaires Fribourg Suisse, 1992, 19–46.

Fontes vitae sancti Thomae Aquinatis notis historicis et criticis illustrati. Edited by Domenicus Prümmer and M. H. Laurent. Toulouse: Saint Maximin, 1912.

Garnerius of Rochefort. *Contra Amaurianos*. Edited by Paolo Lucentini. CCCM 232. Brepols: Turnhout, 2010.

Gerard de Frachet. *Lives of the Brethren of the Order of Preachers 1206–1259*. Translated by Placid Conway, O.P. Edited, with notes and introduction by Bede Jarrett, O.P. London: Blackfriars, 1955. http://www.domcentral.org/trad/brethren/default.htm. Accessed March 2011.

———. *Vitae Fratrum Ordinis Praedicatorum*. Edited by Benedict M. Reichert. Monumenta Ordinis Pradicatorum Historica 1. Louvain: Charpentier and Schoonjas, 1896.

Gerald of Wales. *Itinerarium Kambriae et Descriptio Kambriae*. Edited by James F. Dimock. In *Giraldi Cambrensis opera*, vol. 6. London: Rolls Series, 1868.

Gilbert of Poitiers. *De Discretione animae, spiritus et mentis*. Edited by Nicholas M. Häring. "Gilbert of Poitiers, Author of the *De Discretione animae, spiritus et mentis* commonly attributed to Achard of Saint Victor." *Mediaeval Studies* 22 (1960): 148–92.

Glossa Ordinaria. Ed. Migne, PL 113. Edited by Raymond Étaix. CCCM 141. Turnhout: Brepols, 1999.
Guerric of St. Quentin. *Guerric of Saint-Quentin: Quaestiones de quolibet.* Edited by Walter H. Principe and Jonathan Glenn Black. Introduction by Jean-Pierre Torrell. Toronto: Pontifical Institute of Mediaeval Studies, 2002.
Gundissalinus. *De Anima.* "The Treatise *De Anima* of Dominicus Gundissalinus." Edited by Joseph Thomas Muckle. *Mediaeval Studies* 2 (1940): 23–103.
Heldris of Cornwall. *Silence: A Thirteenth-Century French Romance.* Edited and translated, with introduction and notes by Sarah Roche-Mahdi. East Lansing, Mich.: Colleagues, 1992.
Herbert of Boseham. *Liber Melorum.* PL 190, cols. 1293–1403.
Hildegard of Bingen. *Acta Inquisitionis de virtutibus et miraculis sanctae Hildegardis.* Edited by Charles Daremberg and F. A. Reuss, PL 197:131–40.
Hildegard of Bingen. *Hildegardis Bingensis epistolarium, pars prima.* Edited by Lieven Van Acker. CCCM 91, no. 1. Turnhout: Brepols, 1991.
———. *The Letters of Hildegard of Bingen.* Translated by Joseph L. Baird and Radd K. Ehrman. 2 vols. New York: Oxford University Press, 1994.
Hugh of St. Cher. *De prophetia.* In Jean-Pierre Torrell, *Théorie de la prophétie et philosophie de la connaissance aux environs de 1230: La contribution d'Hugues de Saint-Cher (Ms. Douai 434, Question 481).* Leuven: Spicilegium Sacrum Lovaniense, 1977.
———. *De raptu.* Edited by Barbara Faes de Mottoni. "Il ms. Douai Bibliothéque Municipale 434/II e la questio N. 480 *De raptu*." *AHDLMA* 73, no. 1 (2006), 165–201.
Hugh of St. Victor. *Commentariorium in Hierarchiam Coelestem S. Dionysii*, PL 175:954–55. The critical edition is *Hugonis de Sancto Victore Super Ierarchiam Dionysii* II.1, edited by Dominic Poirel, 443–44. CCCM 178. Turnhout: Brepols, 2015.
———. *De unione corporis et animae.* PL 177, cols. 285–94.
———. *De Sacramentis christianae fidei.* PL 176, cols. 173–618.
Jean de Joinville. *Vie de Saint-Louis / The Life of St. Louis by John of Joinville.* Translated by René Hague. London and New York: Sheed and Ward, 1955.
John of Garland. *Morale Scolarium of John of Garland (Johannes de Garlandia).* Edited, with an introduction on the life and works of the author by Louis John Paetow. Berkeley: University of California Press, 1927.
John of La Rochelle. *Summa de anima.* Edited by Jacques Guy Bougerol. Textes philosophiques du moyen âge XIX. Paris: Vrin, 1995.
———. *Tractatus de divisione multiplici potentiarum animae: Texte critique avec introduction, notes et tables.* Edited by Pierre Michaud-Quantin. Textes philosophiques du moyen âge XI. Paris: Vrin, 1964.
John of Salisbury. *The Metalogicon of John of Salisbury: A Twelfth-Century Defense of the Verbal and Logical Arts of the Trivium.* Translated, with

introduction and notes by Daniel McGarry. Gloucester, Mass.: Peter Smith, 1971.

———. *Policraticus, sive De nugis Curialium et vestigiis philosophorum*. Edited by Clement C. I. Webb. Frankfurt am Main: Minerva, 1965.

John Scotus Eriugena. *Iohannis Scoti Eriugenae Expositiones in Ierarchiam Coelestem*. Edited by Jeanne Barbet. Turnhout: Brepols, 1975.

Jutta and Hildegard: The Biographical Sources. Translated with introduction Anna Silvas. University Park: Pennsylvania State University Press, 1998.

Le "Guide de l'étudiant" d'un maître anonyme de la faculté des arts de Paris au XIIIe siècle. Édition critique provisoire du ms. Barcelona, Arxiu de la Corona d'Aragó, Ripoll 109, ff. 134ra–58va. Edited by Claude Lafleur, in collaboration with Joanne Carrier. Québec: Université Laval, 1992.

Les sermons universitaires parisiens de 1230–1231: Contribution à l'histoire de la prédication médiévale. Edited by Marie-Madeleine Davy. Études de philosophie médiévale XV. Paris: Vrin, 1931.

Lombard, Peter. *Collectanea in omnes epistolas divi Pauli apostoli*. PL 191, cols. 1297–1696.

———. *Libri sententiarum*. Magistri Petri Lombardi Parisiensis episcopi Sententiae in IV libris distinctae. Editio tertia. Ad fidem codicum antiquiorum restituta. 2 vols. Grottaferrata, Rome: Collegii S. Bonaventurae Ad Claras Aquas, 1971–81.

Map, Walter. *De Nugis Curialium: Courtiers' Trifles*. Edited and translated by M. R. James. Revised by C. N. L. Brooke and R. A. B. Mynors. Oxford: Clarendon, 1983.

Paris, Matthew. *Chronica maiora*. Edited by Henry Richard Luard. London: Longman, 1872; *Matthew Paris's English History 1235–1273*. Translated by John Allan Giles. New York: AMS Press, 1968.

———. *Roger Wendover's Flowers of History*. Translated and edited by John Allen Giles. New York: AMS, 1968. Originally published London: Bohun, 1849.

Philip the Chancellor. *Summa de bono* [= SB]. *Philippi Cancellarii Summa de bono*. Edited by Nikolaus Wicki. 2 vols. Bern: Francke, 1985.

Radulphus Ardens. *Speculum Universale I–V*. Edited by Claudia Heinmann and Stephan Herst. CCCM 241. Tournhout: Brepols, 2011.

Renart, Jean [Jehan]. *Le lai de l'ombre*. Translation And Introduction by Adrian P. Tudor. Text edited by Alan Hindley And Brian J. Levy. Liverpool Online Series. Critical Editions of French Texts 8 (2004). https://www.liverpool.ac.uk/media/livacuk/modern-languages-and-cultures/liverpoolonline/ombre.pdf.

———. *The Romance of the Rose or Guillaume de Dole*. Translated by Patricia Terry and Nancy Vine Durling. Philadelphia: University of Pennsylvania Press, 1993.

Richard of St. Victor. *The Twelve Patriarchs: The Mystical Ark, Book Three of the Trinity*. Translation and Introduction by Grover A. Zinn. New York: Paulist, 1979.

Roland of Cremona. "La 'Summa' di Rolando di Cremona, Il testo del prologo." Edited by Giuseppe Cremascoli. *Studi Medievali* 16 (1975): 825–76.

———. Summa [= SR]. *Summa Magistri Rolandi Cremonensis O.P. Liber Tercius*. Editio princeps. Edited by Alois Cortesi. Bergamo: Monumenta Bergomensia, 1962.

Rufus, Richard, Matthew Etchemendy, and Rega Wood. "*Speculum animae*: Richard Rufus on Perception and Cognition," *Franciscan Studies* 69, no. 1 (2011): 53–115.

Salimbene de Adam. *Cronica*. Edited by Giuseppe Scalia. 2 vols. CCCM 125–25A. Turnhout: Brepols, c1998–99.

Schwester Katrei. Translated by Elvira Borgstädt. In *Meister Eckhart, Teacher and Preacher*, edited by Bernard McGinn. The Classics of Western Spirituality. New York: Paulist Press, 1986.

Simon of Tournai. *Les "Disputationes" de Simon de Tournai*. Edited by Joseph Warichez. Spicilegium Sacrum Lovaniense 12. Louvain: Peeters, 1932.

La "Summa Duacensis" (Douai 434), texte critique avec une introduction et des tables. Edited by Palémon Glorieux. Textes philosophiques du moyen âge 2. Paris: Vrin, 1955.

Thomas Celano. *Vita Prima, Vita Secunda, et Tractatus de Miraculis*. In *Analecta Franciscana*, 10:1–331. Rome: Quaracchi, 1926–41. For reasons of inaccessibility I often used the web version of the Latin in *The Franciscan Archive*, http://www.franciscan-archive.org/index2.html.

Thomas of Cantimpré. *S. Theol. Doctoris . . . Bonum Universale de apibus. Opera Georgii, Colvenerii* S. Theol Doctoris. Douai: Baltazaris Belleri, 1627.

Three Latin Comedies. Edited by Keith A. Bate. Toronto: Pontifical Institute of Mediaeval Studies, 1976.

Vitry, Jacques de. *The Historia Occidentalis of Jacques de Vitry: A Critical Edition*, by John Frederick Hinnebusch. Spicilegium Friburgense 17. Fribourg: University Press, 1972.

———. *The Life of Marie d'Oignies by Jacques de Vitry*. Translated by Margot H. King, with introduction and notes by Margot H. King and Miriam Marsolais. Toronto, Ontario: Peregrina, 1993.

Wakefield Walter L., and Austin P. Evans, trans. and eds. *Heresies of the High Middle Ages: Selected Sources*. New York: Columbia University Press, 1991.

William of Auvergne. *De bono et malo*. Edited by J. Reginald O'Donnell. "Tractatus Magistri Guillelmi Alvernensis *De bono et malo*." *Mediaeval Studies* 8 (1946): 245–99.

———. *De bono et malo*. Edited by J. Reginald O'Donnell. "Tractatus secundus Guillelmi Alvernensis *De bono et malo*." *Mediaeval Studies* 16 (1954): 219–71.

———. *De Trinitate*. Edited by Bruno Switalski. Toronto: Pontifical Institute of Mediaeval Studies, 1976.

———. [= GOO] *Guilielmi Alverni Opera Omnia*. 2 vols. Paris, 1674.

William of Auxerre. *Summa Aurea* [= SA]. Edited by Jean Ribaillier. In *Spicilegium Bonaventurianum*, vols. 16–20. Paris: Grottaferrata, 1980–87.

William of Saint-Amour. *De periculis novissimorum temporum*. Edited by Guy Geltner. Leuven: Peeters, 2008.
William the Breton. *Oeuvres de Rigord et Guillaume le Breton. Historiens de Philippe-Auguste. Publiées pour la Société de l'Histoire de France*. Edited by H. François Delaborde. 2 vols. Paris, 1882–85.

SECONDARY LITERATURE

Abate, G., and G. Luisetto. *Codici e manoscritti della Biblioteca Antoniana*, col catalogo delle miniature. Edited by F. Avril, F. d'Arcais, and G. Mariani Canova. Vicenza, 1975.
Aertsen, Jan. "The Medieval Doctrine of the Transcendentals: The Current State of Research." *Bulletin de philosophie médiévale* 33 (1966): 130–47.
———. "The Medieval Doctrine of the Transcendentals: New Literature." *Bulletin de philosophie médiévale* 41 (1999): 107–21.
Aertsen, Jan A., Kent Emery, and Andreas Speer, eds. *Nach der Verurteilung Von 1277: Philosophie und Theologie an der Universität von Paris im letzten Viertel des 13. Jahrhunderts. Studien und Texte*. Berlin and New York: Walter de Gruyter, 2001.
Algazi, Gadi. "Doing Things with Gifts." In *Negotiating the Gift: Pre-Modern Figurations of Exchange*, edited by Gadi Algazi, Valentin Groebner, and Bernhard Jussen, 9–27. Göttingen: Vandenhoeck and Ruprecht, 2003.
Anciaux, Paul. "La date de composition de la Somme de Godefroid de Poitiers." *RTAM* 16 (1949): 165–66.
Anderson, Allan. "Pentecostal-Charismatic Spirituality and Theological Education in Europe from a Global Perspective." *PentecoStudies* 3, no. 1 (2004). http://www.glopent.net/pentecostudies/2004/anderson2004.pdf;. Accessed March 2011.
Anheim, Étienne, and Sylvain Piron. "Le travail intellectuel au Moyen Âge: Institutions et circulations." *Revue de synthèse* 129, no. 4 (2008): 481–84.
Avi-Yonah, Reuven. "Career Trends of Parisian Masters of Theology, 1200–1320." *History of Universities* 6 (1986): 47–64.
Baldwin, John W. *Masters, Princes, and Merchants: The Social Views of Peter the Chanter and His Circle*. Princeton: Princeton University Press, 1970.
———. *The Scholastic Culture of the Middle Ages, 1000–1300*. Lexington, Mass.: Heath, 1971.
———. "Masters at Paris from 1179 to 1215: A Social Perspective." In *Renaissance and Renewal in the Twelfth Century*, edited by Robert L. Benson and Giles Constable with Carol D. Lanham, 138–72. Cambridge, Mass.: Harvard University Press, 1982.
———. *Aristocratic Life in Medieval France: The Romances of Jean Renart and Gerbert de Montreuil, 1190–1230*. Baltimore and London: John Hopkins University Press, 2000.

Barthes, Roland. *The Semiotic Challenge*. Trans. Richard Howard. Berkeley: University of California Press, 1994.
Bartlett, Robert. *The Natural and the Supernatural in the Middle Ages*. Cambridge: Cambridge University Press, 1998.
Bejczy, István Pieter. *Virtue Ethics in the Middle Ages: Commentaries on Aristotle's Nicomachean Ethics, 1200–1500*. Leiden and Boston: Brill, 2008.
Bell, Carl. "States of Consciousness." *Journal of the National Medical Association* 72, no. 4 (1980): 331–34.
Bell, Carl, Belinda Thompson, Kumea Shorter-Goodman, Raymond Mays, and Bambade Shakour. "Altered States of Consciousness Profile: An Afro-Centric Intrapsychic Evaluation Tool." *Journal of the National Medical Association* 77, no. 9 (1985): 715–28.
Bénatouïl, Thomas, and Isabelle Draelants, eds. *Expertus sum: L'expérience par les sens dans la philosophie naturelle médiévale*. Florence: SISMEL Edizioni del Galuzzo, 2011.
Berlioz, Jacques. "La voix de l'évêque: Guillaume d'Auvergne dans les exempla (xiiie–xive siècle)." In *Autour de Guillaume d'Auvergne [mort en] 1249*, edited by Franco Morenzoni and Jean-Yves Tilliette, 9–34. Turnhout: Brepols, 2005.
Berndt, Rainer. "La théologie comme système du monde: Sur l'évolution des sommes théologiques de Hughes de Saint-Victor à Saint Thomas d'Aquin." *RSPT* 78, no. 4 (1994): 555–72.
Bernstein, Alan E. "Magisterium and License: Corporate Autonomy against Papal Authority in the Medieval University of Paris." *Viator* 9 (1978): 291–308.
Bieniak, Magdalena. *The Soul-Body Problem at Paris, ca. 1200–1250: Hugh of St. Cher and His Contemporaries*. Ancient and Medieval Philosophy Series 1.42. Leuven: Leuven University Press, 2010.
Bignami-Odier, Jeanne. "Le manuscrit Vatican latin 2186." *AHDLMA* 11 (1937): 133–66.
Biller, Peter, and Anne Hudson, eds. *Heresy and Literacy*. Cambridge: Cambridge University Press, 1994.
Biller, Peter, and Barrie Dobson, eds. *The Medieval Church: Universities, Heresy and the Religious Life: Essays in Honour of Gordon Leff*. Suffolk, UK, and Rochester, N.Y.: Boydell, 1999.
Bonassie, Pierre, and Gérard Pradalié, eds. *La capitulation de Raymond VII et la fondation de l'université de Toulouse, 1229–1979: Un anniversaire en question*. Toulouse: Université Toulouse-Le Mirail, 1979.
Bono, James J. "Medical Spirits and the Medieval Language of Life." *Traditio* 40 (1984): 91–130.
Bougerol, Jacques Guy. "La glose sur les Sentences du manuscrit Vat. Lat. 691." *Antonianum* 55 (1980): 108–73.
———. "Jean de La Rochelle: Les oeuvres et les manuscrits." *Archivum Franciscanum Historicum* 87 (1994): 205–15.

Bourdieu, Pierre. "Postface" for Erwin Panofsky. *Architecture gothique et pensée scolastique*. Paris: Les Editions de Minuit, 1967, 133–67.
Bourguignon, Erica. "Introduction: A Framework for the Comparative Study of Altered States of Consciousness." In *Religion, Altered States of Consciousness and Social Change*, edited by Erica Bourguignon, 3–35. Columbus: Ohio State University Press, 1973.
Brooke, Rosalind B. *Early Franciscan Government; Elias to Bonaventure*. Cambridge: Cambridge University Press, 1959.
Buffon, Valeria A. "Happiness and Knowledge in Some Masters of Arts before 1250: An Analysis of Aome Commentaries on the Book I of Nicomachean Ethics." *Patristica et Medievalia* 25 (2004): 111–15.
———. "The Structure of the Soul, Intellectual Virtues, and the Ethical Ideal of Masters of Arts in Early Commentaries on the *Nichomachean Ethics*." In *Virtue Ethics in the Middle Ages: Commentaries on Aristotle's Nicomachean Ethics, 1200–1500*, edited by István Pieter Bejczy, 13–30. Leiden and Boston: Brill, 2008.
Burnett, Charles. "The Superiority of Taste." *Journal of the Warburg and Courtauld Institutes* 54 (1991): 230–38.
Burr, David. "Olivi on Marriage: The Conservative as Prophet." *Journal of Mediaeval and Renaissance Studies* 2 (1972): 183–204.
———. *The Persecution of Peter Olivi*. Philadelphia: American Philosophical Society, 1976.
———. "Olivi on Prophecy." *Cristianesimo nella Storia* 17, no. 2 (1996): 369–91.
———. "Did the Beguins Understand Olivi?" In *Pierre de Jean Olivi (1248–1298): Pensée scolastique, dissidence spirituelle et société; Actes du colloque de Narbonne (mars 1998)*, edited by Alain Boureau and Sylvain Piron, 309–18. Paris: Vrin, 1999.
———. *The Spiritual Franciscans: From Protest to Persecution in the Century after Saint Francis*. University Park: Pennsylvania State University Press, 2001.
Bynum, Caroline Walker. *Jesus as Mother: Studies in the Spirituality of the High Middle Ages*. Berkeley and Los Angeles: University of California Press, 1982.
———. *The Resurrection of the Body in Western Christianity, 200–1336*. New York: Columbia University Press, 1995.
———. "Metamorphosis, or Gerald and the Werewolf." In *Metamorphosis and Identity*, 77–111. New York: Zone, 2001.
———. "Monsters, Medians, and Marvelous Mixtures: Hybrids in the Spirituality of Bernard of Clairvaux." In *Metamorphosis and Identity*, 113–62. New York: Zone, 2001.
Capelle, Catherine-Germaine. *Autour du décret de 1210 III: Amaury de Bène*. Paris: Vrin, 1932.
Carroll, Lewis. *Alice's Adventures in Wonderland*. Chicago: VolumeOne, 1998). Originally published in 1865.

Carruthers, Mary. "Sweetness." *Speculum* 81 (2006): 999–1013.
Casagrande, Carla. "Le calame du Saint-Esprit: Grâce et rhétorique dans la prédication au XIIIe siècle." In *La parole du prédicateur, Ve–XVe siècle*, edited by Rosa Maria Dessi and Michel Lauwers, 235–54. Nice: Presses Universitaires de Nice, 1997.
Chenu, Marie-Dominique. "Maîtres et bacheliers de l'Université de Paris v. 1240: Description du manuscrit Paris, Bibl. Nat. lat. 15652." *Études d'Histoire Littéraire et Doctrinale du XIIIe Siècle* 1 (1932): 11–39.
——. *La théologie comme science au XIIIe siècle*. Paris: Vrin, 1957.
Clanchy, Michael T. *From Memory to Written Record: England 1066–1307*. Oxford: Blackwell, 1993.
Colish, Marcia L. "*Habitus* Revisited: A Reply to Cary Nederman." *Traditio* 48 (1993): 77–92.
——. "From the Sentence Collection to the Sentence Commentary and the Summa: Parisian Scholastic Theology, 1130–1215." In *Manuels, programmes de cours et techniques d'enseignement dans les universites medievales: Actes du colloque International de Louvain-la-Neuve (9–11 septembre 1993)*. Edited by Jacqueline Hamesse, 9–29. Louvain-la-Neuve: Institut d'etudes medievales de l'Universite catholique de Louvain, 1994.
Colledge, Edmund. "The Legend of St. Thomas Aquinas." In *St. Thomas Aquinas 1274–1974: Commemorative Studies*, 1:13–28. Toronto: Pontifical Institute of Mediaeval Studies, 1974.
Conlan, William J. "The Definition of Faith according to a Question of MS. Assisi 138: Study and Edition of Text." In *Essays in Honour of Anton Charles Pegis*, edited by J. Reginald O'Donnell, 17–69. Toronto: Pontifical Institute of Mediaeval Studies, 1974.
Contenson, P. M. de. "Avicennisme latin et vision de Dieu au début du XIIIe siècle." *AHDLMA* 26 (1959): 29–97.
——. "La théologie de la vision de Dieu au début du XIIIe siècle: Le De retributionibus sanctorum de Guillaume d'Auvergne et la condamnation de 1241." *RSPT* 46 (1962): 409–44.
Coolman, Boyd Taylor. *Knowing God by Experience: The Spiritual Senses in the Theology of William of Auxerre*. Washington, D.C.: The Catholic University of America Press, 2004.
Corbellari, Alain. *La voix des clercs: Littérature et savoir universitaire autour des dits du XIIIe siècle*. Genève: Droz, 2005.
Corti, Guglielmo. "Le sette parti del Magisterium divinale et sapientiale di Guglielmo di Auvergne." In *Studi e ricerche di scienze religiose in onore dei Santi apostoli Pietro et Paolo nel xix centenario del loro martirio*, 289–307. Rome: Facultas Theologica Pontificiae Universitatis Lateranesis, 1968.
Côté, Antoine. *L'infinité divine dans la théologie médiévale, 1220–1255*. Paris: Vrin, 2002.

Corry, Leo. "Geometry and Arithmetic in the Medieval Traditions of Euclid's *Elements*: A View from Book II." *Archive for History of Exact Sciences* 67, no. 6 (2013): 637–705.
Courtenay, William J. "Dominicans and Suspect Opinion in the Thirteenth Century: The Cases of Stephen of Venizy, Peter of Tarentaise, and the Articles of 1270 and 1271." *Vivarium* 32 (1994): 186–95.
Courtenay, William J., Jürgen Miethke, and David B. Priest, eds. *Universities and Schooling in Medieval Society*. Leiden and Boston: Brill, 2000.
Crombie, Alistair Cameron. *Robert Grosseteste and the Origins of Experimental Science, 1100–1700*. Oxford: Clarendon, 1953.
———. "Grosseteste's Position in the History of Science." In *Robert Grosseteste: Scholar and Bishop*, edited by Daniel A. P. Callus, 98–120. Oxford: Clarendon, 1955.
Crossnoe, Marshall E. "Education and the Care of Souls: Pope Gregory IX, the Order of St. Victor and the University of Paris in 1237." *Mediaeval Studies* 61 (1999): 137–72.
Dahan, Gilbert. "Une introduction à l'étude de la philosophie: Ut ait Tullius." In *L'enseignement de la philosophie au xiiie siècle: Autour du "Guide de l'étudiant" du ms. Ripoll 109*, edited by Claude Lafleur and Joanne Carrier, 3–58. Turnhout: Brepols, 1997.
———. *Le brûlement du Talmud à Paris 1242–1244*. Paris: Cerf, 1999.
———. *L'exégèse chrétienne de la bible en occident médiéval, XIIe-XIVe siècle*. Paris: Cerf, 1999.
Dahan, Gilbert, Pierre-Marie Gy, and Louis-Jacques Bataillon, eds. *Hugues De Saint-Cher (†1263): Bibliste et Théologien; Actes du colloque "Hugues de Saint-Cher, OP, bibliste et théologien" Paris, Centre d'études du Saulchoir, 13–15 mars 2000*. Turnhout: Brepols, 2004.
d'Alverny, Marie Thérèse. "Un fragment du procés des Amauriciens." *AHDLMA* 18 (1950): 325–36.
Davenport, Anne Ashley. *Measure of a Different Greatness: The Intensive Infinite, 1250–1650*. Leiden and Boston: Brill, 1999.
de Bruyne, Edgar. *Etudes d'esthétique médiévale*. 3 vols. Brugge: De Tempel, 1946.
Decker, Bruno. *Die Entwicklung der Lehre von der prophetischen Offenbarung*. Breslau: Müller and Seiffert, 1940.
DeWalt, Kathleen M., and Billie R. DeWalt. *Participant Observation: A Guide for Fieldworkers*. Walnut Creek, Calif.: AltaMira, 2002.
Dewan, Lawrence. "'Obiectum': Notes on the Invention of a Word." *AHDLMA* 48 (1981): 37–96.
Dinzelbacher, Peter. *Vision und Visionliteratur im Mittelalter*. Stuttgart: Hiersemann, 1981.
Dondaine, Hyacinthe-François. "Hugues de Saint-Cher et la condamnation de 1241." *RSPT* 33 (1949): 170–74.

———. "L'objet et le 'medium' de la vision béatifique chez les théologiens du XIIIe siècle." *RTAM* 19 (1952): 60–130.
Dondaine, Hyacinthe-François, and Bertrand-Georges Guyot. "Guerric de Saint-Quentin et la condamnation de 1241." *RSPT* 44 (1960): 225–42.
Dondaine, Hyacinthe-François, and Léon Reid. "Introduction." In Thomas Aquinas, *Expositio super Isaiam ad litteram*, Editio Leonina 28. Rome: Editori di San Tommaso, 1974.
Doucet, Victorin. "La date des condamnations Parisiennes dites de 1241: Faut-il corriger le cartulaire de l'Université?" In *Mélanges Auguste Pelzer: Études d'histoire littéraire et doctrinale de la scolastique médiévale offertes à Monseigneur Auguste Pelzer à l'occasion de son soixante-dixième anniversaire*, 183–93. Louvain: Bibliothèque de l'Université Bureaux du "Recueil," 1947.
———. "A travers le manuscrit 434 de Douai." *Antonianum* 27 (1952): 531–80.
Douglas, Mary. *Natural Symbols, Explorations in Cosmology*. New York: Pantheon, 1970.
Draelants, Isabelle. "Expérience et autorités dans la philosophie naturelle d'Albert le Grand." in *Expertus sum: L'expérience par les sens dans la philosophie naturelle médiévale*, edited by Thomas Bénatouïl and Isabelle Draelants, 89–122. Florence: SISMEL, Edizioni del Galluzzo, 2011.
Dragonetti, Roger. *Le mirage des sources: L'art du faux dans le roman médiéval*. Paris: Seuil, 1987.
Dufeil, Michel-Marie. *Guillaume de Saint-Amour et la polémique universitaire parisienne 1250–1259*. Paris: Picard, 1972.
Durbin, Bertrand. "La crise du lodgement des étudiants à Paris au XIIème siècle." Ph.D. diss. Paris: Université Panthéon-Assas, 2005.
Eco, Umberto. *Art and Beauty in the Middle Ages*. New Haven: Yale University Press, 1986.
———. *The Aesthetics of Thomas Aquinas*. Translated by Hugh Bredin. Cambridge, Mass.: Harvard University Press, 1988.
———. *Baudolino*. Translated by William Weaver. New York: Harcourt, 2002.
Englhardt, Georg. *Die Entwicklung der dogmatischen Glaubenspsychologie in der mittelalterlichen Scholastik vom Abaelardstreit (um 1140) bis zu Philipp dem Kanzler (gest. 1236)*. Münster: Aschendorff, 1933.
———. "Adam de Puteorumvilla, un maître proche d'Odon Rigaud: Sa psychologie de la foi." *RTAM* 8 (1936): 61–78.
Evans, Gillian R. *Mediaeval Commentaries on the Sentences of Peter Lombard: Current Research*. Leiden and Boston: Brill, 2002.
Even-Ezra, Ayelet. "The Conceptualization of Charisma in the Early Thirteenth Century." *Viator* 44, no. 1 (2013): 151–68.
———. "'Qui predicat magister est': Preaching and Teaching in Paris according to Gualterus de Castro Theodorici (d. 1249)." In *Les débuts de l'enseignement*

universitaire à Paris (1200–1245 environ), edited by Olga Weijers and Jacques Verger, 349–57. Tournhout: Brepols, 2013.

———. "Blind Men Speaking of Colors: Paul's Recollection and the Self Image of Early Thirteenth-Century Theologians." *Harvard Theological Review* 107, no. 4 (2014): 425–46.

———. "The *Questio de officio predicacionis* of Gauthier de Château Thierry: A Critical Edition." *AHDLMA* 81 (2014): 385–462.

———. "Schemata as Maps and Editing Tools in Early Thirteenth-Century Scholasticism." *Manuscripta* 61, no. 1 (2017): 21–71.

Faes de Mottoni, Barbara. "Les manuscrits du commentaire des Sentences d'Hugues de Saint-Cher." In *Hugues De Saint-Cher (†1263): Bibliste et theologien; Actes du colloque "Hugues de Saint-Cher, O.P., bibliste et théologien," Paris, Centre d'études du Saulchoir, 13–15 mars 2000*, 273–95. Turnhout: Brepols, 2004.

———. "Guglielmo d'Alvernia e l'anima rapita." In *Autour de Guillaume d'Auvergne, [mort en] 1249 Texte imprimé*, edited by Franco Morenzoni and Jean-Yves Tilliette, 55–74. Turnhout: Brepols, 2005.

———. *Figure e motivi della contemplazione nelle teologie medievali*. Florence: SISMEL, Edizioni del Galluzzo, 2007.

Ferruolo, Stephen C. *The Origins of the University: The Schools of Paris and Their Critics, 1100–1215*. Stanford, Calif.: Stanford University Press, 1985.

Ferté, Jean. "Rapports de la somme d'Alexandre de Halès dans son "De fide" avec Philippe le Chancelier." *RTAM* 7 (1935): 381–402.

Ferzoco, George. "The Changing Face of Tradition: Monastic Education in the Middle Ages." In *Medieval Monastic Education*, edited by Carolyn Muessig and George Ferzoco, 1–6. London and New York: Leicester University Press, 2000.

Fidora, Alexander, and Matthias Lutz-Bachmann, eds. *Erfahrung und Beweis: Die Wissenschaften von der Natur im 13. und 14. Jahrhundert / Experience and Demonstration: The Sciences of Nature in the 13th and 14th Centuries*. Berlin: Akademie Verlag, 2006.

Filthaut, Ephrem. *Roland von Cremona, O.P., und die Anfänge der Scholastik im Predigerorden: Ein beitrag zur geistesgeschichte der älteren dominikaner*. Vechta: Albertus-Magnus-Verlag der Dominikaner, 1936.

Fisher, Nicholas. W., and Sabetai Unguru. "Experimental Science and Mathematics in Roger Bacon's Thought." *Traditio* 27 (1971): 353–78.

Forlivesi, Marco, Riccardo Quinto, and Silvana Vecchio, eds. *"Fides virtus": The Virtue of Faith from the Twelfth to the Early Sixteenth Century*. Münster: Ascendorff, 2014.

Fries, Albert. "De commentario Guerrici de S. Quintino in libros sententiarum." *Archivum Fratrum Praedicatorum* 5 (1935): 326–41.

Fulton, Rachel. "'Taste and See That the Lord Is Sweet' (Ps 33:9): The Flavor of God in the Monastic West." *Journal of Religion* 86, no. 2 (2006): 169–204.

Gauthier, Réné A. "Le cours sur l'Ethica nova d'un maître ès arts de Paris (vers 1235–1240)." *AHDLMA* 42 (1975): 71–141.
———. "Le traité 'De Anima et de potenciis eius' d'un maître ès arts (vers 1225)." *RSPT* 66 (1982): 3–55.
———. "Notes sur les débuts (1225–1240) du premier 'Averoïsme.'" *RSPT* 66 (1982): 321–74.
Gelber, Hester. *It Could Have Been Otherwise: Contingency and Necessity in Dominican Theology at Oxford, 1300–1350.* Leiden and Boston: Brill, 2004.
Geltner, Guy. "Faux Semblants: Antifraternalism Reconsidered in Jean de Meun and Chaucer." *Studies in Philology* 101, no. 4 (2004): 357–80.
———. "William of Saint-Amour's *De periculis novissimorum temporum*: A False Start to Medieval Antifraternalism?" In *Critics and Defenders of Franciscan Life*, edited by Michael F. Cusato and Guy Geltner, 105–18. Leiden: Brill, 2009.
Gieryn, Thomas F. "Boundary-Work and the Demarcation of Science from Non-Science: Strains and Interests in Professional Ideologies of Scientists." *American Sociological Review* 48, no. 6 (1983): 781–95.
Gieysztor, Alexander. "Management and Resources." In *A History of the University in Europe*, edited by Hilde de Ridder-Symoens, 1:116–19. Cambridge: Cambridge University Press, 1992.
Giroux, Henry A., and David E. Purpel, eds. *The Hidden Curriculum and Moral Education: Deception or Discovery?* Berkeley, Calif. McCutchan, 1983.
Glorieux, Palémon. *Répertoire des maîtres en théologie de Paris au XIIIe siècle.* Paris: Vrin, 1933.
———. "Les 572 Questions du manuscrit de Douai 434." *RTAM* 10 (1938): 123–52, 225–67.
———. "Les années 1242–1247 à la Faculté de théologie de Paris." *RTAM* 29 (1962): 234–49.
Goodman, Felicitas D. *Where the Spirits Ride the Wind: Trance Journeys and Other Ecstatic Experiences.* Bloomington: Indiana University Press, 1990.
———. "Ritual Body Postures, Channeling, and the Ecstatic Body Trance." *Anthropology of Consciousness* 10, no. 1 (1999): 54–59.
Goris, Harm. "Tense Logic in 13th Century Theology." *Vivarium* 39 (2001): 161–84.
Gorochov, Nathalie. "The Self-Image of the Masters of Theology at the University of Paris in the Late Thirteenth and Early Fourteenth Centuries." *Journal of Ecclesiastical History* 46 (1995): 398–431.
———. *Naissance de l'université: Les écoles de Paris d'Innocent III à Thomas d'Aquin (v. 1200–v. 1245).* Paris: Champion, 2012.
Grabmann, Martin. *Die theologische Erkenntnis- und Einleitungslehre des hl. Thomas von Aquin.* Fribourg, Switzerland: Paulusverlag, 1948.
———. *Die Geschichte der scholastischen Methode: Nach den gedruckten und ungedruckten Quellen dargestellt.* 2 vols. Basel: Schwabe, 1961.

Graf, Thomas. *De subiecto psychico gratiae et virtutum secundum doctrinam scholasticorum usque ad medium saeculum XIV.* Pars 1/1, *De subiecto virtutum cardinalium.* Rome: Herder, 1934.

Greene, Robert A. "Instinct of Nature: Natural Law, Synderesis, and the Moral Sense," *Journal of the History of Ideas* 58, no. 2 (1997): 173–98.

Gründel, Johannes. "Die Sentenzenglosse des Johannes Pagus (circa 1243–1245) in Padua, Bibl. Ant. 139." *Münchener theologische Zeitschrift* 9, no. 3 (1958): 171–85.

———. *Das "Speculum Universale" des Radulfus Ardens.* Munich: Hueber, 1961.

Grundmann, Herbert. "Sacerdotium—Regnum—Studium: Zur Wertung der Wissenschaft im 13. Jahrhundert." *Archiv für Kunstgeschichte* 34 (1952): 5–21.

Guyon, Catherine. *Les écoliers du Christ: L'ordre canonial du Val des écoliers 1201–1539.* Saint-Etienne: Presses Universitaires de Saint-Etienne, 1998.

Guyot, Bertrand-G. "Quaestiones Guerrici, Alexandri et aliorum magistrorum Parisiensium (Praha, Univ. IV. D. 13)." *Archivum Fratrum Praedicatorum* 32 (1962): 5–125.

Hackett, Jeremiah, ed. *Roger Bacon and the Sciences: Commemorative Essays.* Studien und Texte zur Geistesgeschichte des Mittelalters. Leiden, New York, and Cologne: Brill, 1997.

———. "Experientia, Experimentum and Perception of Objects in Space: Roger Bacon." In *Raum und Raumvorstellungen im Mittelalter,* edited by Jan Aersten and Andreas Speer, 101–20. Berlin: Walter de Gruyter, 1998.

Hadot, Pierre. *Exercices spirituels et philosophie antique.* Paris: Études augustiniennes, 1981.

———. *Philosophy as a Way of Life: Spiritual Exercises from Socrates to Foucault.* Translated by Arnold I. Davidson. Malden, Mass.: Blackwell, 1995.

———. *What Is Ancient Philosophy?* Cambridge, Mass.: Harvard University Press, 2002.

Haley, Peter. "Rudolph Sohm on Charisma." *Journal of Religion* 60, no. 2 (1980): 185–97.

Hamesse, Jacqueline. "Experientia/experimentum dans les lexiques médiévaux et dans les textes philosophiques antérieurs au 14e siècle." In *Experientia: X Colloquio internazionale, Roma, 4–6 gennaio 2001,* edited by Marco Veneziani, 77–90. Florence: Olschki, 2002.

Häring, Nikolaus M. "Gilbert of Poitiers, Author of the *De Discretione animae, spiritus et mentis* commonly attributed to Achard of Saint Victor." *Mediaeval Studies* 22, no. 1 (1960): 148–92.

———. "Die ersten Konflikte zwischen der Universität von Paris und der kirchlichen Lehrautorität." In *Die Auseinandersetzungen an der pariser Universität im XIII Jahrhundert,* edited by Albert Zimmermann, 38–51. Berlin: Walter de Gruyter, 1976.

Harkins, Franklin. "*Filiae Magistri*: Peter Lomard's Sentences and Medieval Theological Education 'On the Ground.'" In *Medieval Commentaries on the*

Sentences of Peter Lombard, edited by Philipp W. Rosemann, 26–78. Leiden: Brill, 2015.
Haskins, Charles H. *Studies in Mediaeval Culture*. New York: Ungar, 1929.
Hasse, Dag Nikolaus. *Avicenna's De Anima in the Latin West: The Formation of a Peripatetic Philosophy of the Soul, 1160–1300*. London: Warburg Institute, 2000.
Hedwig, Klaus. "Roger Bacon's *Scientia experimentalis*." In *Philosophen des Mittelalters*, edited by Theo Kobush, 140–51. Darmstadt: Primus, 2000.
Heinzmann, Richard. *Die "Compilatio quaestionum theologiae secundum Magistrum Martinum."* Munich: Hueber, 1964.
Henquinet, François-Marie. "Les écrits du Frère Guéric de Saint-Quentin." *RTAM* 6 (1934): 184–214, 284–312, 394–410.
——. "Les questions inédits d'Alexandre de Halès sur les fins dernières." *RTAM* 10 (1938): 56–78.
Huss, Boaz. "A New Age in Modern Kabbalah Research" [Hebrew]. *Theoria ve-Bikoret* 27 (2005): 246–63.
Jaeger, C. Stephen. *The Envy of Angels: Cathedral Schools and Social Ideas in Medieval Europe, 950–1200*. Philadelphia: University of Pennsylvania Press, 1994.
Jung, Carl Gustav. "The Face to Face Interview." In *C. G. Jung Speaking: Interviews and Encounters*, edited by William McGuire and R. F. C. Hull, 424–39. Princeton: Bollingen Paperbacks, 1977.
Jussen, Bernhard. "Religious Discourses of the Gift in the Middle Ages: Semantic Evidences (Second to Twelfth Centuries)." In *Negotiating the Gift: Pre-Modern Figurations of Exchange*, edited by Gadi Algazi, Valentin Groebner, and Bernhard Jussen, 173–92. Göttingen: Vandenhoeck and Ruprecht, 2003.
Kantorowicz, Ernst H. "Die Wiederkehr Gelehrter Anachorese im Mittelalter." In *Selected Studies*, 339–51. Locust Valley, N.Y.: Augustin, 1965.
Kawulich, Barbara W. "Participant Observation as a Data Collection Method." *Qualitative Social Research* 6, no. 2 (2005). http://www.qualitative-research.net/index.php/fqs/article/view/466/996. Accessed December 2015.
Kiefer, Thomas. *Aristotle's Theory of Knowledge*. London: Continuum, 2007.
King, Peter. "Two Conceptions of Experience." *Medieval Philosophy and Theology* 11, no. 2 (2003): 203–26.
Köhn, Rolf. "Monastisches Bildungsideal und weltgeistliches Wissenschaftsdenken: Zur Vorgeschichte des Mendikantenstreites an der Universität Paris." In *Die Auseinandersetzungen an der pariser Universität im xiii Jahrhundert*, edited by Albert Zimmermann, 1–37. Berlin: De Gruyter, 1976.
König-Pralong, Catherine. *Le bon usage des savoirs: Scolastique, philosophie et politique culturelle*. Paris: Vrin, 2011.
Lacombe, George. "The Questiones of Cardinal Stephen Langton. Part II." *New Scholasticism* 3 (1929): 113–58.
Lafleur, Claude. *Quatre introductions à la philosophie au XIIIe siècle, textes critiques et étude historique*. Paris: Vrin, 1988.

Landgraf, Artur M. *Dogmengeschichte der Frühscholastik*. 4 vols. Regensburg: Pustet, 1952–56.
———. *Introduction à l'histoire de la littérature théologique de la scolastique naissante*. Translated by Albert M. Landry. Montréal: Institut d'études médiévales, 1973.
Landini, Lawrence. *The Causes of the Clericalization of the Order of Friars Minor 1209–1260 in the Light of the Early Franciscan Sources*. Chicago: Pontifica Universitas Gregoriana, 1968.
Lave, Jean, and Étienne Wenger. *Situated Learning: Legitimate Peripheral Participation*. Cambridge and New York: Cambridge University Press, 1991.
Le Goff, Jacques. *The Birth of Purgatory*. Chicago: University of Chicago Press, 1984.
Le Roi Ladourie, Emanuel. *Montaillou: Village occitan, de 1294 à 1324*. Paris, Gallimard, 1975.
Leclercq, Jean. *The Love of Learning and the Desire for God: A Study of Monastic Culture*. Translated by Catharine Misrahi. New York: Fordham University Press, 1974.
Lerner, Robert E. "Weltklerus und religiöse Bewegung im 13. Jahrhundert: Das Beispiel Philipps des Kanzlers." *Archiv für Kulturgeschichte* 51 (1969): 94–108.
———. "Ecstatic Dissent." *Speculum* 67, no. 1 (1992): 33–57.
Lisska, Anthony J. *Aquinas's Theory of Natural Law: An Analytic Reconstruction*. Oxford: Clarendon, 1996.
Little, Lester K. *Religious Poverty and the Profit Economy in Medieval Europe*. Ithaca, N.Y.: Cornell University Press, 1978.
Lottin, Odon. *Le Droit naturel chez saint Thomas d'Aquin et ses prédécesseurs*. Bruges: Bayert, 1931.
———. "Roland de Crémone et Hugues de Saint-Cher." *RTAM* 12 (1940): 136–43.
———. *Psychologie et morale aux XIIe et XIIIe siècles*. 6 vols. Gembloux: Duculot, 1949–60.
Luscombe, David. "Ethics in the Early Thirteenth Century." In *Albertus Magnus und die Anfänge der Aristoteles-Rezeption im lateinischen Mittelalter: Von Richardus Rufus bis zu Franciscus de Mayronis*, 657–83. Münster: Aschendorff, 2005.
MacDonald, Scott, ed. *Being and Goodness: The Concept of the Good in Metaphysics and Philosophical Theology*. Ithaca, N.Y.: Cornell University Press, 1991.
———. "Goodness as Transcendental: The Early Thirteenth-Century Recovery of an Aristotelian Idea." *Topoi* 11 (1992): 173–86.
Maddox, Donald. *Fictions of Identity in Medieval France*. Cambridge and New York: Cambridge University Press, 2000.
Marenbon, John. *Later Medieval Philosophy (1150–1350): An Introduction*. London and New York: Routledge and Paul, 1987.

———. "Gilbert of Poitiers and the Porretans on Mathematics in the Division of Sciences." In *"Scientia" und Disciplina": Wissentheorie und Wissenschaftspraxis im 12. und 13. Jahrhundert*, edited by Rainer Berndt, Matthias Lutz-Bachmann, and Ralph M. W. Stammberger, 37–69. Berlin: Akademie Verlag, 2002.

———. "Gilbert of Poitiers." In *A Companion to Philosophy in the Middle Ages*, edited by Jorge J. E. Gracia and Timothy B. Noone, 264–66. Malden, Mass.: Blackwell, 2003.

Marrone, Steven P. *William of Auvergne and Robert Grosseteste: New Ideas of Truth in the Early Thirteenth Century*. Princeton: Princeton University Press, 1983.

———. *The Light of Thy Countenance: Science and Knowledge of God in the Thirteenth Century*. Leiden and Boston: Brill, 2001.

McDonnell, Kilian. "Spirit and Experience in Bernard of Clairvaux." *Theological Studies* 58 (1997): 3–18.

McGinn, Bernard, ed. *Three Treatises on Man: Cistercian Anthropology*. Kalamazoo, Mich.: Cistercian, 1977.

———. Review of *Vision und Visionliteratur in Mittelalter*, by Peter Dinzelbacher. *Speculum* 59, no. 1 (1984): 138–40.

———. *The Growth of Mysticism: Gregory the Great through the 12th Century*. Vol. 2 of *The Presence of God: A History of Western Christian Mysticism*. New York: Crossroad, 1994.

———. *The Flowering of Mysticism: Men and Women in the New Mysticism*. Vol. 3 of *The Presence of God: A History of Western Christian Mysticism*. New York: Crossroad, 1998.

———. "The Language of Inner Experience in Christian Mysticism." *Spiritus* 1, no. 2 (2001): 156–71.

Mews, Constant J. "Hildegard and the Schools." In *Hildegard of Bingen in the Context of Her Thought and Art*, edited by Charles Burnett and Peter Dronke, 89–110. London: Warburg Institute, 1998.

Miethke, Jürgen. "Papst, Ortsbichof und Universität in den Pariser Theologenprozessen des 13. Jahrhunderts." In *Die Auseinandersetzungen an der pariser Universität im XIII Jahrhundert*, ed. Albert Zimmermann, 52–94. Berlin: De Gruyter, 1976.

———. "Practical Intentions of Scholasticism: The Example of Political Theory." In *Universities and Schooling in Medieval Society*, edited by William J. Courtenay and Jürgen Miethke, 211–28. Leiden, Boston, and Cologne: Brill, 2000.

Minister, Meredith. *Trinitarian Theology and Power Relations: God Embodied*. New York: Palgrave Macmillan, 2014.

Miramon, Charles de. "La place d'Hugues de Saint-Cher dans les débats sur la pluralité des bénéfices (1230–1240)." In *Hugues De Saint-Cher (†1263): Bibliste et theologien; Actes du colloque "Hugues de Saint-Cher, O.P., bibliste et théologien."* Paris, Centre d'études du Saulchoir, 13–15 mars 2000, 341–86. Turnhout: Brepols, 2004.

Moore, Robert I. *The Formation of a Persecuting Society: Authority and Deviance in Western Europe 950–1250*. 2nd ed. Oxford: Blackwell, 2007.

Morenzoni, Franco. "Parole du prédicateur et inspiration divine d'après les *artes praedicandi*." In *La Parole du prédicateur Ve–XVe siècle*, edited by Rosa Maria Dessi and Michel Lauwers, 271–310. Nice: Collection du centre d'études médiévales, 1997.

Morenzoni, Franco, and Jean-Yves Tilliette, eds. *Autour de Guillaume d'Auvergne, [mort en] 1249: Texte imprimé*. Turnhout: Brepols, 2005.

Mulchahey, Marian Michèle. *"First the Bow is Bent in Study . . .": Dominican Education before 1350*. Toronto: Pontifical Institute of Mediaeval Studies, 1998.

Münster-Swendsen, Mia. "The Model of Scholastic Mastery in Northern Europe c. 970–1200." In *Teaching and Learning in Northern Europe 1000–1200*, edited by Sally N. Vaughn and Jay Rubenstein, 306–42. Turnhout: Brepols, 2003.

———. "Medieval 'Virtuosity': Classroom Practice and the Transfer of Charismatic Power in Medieval Scholarly Culture c. 1000–1230." In *Negotiating Heritage: Memories of the Middle Ages*, edited by Mette B. Bruun and Stephanie Glaser, 43–63. Turnhout: Brepols, 2008.

Murdoch, John E., and Edith D. Sylla, eds. *The Cultural Context of Medieval Learning: Proceedings of the First International Colloquium on Philosophy, Science and Theology in the Middle Ages*, September 1973. Dordrecht: Reidel, 1975.

Murray, Alexander. *Reason and Society in the Middle Ages*. Oxford: Clarendon Press, 1978.

Nardi, Paolo. "Relations with Authority." In *History of the University in Europe*, edited by Hilde de Ridder-Symoens, 1:77–106. Cambridge: Cambridge University Press, 1992.

Nederman, Cary J. "Nature, Ethics, and The Doctrine of '*Habitus*': Aristotelian Moral Psychology in the Twelfth Century." *Traditio* 45 (1989–1990): 87–110.

Parry, Jonathan. "Mauss, Dumont and the Distinction between Status and Power." In *Marcel Mauss: A Centenary Tribute*, edited by Wendy James and N. J. Allen, 151–72. New York: Berghahn, 1998.

Pasnau, Robert. *Theories of Cognition in the Later Middle Ages*. New York: Cambridge University Press, 1997.

Payne, Thomas Blackburn II. "Poetry, Politics, and Polyphony: Philip the Chancellor's Contribution to the Music of the Notre Dame School." Ph.D. diss., University of Chicago, 1991.

Peirce, Charles S. *The Writings of Charles S. Peirce: A Chronological Edition*. Edited by Max H. Fisch. Bloomington: Indiana University Press, 1982.

Pelster, Franz. "Literaturgeschichtliches zur Pariser theologischen Schule aus den Jahren 1230 bis 1256." *Scholastik* 5 (1930): 46–78.

———. "Die Pariser Verurteilung von 1241: Eine Frage der Datierung." *Archivum Fratrum Praedicatorum* 18 (1948): 405–17.
Pennington, Kenneth. "Pluralism and the Canonists in the Thirteenth Century." *Speculum* 51 (1976): 35–48.
———. "Natural Law." In *Dictionary of the Middle Ages: Supplement 1*, 417–20. New York: Charles Scribners Sons–Thompson-Gale, 2004.
———. "*Lex naturalis* and *Ius naturale*." *Jurist* 68 (2008): 569–91.
Peters, Edward. "*Libertas inquirendi* and the *vitium curiositatis* in Medieval Thought." In *La notion de liberté au moyen âge: Islam, Byzance, Occident*. Penn-Paris-Dumbarton Oaks Colloquia, IV, session des 12–15 octobre 1982, edited by Georges Makdisi, Dominique Sourdel, and Janine Sourdel-Thomine, 89–98. Paris: Les Belles Lettres, 1985.
Pitour, Thomas. *Wilhelm von Auvergnes Psychologie: Von der Rezeption des aristotelischen Hylemorphismus zur Reformulierung der Imago-Dei-Lehre Augustins*. Paderborn: Ferdinand Schöningh, 2011.
Post, Gaines. "Alexander III, the *Licentia Docendi* and the Rise of the Universities." In *C. H. Haskins Anniversary Essays*, edited by John I. La Monte and Charles H. Taylor, 255–77. Boston: Houghton Mifflin, 1929.
———. "Parisian Masters as a Corporation, 1200–1246." *Speculum* 9 (1934): 421–45.
Post, Gaines, Kimon Giocarinis, and Robert Kay. "The Medieval Heritage of a Humanistic Ideal: 'Scientia donum dei est, unde vendi non potest.'" *Traditio* 11 (1955): 195–234.
Pouillon, Henri. "Le premier traité des propriétés transcendentals, La 'Summa de bono' du Chancellier Phillipe." *Revue néoscolastique de philosophie* 42 (1939): 40–77.
———. "La beauté, propriété transcendantale chez les scolastiques (1220–1270)." *AHDLMA* 15 (1946): 293–305.
Principe, Walter H. *William of Auxerre's Theology of the Hypostatic Union*. Studies and Texts 7. Toronto: Pontifical Institute of Mediaeval Studies, 1963.
———. *Alexander of Hales' Theology of the Hypostatic Union*. Studies and Texts 12. Toronto: Pontifical Institute of Mediaeval Studies, 1967.
———. *Hugh of Saint Cher's Theology of the Hypostatic Union*. Studies and Texts 19. Toronto: Pontifical Institute of Mediaeval Studies, 1970.
———. *Philip the Chancellor's Theology of the Hypostatic Union*. Studies and Texts 32. Toronto: Pontifical Institute of Mediaeval Studies, 1975.
Quinto, Riccardo. *Doctor Nominatissimus: Stefano Langton (1228) e la tradizione delle sue opere*. Beiträge zur Geschichte der Philosophie und Theologie des Mittelalters 39. Münster: Aschendorff, 1994.
———. "Il codice 454 di Douai, Stefano Langton e Nicola di Tournai." *Sacris Erudiri* 36 (1996): 233–361.
———. "Le commentaire des Sentences d'Hugues de Saint-Cher." In *Hugues De Saint-Cher (†1263): Bibliste et theologien; Actes du colloque "Hugues de*

Saint-Cher, O.P., bibliste et théologien," Paris, Centre d'études du Saulchoir, 13–15 mars 2000, 299–324. Turnhout: Brepols, 2004.

Rashdall, Hastings. *The Universities of Europe in the Middle Ages.* 3 vols. Oxford: Oxford University Press, 1936.

Regan, Frances Carmel. *A Study of the "Liber de spiritu et Anima": Its Doctrine, Sources, and Historical Significance.* Toronto: University of Toronto Press, 1948.

Reynaert, J. "Hadewijch: Mystic Poetry and Courtly Love." In *Medieval Dutch Literature in Its European Context*, edited by Erik Kooper, 208–25. Cambridge University Press, 1994.

Riché, Pierre. *Education and Culture in the Barbarian West, Sixth through Eighth Centuries.* Columbia: University of South Carolina Press, 1976.

Ridder-Symoens, Hilde de, ed. *A History of the University in Europe.* Vol. 1. Cambridge: Cambridge University Press, 1992.

Robson, Michael, and Jens Röhrkasten, eds. *Franciscan Organization in the Mendicant Context: Formal and Informal Structures of the Friars' Lives and Ministry in the Middle Ages.* Berlin: LIT, 2010.

Roest, Bert. *A History of Franciscan Education (c. 1210–1517).* Leiden: Brill, 2000.

Rosemann, Philipp W. *The Story of a Great Medieval Book: Peter Lombard's Sentences.* Toronto: University of Toronto Press, 2007.

Saccenti, Riccardo. *Conservare la retta volontà: L'atto morale nelle dottrine di Filippo il Cancelliere e Ugo di Saint-Cher (1225–1235).* Bologna: Il Mulino, 2013.

Sannino, Antonella. "Guillaume d'Auvergne e i *libri experimentorum*." In *Expertus sum L'expérience par les sens dans la philosophie naturelle médiévale*, edited by Thomas Bénatouïl and Isabelle Draelants, 67–88. Florence: SISMEL Edizioni del Galuzzo, 2011.

Schlosser, Marianne. *Lucerna in caliginoso loco: Aspekte des Prophetie-Begriffes in der scholastischen Theologie.* Paderborn: Schöningh, 2000.

Segal, Allan. *Paul the Convert: The Apostolate and Apostasy of Saul the Pharisee.* New Haven, Conn.: Yale University Press, 1990.

Şenocak, Neslihan. *The Poor and the Perfect: The Rise of Learning in the Franciscan Order, 1209–1310.* Ithaca, N.Y.: Cornell University Press, 2012.

Shantz, Colleen. *Paul in Ecstasy: The Neurobiology of the Apostle's Life and Thought.* Cambridge: Cambridge University Press, 2009.

Sileo, Leonardo. *Teoria della scienza theologica: Quaestio de scientia theologiae di Odo Rigaldi e altri testi inedita (1230–1250).* 2 vols. Rome: Pontificium Athenaeum Antonianum, 1984.

Smalley, Beryl. "Gregory IX and the Two Faces of the Soul." *Medieval and Renaissance Studies* 2 (1950): 179–82.

Smith, Susan L. "Tales of the Mounted Aristotle." In *The Power of Women: A Topos in Medieval Art and Literature*, 66–74. Philadelphia: University of Pennsylvania Press, 1985.

Stock, Brian. "Some Observations on Bernard of Clairvaux." In *The Cultural Context of Medieval Learning: Proceedings of the First International Collo-*

quium on Philosophy, Science and Theology in the Middle Ages, September 1973, 223–25. Dordrecht: Reidel, 1975.
Stover, A. "Hildegard, the Schools and Their Critics." In *A Companion to Hildegard of Bingen*, edited by Beverly Kienzle, George Ferzoco, and Debra Stoudt, 109–36. Leiden: Brill, 2011.
Studerus, Erich, Alex Gamma, and Franz X. Vollenweider. "Psychometric Evaluation of the Altered States of Consciousness Rating Scale (OSV)." *PLoS One* 5, no. 8 (2010). doi:10.1371/journal.pone.0012412.
Tabor, James D. *Things Unutterable: Paul's Ascent to Paradise in Its Greco-Roman, Judaic and Early Christian Contexts*. Studies in Judaism. Lanham, Md.: University Press of America, 1986.
Tatarkiewicz, Wladyslaw. *History of Aesthetics*. 3 vols. The Hague: Mouton, 1970–74.
Teske, Roland J. "William of Auvergne on Philosophy as divinalis and sapientialis." In *Was ist Philosophie im Mittelalter? / Qu'est-ce que la philosophie au moyen age? / What Is Philosophy in the Middle Ages?: Akten Der 10. Internationale Kongress für Mittelalterliche Philosophie vom 25. bis 30. August 1997 in Erfurt in Kurzfassungen*, edited by Jan A. Aersten and Andreas Speer, 475–81. Berlin and New York: Walter de Gruyter, 1998.
Thijssen, J. M. M. H. "Master Amalric and the Amalricians: Inquisitorial Procedure and the Supression of Heresy in the University of Paris." *Speculum* 71, no. 1 (1996): 43–65.
Thorndike, Lynn. *A History of Magic and Experimental Science*. 8 vols. New York: Columbia University Press, 1923.
Tierney, Brian. *The Idea of Natural Rights: Studies on Natural Rights, Natural Law and Church Law 1150–1625*. Atlanta: Scholars Press, 1997.
Tifenbach, Ryan M. "A Combinatorial Approach to Nearly Uncoupled Markov Chains." PhD. diss. Maynooth: National University of Ireland, 2011.
Torrell, Jean-Pierre. *Théorie de la prophétie et philosophie de la connaissance aux environs de 1230: La contribution d'Hugues de Saint-Cher (Ms. Douai 434, Question 481)*. Leuven: Spicilegium Sacrum Lovaniense, 1977.
———. *Recherches sur la théorie de la prophétie au moyen âge, XIIe–XIVe siécles: Études et textes*. Fribourg: Éditions Universitaires Fribourg Suisse, 1992.
Trachsler, Richard, ed. *Moult obscures paroles: Études sur la prophétie médiévale*. Paris: Presses de l'Université Paris-Sorbonne, 2007.
Trail, David A. "Philip the Chancellor and the Heresy Inquisition in Northern France, 1235–1236." *Viator* 37 (2006): 241–54.
Trottmann, Christian. "Psycho-somatique de la vision béatifique selon Guerric de Saint- Quentin." *RSPT* 78 (1994): 203–25.
———. *La vision béatifique: Des disputes scolastiques à sa définition par Benoît XII*. Rome: École française de Rome, 1995.
———. *Théologie et noétique au XIIIe siècle: À la recherche d'un statut*. Paris: Vrin, 1999.

Unguru, Sabetai. "Experiment in Medieval Optics." In *Physics, Cosmology and Astronomy 1300–1700: Tension and Accommodation*, edited by Sabetai Unguru, 163–81. Dordrecht: Kluwer Academic, 1991.
Valois, Noël. *Guillaume d'Auvergne, évêque de Paris (1228–1249): Sa vie et ses ouvrages*. Paris: Picard, 1880.
Van Engen, John, ed. *Learning Institutionalized: Teaching in the Medieval University*. Notre Dame, Ind.: University of Notre Dame Press, 2000.
Veneziani, Marco, ed. *Experientia: X Colloquio internazionale Roma 4–6 gennaio 2001*. Florence: Olschki, 2002.
Verger, Jacques. *Les universités françaises au moyen âge*. Leiden and New York: Brill, 1995.
———. *Les gens de savoir dans l'Europe de la fin du Moyen Age*. Paris: Presses Universitaires de France, 1997.
———. "The First French Universities and the Institutionalization of Learning: Faculties, Curricula, Degrees." In *Learning Institutionalized: Teaching in the Medieval University*, edited by John Van Engen, 5–19. Notre-Dame, Ind.: University of Notre Dame Press, 2000.
———. "Hugues de Saint-Cher dans le contexte universitaire Parisien." In *Hugues De Saint-Cher (†1263): Bibliste et theologien; Actes du colloque "Hugues de Saint-Cher, O.P., bibliste et théologien,"* Paris, Centre d'études du Saulchoir, 13–15 mars 2000, edited by Gilbert Dahan, Louis-Jaques Bataillon, and Pierre-Marie Gy, 13–22. Turnhout: Brepols, 2004.
Véronèse, Julien. *"L'Ars notoria" au Moyen Âge: Introduction et édition critique*. Florence: SISMEL, Edizioni del Galluzzo, 2007.
Weber, Max. *The Theory of Social and Economic Organization*. Translated by A. M. Henderson. New York: Oxford University Press, 1947.
———. *Max Weber on Charisma and Institution Building: Selected Papers*, edited by Shmuel N. Eisenstadt. Chicago: University of Chicago Press, 1968.
Wei, Ian P. "From Twelfth-Century Schools to Thirteenth-Century Universities: The Disappearance of Biographical and Autobiographical Representations of Scholars." *Speculum* 86, no. 1 (2011): 42–78.
———. *Intellectual Culture in Medieval Paris*. Cambridge: Cambridge University Press, 2012.
Weigand, Rudolf. *Die Naturrechtslehre der Legisten und Dekretisten von Irnerius bis Accursius und von Gratian bis Johannes Teutonicus*. Munich: Max Hueber, 1967.
Weijers, Olga. *Terminologie des universités au XIIIe siècle*. Rome: Ateneo, 1987.
———. "Quelque réflexions sur le travail intellectuel au Moyen Âge: À propos d'un numéro récent de la *Revue de Synthèse*." *Bulletin de philosophie médiévale* 51 (2009): 221–28.
Weisheipel, James A. *Friar Thomas d'Aquino: His Life, Thought and Work*. Oxford: Blackwell, 1973.

Weisweiler, Heinrich. "Théologiens de l'entourage d'Hugues de Saint-Cher." *RTAM* 8 (1936): 389–407.
Wenger, Étienne. *Communities of Practice: Learning, Meaning, and Identity.* Cambridge and New York: Cambridge University Press, 1998.
Wesjohann, Achim. "'Simplicitas' als franziskanisches Ideal und die Prozess der Institutionalisierung des Minoritenordens." In *Die Bettelorden im Aufbau: Beiträge zu Institutionalizierungsprozessen im mittelalterichen Religiosentum*, edited by Gert Melville and Jörg Oberste, 107–67. Münster: LIT, 1999.
Whitehead, Christiania. "Making a Cloister of the Soul in Medieval Religious Treatises." *Medium Aevum* 67 (1998): 1–29.
Wicki, Nikolaus. *Die Lehre von der himmlischen Seligkeit in der mittelalterlichen Scholastik von Petrus Lombardus bis Thomas von Aquin.* Fribourg, Switzerland: Universitätsverlag, 1954.
———. "Philipp der Kanzler und die pariser Bischofswahl von 1227/1228." *Freiburger Zeitschrift für Philosophie und Theologie* 5 (1958): 318–26.
———. *Die Philosophie Philipps des Kanzlers: Ein philosophierender Theologe des frühen 13. Jahrhunderts.* Fribourg: Academic Press, 2005.
Wieland, Georg. *Ethica, scientia practica: Die Anfänge der philosophischen Ethik im 13. Jahrhundert.* Münster: Aschendorff, Bonn, 1981.
Young, Spencer E. "Paris BNF MS Lat. 14726—Peter Bar, Stephen Berout and Master G.: A New Witness to William of Auxerre?." *Bulletin de Philosophie Médiévale* 50 (2008): 53–82.
———. *Scholarly Community at the Early University of Paris: Theologians, Education and Society, 1215–1248.* Cambridge: Cambridge University Press, 2014.
Yukio, Iwakuma. "*Enuntiabilia* in Twelfth-Century Logic and Theology." In *Vestigia, imagines, verba: Semiotics and Logic in Medieval Theological Texts*, edited by Costantino Marmo (Turnhout: Brepols, 1997).
Zink, Michel. *The Invention of Literary Subjectivity.* Translated by Davis Sices. Baltimore: John Hopkins University Press, 1999.
Zumthor, Paul. *Merlin le prophète: Un thème de la littérature polémique de l'historiographie et des romans.* Lausanne: Payot, 1943.

INDEX

Abelard, 128, 161
Abraham, 119, 125
abstraction, 8–10, 25, 38, 42, 44, 46–49, 53, 56, 74, 195
"active" visionaries, 51
Adam, 46–49, 46f, 220n78; Eve and, 169, 201, 244n56
Adam of Puteorumvilla, 122, 215n6; on *habitus*, 149–50
Aelred of Rievaulx, 102
affective knowledge, 57, 175, 191, 196, 261n122
affective psychological powers, 158
affectus, 47, 123, 185, 187, 238n71. *See also* intellect
Alan de Lille, 113, 240n5, 241n21, 256n61
Albert of Pisa, 253n22
Alchemy, 75–76
Alcher of Clairvaux, 31, 192
Alexander of Hales, 13–14; affective psychological powers, 158; comparisons of visions, 45–47, 46f, 54, 57; on definitions, 71; on direct vision of God, 84, 97, 109; on faith, 85, 119–20, 122–23, 242n28; *Glossa* of, 46, 231n14, 242n34, 254n36, 256n60, 261n123; on mediators, 59; on NGF, 172; on Paul's doubt and rapture, 36–37, 41–2, 45, 49–158, 219n58, 231n15; on persuaded faith, 119; Philip the Chancellor and, 196; on preaching, 172, 185; on prophetic vision, 166; threefold approach to cognition on, 97; on unformed faith, 167–68
Alexander of Nequam, 168
Alexander the Great, 161–62
altered states of consciousness, 3, 12, 15–19; drug culture and, 53
Amalricians, 5–7, 83, 112, 132, 171–72
Amaury of Bena, 5–7, 208n17, 209nn20,22

Ambrose, 109, 246n4
Andreas Capellanus, 70
Angelo Clareno, 153
angels: Aristotle's knowledge of, 78; faith of, 86–87; as mediators, 59, 92; object of theological inquiry, 54, 189; seen by Paul, 78, 89–91, 233n30; vision and knowledge of God, 18, 26, 30, 33, 37, 39–42, 43t, 44–46, 50–52, 53t, 57, 60, 82, 84–85, 89–91, 165, 169, 195, 217n29
Antichrist, 44
Anticlaudianus (Alan de Lille), 113
Arianism, 129–30
Aristotle, 94, 97, 191–92; Amaury of Bena related to, 6–7; *Categories*, 20–21; epistemology of, 83; *Ethics* of, 20–21, 184–85, 253n14; *experientia* and, 77–78; faith and, 19, 77; on good, 179, 193; grace and, 98–99; on *habitus*, 20–22, 213n57; on intellect, 89–90; on medium, 114; on memory, 63; *Metaphysics*, 89, 181; perception of *scientia* of, 142; *Physics*, 63, 79, 178, 192–93; *Posterior Analytics* of, 62, 64, 74, 77, 121, 141–42; *Topics*, 20, 70; on "undemonstrative knowledge", 117, 241n18; on virtue, 161–62, 176–77, 253n14
Artes praedicandi, 172–73
Articles of faith, 71, 77, 86–87, 115, 117, 121–26, 131, 138, 141, 145, 149, 168, 200t
astronomers, 75, 140–42, 144, 151
Augustine, 31, 59, 88, 97, 102, 212n51, 228n50; on belief and knowing, 140; classification of visions, 17–18, 25–29, 30, 35–36, 53, 55–56, 59–61, 88; II Cor. 12:1–5 and, 28; *De genesi ad litteram*, 27; delight and, 179–80; on good and virtue, 179; Paul's doubt and, 27–29, 29f

291

authority, 19, 189; belief and, 138–39; estrangement from, 103; faith and, 113, 118, 125–26, 149, 242n28; heresy and, 129–34, 245n70, 246nn73,75; immediacy and, 111–15, 240n9; inspiration and, 191; in Numbers 12:1–8, 111; of Paul the Apostle, 23, 27, 78; preaching and, 175–76; regulation of, 159; self and, 113–14. *See also* magisterial authority
Avicenna, 16, 84, 144, 176, 178, 191–92, 212n51, 259n93

Baldwin, John, 12–13, 105
Baldwin of Ford, 77
Barthes, Roland, 23, 53
Beatific vision, 10, 12, 15, 58, 83–84, 87–88, 91–93, 95, 97–99, 119, 139, 144–45, 156. *See also* glorified souls; immediacy; medium
beauty, 84, 104, 179–81, 188, 192
being, goodness and, 178, 258n85
belief, 140–41; authority and, 138–39; cognition and, 20; Euclid and, 138, 247n9; faith and, 201t–202t; knowing compared to, 137–38; knowledge compared to, 59. *See also* faith
believers, 26, 190; theologians compared to, 142; vision of, 44, 46f, 47, 50, 53, 53t
Bernard Gui, 8, 10–11
Bernard of Clairvaux, 4, 76–77, 150, 192
binaries, 32
Blanche of Castille (queen), 249n44
"blind men's knowledge," 62–65, 78–79
Blund, John, 102–3, 192
Boethius, 127, 242n21
Bonaventure, 14, 196, 253n22
Bono, James, 31
"boundary-work," 16, 26, 190
Bourdieu, Pierre, 21, 213n57
Bourguignon, Erica, 53, 214n3
Brooke, Rosalind, 152–53
Bruno the Carthusian (saint), 217n29
Bynum, Carolyn Walker, 25, 32, 42, 137, 150

Caesar of Heisterbach, 6, 55, 172, 209nn20–21
Calo (hagiographer), 7–8, 10
caritas. See love
Carroll, Lewis, 1
Cassiodorus, 71, 164
Categories (Aristotle), 20–21
charisma, 251n4; of itinerant preachers, 131, 133, 245n70; preaching and, 131, 133, 173–75, 245n70
Christ. *See* Jesus Christ
Chronica maiora (Matthew Paris), 151
Cistercians, 42, 74, 76–77, 103, 192
classifications, Chapter 1
coexisting *habitus*, Chapter 4
cognitions, 196; "accidental," 141; of altered states of consciousness, 18–19; aspects of, 87; belief and, 20; clarity of, 157; classification of, 144; competition of, 136–40, 246n4, 247n8; Chapter 4; Chapter 6; double, 139–42; love and, 158; "natural," 141; *nominalis* vs. *realis*, 62; rapture and, 49; threefold perception of, 85; trance experiences as, 20; transition of, Chapter 4, 19–20, 135–36; types of, Chapter 1
communities: "community of practice," 12; internal differences in, 194–96; of professionals, 12–13; within university life, 161
comprehensor vision, 30–31, 31f, 35–36, 41
condemnations: 5, 82–85, 94–95, 99–100
confession, 6, 153
constitutions, Pre-Narbonian, 163
contemplation and contemplators, 1, 43, 45–47, 49, 50–52, 53t, 54–55, 57, 80, 151, 164, 184–85
Contenson, P. M. de, 82–84, 95
Contra Amaurianos (Garnerius of Rochefort), 172
Coolman, Boyd Taylor, 77
corporeal vision, 28–29, 29f, 31f
correlation awareness, 27–28, 32–35
Council of Reims, 4
courtly love, 105–6
courtly self, 105
curialitas, 252n12

INDEX   293

David of Dinant, 83
De anima (Aristotle), 94, 99, 235n43, 237n65, 258n89
De anima (William of Auvergne), 42, 53, 156, 180, 182–83, 192, 220nn65,68, 223n100, 228n52, 233n27–28, 237n66, 240n9, 251n60, 259n103, 260n104
De anima et potenciis eius, 237n65
De bono et malo (William of Auvergne), 124–25, 180–81
De discretione animae, spiritus et mentis (Gilbert of Poitiers), 32
De fine actionum spiritualium (anonymous quaestio), 186
De genesi ad litteram (Augustine), 27
De prophetia (Alexander of Hales), 47
De retributionibus sanctorum (William of Auvergne), 94–95, 263n7
De spiritu et anima (Alcher of Clairvaux), 31, 192
De trinitate (Augustine) 215n14
De trinitate (Boethius) 242n21
De trinitate (William of Auvergne), 145–46, 188
De universo (William of Auvergne), 188
De virtutibus (William of Auvergne), 259n103, 261n122, 263n7
deaf: faith and salvation of, 120, 133
definitions, 3, 12, 18, 62, 64, 70–72, 79, 113, 184; of faith, 72, 115–16; of rapture 57
delight, 179–80, 188
demons, 114
demonstrative knowledge, 114, 117, 125, 141, 143–44
Dewan, Lawrence, 87
Dialogue on the Soul (Aelred), 102
Dialogus Miraculorum (Caesar of Heisterbach), 55
Dinzelbacher, Peter, 22
Dionysius the Areopagite, (Pseudo-), 82, 84, 94, 217n29, 237n64
Disciplina scolarium (Ps. Boethius), 127
dissociation, 25
divine presence, 52
divine word, 35–36, 89, 233n29
Dominicans, 10, 38, 40, 131, 163, 188, 195–96. *See also* Guerric of St. Quentin; Hugh of St. Cher; Roland of Cremona
Dondaine, Hyacinthe-François, 82–83, 95
Douai BM$_{434}$, 215n6, 233n30, 235n50, 236n56, 255n46, 263n2
double cognitions, 139–42, 144–45, 248n24
doubts: classifications of, 29–32, 30t, 31f; heresy and, 130, 132–34; about immediacy, 81. *See also* Paul's doubt
Douglas, Mary, 25
Dragonetti, Roger, 109
drug culture, 53

ecstasy, ecstatic, 1, 3, 5–12, 16, 24, 26, 28, 34, 46, 49, 53–56, 61, 69, 74, 80, 97, 111–13, 135, 150, 193; soul related to, 227n38. *See also* rapture
Englhardt, Georg, 113, 116, 118
enraptured, 7, 18, 42, 44–52, 57, 69. *See also* rapture; Vision
Eriugena, John Scotus, 82–84, 95, 231n5
essence, 100; accident and, 81; face-to-face and, 101; of God, 83–84; seeing, 108; of soul, 99, 101, 237n64
ethics: *habitus* and, 21; Philip the Chancellor and, 181–82; theology as, 182–88, 187t, 259n103, 260nn108,111–12, 261nn122–23; in university life, 161–62, 253n14
Ethics (Aristotle), 20–21, 184–85, 253n14
Euclid, 112–13; belief and, 138, 247n9
Eugenius III, 4
Eve, 244n56
Exemplar of all things, 36, 39, 50
Exemplum, exempla, 55, 72–73, 89–92, 94, 134, 187, 227n36
Exodus 33:20, 35–36
experience (*experientia, experimentum*), Chapter 2; 70, 72, 227n41; knowledge from, 74–79, 227n41, 228nn46,50,52. *See also* personal experience; trance experiences

294 INDEX

face-to-face vision, 30, 30*t*, 35–36, 38, 49–50, 55–56, 59–60, 88, 101, 135–36, 140, 159; essence and, 101; in Numbers 12:1–8, 111
faith: Alexander of Hales and, 85, 119–20, 122–23, 242n28; argument and, 115–18, 122, 240n13; Aristotle and, 19, 77; articles of, 200*t*; authority and, 113, 118, 125–26, 149, 242n28; belief and, 201*t*–202*t*; cognitive, 98; comparisons to other cognitions and visions, 48, 48*f*, 71–72; definitions of, 200*t*–201*t*; enigma of, 118–19; Godfrey of Poitiers on, 140, 143, 150; Guerric of St. Quentin on, 87; *habitus* of, 37, 41, 45, 47, 135, 137, 139, 147, 150, 201*t*, 231n16; Hugh of St. Cher and, 122, 200*t*–202*t*; knowledge and, 77–78, 138, 147, 247n8; love and, 118, 123, 149; Philip the Chancellor and, 86, 119–20, 122–23, 167–68, 242n28; reason related to, 138, 147, 247n8; Roland of Cremona on, 119–21, 167, 200*t*–202*t*; science and, 117–18, 121–22, 142, 147, 241n21; seeing itself, 98, 236nn56–57; SH on, 86–87, 120, 232n18; struggle of, 123–24; theologians and, 146–50; truth and, 113, 118, 201*t*; understanding and, 141–42; unformed, 118, 137, 139, 145, 167–68, 170–71, 182; virtue of, 165, 167–68, 180, 259n93; visions and, 87, 232n19; William of Auxerre and, 77, 115–20, 141–42, 147, 150, 167, 180, 200*t*–202*t*, 231n16, 232n19, 241n21, 242n28, 259n93; wisdom and, 119
Filia Magistri, 188
First principles, 19, 60, 77, 112, 118, 121–25, 144, 149, 192
Francis of Assisi, 26, 43, 146, 225n21; charisma of, 174; simplicity and, 152–54, 251n57; *stigmata* of, 69, 80
Franciscans, Friars Minor, 11, 34, 36–38; 152, 163. *See also* Alexander of Hales; Francis of Assisi; John of La Rochelle; Odo Rigaldi
Frederick II (emperor), 163
French romance, 104–10, 239nn83,88
Fulk of Neuilly, 146; preaching of, 173

Galen, 32, 39
Garnerius of Rochefort, 172
Gauthier of Chateau-Thierry, 175–76
Gerard of Frachet, 151–52, 164–65, 218n45
Gerardus Novariensis, 168
ghost stories, 73–74, 81
Gieryn, Thomas F., 16
gifts: John of La Rochelle on, 170; preaching and, 172–76, 256n65, 257n73; of prophecy, 164–68, 254n38; of understanding and wisdom, 14, 26, 47, 57, 78–79, 141, 145; virtues related to, 167; and visions, 159. *See also* nongratifying gifts
Gilbert of Poitiers, 3–4, 112
Giles of Assisi, 153
Glorieux, 215n6, 220n78, 259n97
glorified souls, 45, 47–51, 85, 93, 96. *See also* beatific vision
Glossa in quatuor libros Sententiarum Petri Lombard (Alexander of Hales), 46, 231n14, 242n34, 254n36, 256n60, 261n123
God, 190; altered states of consciousness and, 19; *comprehensor* and, 35; essence of, 83–84; images and, 64; intellect and, 124–25; knowledge and, 145–46, 185, 260n111; seeing, 94; self and, 110; soul and, 89, 93, 235n50; *species* of, 83–84
Godfrey of Poitiers, 13; on faith, 71, 86, 140, 143, 150; against heresy, 132; on knowledge, 34, 56; on love, 158; on medium, 60, 88; on prophecy, 44–45, 53, 55–56, 168–69; on rapture, 33–37, 56, 60; on *spiritus*, 32; on theology, 132, 147–48
Golden Summa. See *Summa aurea*
Good, goodness: Aristotle on, 179, 193; being and, 178, 258n85; intellect and, 182; knowledge and virtue and, 178–80, 258n85
Gorochov, Nathalie, 13, 210n40
Grabmann, Martin, 117
grace, 255n49; Aristotle and, 98–99; Philip the Chancellor on, 169; of preaching, 172–73; prophecy and, 20, 172–73. *See also* gifts; nongratifying gifts
Graf, T. A., 98

INDEX 295

Gregory IX (pope), 147, 163, 230n3, 248n32
Guerric of St. Quentin, 13, 14, 40, 212n49, 218n51, 256n65; on faith, 87, 121, 132; on love, 47–48, 95–96, 235n47; on medium in the vision of God, 95–97; on recollection, 67, 68t; on rapture, 40–41, 53, 67, 69
Guiard of Laon, 13, 98
Guillaume de Dole (*Roman de la Rose*) (Renart), 106
Guillaume of Breton, 6
Guyot, Bertrand-G., 95

habitus, 20, 213n57; choice of, 107; coexistence of, 143–45, 153–54, 248n24; of cognitions, 141, 194; contradiction of, 144–45; description of, 21–22; ethics and, 21; of faith, 37, 41, 45, 47, 135, 137, 139, 147, 150, 201t, 231n16; of glory, 109; identity and, 21–22, 135–36; knowledge and, 21, 75–76, 111, 143, 154; medium and, 91, 96; Odo Rigaldi on, 149–50; of rapture, 67; recollection and, 65–66; seeing and, 85; simultaneity of, 58; transition of, 141; virtues and, 21–22, 164–65
habitus sapientialis, 76–77
habitus scientialis, 76
hearing, 113, 120
Hebrews 11:1, 71, 115
Heldris of Cornwall, 105–10
Henri d'Andeli, 103, 161–62
Henri Le-Mans, 245n70
Herbert of Auxerre, 169
Herbert of Bosham, 72
heresy: Amalricians, 83, 112, 171–72, 256n63; arguments related to, 131–32; authority and, 129–34, 245n70, 246nn73,75; charismatic itinerant preachers and, 131, 133, 245n70; doubt and, 130, 132–34; heart and, 133–34; Hugh of St. Cher and, 132–33; literacy related to, 133; mental capacity and, 129–30; theology and, 133
Hezekiah (king), 3
Hilary of Poitiers, 130
Hildegard of Bingen, 2–5, 22, 26, 54, 74, 112, 208n15

Holy Spirit, 2, 6–8, 112, 115, 119, 132–34, 141, 154, 170, 172. *See also* gifts; grace; nongratifying gifts
Honorius III (pope), 129, 131–32, 163, 231n5
Hortus deliciarum, 263n3
Hugh of St. Cher, 13, 22, 195, 199; on coexisting *habitus*, 145, 248n24; comparison of visions 52, 55; definitions, 71; on faith, 122, 200t–202t; on heresy, 132–33; on Paul's memory, 67–68, 68t; on prophecy, 90–91; 219n62; on rapture 41–42; on theologians, 132, 188
Hugh of St. Victor, 31, 92, 94, 113, 192, 227n38
Humbert of the Romans, 152, 173
hypocrisy, 155

identity: communal, 13, 136, 147, 192; *habitus* and, 21–22, 135–36; hypocrisy, 155; individual, 1, 15, 19, 32, 194–95; role-switching of, 154–55, 251n57; taxonomy and, 53–58
illumination, 11, 19, 41, 44, 50, 57, 77, 89–90, 113, 133, 141, 148, 166, 168, 192–93; for learning, 115–26, 240n13, 241nn15,18,21, 242n28, 243n36, 244nn52,56
images, 18–19, 82, 84; devil and, 114; of knowledge, 163–64, 193; lion, 94, 235n43; in literature, 106, 108; recollection and, 61–69, 80; seeing through, in rapture and the beatific vision, 28, 29, 46, 50, 59–60, 88–90, 92–95, 106–10; self-, 70–72, 233nn29–30, 234n34; simplicity as, 154–55
imagination, 36, 46–47, 53t, 60, 97, 185; memory and, 63–64
immediacy: authority and, 111–15; faith and, 120–23, 148; of first principles, 77, 117, 240n9; of truth, 123, 126–27, 147; of vision of God, Chapter 3, 18, 33, 37, 41, 60–61, 69, 79, 81, 88, 91, 95–97, 194
Innocent III (pope), 129, 163, 230n1
inspiration, 7–8, 10, 44–45, 51, 55, 71, 82, 104; authority and, 111, 191; Chapter 4; formal learning and, 19, 34

intellect, 160; *affectus* and, 185, 187–88, 187t, 260n112; Alexander of Hales on, 185; Aristotle on, 89–90; God and, 124–25; good and, 182; love and, 182; Philip the Chancellor on, 187–88, 187t, 261n122; preaching related to, 185; in *quaestio* 230, 158; rapture and, 48–51; struggle of, 124–26; theology and, 187–88; virtues and, 165, 181; will compared to, 182–83, 259n103; William of Auxerre on, 88–89, 91, 96, 124–26. *See also* practical intellect; speculative intellect

intellectual visions, 28–29, 29f, 31f, 51, 60n. *See also* immediacy; seeing through images

intellectus cognitionis, 158, 187–88, 187t

intellectus operationis, 158, 165, 187, 187t

intermediary vision (*visio mediastina*), 30–31, 31f; 33, 36–40, 44, 46–48, 55, 219n62, 220n64

interpreters of scriptures (exegetes), 90, 137; as seers of God, 44–45, 47, 48f, 53–55, 79, 217n29

introspection, 60–6, 88; limits of, 97–101, 237n64

intuition, 52, 53t, 55, 57, 111, 113

Isaiah, 29, 165, 168; Thomas Aquinas' commentary on, 7–8

Jacques de Vitry, 43, 146, 161, 174, 183; on knowledge, 162–63; on preaching, 173

Jacques Le Goff, 32

Jaeger, Stephen, 127–28, 160

James of Venice, 62

Jean of Joinville, 115, 124, 126

Jesus Christ, 2–3, 6, 9, 23, 26, 45, 76, 87, 139–40, 152–54, 162, 164, 169, 189; cognition of, 18, 47, 49–52, 54, 144; as mediator, 60; *stigmata* of, 69; wisdom from, 104

Joachim of Fiore, Joachimite 2, 5, 7, 44, 74

John of Damascus, 120

John of Garland, 252n12

John of La Rochelle, 13, 41–42, 19; definitions and, 71; on gifts, 170, 172; on medium, 93; on soul, 103–4; *Summa de Anima* of, 71, 192; Vat. Lat. 691, 14, 132, 212n49.

John of Salisbury, 128, 225n14

John of St. Gilles, 40

John of Treviso, 169

John Pagus, 82, 97–98, 186, 230n3

Jonah's prophecy, 90

Jordan of Nemours, 112–13

Jung, C. G., 135

King, Peter, 74, 79

knowing, 140–41; belief compared to, 137–38; living compared to, 189; modes of, 145–46; William of Auvergne on, 145–46, 248n24

knowledge, 56; affective, 57, 175, 191, 196, 261n122; belief compared to, 59; of blind men, 62–65, 78–79; character and, 158–59; and Dominicans, 163, 195–96; dualist position of, 260n111; from experience, 74–79, 227n41, 228nn46,50,52; faith and, 77–78, 138, 147, 247n8; Gerard of Frachet on, 165; God and, 145–46, 185, 260n111; *habitus* and, 21, 75–76, 111, 143, 154; hierarchy of, 74–75; identity related to, 1; images of, 60, 163–64; Jacques de Vitry on, 162–63; legitimacy of, 75–76; levels of, 33–34, 217n31; love and, 153, 158, 176–82, 258n85, 259nn93–94, 97; from mediators, 59–60; NGF and, 171–72, 256n60; objects of, 60; Odo Rigaldi and, 185, 260n112; of Paul the Apostle, 27–28; Paul the Apostle doubt and, 37, 39; of prophets, 145–46; simple, 185; soul and, 188; speculative, 191; sweetness related to, 164; systematization of, 75; through signs, 106; of truth, 172; undemonstrative, 117, 241n18; William of Auvergne on, 76, 156, 188, 228n52; from words, 62–63. *See also* cognitions; visions

knowledge and virtue: good and, 178–80, 258n85; Philip the Chancellor on, 177–78, 181–82, 259n97; William of Auvergne on, 180–81, 259n94; William of Auxerre on, 177, 179–80, 259n93

INDEX 297

Lai d'Aristote (Henri d'Andeli), 161–62
Lai de l'ombre (The Song of the Shadow) (Renart), 105
laicus (layman), 152, 156–57, 175
Lambert le Begue, 245n70
Landgraf, Artur M., 170, 212n49
Lave, Jean, 12
law, 121; science and, 112–13
learning, 19, 114, 240n9; illumination for, 115–26, 240n13, 241nn15,18,21, 242n28, 243n36, 244nn52,n56
Lerner, Robert E., 112
levitation, 9
light, 222n92; perfection of, 88–89; soul and, 96; in visions, 65–66. *See also* illumination; medium
lion: image of, 94, 235n43
literacy, 132–33, 155
Louis IX (king, saint), 8, 115, 124, 126, 244n52
love (*caritas*), 41, 44, 127–28, 192; of Alexander the Great, 161–62; beauty and, 180; cognition and, 158; courtly, 105–6; definition of, 226n25; faith and, 118, 123, 149; Guerric of St. Quentin on, 95–96, 235n47; intellect and, 182; knowledge and, 153, 158, 176–82, 258n85, 259nn93–94,97; Paul the Apostle on, 136–37, 246n4; priority of, 159

MacDonald, Scott, 181, 258n85
magisterial authority: erosion of, 128; institutionalization of, 128–29; love in, 127–28; nascent university and, 126–29, 160–61, 190
Marrone, Steven P., 213n56
Martin (Master), 30; on prophecy, 168
masters, 105, 112, 115, 124–25; Parisian regent, 12–13, 160–61, 252n8
Mathew de Scotia, 163
Matthew Paris, 82, 151, 230n2, 249n44
Mauss, Marcel, 174
McGinn, Bernard, 69
medium, 83–85, 88, 235n50; Aristotle on, 114; between body and soul, 31, 40; Godfrey of Poitiers on, 60; Guerric of St. Quentin on, 95–96; interiority and,

88–101; John of La Rochelle and, 93; Roland of Cremona on, 65; in vision, Chapter 2, Chapter 3; William of Auxerre on, 63, 90–92, 233n30; William of Auvergne on, 83. *See also* images; immediacy
memory, 223n2; imagination and, 63–64. *See also* recollection
mendicant orders, 42–44, 43t, 213n54; integration of, 151–56; poverty of, 155; records from, 13; religiosity of, 151–52. *See also* Dominicans; Franciscans
mental phenomena, modern classification of, 24, 214n4
Merlin, 2, 5, 107–8
metaphor, 182–83, 259n103
Metaphysics (Aristotle), 89, 181
Mews, Constant, 4, 208n15
miracles, 39; faith relying on, 113, 118, 120, 134, 141; gift of 169;
mirror: of creation, 119; of eternity, 35–36, 39, 45–47, 50–51, 53t, 55–56, 89–91, 94, 169, 217n39, 239n88; divine word as, 233n29; seeing through, 30, 35, 46, 56, 59, 118
monasticism, 43, 55, 160, 183, 263n3
Moore, Robert, 132
moral education, 160
Morenzoni, Franco, 172–73
Moses, 18, 31, 35, 45–47, 48f, 49–50, 54, 67, 111, 132–33; Thomas Aquinas compared to, 10, 210n37
MS Vat. Lat. 782, 185–86, 261n115
Mulchahey, Marian Michel, 163, 260n107
Münster-Swendsen, Mia, 127–28
Murray, Alexander, 146

natural and supernatural, 50, 168, 254n38
"natural" cognitions, 141
natural law, 121
nature, 57, 69–70; *habitus* and, 21–22; rapture and, 48, 50–51
Nature and Nurture, 106–8
navigation, 142
Ne transgrediaris, 168
NGF. *See* nongratifying gifts
Nicholas de Flavigny, 227n37

298 INDEX

Nicholas of Lyre, 209n31
nongratifying gifts (NGF), 255nn46,49–50, 256n54; gratifying gift compared to, 170, 256nn60–61; knowledge and, 171–72, 256n60; Philip the Chancellor on, 168; SH on, 169; spirit and, 170; "spirit of truth" and, 171
Numbers 12:1–8, 111

obedience, 125–27, 134, 146, 153, 181
Odo of Soissons, 3–4
Odo Rigaldi, 13, 149–50, 215n6; on faith, 126, 149; on theology, 121–22, 185
Odon Lottin, 212n49
On the Soul (Aristotle). See *De anima*
Order of the Valley of Disciples (*Val Scolarium*), 37–38

Panofsky, Erwin, 213n57
Paris. *See* university faculty
Parry, Jonathan, 174
Pasnau, Robert, 15
Paul of Aquilla, 10
Paul the Apostle. *See specific topics*
Paul's doubt: Augustine and, 27–29, 29*f*; *comprehensor* vision and, 30, 35, 41; correlation awareness and, 27–28, 32–35; earth and heaven related to, 29–30, 30*t*; intermediary vision and, 30–31, 31*f*, 33, 36–39, 44, 219n62; joy and, 39; knowledge and, 37, 39; love and, 41; mendicant analogy on, 42–44, 43*t*; "mirror of eternity" and, 35–36; soul and, 30–32, 30*t*, 38–39; soul-body and, 40–42, 219n56, 220n64; third heaven and, 28–29, 33, 37, 41, 217n29; visions and, 28–29, 29*f*
Peirce, Charles S., 68, 68*t*
perfection, 25, 178, 181–84, 187–88, 196; of light, 88–89
personal experience: soul and, 102–4, 238n71; in university life, 72–74, 227nn36–38
Peter (saint), 8, 139, 144
Peter John Olivi, 11, 44
Peter Lombard, 85, 231n15; *Sentences* of, 26, 132, 157, 186–88, 187*t*, 215n6

Peter of Corbeille, 116, 118, 122
Peter the Chanter, 12
Philip the Chancellor, 14, 54, 71, 233n30; Alexander of Hales and, 196; on angels, 169; on ethics, 181–82; on faith, 86, 119–20, 122–23, 167–68, 242n28; on grace, 169; against heresy, 132; on intellect, 187–88, 187*t*, 261n122; on Jonah, 90; on knowledge and virtue, 177–78, 181–82, 259n97; on the mirror of eternity, 90–91; on NGF, 168; on prophecy, 166–67, 169, 255n42; on transcendentals, 179; on unformed faith, 167–68
philosophers, 16, 18, 26, 66, 74, 103, 133; vision of, 52–55; old women and, 146–50, 248n32, 249n42
philosophy (natural), 6, 56, 63, 75, 131, 147, 163, 178, 207n7
Physics (Aristotle), 63, 79, 178, 192–93
Pierre Clergue, 245n70
Posterior Analytics (Aristotle), 62–64, 74, 77, 112–18, 121–22, 141–43, 193
practical intellect, 158, 165, 187, 187*t*
Praepositinus of Cremona, 33, 168, 256n61
Prague Univ. IV D 13, 86–87, 95
preaching: authority and, 175–76; charisma and, 131, 133, 173–75, 245n70; Gauthier of Chateau-Thierry on, 175–76; gifts and, 172–76, 256n65, 257n73; grace of, 172–73; intellect related to, 185; reciprocity and, 174–75, 257n73; teaching compared to, 185–86; by women, 175–76
Pre-Narbonian constitutions, 163, 253n23
presence, divine, 52, 56, 58, 60–61, 67, 85, 88–89, 92–94; of the Holy Spirit or Christ in the soul, 115, 140, 170, 172
prophecy, 4, 12–15, 26, 50, 220n77, 256n61; comparisons with other visions, 48*f*, 223n102; definition of, 71, 164; gift of, 164–68, 254n38; Godfrey of Poitiers on, 44–45, 168–69; grace and, 20, 172–73; rapture compared to, 51; speaking in tongues compared to, 159; Stephen Langton on, 168, 255n42; virtue and, 164–67

prophetic vision, 45–46; *scientia* and, 114; types of, 166; virtue and, 166
prophets, 2, 46*f*, 47, 53*t*, 55; designation of, 44–45; knowledge of, 145–46; Merlin as, 107–8; William the Goldsmith as, 6–7
prudence, 177–78, 181
purgatory, 32

Quaestio 9, 91, 95–96, 99, 234n34
Quaestio 12, 202b
Quaestio 28–129, 263n2
Quaestio 45, 145, 237n58, 243n34
Quaestio 230, 42, 51, 158, 220n71
Quaestio 260, 220n78
Quaestio 337, 233n30
Quaestio 338, 42, 50–52, 54, 56
Quaestio 454, 42, 49–50, 54, 65–68, 80, 93, 95–96, 158
Quaestio 480–481. *See* Hugh of St. Cher
Quaestio 500. *See* Guiard of Laon
Quaestio 501, 87, 98, 145
Quaestio 520. *See* William of Durham
Quaestio 530, 87, 145, 243n34
Quaestio 531, 234n34
Quaestio 540, 166
Quaestio de divina scientia (Prague IV D 13), 121, 148, 186
Quaestiones 498–99, 247n6
Quinto, Riccardo, 222n90

Radulfus Ardens, 259n97
rapture, 11–14, 45, 57, 184, 190–91, 195; cognition and, 49; communication of, 80; comparisons and, 46–49, 48*f*; confusion related to, 17; faith and, 137, 144, 158; *habitus* of, 67, 195; intellect and, 48–51; memory of, Chapter 2; nature and, 48, 50–51; prophecy compared to, 51, 195; status and, 49–50; taxonomy regarding, Chapter 1; of Thomas Aquinas, 7–10; trance and, 214n3; visions and, 49, 53. *See also* enraptured
Reason and Society in the Middle Ages (Murray), 146
reasoning, 53*t*

recollection, Chapter 2; 18, 79–80; *habitus* and, 65–66; images and, 67–69; purpose of, 80; Roland of Cremona on, 68–69, 68*t*. *See also* memory
reflection, 105, 215n6. *See also* mirror of eternity
Reginald of Piperno, 7–8, 11
Renart, Jean, 105–6
revelation, 6–7, 10, 23–24, 33, 45, 53*t*, 63, 71, 89, 104, 111–12, 114, 118, 120, 145, 171
Richard of St. Victor, 55, 72, 223n2
Richard Rufus, 103
Robert of Courçon, 162, 168
Robert of Melun, 233n29
Roest, Bert, 152
Roland of Cremona, 38–41, 53–54, 56, 195, 218n45, 225n20; Aristotle and, 253n14; on blind men's knowledge, 62–65, 78–79; on coexisting habitus, 143–44, 150; on demons, 114; on *experientia*, 77–79; on faith, 86, 116, 119–21, 167, 200*t*–202*t*; on heresy, 130–32, 134, 246n75; on medium, 93, 96; on memory, 63–70, 68*t*; prophecy and, 169; on simplicity, 157; *stigmata* and, 69; on theologians, 178, 188; on unformed faith, 167
Roman de la Rose (*Guillaume de Dole*) (Renart), 106
Romans 10:17, 120
Rosemann, Philipp W., 261n123
Ross, William D., 62

Salimbene de Adam, 153, 156, 163, 173
salvation, 20, 72, 87, 120, 129, 156, 162–63, 167–68, 170, 172, 254n38
Samaritan woman, 140, 148–49
Samuel, 16, 166
sapientia morum, 187
Schlosser, Marianne, 15, 212n51, 213n54, 223n102
Schwester Kathrei (*Sister Katherine*), 189
science and *scientia*, 148, 186; definitions of, 33, 75; faith and, 117–18, 121–22, 142, 147, 241n21; law and, 112–13; prophetic vision and, 114; recollection and, 80; theology as, 121, 147, 184; virtue and, 176–77. *See also* knowledge

scripture(s), 4, 36, 39, 44–45, 54–56, 76, 79, 104, 113, 120–21, 131–32, 141, 149, 153, 159, 186. *See also* interpreters
secundum pietatem, 150, 167, 176, 184, 196
seeing, 94, 98, 236nn56–57; by angels, 90–91, 233n30; argument and, 115; essence, 108; *habitus* and, 85; likeness and, 92–93; recollecting compared to, 65. *See also* images
self, 11, 15, 17, 19–22, 134–35, 194, 236nn56–57; alienation from, 24; continuity of, Chapter 2, Chapter 5; in courtly romance, 104–9; experiencing self, 24, 80; fighting against, 162; God's self-knowledge, 97–98; ignorance of, Chapter 1; as locus of presence and certitude, 60, 89; manipulation of, Chapter 5; as medium, 91, 96; as potency alone, distinct from habitus, Chapter 3; recollection as self-awareness, 69; in society, Chapter 6; as source of authority, Chapter 4; subjectivity and, 110; "super-self," 165, 168, 255n39; transformation and, 194; two orders within, 150–51
self-definition of theologians, 13, 16–17, 70–72, 184, 233nn29–30, 234n34
sense experience. *See* experience
senses, 46f, 100–1
Sentences (Peter Lombard), 26, 132–33, 149, 157, 186–88, 215n6; intellect and, 186–87, 187t. *See also* Hugh of St. Cher; Vat. Lat. 691; Alexander of Hales (Gloss); John Pagus; Adam de Puteorumvilla
Sepculum animae (Richard Rufus), 103
Seraphim. *See* angels
sermons, 2, 72, 154, 161, 172–74, 227n36
SH. *See Summa Halensis*
shamans, 1–2, 8
Shantz, Colleen, 193, 214n1
signs, 69, 100; knowledge through, 106; theory of, 68, 68t
Silence (Heldris of Cornwall), 105–10
Simon d'Authie, 14
Simon of Tournai, 138
Simony, 2

simplicity, 20, 34, 136, 142, 146–47, 151–56, 191, 249n44, 251n57; divine simplicity 236n56
sin, 45, 88, 129–30, 166, 172, 181, 185–86; of theologians, 147, 186
sinner, 4, 20, 166, 168, 171
social positions, 25, 53t, 112, 157, 183, 189, 194
Sohm, Rudolf, 251n4
Song of Songs, 104, 131–32, 192
Song of the Shadow, The (*Lai de l'ombre*) (Renart), 105
soul-body, 40–42, 219n56, 220n64
souls, 33, 48–49, 51, 100, 192; affect on, 102–4, 238n71; different parts of, 261n122; ecstasy related to, 227n38; essence of, 99, 101, 237n64; glorified, 48–49, 51; God and, 89, 93, 235n50; *habitus* and, 21–22; image and, 90; John of La Rochelle on, 103–4; knowledge and, 188; light and, 96; Paul's doubt and, 30–32, 30t, 38–39; personal experience and, 102–4, 238n71; representation and, 84; *species* and, 83; structure of, 178; virtue and, 167
speaking in tongues, 159, 220n77
speculative intellect, 158, 187–88, 187t
Speculum Universale (Radulfus Ardens), 259n97
Spirit. *See* Grace; Holy Spirit; Nongratifying gifts; *spiritus*
spirit possession, 61
spiritual-imaginary vision, 28–29, 29f, 31f
spiritus (subtle matter), 32
spiritus adoptionis ("spirit of adoption"), 170, 256n54
spiritus veritatis ("spirit of truth"), 170–71, 256n54
statutes: of 1215, 161, 252n8; of 1231, 252n11
Stephanus, presbyter of Celle, 209n22
Stephen (Étienne) de Bourbon, 72–73, 218n51
Stephen Langton, 30, 33, 116, 163, 168, 171, 255n50; prophecy and, 168, 255n42
stigmata, 65, 68t, 69, 80

Stover, A., 4–5
Summa against the Gentiles (Aquinas), 7–8
Summa aurea (*Golden Summa*; *Summa magistri Guillelmi*) (William of Auxerre), 35–36, 64, 165, 217n36. See also William of Auxerre
Summa Basiliensis, 169
Summa de Anima (John of La Rochelle), 71, 192, 226n31
Summa Douacensis, 91, 196, 212n48, 255n49, 259n97
Summa Halensis (SH), 14, 26–27, 70, 169–70, 231n15; on double cognitions, 144–45; on faith, 86–87, 120, 232n18
Summa magistri Guillelmi. See *Summa aurea*
supernatural, 56, 167–68, 254n38, 255n39

Theodor (hagiographer), 22
theologians, 55–56, 223n102; academic, 54, 70–72, 233nn29–30, 234n34; arguments of, 149; believers compared to, 142; careers, 183; decrees of, 61; faith and, 146–50; positions of, 189, 191; self-definition of, 184; struggle of, 124
theology, 2–3, 76; end of, 184; as ethics, 182–88, 187t, 259n103, 260nn108,111–12; 261nn122–23; of Godfrey of Poitiers, 147–48; heresy and, 133; intellect and *affectus* and, 187–88, 187t, 261nn122–23; Odo Rigaldi on, 185, 260n112; philosophy and, 147; practicality of, 260n112; *quaestiones* and, 26–27; as science, 121, 147, 184; truth and goodness related to, 186–88, 261nn122–23, 262n128
third heaven, 40; Paul's doubt and, 28–29, 33, 37, 41, 217n29
Thomas Aquinas, 7–8, 11, 112, 209n31; ghost stories and, 73–74, 81; with Jesus Christ, 9; Moses compared to, 10, 210n37; raptures of, 9–10
Thomas Celano, 69, 225n21; on Francis of Assisi, 174; on simplicity, 152–56
Thomas Chobham, 173
Thorndike, Lynn, 75

threefold approach to knowing, 88, 200t–202t, 232nn18–20; distinctions in, 85–87, 231nn15–16
threefold self-vision, 98
Tocco (hagiographer), 7–9, 210n37
Topics (Aristotle), 20–21
Torrell, Jean-Pierre, 91
trance, 190, 214n3; academic study of, 1, 194; as cognition, 20; perfection and, 25; recollection of, 18; society related to, 25; spirit possession compared to, 61; tensions and, 25. See also visions
transcendentals, 179
transformation, 19, 22, 137–38, 150, 194–97
transition of virtues (transitus virtutum), 137; Chapter 5
Trinity, 6, 41, 48, 54, 93, 99, 119, 138, 168, 189
Trottman, Christian, 84, 230n4, 235n47
truth, 4, 6, 8–9, 11, 92–94, 124, 126–27, 165–66; beauty and, 180; faith and, 86, 113, 117–19, 121, 130–34, 138, 140–41, 145–48, 154, 201t; fiction and, 106–9; hypocrisy and, 155; immutable, immobile 44, 71; knowledge of, 172; prophecy and, 44, 90, 164; "spirit of," 170–71, 256n54; theology and, 260n112; union with, 84
truth and goodness, 99, 167, 180–84; intellect and *affectus* related to, 185–88, 187t, 261nn122–23, 262n128; theology and, 186–88, 261nn122–23, 262n128

"undemonstrative knowledge," 117, 241n18. See also First principles
unformed faith, 118, 137, 139, 145, 167–68, 170–71, 182, 203t
universities, 2, 11–12. See also specific topics
university faculty, 18, 196; autonomy of, 182–83; perception and, 20; theologian careers of, 183, 260n108. See also magisterial authority
university life, 196–97; communities within, 161; conduct within, 161, 252nn11–12; economics of, 162; ethics in, 161–62, 253n14; personal experience in, 72–74, 227nn36–38; privileges within, 183, 260n107

Val Scolarium (Order of the Valley of Disciples), 37–38, 43
Vat. Lat. 691, 14, 132, 144, 188, 212n49, 236n54, 242n28, 247n18
viatores (wayfarers), 29–30, 30*t*, 37, 47, 57
Virgin Mary, 139–40, 144–45, 164–65, 240n13
virginal birth, 240n13
virginity, 4, 106
virtue (*virtus*): Aristotle on, 161–62, 176–77, 253n14; of faith, 165, 167–68, 180, 259n93; gifts related to, 167; *habitus* and, 21–22, 164–65; intellect and, 165, 181; practical intellect and, 165; prophecy and, 164–67; prophetic vision and, 166; of prudence, 177–78; science and, 176–77; soul and, 167; "transition of," 137; unformed faith as, 167–68; virginity, 106. *See also* knowledge and virtue
visio comprehensoris. See *comprehensor* vision
visio mediastina. See intermediary vision
visions, 14–15, 93–94, 98, 191; of believers, 44, 46*f*, 47, 50, 53, 53*t*; categories of, 17–18, 52; contemplation with, 55; corporeal, 28–29, 29*f*, 31*f*; faith and, 87, 232n19; gifts from, 159; "immediate," 96; light in, 65–66; marks and, 225n21; mastery related to, 25–26; quadripartite model of, 66, 68–69, 68*t*; rapture and, 49, 53; types of, 165–66. *See also* cognitions; intermediary vision; Paul the Apostle; prophetic vision
Vitae fratrum (Gerard of Frachet), 151–52

Waldensians, 34, 131, 146, 217n31
Walter Map, 34, 146, 217n31
Weber, Max, 251n4
Wenger, Étienne, 12
will: intellect compared to, 182–83, 259n103
Willermus, (master) 184, 186, 215n6
William of Auvergne, 14, 53, 84, 194–95, 230n3; actions and, 100; common sense of, 100–1; *De anima* of, 156, 182–83, 240n9, 259n103; *De Trinitate* of, 145–46, 188; *De virtutibus* of, 259n103, 261n122; Eriugena and, 95; faith and, 120–23, 156, 243n36; judgment of, 99; on knowing, 145–46, 248n24; on knowledge and virtue, 180–81, 259n94; knowledge of, 76, 156, 188, 228n52; on learning, 240n9; on love, 44; on magisterial authority, 127; metaphor of soul, 182–83, 259n103; on mirror, 90; on scientific knowledge, 156; on soul, 99–100; on virtue, 165; on vision, 93–94
William of Auxerre, 5, 42, 56, 192, 217n35, 218n40; Augustine and, 88; on beauty, 179–80; on belief and knowing, 140–41; on cognition, 61–62, 141–42, 144–45, 157; *comprehensor* vision and, 35–36; on double cognition, 141–42, 144–45; faith and, 77, 115–20, 141–42, 147, 150, 167, 180, 200*t*–202*t*, 231n16, 232n19, 241n21, 242n28, 259n93; good and, 179; on heresy, 129–30, 132–34; intellect and, 88–89, 91, 96, 124–26; on magisterial authority, 126–27; on medium, 91–92, 233n30; prophecy and, 169; on recollection, 68*t*; Roland of Cremona and, 38, 78–79, 157, 195; Salimbene de Adam on, 173; *Summa aurea* of, 35–36, 64, 165, 217n36; theologian career of, 260n108; on threefold self-vision, 98; transcendentals and, 179; on unformed faith, 167; on veils, 88, 96; on virtue, 165, 177
William of Champeaux, 43
William of Durham, 13, 98, 202*b*, 235n43, 236n56
William of St. Amour, 8, 155
William the Goldsmith, 6–7
Wisdom (gift). *See* gifts
women: preaching by, 175–76; Virgin Mary, 139–40, 144, 164, 240n13; virginity of, 106. *See also* philosophers

Zachariah, 45
Zink, Michel, 109

FORDHAM SERIES IN MEDIEVAL STUDIES

Ronald B. Begley and Joseph W. Koterski, S.J. (eds.), *Medieval Education*
Teodolinda Barolini and H. Wayne Storey (eds.), *Dante for the New Millennium*
Richard F. Gyug (ed.), *Medieval Cultures in Contact*
Seeta Chaganti (ed.), *Medieval Poetics and Social Practice: Responding to the Work of Penn R. Szittya*
Devorah Schoenfeld, *Isaac on Jewish and Christian Altars: Polemic and Exegesis in Rashi and the "Glossa Ordinaria"*
Martin Chase, S.J. (ed.), *Eddic, Skaldic, and Beyond: Poetic Variety in Medieval Iceland and Norway*
Felice Lifshitz, *Religious Women in Early Carolingian Francia: A Study of Manuscript Transmission and Monastic Culture*
Sam Zeno Conedera, S.J., *Ecclesiastical Knights: The Military Orders in Castile, 1150–1330*
J. Patrick Hornbeck II and Michael van Dussen (eds.), *Europe After Wyclif*
Laura K. Morreale and Nicholas L. Paul (eds.), *The French of Outremer: Communities and Communications in the Crusading Mediterranean*
Ayelet Even-Ezra, *Ecstasy in the Classroom: Trance, Self, and the Academic Profession in Medieval Paris*

www.ingramcontent.com/pod-product-compliance
Lightning Source LLC
Chambersburg PA
CBHW030435300426
44112CB00009B/1007